CIB PUBLISHING

The Monetary and Financial System

4th edition

David Goacher

BA (Econ.), PhD

institute of financial services

First published in 1991
2nd edition 1994
3rd edition 1996
4th edition 1999

CIB Publishing
c/o The Chartered Institute of Bankers
Emmanuel House
4-9 Burgate Lane
Canterbury
Kent
CT1 2XJ
United Kingdom

Telephone: 01227 762600

CIB Publishing publications are published by The Chartered Institute of Bankers, a non-profit making registered educational charity.

Typeset by Intype London Ltd
© David Goacher 1999

ISBN 0-85297-540-6

Contents

Contents

Introduction

The Concept of the Course

This workbook has been written for students studying *The Monetary and Financial System* for the CIB/UMIST BSc (Hons) Financial Services and the Associateship of The Chartered Institute of Bankers. The workbook aims to cover all key topics contained in the CIB/UMIST Syllabus, the major areas of which are:

- The Properties and Pricing of Financial Assets
- Financial Institutions
- Financial Markets
- Derivative Instruments
- The Regulation of Financial Institutions and Financial Markets
- The Analysis of Interest Rates
- Monetary Policy
- The Analysis of Exchange Rates
- Portfolio Theory
- Corporate Sector Finance
- Personal Sector Finances and the Housing Market.

Each of Units 1 to 11 is divided into sections and contains:

- A statement of learning objectives
- Concise topic-by-topic coverage of the key concepts and principles
- Contemporary examples and data to illustrate the application of theory
- Study activities to reinforce assimilation of the text material
- Self-assessment questions to test knowledge and reinforce understanding.

Unit 12 contains a bank of examination questions, which may be used for examination practice and self-assessment. Suggested answers to each of these examination questions are given in Appendix 2.

Learning Activities

Each of Units 1 to 11 consists of study notes designed to focus attention upon the key aspects of the subject matter. These notes are divided into convenient sections for study purposes. Following each small group of sections there is a *Study Activities* session, which is intended to encourage students to think about what they have studied in the preceding few sections and to consolidate their knowledge. These *Study Activities* comprise a series of short questions for each of which a reference is given to the precise part of the preceding text where the answer may be found. Students are strongly encouraged to use these Study Activities in order to test their understanding of the material. Students should also note their areas of weakness and re-read the relevant parts of the text as necessary. At the end of these Units there are *Self-Assessment Questions*. These comprise short answer questions and multiple-choice questions. The answers to all of these questions are to be found in Appendix 1.

The inclusion of examination questions, in Unit 12, is crucial, as many students fail the examination not because of a lack of knowledge, but rather because of a failure to structure and apply this knowledge when answering questions. The answers provided in this workbook are only suggested answers to questions, and it must be emphasised that for many questions there is no single correct answer. Students may obtain a pass mark for any given question through several different answers. However, in order to obtain a high mark, it is vital that answers deal concisely and thoroughly with the core subject matter and answers should cover all issues raised by the questions.

The approach taken throughout this workbook is one of preparing the student for an examination. However, it must be emphasised that it is dangerous for students to try to spot questions and attempt to memorise answers by rote learning. The chances of success can be increased only by thorough and careful preparation.

It is important to emphasise that completion of this workbook alone is not sufficient preparation for the examination. The depth and breadth of knowledge and skills required to complete successfully a course that equates to one-quarter of a year of full-time honours degree study (half of which is at final year level) mean that substantially more is required. Whilst this workbook is designed to provide a sound base for study, it must be supplemented by reading other literature and, ideally, by participating in either a college-based course or an approved distance learning programme. Also, as with most topics, certain aspects of *The Monetary and Financial System* subject fields are constantly developing. Therefore, it is of great importance that students should keep up-to-date with contemporary developments in the key areas of the syllabus. There is no real substitute for reading relevant articles in *The Economist, The Banker, Bank of England Quarterly Bulletin and the Financial Times* and other quality newspapers.

Study Guide

Studying

When preparing for any examination, an organised and disciplined study plan is vital. You should devise an approach that will enable you to complete this workbook and still leave time for revision of this and any other subject you are taking at the same time. Many candidates find that six weeks is about the right period of time to leave for revision – enough time to get through the revision material, but not so long that it is no longer fresh in your mind by the time you reach the examination.

This means that you should plan how to get to the last unit by, say, the end of March for a May sitting or the end of August for an October sitting. This includes not only reading the text, but also making notes, working through the study activities and answering the illustrative examination questions. In addition, you should be undertaking additional reading and attending courses as indicated above during the period of study.

The following suggestions are offered as a starting point for approaching your study:

- *Plan time each week* to study a part of this workbook. Make sure that it is 'quality' study time. Let it be known that you are studying and that you should not be disturbed.

- Set a *clearly defined objective* for each study period. You may simply wish to read through a unit for the first time or perhaps you may want to make some notes on a unit that you have already read a couple of times. Don't forget to work through the study activities, self-assessment questions and any relevant examination questions.

- *Review your study plan.* Devise a study checklist and timetable so that you can schedule and monitor your progress. Don't panic if you fall behind your schedule, but do think how you will make up for lost time.

- Look for *relevant examples* of what you have covered in the 'real' world. If you work for a financial organisation, this should provide them. If you don't, then think about your experiences as an individual bank or building society customer or perhaps about your employer's position as a corporate customer of a bank. Keep an eye on the quality press for reports about relevant developments.

Revising

The period that you have earmarked for revision is a very important:

- *Make use of a timetable.*

- *Clear objectives should be set for each revision session*

- *Use time sensibly.* How much revision time do you have? Remember that you still need to eat, sleep and fit in some leisure activities!

- *Allocate the available time to maximise the impact on your preparation.* What are your weaker topic areas? You will probably need to put extra effort into some topics, whilst others you may absorb relatively easily. You will also need to plan your revision around your learning style.

● *Believe in yourself.* Are you cultivating the right attitude of mind? There is absolutely no reason why you should not pass the exam if you adopt the correct approach. Be confident, you have passed exams before so you can pass this one.

Passing examinations is half about having the required knowledge, understanding and skills, and half about the right *technique in the examination.*

Taking the examination

First, make sure that you satisfy the examiner's requirements:

● *Read the instructions on the front of the exam paper carefully.* Check that the exam format is what you expect. It is surprising how often examiners' reports remark on the number of students who attempt too few – or too many – questions, or who attempt the wrong number of questions from different parts of the paper. Make sure that you are planning to answer the right number of questions drawn from the correct parts of the question paper.

● *Read all the questions on the exam paper before you start writing.* Come to some view on the preferred ordering of questions that you intend to attempt in the light of your preparation. Look at the weighting of marks given to each part of the question. This will give an indication of the distribution of effort required.

● *Don't produce irrelevant answers.* Make sure you answer the question set, and not the question you would have preferred to be set.

● *Produce an answer in the correct format.* If a question asks for a diagram or an example, give one. If a question does not specifically asks for a diagram or example, but it seems appropriate, give one.

Second, observe the following simple rules to ensure that your script is acceptable to the examiner:

● *Present a tidy paper.* You are a professional and it should always show in the presentation of your work. Candidates may be penalised for poor presentation and so you must make sure that you write legibly, label diagrams clearly and lay out your work professionally. Assistant examiners each have dozens of papers to mark; a badly written scrawl is unlikely to help your chances of receiving any benefit of the doubt.

● *State the obvious.* Many candidates look for complexity that is not required and consequently overlook the obvious. Make basic statements first. Plan your answer and ask yourself whether you have answered the main parts of the question.

● *Use examples.* This will help to demonstrate to the examiner that you keep up-to-date with the subject. There are lots of useful examples scattered through this workbook and you can read about others if you dip into the quality press or take notice of what is happening in your working environment.

Finally, make sure that you give yourself the opportunity to do yourself justice:

- *Select questions carefully.* Read through the paper once, then quickly jot down any key points against each question in a second read through. Reject those questions against which you have jotted down very little. Select those where you are reasonably confident about what is required.

- *Plan your attack carefully.* Consider the order in which you are going to tackle questions. Many students decide to tackle first the question that they believe will be easiest for them to answer. This can be a useful confidence builder.

- *Read the question carefully and plan your answer.* Read through the question again very carefully when you come to answer it.

- *Gain the 'easy' marks.* Include the obvious if it answers the question and do not spend valuable time trying to produce a perfect answer at the expense of 'easier' marks from other questions.

- *Avoid getting bogged down in small parts of questions.* If you find a part of a question difficult, get on with the rest of the question. If you are having problems with something the chances are that everyone else is too.

- *Don't leave the exam early.* If you finish early, use your spare time to check and recheck your script.

Acknowledgement

The author and publishers wish to thank Mr Alastair Tyler (of Abbey National Treasury Services plc) and Mr Paul Cowdell (Yorkshire Bank Principal Lecturer, Sheffield Hallam University) for their valuable and constructive comments on the first draft of this 4th edition of this Workbook.

1

THE PROPERTIES AND PRICING OF FINANCIAL ASSETS

Objectives

After studying this unit, you should be able to:

- describe the nature of financial assets and appreciate their principal economic functions;

- understand the nature, characteristics and functions of money;

- describe the importance of the banking system to the determination of the money supply;

- understand the impact of money on prices and output;

- explain the principles of the pricing of financial assets;

- understand the concept of risk associated with financial assets;

- appreciate how risk may be managed through portfolio diversification.

1 The nature and economic functions of financial assets

1.1 An asset is any possession that has value to the owner. An asset may be a physical possession (e.g. land, buildings or jewellery) or a claim on something or somebody (e.g. a mortgage, a book debt, or a loan to or a deposit with a third party). It could also be intangible, and yet still have significant value; for example a brand name (such as Pepsi or Black Magic) or goodwill, which, in effect, is the value of a business's existing customers and reputation.

1.2 A financial asset is an intangible asset that may be defined as a claim that is expressed in terms of money. By contrast, real assets, termed tangible assets, have physical substance.

1.3 Financial assets have one similarity with physical assets, in that they both yield a return for their owners. In the case of financial assets, the return is normally in the form of interest, profits or dividends. Physical assets such as machinery are used to produce output, which, in turn, generates sales revenue. Residential property generates housing services, a car generates transportation services, and so on, each of which has value to the owner. Also, financial and physical assets may be linked because a financial asset may be issued as a means of raising funds to purchase a physical asset. Cash and other non-interest-bearing elements of the money supply do not generate any monetary return for their holder; rather these financial assets have value in terms of what they will purchase and the convenience that they embody.

1.4   Most financial assets generate a stream of income and other receipts – they generate a cash flow – for their owners, for example:

- Mortgage loans – interest and repayment of principal.

- Company shares – half-yearly dividends, a rise in share prices (bringing in cash when the shares are sold).

- Bonds (or gilt-edged securities) – interest plus capital repayment on maturity.

- Bills – discount (= excess of maturity value over purchase price) plus capital repayment on maturity.

- Trade debt – eventual payment plus any interest if specified in contract of sale.

- Bank deposits – most, but not all, pay some interest and the sum deposited is available for withdrawal (perhaps following a period of notice).

- Building society deposits – almost invariably these pay interest and again the funds may be withdrawn.

- Cash (bank notes and coin) – no interest is paid and the entire return is non-monetary.

The functions of financial assets

1.5   Financial assets have two main functions. These are to:

- Transfer funds from people and organisations with surplus funds to those who need funds – often so that they can purchase tangible assets.

- Redistribute the unavoidable risk associated with the cash flows generated by tangible assets. For example, a company may be financed partly by equity shares (which pay a dividend according to the company's profitability and hence its ability to pay) and partly by loan stock which has a fixed coupon (and hence entails a regular servicing requirement).

Study Activities 1

1. What is the key characteristic of all assets? *(Paragraph 1.1)*

2. Define a financial asset. *(Paragraph 1.2)*

3. How are financial assets related to real (physical) assets? *(Paragraph 1.3)*

4. What is meant by the cash flow of a financial asset? *(Paragraph 1.4)*

5. Give three examples of financial assets and the nature of the cash flows that they generate. *(Paragraph 1.4)*

6. What are the major economic functions of financial assets? *(Paragraph 1.5)*

2 The properties (characteristics) of financial assets

2.1 The key characteristics of financial assets are normally listed as follows:

Liquidity

2.2 An asset is defined as being liquid if it may be converted into cash quickly, without capital loss and without loss of interest. A market is said to be liquid when assets can be sold on it without their losing much capital value or there being much delay or expense. Therefore, liquidity may be derived from the market for an asset or from the contractual nature of the asset.

Cost of convertibility into and out of cash

2.3 This relates to the cost of investing in an asset and then subsequently converting the asset back to cash. For example, shares in leading companies may be easy to buy and sell in an active market, but there are costs involved in these transactions, including the 'bid-offer spread', broker's commission, stamp duty and other charges. These costs may be termed the 'round-trip costs'. Apart from any loss of interest, there is normally no round-trip cost associated with a bank deposit, although there will be other (usually small) transaction costs.

Divisibility and denomination

2.4 A financial asset may be divisible into very small units; for example, most bank deposits may be made or withdrawn in any amount (in theory, down to one penny). Other financial assets may only be traded in their original large denominations of issue; for example, the minimum issue denomination of a sterling certificate of deposit may be £50,000.

Associated cash flow

2.5 This was mentioned and illustrated in paragraph 1.5 but it is important to appreciate how inflation can eat into the expected cash flow from an asset. Thus, as well as looking at nominal cash flows (returns), analysts and investors examine real returns, i.e. after allowing for anticipated inflation. It is possible to subtract the inflation rate from the nominal interest rate on an asset to get an approximation of the real rate of interest. In many countries a number of financial assets are index-linked, so that their real returns rise in line with inflation. In the UK, for example, certain gilt-edged securities are index-linked, in regard to both capital and repayment.

Term to maturity

2.6   This characteristic relates to the time period that must elapse before the full nominal or face value of a financial asset is returned to the holder by the issuer of the asset. For example, a gilt-edged security may be issued with an original maturity of ten years. On the day of issue, that security has a term to maturity of ten years. Nine years after the date of issue, the security has a (residual) term to maturity of one year.

Contractual convertibility

2.7   Within the terms of the contract that created them, some financial assets may be exchanged for or converted into other forms of financial asset. For example, a convertible loan stock may, on certain specified dates, be converted into ordinary shares at a stated price.

Uncertainty of return

2.8   There is nearly always some uncertainty related to the cash flow associated with a financial asset. In the UK, gilt-edged securities are the only financial asset whose associated return is regarded as being without risk. However, inflation can eat into the real purchasing power even of this guaranteed income stream. Accordingly, the UK government issues index-linked gilt-edged securities, which removes this particular risk for investors (but replaces it with an uncertain nominal yield – as inflation cannot be predicted with complete accuracy).

Currency of denomination

2.9   Most financial assets are denominated in a single currency; e.g. sterling or the US dollar. However, they may also be denominated in terms of a basket of currencies. For example, prior to the introduction of the Euro, some UK Treasury bills were denominated in ECU (a composite basket of EU members' currencies). Some financial assets also allow investors some discretion over the currency of denomination of the returns.

Tax status

2.10   This is an important characteristic of an asset, because most income flows and some capital gains are subject to tax. However, rates of tax can change annually, while the underlying principles of each country's tax system can also change, although usually less frequently. In the UK, some assets are completely free of income tax and capital gains tax, e.g. National Savings Certificates, although they are still subject to inheritance tax. Obviously, the liability of its cash flow to taxation does reduce the attraction of an asset to potential investors who are subject to that tax.

Study Activities 2

1. Compare the liquidity of an asset with the liquidity of a market. *(Paragraph 2.2)*

2. What is meant by 'the cost of convertibility of a financial asset'? *(Paragraph 2.3)*

3. Explain why denomination is important if an asset is not divisible. *(Paragraph 2.4)*

4. Distinguish between nominal and real yield (cash flow). *(Paragraph 2.5)*

5. What is meant by 'residual term to maturity'? *(Paragraph 2.6)*

6. Is convertibility a characteristic given to an asset by the market in which it is traded? Explain your answer. *(Paragraph 2.7)*

7. In what sense is the return on index-linked gilt-edged securities uncertain?
(Paragraph 2.8)

8. Why is an investor's tax status of importance to his or her choice of financial assets?
(Paragraph 2.10)

3   Money

Definition

3.1   Money may be defined as any asset that is generally acceptable as a medium of exchange or for the settlement of debts. Today, money is normally a financial asset, i.e. a claim on the issuing organisation (bank or government). In the past commodities were used as money. People may revert to using physical assets as money if there is a breakdown of confidence in the acceptability of notes and coin (token money) and transfers of bank deposits (representative money).

Characteristics of money

3.2   The essential characteristic of money is that it must be generally acceptable. Unless the vast majority of people are willing to accept an asset in exchange for goods, services or other assets, then that asset is not money. In a modern economy, most people will accept bank notes and coin, bank deposits and building society deposits as media of exchange and in discharge of debt.

3.3   In addition to being generally acceptable, it is desirable for assets functioning as money to posses some or all of the characteristics listed as follows:

Stability of value

3.4 Money has been criticised as being 'a financial tape measure made of elastic' because its value (its purchasing power) changes over time – and usually downwards. This is the problem, of course, caused by inflation – a rising level of prices in general. Countries that have experienced exceptionally high rates of inflation (known as hyperinflation), leading to a complete breakdown of confidence in the country's money, have sometimes felt it necessary to replace their currency with a new one.

3.5 Another way of coping with the declining value of money (the result of ever-rising prices) is to index-link some financial assets, social security benefits and taxes. In the UK, the usual link is with the general (headline) index of retail prices (RPI).

Scarcity

3.6 In the past, countries have often chosen precious metals to be their money, e.g. silver and gold. Countries do not choose assets that are in plentiful supply. Today, a major concern of the authorities of all countries is ensuring that the money supply does not expand too rapidly. The increased sophistication of the financial system has not made this task any easier.

Portability

3.7 Originally, this meant 'easy to carry' but today it encompasses 'easy to transfer, in person, or in writing, or by telephone or by electronic means'.

Durability

3.8 Silver and gold were used as money not only because they are scarce but also because they are long lasting. Coins have a very long life span. However, paper bank notes in circulation need to be renewed fairly regularly. Where money is in the form of book entries (e.g. bank deposits) the life span is technically infinite.

Divisibility

3.9 Most countries use units of 1, 2, 5, 10, 20 and 50 (and often higher values of 100 and multiples thereof) to denominate their notes and coin. By including some very low value denominations, all amounts can be paid in a currency.

3.10 Most cheques can, of course, be written for any amount, although some bank accounts (usually earning a premium rate of interest) do not permit cheques below (say) £250 to be drawn. It should, however, be remembered that cheques are not money, but merely instructions to a bank (or building society) to transfer a financial asset (a credit balance) or to increase a financial liability (an overdraft or loan) by transferring a financial asset to the payee.

Recognisability

3.11   For ease of day-to-day business, money must be easily recognisable as such. Most of us can recognise notes and coin from many countries but it may be harder to recognise a foreign cheque, payment order or giro transfer.

Homogeneity

3.12   All, or nearly all, elements of the money supply must be alike. For instance, a bank deposit should be money whether it is with, say, Barclays Bank or Bank of Scotland.

Study Activities 3

Compare and contrast the characteristics of (a) financial assets in general, and (b) money in particular.   *(Paragraphs 2.2 – 2.10 and 3.2 – 3.12)*

Functions of money

A medium of exchange

3.13   Before the introduction of money, goods were exchanged directly for goods. In other words, trading took place via a process of barter. With the use of money, exchange became indirect. Today, people exchange goods/services, first into money and then from money into another good or service or into a financial asset (other than money). Money is the medium by which the exchange is completed.

A liquid store of value

3.14   People may hold wealth in the form of money. They may choose to exchange physical assets into money and then to store that money for future exchange back into a physical asset or another financial asset. In this context, the importance of the durability and, particularly, the stability of value of money should be noted.

A standard of deferred payment

3.15   Money may be used to denominate commitments to make payments at future dates. In most cases an agreement to pay money is likely to be more acceptable to a creditor than an agreement to hand over a physical asset or to perform a service at a future date. Once again, the impact of inflation needs to be recognised.

A unit of account

3.16   In all forms of trade it is useful to be able to compare directly the value of one type of commodity or service against another. Money can be used for such a comparison. In addition money, being a unit of account, enables assets to be valued for insurance or tax purposes. Other (non-money) assets such as barrels of oil or ounces of gold can perform the function of a unit of account. The major problem of money as a unit of account is that its value is eroded by inflation. This is particularly apparent when it is desired to fix the prices of certain items only periodically. When non-financial assets such as barrels of oil are used the problem can be overcome, unless the value of oil begins to fluctuate violently.

The link between liquidity and money in a modern economy

3.17   There has been much argument amongst economists as to just what items constitute money. Some liquid assets are not counted as money, although any item that can be classed as money must be a liquid asset. Banknotes and coin in the UK must be classed as money because they are legal tender that is readily accepted as a medium of exchange. However, nowadays many transactions involve transfers of bank or building society deposits using cheques or electronic funds transfer. Therefore, whilst there is some risk of payment being refused, transfers of bank and building society deposits are undoubtedly a widely accepted means of payment, and hence the deposits should be considered as money.

3.18   The distinction between current accounts and deposit/savings accounts is blurred. Most banks and building societies will transfer funds from deposit/savings accounts to current accounts on demand, making an appropriate deduction of interest in lieu of a period of notice of withdrawal. Hence, bank and building society deposit/savings accounts also tend to be treated as money.

3.19   Once it is generally accepted that liquid assets other than cash may be classed as money, an extremely important concept begins to emerge regarding what constitutes money. Whilst opinions differ as to the precise items that constitute money, many economists now tend to regard money as a group of assets which embody a high level of liquidity and which reflect private sector purchasing power. In this context, the importance of liabilities of the banking sector (i.e. bank deposits) cannot be overstated. In the UK the most widely used broad definition of the money supply (M4) is composed primarily of bank deposits.

Technical definitions of money in the UK

3.20   There are currently four official monetary aggregates used in the UK:

M0   Notes and coin in circulation outside of the Bank of England + banks' operational deposits with the Bank of England.

M2   M4 private sector holdings of notes and coin + M4 private sector holdings of sterling retail deposits with UK banks + M4 private sector holdings of sterling retail deposits and shares with UK building societies.

M4   M4 private sector holdings of notes and coin + M4 private sector holdings of sterling deposits (including sterling certificates of deposit) with UK banks + M4 private sector holdings of sterling shares and deposits (including sterling certificates of deposit) with UK building societies.

M3H   M4 + M4 private sector holdings of foreign currency deposits with UK banks and building societies + sterling and foreign currency deposits held by UK public corporations with UK banks and building societies.

Note that in respect of the above definitions:

(a) M4 private sector means the UK non-bank non-building society private sector.

(b) Notes and coin relate exclusively to holdings of sterling.

(c) Banks' 'retail' deposits are defined as deposits that arise from a customer's acceptance of an advertised rate (including nil) for a particular product.

(d) Building societies' 'retail' shares and deposits include all shares held by, and sums deposited by, individuals. Also included are shares and deposits placed with societies in accordance with the terms of contractual saving schemes operated by banks and friendly societies acting as intermediaries for individuals and, where a building society has so elected, shares and deposits of under £50,000 from corporate bodies.

3.21   M0 is a narrow definition of money, sometimes referred to as the 'wide monetary base'. The income velocity of circulation of M0, that is the ratio of gross domestic product (GDP) to M0, rose during the 1970s and the 1980s because people used notes and coin more economically as they increasingly used bank services. More recently, the velocity has stabilised as the pace of relevant financial innovation has slowed.

3.22   M4 is the most widely used broad definition of money. The income velocity of circulation of M4, that is the ratio of GDP to M4, declined sharply during the 1980s, again due to financial innovation (making bank and building society accounts more attractive repositories of wealth). During the first half of the 1990s the velocity stabilised, as did the pace of financial innovation (as far as it affected desired holdings of M4), but since 1995 further reductions in the velocity have been observed. It would appear that much of the more recent trend has been due to increased holdings of bank deposits by other financial institutions active in trading securities and derivative instruments. Hence wholesale financial factors, rather than personal expenditure factors, are to blame for this trend.

Study Activities 4

1. Compare and contrast the functions of financial assets used as money with those of all financial assets. *(Paragraphs 1.5 and 3.13 – 3.16)*

2. Distinguish between narrow and broad measures of money. *(Paragraphs 3.20 – 3.22)*

3. What factors might explain recent changes in the trends of the income velocities of circulation of M0 and M4? *(Paragraphs 3.21 and 3.22)*

4 Inflation

The definition of inflation

4.1   Inflation may be defined as a sustained increase in the general level of prices. A one-off increase in the general price level or a sustained increase in just a small number of prices does not constitute inflation.

4.2   In a barter economy, where goods are traded directly for goods, prices in general cannot rise. For example, if the price of bread in terms of milk doubles, then, by definition, the price of milk in terms of bread must have halved. In a modern economy, where money is used as a medium of exchange, there is no reason why the prices of both bread and milk cannot rise simultaneously. It is for this reason that inflation and money are inextricably linked, and this explains why some commentators suggest that inflation is necessarily a monetary phenomenon. It also provides some explanation of why much of the discussion of the control of inflation is concerned with monetary conditions.

4.3   Given the relationship between money and inflation, the definition of inflation may be turned around to emphasise its monetary aspects. Hence, inflation may be defined as a persistent fall in the purchasing power of money. Inflation may, therefore, be viewed as the erosion of the real value of a unit of money, in terms of the volume of goods and services that it may buy.

The problems caused by inflation

4.4   One of the major effects of inflation is the erosion of the real value (purchasing power) of money and of the real value of financial assets that are denominated in money terms. Cash and certain other financial assets such as bank deposits that pay no interest are subject to the full eroding effect of inflation on their real value. One of the problems of inflation is, therefore, that it undermines the ability of money to act as a *store of value*, one of the functions of money identified earlier. When extremely high rates of inflation (known as 'hyperinflation') are experienced, the destruction of the store-of-value function of money becomes so great that people refuse to hold money or to accept it as payment for goods and services, so that it also loses its function as a *medium of exchange*. In these circumstances people revert to the use of barter. Even with quite moderate rates of inflation, however, attempts are made to economise on the volume of cash and non-interest-bearing assets, which leads to a loss of efficiency within the economic system.

4.5   Some compensation for the erosion of real purchasing power caused by inflation may be obtained from the payment of *interest*. If inflation is running at a rate of 8% pa, but 10% pa is obtainable by investing in a particular financial asset, then an individual will, at the end of the period, have received a 2% pa real return on his or her funds. There are, however, several problems here. *First*, the inflation rate may well be higher than the available interest rate on an investment, so that the individual can only receive a partial compensation for the effects of inflation. *Second*, an interest rate to match or exceed the inflation rate may only be achieved by investing in assets of a very low liquidity. Assets offering a high level of liquidity tend to offer lower interest rates, and so the investor is faced with the choice either of achieving good protection from inflation or of achieving an acceptable level of liquidity. *Third*, the level of inflation will not be known in advance. On the basis of the *current* rate of inflation, an investor may invest in an asset that offers complete protection from inflation, but if there is an *unexpected increase* in the inflation rate, the protection from inflation will be accordingly reduced. *Fourth*, the prevalence of inflation may, by itself, increase the risk associated with financial assets purchased by investors seeking protection from the effects of inflation.

4.6   It is common for many financial assets to suffer declines in their real value in times of inflation. Cash and non-interest-bearing bank deposits will inevitably incur falls in their real value due to inflation, but interest-bearing assets may also do so. The majority of bonds issued by the government are issued at a fixed rate of interest, and consequently when the inflation rate rises above that interest rate, real capital losses are likely to be incurred by the holders of the bonds. Much of the debt issued by companies is also of a fixed-interest type, and hence the holders of that debt are in the same position. In practice, the major investors in government and corporate fixed-interest debt are pension funds and insurance companies, and hence the members of pension funds and the holders of insurance policies will suffer losses as a result.

4.7   The holders of fixed interest financial assets that are expressed in money terms are likely to be losers in times of unexpected inflation. In broad terms, these will be the *lenders* of money in an economy. By contrast, those who gain from unexpected inflation will be the *borrowers* in an economy. A government, with a large debt outstanding and a budget deficit financed by borrowed funds, is therefore a major beneficiary of inflation. The corporate sector will also benefit from unexpected inflation to the extent that it is a net borrower. Personal sector debtors with mortgage loans, who over many periods of time have seen increases in the prices of their homes substantially above the inflation rate, have tended to benefit at the expense of those individuals with savings in building societies and other mortgage providers. Of course, if interest rates are variable and adjust to compensate for changes in the rate of inflation, this unintended redistribution of income may be largely removed.

4.8   Unexpected inflation, therefore, causes an arbitrary *redistribution of income and wealth* from lenders to borrowers. There are also lesser problems associated with inflation, including:

●   *Uncertainty*. Inflation introduces uncertainty since in the case of longer-term contracts that are expressed in money terms, the *real* return from any such contract will be affected by future inflation rates that are, of course, unknown. The response may then be for people and business organisations to *avoid* longer-term contracts and to place emphasis on short-term returns, which may well lower the efficiency and growth rate of the economy.

- *Inflation illusion.* During periods of inflation, there is a tendency for people to *think* that their real purchasing power is falling due to increases in prices, and to forget to consider what is happening to their incomes which, if wages or salaries, are almost invariably rising by a similar rate as inflation.

- *Costs of changing prices.* The costs of frequent changes in price lists, of changing vending machines, payphones and so on, as a consequence of inflation are costs that may be substantial, particularly for certain industries.

- *Costs of learning prices.* The presence of inflation will cause an individual's knowledge of prices to become out-of-date very quickly. With frequent purchases this will not present a difficulty unless inflation is very rapid. With infrequent purchases, however, an individual will have little idea of an appropriate price, and will have to devote time and effort to re-learning the appropriate price for a product or service by surveying the market.

The problems caused by inflation ensure that it is a general cause of concern, and hence most governments (and especially central banks) devote considerable effort to deriving policies aimed at keeping the rate of inflation low.

The relationship between money, prices and output

4.9　A useful starting point for the analysis of the relationship between money and inflation is the *Fisher equation* (also known as the 'equation of exchange'). This may be stated as

$$MV = PT$$

where　　M = money stock

V = velocity of circulation of money

P = average price level of transactions

T = number of transactions per period.

4.10　Strictly speaking, the Fisher equation is an identity because it is necessarily true. This may be appreciated by noting that MV represents the total value of all expenditures in a period, while PT represents the total value of all sales in a period. Since expenditures must be matched by sales of equal value, the two sides of the equation must always be equal.

4.11　In order to turn the Fisher equation into a theory of inflation, the so-called 'monetarist' school of thought asserts that

(a) V is predictable and that its long-term trend is stable;

(b) T has a long-term value determined by forces within the real economy. The basis of this view is that market forces will push the economy towards a position of full employment, although there may be short-term rigidities and disruptions that allow unemployed resources to occur in the shorter term.

4.12   These assertions suggest that, in the short-run, an increase in the money supply may result in an increase in the level of output and employment. Also there may be a reduction in nominal interest rates, due to the fact that some of the additional money supply may be used to purchase financial assets, driving their prices up and their yields down. In the longer-term, however, adjustments will take place in the real economy such that there will be no effect on the real levels of output or employment. The only long-term effect will be to raise the general price level.

4.13   An alternative school of thought flows from the so-called 'Keynesian' doctrine. This maintains that V is volatile due to a number of factors. For example, changes in interest rates may cause people to hold varying money balances in bank and building society accounts as the opportunity cost of doing so alters. Also, it is emphasised that there are significant problems in defining M in a modern economy. Consequently, the monetarist view that inflation may be controlled via manipulation of M is strongly criticised. Although it must be recognised that Keynesians do accept that significant increases in the money supply are not only likely to boost the level of demand and output in the short-term, but also are likely to result in a higher long-term price level.

4.14   Irrespective of the position taken on theory there is no mistaking the practical importance of the banking sector in the determination of the price level and output. Bank deposits dominate the broad measures of the money supply most widely regarded by economists as being relevant for spending decisions. Therefore, as bank lending is the main determinant of deposit growth, the lending policy of banks is crucial to the determination of the rate of inflation (at least in the longer term). In the shorter-term, bank lending may drive economic growth through consumer and investment expenditure financed by borrowing. Financial innovation initiated by banks may also influence V, so influencing the inflationary impact of a given increase in M. The implications for controlling inflationary forces are clear (and will be taken up in Unit 6).

Study Activities 5

1. How does inflation affect the use of money as a medium of exchange and a store of value?   *(Paragraph 4.4)*

2. Need money always be a poor store of value? Why?   *(Paragraph 4.5)*

3. In what sense may borrowers gain from inflation?   *(Paragraph 4.7)*

4. In addition to the problems implied by questions 1 – 3, what other problems are caused by inflation?   *(Paragraph 4.8)*

5. Specify the equation of exchange and explain what it signifies.   *(Paragraph 4.9)*

6. According to the monetarist school of thought, what are likely to be the short-term implications of an increase in the money supply?   *(Paragraph 4.12)*

7. What is the long-term impact of an increase in the money supply according to the monetarists? Relate your explanation to the equation of exchange.   *(Paragraph 4.12)*

8. In what ways does the Keynesian analysis of the impact of an increase in the money supply differ from the monetarist analysis?   *(Paragraphs 4.12 and 4.13)*

9. Outline the role of banks in the relationship between money, prices and output.
         (Paragraph 4.14)

5   Discount rates and the value of financial assets

5.1   In technical terms, the *true* or *correct* price of an asset equates to the present value of all expected future cash flows associated with the asset. For example, a government bond may pay a £500 coupon (interest payment) at the end of each of five years, and the maturity value of the bond may be £10,000. The true or correct price of the bond is the present value of that stream of cash – that is, £500, £500, £500, £500 and £10,500. However, as an amount of money at a future date is generally not regarded as having the same value as the same amount of money today, the future cash flows must be *discounted* in order to determine their present value. It would only be if a zero discount rate was to applied to the future cash flow that the present value of the bond in the above example would be the sum of the cash flows, i.e. £12,500.

5.2   The formula that is applied to a set of expected future cash flows in order to determine their present value is expressed as follows:

$$PV = \frac{CF_1}{(1+r)} + \frac{CF_2}{(1+r)^2} + \frac{CF_3}{(1+r)^3} + \ldots\ldots + \frac{CF_n}{(1+r)^n}$$

where PV = the true (or correct) price of a financial asset

CF_t = the cash flow associated with the asset in years $t = 1, 2, \ldots, n$

n = the years to maturity of the financial asset

r = the discount rate to be applied.

It will be noted that, taking each element of the cash flow separately, the formula derives from the compound interest calculation. Effectively, the calculation involves determining the amount of money that would need to be invested today at the appropriate market rate of interest in order to generate the expected future cash payments. This provides a clue to the practical determination of the discount rate; i.e. the appropriate market rate of interest may be used.

5.3　　As an example, a discount rate of 10% may be applied, and assuming that the cash is received at the end of each year, the present value of the bond quoted above would be

$$PV = \frac{500}{(1 + 0.1)} + \frac{500}{(1 + 0.1)^2} + \frac{500}{(1 + 0.1)^3} + \frac{500}{(1 + 0.1)^4} + \frac{10,500}{(1 + r)^n}$$

$$= £(454.5 + 413.2 + 375.6 + 341.5 + 6,519.7) = £8,104.5$$

Clearly, this value is considerably less than the crude summation of the expected cash flows. The greater the discount rate applied, the smaller the present value becomes. Intuition provides some explanation of why an expected future cash flow has a value to the recipient that is less than the same amount received today, but the determination of the discount rate is more complex than just finding a value to reflect human nature.

5.4　　In theory, the discount rate recognises six factors that cause people to discount the value of expected future cash flows relative to cash in hand. These factors may be summarised as follows:

(a) The reward required by lenders/investors for forgoing current consumption. This may be thought of as the real rate of interest required on the asset.

(b) Compensation required for expected inflation, which may erode the purchasing power of money lent.

(c) Default risk premium, which is required to cover the risk that the borrower will fail to meet interest payments and/or principal repayments.

(d) Liquidity premium, which is required to cover the risk that marketable assets may need to be sold at an unfavourable price in order to redeem the funds prior to maturity (assuming that the asset has an associated maturity date).

(e) Compensation required by the lender when funds cannot be accessed for a fixed period of time.

(f) Premium required in respect of the risk associated with assets denominated in a foreign currency as a result of unexpected exchange rate movements.

5.5　　It is easy to see that should the investor's financial requirements or perception of the financial environment alter, the discount rate is also likely to alter. For example, if expectations of future inflation are adjusted upwards, so too will be the discount rate. Hence, any given sequence of cash flows associated with an asset will generate a smaller present value. In other words, the true or correct value of the asset will fall. It should also be noted that the appropriate discount rate may alter from period to period as the events and expectations associated with different periods of time alter. Consequently, the individual elements of a stream of cash flows may be discounted at different rates. As stated above, in practice appropriate market-determined rates of interest will be used as a guide to the discount rates to be applied to any particular asset's expected cash flows.

Study Activities 6

1. In what circumstances would the present value of an asset equate to the sum of the expected cash flows from the asset? *(Paragraph 5.1)*

2. Specify the formula for calculating the present value of a stream of annual cash flows expected over a four-year period. *(Paragraph 5.2)*

3. What factors influence the discount rate that an investor might apply in the calculation of the true or correct price of a financial asset? *(Paragraph 5.4)*

4. Explain why the upward adjustment of expectations of future inflation may lead to a downward adjustment in the present value of a financial asset. *(Paragraph 5.5)*

6 Risk and diversification

6.1 All financial assets embody some degree of risk in the sense that there is always some chance that the expected return from them will not materialise. On some assets the risk of outright default on payment of interest or repayment of principal is very small. For all practical purposes bonds issued by the governments of the leading industrial states are free of default risk. Holdings of such bonds are not, however, free of risk entirely, as capital losses may accrue if the bonds have to be sold at a time when market conditions are adverse. Unexpectedly high rates of inflation and movements in exchange rates (in respect of foreign currency bonds) also pose risks to holders of default-free assets.

6.2 The risks faced by holders of financial assets, which are both explicit and implicit in the factors influencing the determination of discount rates (as discussed above in 5.4), may be divided into two broad types: unsystematic risk and systematic risk.

6.3 Unsystematic risk (which may also be referred to as specific risk, variant risk, idiosyncratic risk or diversifiable risk) is the risk that the borrower or the issuer of a particular security will default on the obligations. This risk may itself be sub-divided into various other risks, which effectively identify the root causes of the problem. Some commonly cited examples include:

(a) *Business risk*, which occurs as a result of revenues being insufficient to cover the fixed costs of operations. The greater the proportion of fixed costs faced by the firm, the greater is the susceptibility of the firm to variability of revenues.

(b) *Financial risk*, which occurs as a result of revenues being insufficient to cover fixed charges such as interest payments on debt. The greater is the firm's reliance on interest-bearing debt relative to equity (i.e. the higher is its financial gearing), the more exposed it is to variability in revenues.

(c) *Management risks*, which arise when the managers of a firm are inexperienced or incompetent and prove to be unable to run the business profitably.

(d) *Collateral risk*, which is related to the possible inadequacy of the claims that a lender may have on a borrower. In the case of a company going into liquidation, an ordinary shareholder faces a much higher level of collateral risk than does a creditor whose claim is secured against fixed assets of the company.

6.4   So long as unsystematic risk is independent of economic developments in general, it can be reduced and at the extreme eliminated via portfolio diversification. Basically, this means that so long as the unsystematic risk associated with assets held within a portfolio are not correlated, the positive and negative variations around the expected returns on the assets should largely cancel each other out. Portfolio theory is discussed in more detail in Unit 9. At this stage, suffice it to say that in an efficient market there will be no premium paid for unsystematic risk.

6.5   By contrast, systematic risk (also known as market risk, covariant risk or non-diversifiable risk) cannot be removed via the holding of a diversified portfolio of assets. This is because this type of risk is derived from general market conditions which affect all borrowers and issuers of securities. For example, if the economy moves into a period of recession the earnings of most businesses are likely to suffer, and personal incomes are likely to fall. Consequently, it is almost impossible to avoid this risk, and the values of financial asset portfolios may be adversely affected, irrespective of the number of different assets held therein.

6.6   Systematic risk affects different types of financial assets differently:

(a) A *reinvestment risk* is associated with fixed-term fixed-capital value deposits. This means that upon maturity funds may have to be reinvested at a lower rate of interest. The greater are fluctuations in the general level of interest rates, the greater is this risk.

(b) Fluctuations in the market rate of interest also affect the market value of bonds. This *interest rate risk* arises because of the fixed interest (coupon) payments attached to bonds, which may become more or less attractive as market rates of interest fall or rise. The relative attractiveness of the income stream will, of course, affect the demand for bonds and hence their market values. The extent to which the market value of a bond alters in response to a given change in interest rates is known as its *duration*. The greater is the response the greater is the duration, and hence the greater is the systematic risk.

(c) Fluctuations in corporate earnings have a major influence on the values of equity shares (i.e. claims on the residual income and net worth of companies). The more volatile are a company's earnings relative to the market as a whole, the greater is the *beta* value associated with that company's shares. If a company has a beta value of unity, this means that its earnings fluctuate in line with the average fluctuation of earnings in the market as a whole. A beta value of less than unity means that earnings are less volatile than average volatility of all shares, and a beta value above unity means that they are more volatile. Therefore, the greater is the beta value associated with a company's shares, the greater is the systematic risk of those shares.

6.7   As systematic risk cannot be removed by portfolio diversification, the existence of this form of risk will always be factored into the required return that investors and lenders seek. Hence it will influence the discount rate to be applied to an expected cash flow from an asset, and consequently the true or correct price of the asset.

Study Activities 7

1. How can British government bonds be both risk-free and yet risky? *(Paragraph 6.1)*

2. What is meant by unsystematic risk? Give some examples of the causes of unsystematic risk.   *(Paragraph 6.3)*

3. In what circumstances will there be no premium paid to cover unsystematic risk?
    (Paragraph 6.4)

4. What is meant by systematic risk?   *(Paragraph 6.5)*

5. Explain the terms reinvestment risk, interest rate risk, duration and beta value.
    (Paragraph 6.6)

6. Why does the existence of systematic risk affect the true or correct price of an asset?
    (Paragraph 6.7)

Summary

Now that you have completed this unit, you should be able to:

● describe the nature of financial assets and appreciate their principal economic functions;

● understand the nature, characteristics and functions of money;

● describe the importance of the banking system to the determination of the money supply;

● understand the impact of money on prices and output;

● explain the principles of the pricing of financial assets;

- understand the concept of risk associated with financial assets;

- appreciate how risk may be managed through portfolio diversification.

Self-assessment questions

Short-answer questions

1. What characteristics are desirable for a good form of money?

2. What is the essential function of money? What other functions can money perform?

3. Why might an investor be faced with a choice between holding a good store of value or holding an asset that has a high degree of liquidity?

4. Summarise the basic principles of pricing a financial asset.

5. 'The market will offer compensation for some risks associated with financial assets, but not for other risks'. Explain.

Multiple-choice questions

1. The two major functions of financial assets are to:

   (a) create risk and redistribute risk

   (b) transfer funds from lenders to borrowers and redistribute risk

   (c) transfer funds from borrowers to lenders and redistribute risk

   (d) aggregate funds and assume risk

   (e) display price information and create incentives.

2. Inflation is normally defined as:

   (a) the occurrence of price rises within the economy

   (b) a sustained increase in the general level of prices

   (c) an increase in the nation's money supply

   (d) a sustained increase in the prices of some goods

   (e) a sustained increase in the price level of manufactured goods.

3. With regard to the Fisher equation, modern monetarists argue that:

   (a) V is constant

   (b) V and T are both constant

   (c) V has a stable long-term trend

   (d) V is unpredictable in the long-term

   (e) M and P are both fixed in the short-term.

4. A financial asset generates cash flows of £500 in Year 1, £500 in Year 2 and £1,000 in Year 3. Applying a discount rate of 10% to the cash flows, the true or correct price of the asset is:

   (a) £2,000

   (b) £2,200

   (c) £1,350

   (d) £1,821

   (e) £1,619

5. Unsystematic risk:

   (a) arises from events that affect the market as a whole

   (b) may be ignored by an investor

   (c) allows borrowers to raise funds more cheaply than would otherwise be the case

   (d) may be reduced via the holding of a diversified portfolio of assets

   (e) relates exclusively to the valuation of equity shares.

2
Financial Institutions

Objectives

After studying this unit, you should be able to:

● understand the difference between financial institutions and financial intermediaries;

● understand the nature and economic significance of financial intermediaries;

● appreciate the Bank of England's role in liquidity management and monetary policy;

● appreciate the difference between retail and wholesale activities of financial institutions;

● understand the main operations of banks and building societies, and appreciate the competitive environment within which they operate;

● describe the activities of the other deposit-taking financial intermediaries;

● compare and contrast deposit-taking and investing financial intermediaries;

● understand the roles and operations of insurance companies and pension funds;

● appreciate the operations of unit trusts and investment trusts.

1   Services provided by financial institutions

1.1   Financial institutions are organisations that provide services in connection with one or more of the following:

● Financial intermediation, linking ultimate providers of funds with ultimate users and creating new financial assets in the process.

● Exchanging financial assets on behalf of their customers, i.e. acting as brokers or agents for clients.

● Exchanging financial assets for their own accounts – proprietary dealers, as they are termed.

● Helping to create financial assets for their customers, and then selling these assets to others in the market – underwriting new share issues, for example.

● Providing investment advice to others, e.g. to people seeking a personal pension or to firms on mergers and takeovers.

- Fund management – managing the whole or part of a pension fund, for example.

1.2   Some large non-financial companies have their own financial subsidiaries. For example, in the UK there is Ford Motor Finance and Marks & Spencer Financial Services. Also in the UK there is the National Savings Bank, which is wholly owned by the Government and where deposits are used by its owner to help finance budget deficits.

2   Definition of financial intermediation

2.1   Financial intermediation is the process of channelling funds between those who wish to lend or invest and those who wish to borrow or require investment funds. Financial intermediaries act as principals, creating new financial assets and liabilities. They do not act solely as agents, charging a commission for their services.

2.2   Given that definition, it is important to note that a wide range of financial institutions is engaged in financial intermediation and that this activity is by no means restricted to banking institutions. Any institution standing between the ultimate provider of funds and the ultimate user of funds is engaging in financial intermediation.

2.3   At the same time it is important to remember that many of the services offered by financial institutions are *not* intermediation activities. Financial advisory services provided by many financial institutions, fund management services and advice on takeovers and mergers provided by merchant banks are all examples of non-intermediary services. Also, insurance agents are sometimes called 'intermediaries' but, in reality, they are only agents and not principals who deal in their own name.

2.4   An important distinguishing characteristic of financial intermediation is that new financial assets and liabilities are created. When money is lent to a financial intermediary the lender holds a claim against that financial intermediary, while if money is borrowed from the financial intermediary, that financial intermediary will be holding a claim against the ultimate borrower. Had the ultimate lender lent directly to the ultimate borrower, only one claim and one liability would have been created. Lending through the financial intermediary results in two claims and two liabilities.

2.5   In the case of a bank or building society deposit, the nature of the claims and liabilities created is usually straightforward. The depositor has a claim for a given amount of money, perhaps to be repaid on demand, while the bank has a matching liability to repay a given amount of money. If the bank on-lends that deposit it has a claim against the borrower for a given amount of money, perhaps to be repaid (with interest) at a given point in time in the future. The borrower, naturally, has a liability to repay that sum of money with interest on the specified date.

2.6   With other financial intermediaries the nature of the claims and liabilities created may not be so straightforward. An individual who buys a long-term insurance policy, for example, may have a claim against the insurance company for a capital sum at a date in the future or on death if that occurs earlier. The insurance company may use the premiums from that policy to purchase a range of different assets, including perhaps ordinary shares in companies (equities), whereby the insurance company will have a claim on the profits earned by the companies involved. The essential point is that not only does financial intermediation involve the creation of additional assets and liabilities, but it may also involve the creation of financial assets and liabilities of a wholly different nature.

3   The requirements of lenders and providers of finance from financial intermediation

3.1   The fact that financial intermediation takes place on a wide scale suggests that both lenders and borrowers have certain requirements that cannot be met by the lender dealing directly with the borrower but that can be met by the use of a financial intermediary. We look first at the requirements of lenders.

3.2   The relative importance of the different requirements on the part of the lender will depend on factors such as income, wealth, the existing holdings of financial assets, etc. However, we may identify four areas that will feature in the requirements of any lenders:

- Expected return;
- Risk;
- Liquidity;
- Transaction costs.

Expected return

3.3   Any lender will only engage in lending because of the profit to be gained from doing so. Lenders will, therefore, be seeking to maximise the return on their loaned funds, other things being equal.

Risk

3.4 Lenders will be concerned to gain a high return on their loaned funds while at the same time minimising the risk involved in the lending. As explained in Unit 1, risk associated with lending money may come in a variety of forms:

Default risk

3.5 This is the risk that the borrower will not repay the sum borrowed or the interest charged when such payments are due. All loans carry a default risk although the extent of the risk will vary. Loans to commercial companies, for example, will carry a higher risk than the negligible default risk associated with securities issued by the UK government.

Risk of capital loss

3.6 This is the risk associated with an increase in the market rate of interest causing a fall in the price of fixed-coupon marketable securities. Governments and private companies often issue such securities as the counterpart to loans received.

Inflation risk

3.7 This is the risk that unexpected increases in the rate of inflation during the life of the loan will reduce the real value of the sum lent, and of the interest payments, below what was anticipated at the time of the loan.

Portfolio risk

3.8 This is the risk that the initial choice of lending opportunities will prove to be poor, in that some of the alternative opportunities that were rejected will turn out to yield higher returns than those selected.

Liquidity

3.9 A liquid asset may be defined as an asset that can be turned into cash quickly and without capital loss or interest penalty. Most bank deposits are therefore very liquid, but investment in, for example, property is highly illiquid. The liquidity that is required by a lender will depend on a number of factors, including in particular the range of liquidity inherent in other securities held. Other things being equal, however, lenders will wish to have a high level of liquidity in their loans.

Transaction costs

3.10 Lenders will be seeking to keep as low as possible the costs associated with seeking out and taking up lending opportunities. They will also, in the case of marketable securities, be taking into account the costs of selling the securities when they wish to withdraw from the loan. Such transaction costs need to be viewed in broad terms, since they will include not only the fees or commissions associated with the purchase and sale of many assets, but will also include the time and trouble involved in identifying and evaluating lending opportunities.

4 The requirements of borrowers from financial intermediation

4.1 Corresponding to the requirements that *lenders* seek to meet by using financial intermediation, *borrowers* will also be seeking to fulfil certain requirements. We may identify five areas that will be of importance to borrowers:

- Interest payable;

- Term of the loan;

- Transaction costs;

- Size of the loan;

- Risk.

Interest payable

4.2 Borrowers will be seeking to minimise the amount of interest that they will pay on their borrowed funds. In this regard, their objectives will be exactly opposite to those of lenders, who will be seeking to maximise the interest return on their loans.

Term of the loan

4.3 An important consideration for borrowers will be the date on which the loan is due to be repaid. In general, borrowers would prefer to have a long period of time before a loan has to be repaid, since this provides them with additional flexibility and reduces the risk of having difficulty in repaying the loan. In this regard also, therefore, the interests of borrower and lender are opposed, since lenders will generally prefer a high level of liquidity.

Transaction costs

4.4 As with the lenders of funds, borrowers will be seeking to minimise the whole range of transaction costs involved in setting up a loan.

Size of loan

4.5 Many borrowers will require relatively large sums of money. This is true of the government, which has in the past required large sums of money to fund its borrowing requirement, and of businesses wishing to fund specific projects, e.g. the Channel Tunnel. It is common, therefore, for the amount of money that a potential borrower wishes to borrow to exceed substantially the amount that any individual lender will wish to lend.

Risk

4.6 Any borrower will need to be aware of the risks associated with a loan, in particular:

- Difficulties involved in renewing a loan if the original loan is for a shorter period than the total required;

- Difficulties and costs caused by the early recall of a loan, if the conditions of the loan allow for this;

- Finding that, due to changed circumstances, the loan is for a smaller amount than required (and that additional funds are necessary), or that it is larger than required (so that interest is being paid on unnecessary funds);

- Obtaining a loan to commence from the date needed;

- Penalty payments may be incurred if the borrower wishes to repay a loan earlier than originally agreed.

As a consequence of these risks, any borrower will be seeking to build in several aspects of flexibility to the conditions of the loan.

Study Activities 1

1. State the functions of financial institutions. *(Paragraph 1.1)*

2. Define the term financial intermediation. *(Paragraph 2.1)*

3. Explain how financial intermediation leads to the creation of new financial assets and liabilities. *(Paragraph 2.4)*

4. Give some examples of assets and liabilities created by the financial intermediation process. *(Paragraphs 2.5 and 2.6)*

5. List the factors that are likely to be considered by a person contemplating lending funds. *(Paragraphs 3.2–3.9)*

6. List the factors that are likely to be considered by a person contemplating borrowing funds. *(Paragraphs 4.1–4.6)*

5 Financial intermediation as a means of accommodating the needs of lenders and borrowers

5.1 Plainly, what potential lenders are seeking on one side and what potential borrowers are seeking on the other will create difficulties in matching borrowers and lenders. When a potential lender is brought together with a potential borrower it may be, for example, that the risk the potential lender is prepared to take on is less than the perceived risk involved in lending to that particular borrower. Alternatively, it might be the case that the borrower wishes to borrow for a much longer period of time than the lender is wishing to lend, or that the borrower requires a much larger loan than the lender wishes to provide. The consequence of this is that even if potential borrowers and lenders are brought together on a widespread scale, so that in principle they could arrange a loan directly between themselves, their conflicting objectives are likely to lead to their being unable to agree terms. The result of this, in turn, is that there will be both unsatisfied demand and unsatisfied supply of loans.

5.2 To a limited extent the different objectives of borrowers and lenders may be accommodated through negotiation over the interest rate on the loan. Payment of a high interest rate on the loan might induce a lender to make a loan that is larger, of longer duration or carries a higher perceived risk than would otherwise be desired. On the other side of the negotiations, the higher interest rate may cause the borrower to reduce the size of the loan or to make it of shorter duration, to bring it into line with what the lender may be offering. In order to avoid paying a higher interest rate the borrower may also be prepared to offer collateral to reduce the risk on the loan, or may offer greater flexibility with regard to repayment.

5.3 In some circumstances negotiation over the interest rate may, therefore, accommodate the differing objectives of borrowers and lenders. However, often the differences are too large for resolution by adjusting the interest rate. In any event, this process assumes that the prospective lenders and borrowers can be brought together in the first place, which may be an unrealistic assumption. In practice lenders and borrowers are distributed throughout the country (or even in different countries), and hence there may be serious problems associated with bringing the two parties together. In addition, it remains the case that even if the practical problems could be overcome, the costs of doing so would substantially reduce the desired volume of borrowing and lending activity. Since that would, for example, leave many businesses short of funds, the result would be a lower level of activity within the economy.

5.4   The alternative method of accommodating the needs of lenders and borrowers is by means of financial intermediation. As we have seen, financial intermediation involves channelling funds between the ultimate lender and the ultimate borrower, and as a consequence of this activity it results in four major outcomes:

- Aggregation of savings;
- Pooling of risk;
- Maturity transformation of funds;
- Reduction of transaction costs.

Aggregation of savings

5.5   As we noted earlier, it is common for lenders to wish to lend smaller amounts of money than borrowers commonly wish to borrow. One outcome of financial intermediation, therefore, is that a number of relatively small deposits from ultimate lenders can be aggregated in order to satisfy the needs of potential borrowers. In this way financial intermediation can overcome one of the problems associated with borrowing and lending directly, by providing a system whereby lenders deposit only modest amounts but borrowers may borrow what could constitute very large amounts.

5.6   The reverse process – *disaggregation* – can occur. For example, a wholesale lender may not wish to incur the expense of processing a large number of mortgage loans, so it may lend a large amount of funds to a financial intermediary which has the necessary administrative backup to provide mortgage loans to the ultimate borrowers. Disaggregation is also helpful to these mortgage lenders, who can raise finance more quickly in the wholesale markets than in the retail markets, thereby enabling them to increase their share of the mortgage market.

Pooling of risk

5.7   A second problem associated with lending and borrowing directly is that the various elements of risk associated with a loan may be too high for the individual lender to accept. For example, the entire risk of default is borne by the single lender. If, however, the loan to the ultimate borrower was to be made by a financial intermediary, then that risk is spread over all the depositors with the financial intermediary. In consequence, the risk of any one depositor losing all his/her funds is substantially reduced, although the risk of losing some funds is increased. It should be noted that financial intermediation does not in itself reduce the risk of a loan going into default but that risk is spread over all the depositors with the intermediary.

5.8   In order to see this process more clearly consider the following simple example. Suppose that on average one in every 10 loans goes into default, with the lender receiving no compensation. Any individual lender (particularly if s/he has only limited wealth and is only able to make one loan at a time) may find the 10% risk of losing the whole loan too great. If, however, the loan is initially to a financial intermediary which is lending to a large number of different borrowers, the risk of losing the whole of one loan is transformed into the near-certainty of losing 10% of the whole portfolio of loans. For the individual lender, therefore, the risk of losing the whole of the loan is virtually zero, but is replaced by the near-certainty of losing 10%. In principle, the 'law of large numbers' operates, not to *eliminate* risk (since the risk of loans going into default is unaltered), but to *transform* it from the point of view of the individual lender to the financial intermediary. In practice, the default risk will be reflected in the difference between the interest rate paid on deposits and the interest rate charged to borrowers; the differential is used in part to absorb the default losses.

5.9   While the *pooling* of the risk involved with lending is the most important consequence of financial intermediation with regard to risk, note that there may be other consequences.

- The financial intermediary will be able to *diversify* the lending across different types of asset, which an individual may not be able to achieve due to a lack of funds. Hence, losses on one type of asset will be offset by gains on another type, so that the risk is reduced further.

- The financial intermediary is likely to have the *expertise and resources to make a much better evaluation* of the risk involved in lending opportunities than individuals would be able to achieve on their own, and consequently the risk taken by the financial intermediary will be *less than the average risk* involved in all lending opportunities.

- In many cases, the *reserves or shareholders' capital* of the financial intermediary will be available to make up deficiencies in the value of deposits should an unusually high rate of defaults occur.

- When supplemented by certain *guarantees initiated by the government*, the risk to the individual lender is reduced further. However, such protection is never for 100% of the amount, to ensure that investors and depositors avoid the most risky propositions (termed the 'moral hazard' of complete protection).

Maturity transformation of funds

5.10   We have noted that borrowers typically want to borrow for a longer period of time than lenders wish to lend. A major feature of financial intermediaries is that they are able to accommodate these different requirements; in general, the claims on a financial intermediary by the lenders are much more liquid than the claims by the financial intermediary on its borrowers. The classic example of this is provided by a building society, where the majority of the funds are repayable on demand yet the society is able to make loans with an initial maturity of, usually, 25 years. However, not all mortgages run their full 20–25-year term and their average length has been eight to 10 years (when the house is sold and the mortgage loan repaid). While building societies provide an extreme example, the principle is also true of, say, banks where the average period of notice to return deposits is very much less than the average time to maturity of its outstanding loans.

5.11   Financial intermediaries are able to do this by virtue of the 'law of large numbers'. The principle involved is that where there is a large number of lenders, the probability of all of those lenders wishing to withdraw the maximum amount of their deposits at the same time is extremely small. While there will be *individual* depositors who do wish to withdraw the whole of their deposits on a particular day, this will be balanced by new deposits and by the majority of deposits being left untouched. Day-to-day variations in the amount withdrawn relative to the amount deposited can be met by changes in the volume of cash or other liquid assets held, and the intermediary will learn from experience what proportion of total deposits needs to be kept as reserves for this purpose. The majority of funds are, however, available for longer-term loans on which the interest rate chargeable will frequently be higher. In summary, it is clear that the financial intermediary has *transformed the maturity* of the short-term deposits into longer-term loans without sacrificing solvency.

5.12   Note that there are certain prerequisites for this maturity transformation of funds to operate smoothly. In particular:

● The number of individual depositors must actually be large enough for the law of large numbers to apply. If the numbers are low, other things being equal, the intermediary will have to hold a large proportion of deposits as cash or other liquid assets.

● Depositors must have confidence that the intermediary will be able to repay funds when required. If this confidence lapses, then depositors *will* seek to withdraw all their funds at the same time and the law of large numbers ceases to be of relevance.

- In order to keep the proportion of cash and other liquid assets low, the intermediary must be able to acquire funds when random fluctuations cause the ratio to fall below the target. For a building society this might involve raising interest rates to attract savings or borrowing funds on the wholesale money market.

5.13   Certain financial intermediaries (notably wholesale banks) have only a small number of depositors, and hence cannot rely on the law of large numbers in order to create maturity transformation of funds. Such institutions will, however, achieve maturity transformation by means of heavy reliance on obtaining funds as and when required and, perhaps, by accepting a higher level of risk than other institutions.

Reduction of transaction costs

5.14   Given the size of the majority of financial institutions, they are able to benefit from economies of scale in a number of areas. These will include:

- Economies in the administration associated with taking in deposits and making loans, due to these transactions becoming routine.

- Economies in the employment of specialist personnel, since the volume of business will allow such people to be fully employed.

- Economies in the acquisition and interpretation of financial information.

Study Activities 2

1. Even if potential borrowers and lenders can be brought together, they may not be able to arrange loans between themselves. Why?   *(Paragraph 5.1)*

2. What is the role of interest rates in accommodating the needs of borrowers and lenders?   *(Paragraph 5.2)*

3. What is the importance of financial intermediaries' ability to aggregate savings?   *(Paragraph 5.5)*

4. What effect do financial intermediaries have on the risk faced by a lender?   *(Paragraphs 5.7–5.9)*

5. What is meant by the maturity transformation of funds within the context of financial intermediation?   *(Paragraphs 5.10–5.11)*

6. What are the prerequisites for the maturity transformation of funds to operate smoothly?   *(Paragraph 5.12)*

7. In what ways do financial intermediaries reduce transaction costs?   *(Paragraph 5.14)*

6 The benefits of financial intermediation

6.1 As a recap, it is now appropriate to review the *benefits* that accrue from financial intermediation. We may consider these in terms of the benefits to the *ultimate lender*, to the *ultimate borrower* and to *society as a whole*.

The benefits to the ultimate lender

6.2 These are:

- *Greater liquidity* is generally achieved by lending to a financial intermediary rather than to the ultimate borrower.

- *Less risk is involved*, due to the pooling of risk inherent with financial intermediation, the improved risk assessment that such intermediaries are able to undertake and the portfolio diversification that can frequently be achieved. This reduction in risk may be reflected in guaranteed interest rates on deposits with a financial intermediary.

- *Marketable securities* may be created. Lending to a financial intermediary will normally give rise to greater liquidity than direct lending to the ultimate borrower. However, additional liquidity (in its broader sense) will be created when the intermediary issues marketable securities in return for deposits. The depositor, instead of waiting until maturity of the security, may sell it in a secondary market to regain the cash.

- A *guaranteed return* may be offered to the lender by a financial intermediary, in contrast to the variable returns more likely to be obtained from lending directly to the ultimate borrower.

- The *lending decision is simplified*, since there are fewer lending opportunities to financial intermediaries than there are to ultimate borrowers. In addition, the assessment of the opportunities for lending to intermediaries is generally a simpler procedure than the individual assessment of the opportunities for lending to ultimate borrowers.

The benefits to the ultimate borrower

6.3 These are:

- Loans will generally be available for *a longer time period* from a financial intermediary than from the ultimate lenders.

- Financial intermediaries will generally be prepared to make loans of *larger amounts* than will ultimate lenders.

- Using financial intermediaries will generally be *cheaper and quicker* than approaching ultimate lenders directly.

- The *interest rate* will generally be *lower* when borrowing from a financial intermediary, compared with borrowing directly from the ultimate lender.

- When borrowing from a financial intermediary, there is a greater likelihood that loans will be *renewed* when required.

The benefits to society as a whole

6.4 Financial intermediation is considered likely to:

- Cause a *more efficient utilisation of funds within an economy*, since the evaluation of lending opportunities will be improved.

- Cause a *higher level of borrowing and lending to be undertaken*, due to the lower risk and costs associated with lending to a financial intermediary.

- Cause an *improvement in the availability of funds to higher-risk ventures*, due to the capability of financial intermediaries to absorb such risk. High-risk ventures are widely considered to be important for creating the basis of future prosperity for an economy.

Study Activities 3

1. What are the benefits generated for lenders by financial intermediaries?
(Paragraph 6.2)

2. What are the benefits generated for borrowers by financial intermediaries?
(Paragraph 6.3)

3. What are the benefits generated for society as a whole by financial intermediaries?
(Paragraph 6.4)

7 The classification of financial intermediaries

7.1 For purposes of analysis it is important to have an operational classification of the wide variety of financial intermediaries found within a modern economy. A conventional approach is to divide financial intermediaries into *bank financial intermediaries* and *non-bank financial intermediaries*. Using the general business operations of the institutions as the basis for classification, bank financial intermediaries comprise retail banks, merchant (or investment) banks and other wholesale banks. In the UK, non-bank financial intermediaries include building societies, the National Savings Bank, finance houses, insurance companies, pension funds, unit trusts and investment trust companies.

7.2 A more refined classification of financial intermediaries formulated on a functional basis is as follows:

Deposit-taking financial intermediaries

These are classified as follows:

- *Retail banks.*
- *Wholesale banks:*
  - British merchant banks (investment banks)
  - Other British banks
  - Overseas banks.
- *Deposit-taking non-bank financial intermediaries:*
  - Building societies
  - Finance houses
  - Credit unions

Investing financial intermediaries

7.3 These *non-deposit-taking non-bank financial intermediaries* include:

- Insurance companies
- Pension funds
- Unit trusts
- Investment trust companies
- Friendly societies.

8 Business aspects of financial intermediation

8.1 Before leaving the topic of financial intermediation, we should consider the business aspects of the process. In common with any business, financial intermediaries will only undertake an activity if it is profitable to do so, which means that the revenues generated by the activity are greater than the costs.

8.2 The *revenues* are the interest payments, dividends and capital gains resulting from the funds that they have lent or used to buy securities.

8.3 The *costs* of financial intermediation arise in three principal areas, the:

- Interest payments or other income flow that has to be allocated to the providers of the funds;
- Operating costs of the institution, which will include salaries and expenses of its employees, rental of buildings and equipment, rates, payment for telecommunications services, VAT and so on. With regard to the retail banks and

some building societies, included here will be the costs of operating the money transmission system;

● Losses caused by borrowers of funds going into default with regard to either interest or principal or both.

8.4 Given that Profit = Revenue – Cost, the profit of a deposit-taking financial intermediary may therefore be enhanced by one or more of four ways, by:

● Increasing the margin between the interest rate paid to lenders and the interest rate charged to borrowers;

● Minimising the operating costs of the institution, and striving to increase efficiency, especially in the utilisation of staff which invariably constitutes the largest proportion of costs;

● Minimising the losses due to default, which may justify the employment of specialist staff and techniques in order to assess risk;

● Pursuing profitable activities not requiring the use of depositors' money, e.g. selling insurance policies. Another name for such activities is 'non-funds-based products'.

8.5 With regard to the interest rate margin competitive forces are important. Thus, if the interest rate on deposits is lowered and that on loans is increased, the intermediary may end up driving business in the direction of its competitors, thereby reducing balance sheet growth and hence profits. As a consequence, intermediaries will place great emphasis on controlling costs and limiting default losses in order to increase profitability.

8.6 Finally, although this unit has been concerned until now with the nature of financial intermediation, it should be noted that many of the services offered by financial intermediaries are *not* intermediary services. Many of them – such as money transmission by the retail banks and building societies – are provided as an adjunct to the intermediary services, either because they are cheap to provide alongside those intermediary services, or because the institution has certain marketing advantages. Frequently these non-intermediary services are provided on a fee basis, and allow the institutions to make better use of some aspect of their resources and expertise.

Study Activities 4

1. What is now the normal basis for the classification of UK financial intermediaries?
(Paragraph 7.1)

2. List the groups of banks included amongst wholesale banks. *(Paragraph 7.2)*

3. List the groups of institutions included under the heading of non-bank financial intermediaries. *(Paragraphs 7.2 and 7.3)*

4. What types of revenues may be derived by a financial intermediation business?

(Paragraph 8.2)

5. What types of costs are associated with a financial intermediation business?

(Paragraph 8.3)

9   The Bank of England

9.1   Most countries with developed financial systems have a central bank of one form or another. Central banks have many specialised functions to perform, and at different times and in different countries the significance attached to any particular function depends upon the characteristics of the financial and economic environment and upon government policy. However, there is little disagreement with the view that the efficient and effective operation of a country's central bank is crucial to the smooth running and stability of that country's monetary and financial system.

9.2   The UK's central bank is the Bank of England. The Bank states that its core purposes are maintaining the integrity and value of sterling; maintaining the stability of the financial system, both domestic and international; and seeking to ensure the effectiveness of the UK's financial services. In order to achieve its objective the Bank of England undertakes a wide range of functions, which, for purposes of analysis, may be divided into monetary policy, banking, market and registration services, and financial system development and support. It is important to appreciate that the Bank of England has recently been experiencing one of the most significant periods of change in its operations and responsibilities to have occurred during its entire history. Of particular note are the changes announced in May 1997 giving the Bank operational independence in respect of monetary policy and removing from it responsibility for banking regulation and supervision. On 1 June 1998 the Bank of England Act 1998 came into force, providing the new framework within which the Bank must now operate and transferring its responsibility for the regulation and supervision of banks and wholesale markets to the Financial Services Authority.

The Bank of England's role in liquidity management and monetary policy formulation

9.3   For many years the Bank of England has provided liquidity to the money markets and, hence, to the financial system as a whole. The Bank's objective has been to maintain the stability of the financial system and, in particular, the stability of short-term rates of interest. For historical reasons, this activity is often been referred to as the Bank's *lender of last resort* function. Formerly, the Bank would lend funds to the discount houses (a small group of specialist intermediaries standing between the Bank and the commercial banks) against the collateral of bills and other short-term instruments. The discount houses would then on-lend funds to the commercial banks or would use the funds to purchase bills from them.

9.4 The lender of last resort function, as described above, should not be confused with the Bank's very occasional involvement in bailing out individual banks that have got into difficulties. This type of operation would only be undertaken if the Bank felt it to be necessary in the interests of financial stability as a whole. It cannot be assumed that the Bank will automatically go to the aid of a bank that appears to be at risk of failing.

9.5 Whilst the basic purpose of day-to-day lender of last resort market intervention is to maintain financial system stability, this activity also has implications for monetary policy. For example, if a shortage of liquidity in the money markets is not rectified there will tend to be upward pressure on short-term interest rates as banks compete for the available funds. Alternatively, an excessive amount of liquidity in the markets may push down short-term interest rates, leading to monetary expansion and consequent inflationary pressures within the economy. In practice, the Bank of England's money market intervention may be used expressly to pursue official monetary policy objectives. In other words, harnessing the flows of funds between the Bank and the money markets is a means of implementing monetary policy.

9.6 Traditionally, the Bank of England undertook monetary policy at the behest of the government. In May 1997 this changed fundamentally, with the Bank of England being given operational freedom in respect of the implementation of the government's monetary policy. The most important practical implication of this occurrence is that the Bank's Monetary Policy Committee now determines whether or not changes should be made in short-term interest rates in pursuit of the goal of a target rate of inflation (currently set at 2.5% +/- 1%) as specified by the government. [Details on the mechanics of monetary policy implementation are given in Section 5 of Unit 3.]

Study Activities 5

1. What broad factors may influence the functions performed by central banks at any given time? *(Paragraph 9.1)*

2. State the core purposes of the Bank of England. *(Paragraph 9.2)*

3. List the broad functions of the Bank of England. *(Paragraph 9.2)*

4. What is the Bank of England's 'lender of last resort' function?
 (Paragraphs 9.3 and 9.4)

5. Why is the lender of last resort function important for money market stability?
 (Paragraph 9.5)

6. In what fundamental way did the Bank of England's monetary policy role alter in May 1997? *(Paragraph 9.6)*

10 Retail and wholesale activities of financial institutions

10.1 Before looking at the activities of each of the main groups of financial institutions, it is useful to consider the difference between the retail and wholesale activities of financial institutions.

10.2 The major distinction between retail and wholesale activities undertaken by financial institutions is in the *size of transactions* involved. Retail activities are concerned with deposits and loans that are of relatively low value, and wholesale activities are concerned with high-value deposits and loans. While no hard distinction between retail and wholesale is possible, a transaction of less than £100,000 would usually be regarded as a retail transaction.

10.3 The distinction between retail and wholesale activities also relates to the *type of customer* involved. Predominantly, retail activities of banks will involve taking in deposits from and making loans to personal customers and small businesses. Notwithstanding this, note that *very large* organisations will often also need to make use of the retail financial services offered by banks. For example, if an organisation has a number of retail outlets, it will make use of local branches of banks in order to deposit cash and cheques.

10.4 A third aspect of the distinction between the retail and wholesale activities of financial institutions relates to the *distribution system* for the services provided. Usually, the provision of retail activities has involved *branch networks* – best typified by the retail banks and by building societies. Although this is the usual format, developments in technology, in particular, are enabling many retail financial services to be provided without a branch network, while some institutions – such as unit trusts – have never operated a branch network. Thus, telephone banking has been developed, while some banks and building societies have launched 'postal accounts', and retail financial services are now becoming increasingly available on the Internet.

10.5 A consequence of retail activities involving transactions of relatively low value is that the *volume* of such transactions will generally be very high. The banks, and increasingly the building societies, are as a consequence partly involved in *money transmission facilities* (such as cheque book accounts, electronic funds transfer and so on) to enable the transfer of funds from one individual or business to another to take place.

10.6 Wholesale activities, being concerned with high-value transactions, typically involve large business customers or other financial institutions. Since these high-value transactions are of limited *volume*, a branch network to support such activities is unnecessary. Also, the interest rates on wholesale transactions are generally market-related rates and are usually at a much finer margin in comparison to retail transactions. The reasons for this occurrence are the high level of competition found in wholesale markets and the lower total costs arising from dealing with limited numbers of high-value transactions.

10.7   Although the distinction between retail and wholesale activities is a useful one, it is important to remember that the distinction is in relation to *activities* rather than institutions. Many financial institutions will be engaged in both wholesale and retail activities. The retail banks, for example, are heavily engaged in wholesale activities, both in terms of obtaining funds and in lending. The larger building societies typically obtain a proportion of their funds from wholesale sources. The basis of classification is therefore in terms of an institution's *dominant* activity, rather than on its *exclusive* activity.

Study Activities 6

1. In relation to size of transactions and types of activities, what are the differences between retail and wholesale activities undertaken by financial institutions?
(Paragraphs 10.2 – 10.7)

2. What is the normal form of distribution channel for retail financial services?
(Paragraph 10.4)

3. For what reasons may wholesale banking activities operate on narrower margins than retail banking activities? *(Paragraph 10.6)*

4. Explain why some financial institutions might be difficult to categorise as either retail or wholesale institutions. *(Paragraph 10.7)*

11   Retail banks

11.1   The term *commercial banks* is used to describe banking institutions that are involved in the traditional banking business of accepting deposits and making loans. This business may be divided into retail activities (which are examined in this section) and wholesale activities (which are dealt with in Section 12 below) according to the scale and nature of the transactions undertaken. In the UK, retail banks comprise a rather diverse set of institutions that vary substantially in terms of their size and scope of operations.

11.2   Some retail banking institutions, notably the London clearing banks such as Barclays and NatWest, have been established as banks for a very long time. Other institutions have only short histories as retail banks, although their origins may be traced back many years. Good examples of this type of institution are the recently converted building societies, such as Halifax and Abbey National.

11.3 The scope of the activities of the institutions varies substantially. The largest clearing banks, for example, all have very extensive wholesale activities, while those of the smaller, more regionally focused retail banks are much more limited. Institutions such as Halifax, Alliance & Leicester and Woolwich undertake activities that are closer in nature to the activities of building societies than to those of the longer-established banks in the group. This is unsurprising given that they only recently converted to banks from mutual building society status.

11.4 Despite these differences, all the institutions offer banking services at a retail level, which involves large numbers of low-value transactions. All the long-established institutions have large dedicated branch networks. By contrast, Girobank (now a subsidiary of Alliance & Leicester) has outlets in post offices. A number of newer entrants to retail banking, such as Prudential Banking, Tesco Personal Finance and Direct Line Financial Services, have no branch networks as such, but rely on telephone, postal and Internet delivery of services, or utilise their parent companies' retail store or office chains to sell their services.

Services

11.5 A key function of the traditional retail banks, which their large branch networks support, is to offer current accounts. The major purpose of current accounts – from the point of view of the account-holder – is that they allow the settlement of debts by means of the transfer of funds from one bank account to another. To allow these transfers of funds, the retail banks have to provide, in conjunction with the current accounts, *payments services*. To achieve this, they offer cheque payment services (supported by cheque guarantee cards to improve acceptability), bank giro credit facilities, direct debits, standing orders and electronic funds transfer via the Bankers' Automated Clearing Service (BACS) and the Clearing House Automated Payments System (CHAPS), together with debit and credit card facilities.

11.6 Retail banks also offer a wide range of other banking services directed particularly at *personal customers*. These services include:

- A range of savings accounts;

- Personal loans, both secured and unsecured;

- Mortgage loans;

- Overdraft facilities;

- Automated teller machines (to allow cash dispensing and other banking services out of normal banking hours);

- Home banking by telephone (to allow transactions to be initiated away from branches and outside normal banking hours);

- Travellers' cheques and foreign currencies;

- Advice on taxation and financial matters;
- Executor and trustee facilities;
- 'Private banking' for high-net-worth individuals.

11.7   Directed particularly at *corporate customers*, retail banks' services include:

- Overdraft facilities and loans, ranging from short-term working capital facilities to long-term secured loans;
- Cash management schemes;
- Electronic banking, using electronic data interchange (EDI) techniques;
- Leasing and hire purchase, often through subsidiaries;
- Export and import financing facilities;
- Payroll services;
- International financial transfers;
- Financial management advice.

11.8   Naturally, not all retail banks offer all these services. In particular, some of the retail banks concentrate on services to *personal* and *small business* customers. Furthermore, the activities listed above relate to *banking* services, although the retail banks are increasingly offering a range of *non-banking* services, including unit trust operations, life and general insurance, and fund management. Profit margins are often higher on such products and services than are available on traditional banking services.

Study Activities 7

1. Outline the key characteristics of the retail banks.   *(Paragraphs 11.2 – 11.5)*

2. Name 10 different types of services provided by a typical retail bank for its personal customers.   *(Paragraph 11.6)*

3. State 10 different types of services provided by a typical retail bank for its corporate customers.   *(Paragraph 11.7)*

The balance sheets of the retail banks

11.9   A good insight into the operations of retail banks may be obtained from an examination of the aggregate balance sheet for the group. The broad structure, in terms of a listing of the key component elements, is given in Table 2.1. (Illustrative figures may be taken from the accounts of any of the UK's major retail banks.) The following analysis relates to the broad distribution of balance sheet items for retail banks in general in recent years. However, it must be recognised that, in practice, individual retail banks may differ significantly from the norm in respect of certain balance sheet items, and the broad balance of items may itself alter over time.

Assets

(i) Sterling assets

11.10 Sterling assets represent about 70% of total assets. It is clear that they dominate the business of the retail banks. The components of those sterling assets are as follows:

11.11 *Cash and balances with the Bank of England.* Despite being the most vital asset for the day-to-day operations of the retail banks, the latter manage to keep the total holdings relatively small. They do so because cash and balances at the Bank of England bring them no income. The balances with the Bank of England are partly operational balances used to meet commitments arising from payments-clearing operations, though they also include the cash ratio deposits that all banks are required to hold with the Bank of England under the provisions of the Bank of England Act 1998. The cash ratio deposits earn no interest and are used by the Bank of England to generate income that is used to pay for activities from which the banks benefit. Only the operational balances are liquid assets for the banks.

11.12 *Market loans.* These account for about 20% of sterling assets, and consequently represent a significant proportion of the retail banks' assets. The 'market' aspect of these loans refers to the fact that they are wholesale loans that are usually made at market-related rates of interest and usually to other banking institutions. The majority of market loans are very liquid; i.e. they have only a short period to maturity, and hence represent an important means of holding interest-bearing assets that are also very liquid. They form the greater part of the banks' liquid assets.

11.13 *Acceptances granted.* Since 1998 all banks have been required to include in their balance sheets both the claims and the liabilities that arise from acceptance activity. The underwriting commitment associated with the acceptance of commercial bills may generate a drain on a bank's resources if the debtor defaults on the bill and the holder of the bill seeks payment from the bank. This liability is balanced by the claim held by the bank on the party whose bill has been accepted. These pairs of liability and asset entries appear under both sterling and foreign currency sections of the balance sheet. Acceptance activity has tended to represent only a small proportion of the retail banks' balance sheets in recent years.

11.14 *Bills.* These account for only about 3 or 4% of sterling assets. As such, they now constitute only a fairly minor element of the retail banks' business, though their importance has been higher in the past. The largest element of these bills is 'eligible bank bills', so called because they are commercial bills that have been accepted (underwritten) by banks which have eligibility status with the Bank of England. To achieve eligibility status, banks have to meet certain criteria set by the Bank of England, relating to the quality of their acceptance business. The significance of eligible bank bills lies in the fact that they are eligible for re-discounting at the Bank of England. A commercial bill that has been accepted by a bank without eligibility status is a normal bank bill and will be included in this category of bills, along with Treasury bills and local authority bills. With a liquid secondary market in bills, these also represent liquid assets that yield an investment return.

11.15 *Claims under sale and repurchase agreements*. These assets have only recently appeared on retail banks' balance sheets. In 1996, an open repo (as these facilities are known) was introduced to the gilt-edged securities market. Banking statistics now show repo claims as a separate asset, with repo liabilities also being shown separately. These claims arise where the banks have bought assets (bills or gilt-edged securities) in sterling from other parties, who must later complete the transactions by buying back the assets from the banks with cash.

11.16 *Advances*. Accounting for around two-thirds of sterling assets, sterling advances clearly represent the most important element of retail banks' assets. Advances constitute the lending made predominantly to the UK private sector, either in the form of overdrafts or loans for fixed periods of time. If the lending is for a fixed period of time, the original maturity may range from a few months to 10 years or more; in the case of mortgage loans, the original maturity is normally for 25 years. The arrangements for the interest rate charged on advances will be either floating (changing with the bank's base rate or the sterling London inter-bank offered rate – LIBOR), or fixed over the duration of the loan, or a hybrid of the two with rates fixed for a certain period of time. In addition, the interest rate charged will vary with the size of the sum borrowed, the creditworthiness of the borrower, the maturity of the loan, the arrangements for repayment, and so on.

11.17 Advances represent the least liquid element of the retail banks' financial assets but also represent the most important source of profit to a retail bank since, subject to competitive forces, the interest margin is greatest on these assets. In order for advances to be profitable, however, the banks need to control the costs of originating and administering the advances and to minimise losses through defaults. Given the lack of liquidity associated with advances, the importance of a substantial proportion of liquid assets – that is, cash, operational balances with the Bank of England, market loans and bills – within the total sterling asset portfolio can be appreciated.

11.18 *Investments*. Traditionally, a large proportion of these investments has been accounted for by securities issued by, or guaranteed by, the British government. An important aspect of British government securities is that they are highly marketable and hence the underlying investment can be realised quickly. Their value changes, however, in the opposite direction to changes in interest rates. Investments account for around 10% of total sterling assets.

(ii) Foreign currency assets

11.19   Foreign currency assets constitute around one quarter of the total assets of the retail banks. The significance of this figure is that the retail banks are not only dealing in sterling at a retail level, but also their business involves a significant foreign currency element.

11.20   The components of the foreign currency assets are very similar to those for sterling assets. A notable figure is that for *market loans and advances to the overseas sector,* demonstrating the point that not only is a substantial element of the business of the retail banks expressed in foreign currency, but also a significant element of that business is non-domestic in nature. In practice market loans are the dominant element. *Sale and repurchase agreements* are available in foreign currencies, although their significance is still relatively modest for the retail banks.

(iii) Miscellaneous assets

11.21   This figure on the asset side of the balance sheet consists of items such as the retail banks' own branch premises and equipment and the value of cheques that have been credited to customers' accounts but which have not been presented for payment to other banks. It includes assets in both sterling and foreign currencies.

Liabilities
(i) Sterling liabilities

11.22   Sterling liabilities represent about two-thirds of total liabilities. This is slightly lower than the proportion of sterling assets in total assets, but account needs to be taken of the 'miscellaneous' items in the balance sheet.

11.23   *Notes issued.* These constitute a relatively small value and represent the notes that are issued by the Scottish and Northern Ireland banks, which are backed, pound for pound, by notes issued by the Bank of England.

11.24   *Sterling deposits.* These account for almost two-thirds of total liabilities, with deposits from the UK private sector (both individuals and businesses) dominating. In addition, around 10% of sterling deposits are in the form of certificates of deposit and other short-term paper. (Sterling certificates of deposit are negotiable bearer securities of fixed term (usually between 28 days and five years), carrying a fixed rate of interest and issued in denominations of £50,000 or more.)

11.25   Around 50% of sterling deposits are in the form of *sight deposits* repayable on demand, with around 80% of these being interest-bearing. The maturity of *time deposits* range from a few days up to several years, and are derived from both retail and wholesale sources. In practice, however, a significant number of the time deposits are repayable on demand (albeit with an interest penalty), and a significant number also have only a short period to maturity. The overall picture facing the retail banks, therefore, is that their sterling liabilities are highly liquid, emphasising their dependence on the 'law of large numbers' to enable them to provide loans and other advances.

11.26 *Liabilities under sale and repurchase agreements.* These arise when a bank has sold assets (bills or gilt-edged securities) in return for cash under sale and repurchase agreements. As part of the contracts, the banks have liabilities to repurchase these bills or gilt-edged securities at some date in the near future.

(ii) Foreign currency deposits

11.27 Foreign currency deposits originate primarily in the form of wholesale deposits, with a high proportion, not surprisingly, coming from the overseas sector. Certificates of deposit are also issued in foreign currencies.

(iii) Miscellaneous liabilities

11.28 These include credit balances received but not yet credited to customers' accounts, and standing orders and credit transfers debited to customers' accounts but not transferred to the payee. These miscellaneous liabilities, however, are normally defined also to include the important element of shareholders' funds, the vast majority of which are denominated in sterling. This item may be sub-divided into equity funds, raised via the issue of share capital, and reserves accumulated via the retention of profits, revaluation of assets and so on. In addition, banks may issue loan stock and debentures to supplement their capital bases. Like any business, a bank needs capital backing for its business operations; in addition to the capital required for premises and equipment and for working capital, shareholders' funds are required to cover the possibility of defaults on loans and capital losses on investments. The size of shareholders' funds relative to total assets therefore represents the ability of a bank to absorb losses, and therefore its ability to repay depositors when it does incur losses.

Table 2.1 Structure of banks' balance sheets: broad categories

ASSETS

Sterling

Cash and balances at the Bank of England
Market loans
Acceptances granted
Bills
Claims under sale and repurchase agreements
Advances
Investments

Foreign currency
>   Market loans and advances
>   Acceptances granted
>   Bills
>   Claims under sale and repurchase agreements
>   Investments

Miscellaneous assets (in sterling and foreign currencies)

TOTAL ASSETS

LIABILITIES

Sterling
>   Notes issued
>   Sterling deposits
>   Acceptances granted
>   Liabilities under sale and repurchase agreements

Foreign currency
>   Foreign currency deposits
>   Acceptances granted
>   Liabilities under sale and repurchase agreements

Miscellaneous liabilities (in sterling and foreign currencies)
>   (including shareholders' funds; i.e. the banks' capital)

TOTAL LIABILITIES

Study Activities 8

1. What are eligible bank bills?   *(Paragraph 11.14)*

2. What is the significance of eligible bank bills for retail banks?   *(Paragraph 11.14)*

3. What is the significance of foreign currency assets for retail banks?
                                                              (Paragraphs 11.19–11.21)

4. Describe the structure of a typical retail bank's portfolio of liabilities.
                                                              (Paragraphs 11.22–11.28)

5. Distinguish between claims and liabilities under sale and repurchase agreements.
                                                              (Paragraphs 11.15 and 11.26)

The changing environment and activities of the UK retail banks

11.29   The analysis of the activities and of the aggregate balance sheet of the retail banks
         in the previous paragraphs provides an overview of what the banks currently do,
         but not of how this has changed over time and is likely to change in the future.
         The following sections provide a brief overview of the way in which the

environment, and hence the activities, of the retail banks has changed in recent years.

Competition

11.30 The major change in the environment within which the retail banks operate is that it has become much more *competitive*. This has come about not only as a consequence of deregulation within financial markets, but also as a consequence of innovation by participants within those markets. The result of this has been that the domination of the market for banking services by the traditional retail banks in the UK has come under attack. With regard to the market for personal customers, a major source of increased competition has been the building societies. Mainly as a consequence of the changes brought about by the Building Societies Act 1986, these institutions have started to offer a much more comprehensive range of banking services including, on a limited basis, personal loans for purposes other than house purchase. It has also been suggested that the general public have much more financial sophistication than they had, say, ten years ago. Consequently, they are now better able to evaluate alternative financial products and are more willing to move funds between different financial institutions to take advantage of better interest rates or other facilities.

Personal customers

11.31 The ability of the retail banks to attract funds from their personal customers was seen to be under threat, and they have responded in a number of ways:

- Instead of offering just the one type of savings account, the 7-day deposit account, a range of savings accounts with competitive interest rates are now offered with, often, improved access to the funds by the customer.

- Improved current account facilities, in the form of interest-bearing current accounts, free banking subject to certain (more generous) criteria, facilities such as automatic overdrafts, and the provision of debit cards.

- Improved access to current account funds, by means of automated teller machines, longer opening hours and home banking facilities.

- Expanded advertising and marketing to increase customer awareness and to improve the image of the retail banks.

- Purchases of building societies by some banks: Lloyds bought Cheltenham & Gloucester; Abbey National bought National & Provincial; and the Bank of Ireland bought Bristol & West.

Corporate customers

11.32 In the market for corporate customers, the changing environment has also manifested itself primarily in the form of increased competition, brought about again by deregulation. The deregulation of the capital markets has enabled corporate borrowers to raise funds from sources other than banks, while increased competition has extended the range of alternative means of finance available from the capital market and has lowered the cost of such finance relative to bank finance.

11.33 The *response* by the retail banks to the increased competition for corporate customers has taken a number of forms:

- Improvement of existing facilities for corporate customers. Given that the cost of funds lies largely outside a bank's control, however, their ability to improve existing facilities is necessarily limited and is concentrated on increasing the flexibility offered to such customers.

- Greater involvement in the securities markets. For some retail banks this has meant acquiring firms operating as brokers or market-makers within the capital markets, but they have also become increasingly involved in merchant and investment banking via their subsidiaries and directly involved in, for example, managing issues of commercial paper.

- Development of particular segments of the market for corporate customers, and in this respect small- and medium-sized businesses have become the focus of attention, since the ability of such businesses to take advantage of deregulation and increased competition within the capital market is limited by their size.

11.34 For both the market for personal customers and that for corporate customers, an additional response to the changing environment has been a movement away from their financial intermediary services towards the whole range of non-intermediary financial services. These activities do not require the banks to obtain and then on-lend funds, allowing the banks to benefit from the interest margin; rather, they generate fees or commissions for the bank concerned, and to some extent are subject to less competition. Many of these activities enable the banks to make more intensive use of their branch networks and hence to lower average costs. They include the selling of insurance, unit trust operations, acting as agent for the sale and purchase of shares and estate agency operations. They are sometimes called 'non-funds-based products'.

Study Activities 9

1. Examine the importance of the Building Societies Act 1986 for UK retail banks.
(Paragraph 11.30)

2. It is sometimes suggested that the general public have become more sophisticated in their financial requirements. How might this fact have affected the operations of retail banks? *(Paragraph 11.30)*

3. Discuss some of the improvements which retail banks have made to their facilities in recent years in order to enhance their position in attracting personal customers.
(Paragraph 11.31)

4. In what ways have retail banks attempted to improve their facilities for corporate customers in recent years? *(Paragraph 11.33)*

5. For what reasons might retail banks move into the provision of non-intermediation financial services? *(Paragraph 11.34)*

12 Wholesale banks

12.1 The wholesale banks represent a diverse group of institutions within the UK financial system. They comprise three broad groups:

● British merchant banks;

● Other British banks;

● Overseas banks.

12.2 The aggregate balance sheet of the wholesale bank sector is *far larger* than that of the retail bank sector. However, while the retail bank sector consists of around 30 institutions (depending upon the definition used), the wholesale bank sector comprises over 500 institutions, and the *average* size of a wholesale bank is appreciably smaller than that of a retail bank. Moreover, within the wholesale sector there is a considerable amount of inter-bank transactions; if net figures excluding inter-bank business are examined, then the wholesale sector does not appear so big relative to the retail sector.

12.3 The broad structure of a typical wholesale bank's balance sheet, in terms of component elements, is basically the same as that shown in Table 2.1, although the wholesale banks have no 'notes issued' under their sterling liabilities. The wholesale banks have a *much greater involvement in foreign currency business* than do the retail banks. Examination of the aggregate balance sheet for the wholesale banks reveals that about three-quarters of the assets of wholesale banks are denominated in foreign currency. Furthermore, over 50% of the liabilities of the wholesale banks are attributable to *overseas* residents, which serves to underline the *international* nature of the wholesale banking sector in the UK.

12.4 Given the overwhelmingly wholesale nature of the activities of the banks in this group, *holdings of cash and balances at the Bank of England are extremely small* representing only a tiny fraction of total assets. Also, only around 15% of sterling deposits with wholesale banks are sight deposits, the bulk therefore constituting time deposits.

12.5 *Market loans and advances dominate both sterling and foreign currency assets*, with bills and investments, both in sterling and in foreign currencies, constituting only about one-eighth of total assets. This is to be expected, given the wholesale nature of their activities, and is consistent with the low proportion of sight deposits within the liability portfolio.

12.6   Sale and repurchase (repo) transactions feature prominently in the aggregate balance sheet, with foreign currency repo business approaching the total of investments denominated in foreign currencies.

12.7   In summary, it is clear that the major activity of the wholesale banks is in taking in term deposits and using them to make term loans. Taking this in conjunction with the fact that the transactions are *wholesale* in nature (that is, small numbers of high-value transactions) leads to the result that the wholesale banks cannot rely on the 'law of large numbers' to apply. The fact that a large number of *different currencies* are involved compounds this problem.

12.8   Consequently, there has to be a degree of *matching* of assets and liabilities. The matching will be in terms both of matching the term to maturity of loans and deposits, and of the currency of denomination. However, the matching is not perfect. If it were, the bank would in effect be acting as a broker rather than as a bank. A mismatch of either the term to maturity or of the currencies involved will potentially allow the bank to gain higher profits, and hence the choice is frequently between lower risk and higher profits. The risk associated with mismatching is alleviated to some extent by the existence of the inter-bank market, where a bank can obtain funds as and when necessary – at a cost. The risk involved in the mismatching of assets and liabilities lies less, therefore, in the threat to solvency than in the loss to profits that might be incurred as a consequence of adverse interest rate or exchange-rate movements.

Study Activities 10

1. List the main categories of wholesale banks to be found within the UK financial system.   *(Paragraph 12.1)*

2. Taking the wholesale banks as a group, what are the three most important types of assets to be found on their balance sheet?   *(Paragraphs 12.3 and 12.5)*

3. For the wholesale banks as a group, what is the most important liability on their balance sheet?   *(Paragraph 12.3)*

4. In general terms, what is the size of the typical wholesale bank compared with the typical retail bank?   *(Paragraph 12.2)*

5. Examine the main characteristics of wholesale banking operations.
                                                                                          (Paragraph 12.7)

6. Why do wholesale banks match their assets with their liabilities according to maturity?
                                                                                  (Paragraphs 12.7 and 12.8)

British merchant banks

12.9   The group of wholesale banks called the British merchant banks comprises around 40 institutions. Historically, a major element of their business lay in the 'acceptance' of bills of exchange. This involves the bank in guaranteeing payment of the bills upon maturity to whoever is then holding the bills. The bank receives a fee for fulfilling this underwriting role, and hence acceptances are an early example of a bank providing non-intermediary services. Once a bill is accepted by a reputable bank it becomes much more marketable, and as a consequence the merchant banks facilitate the use of bills as a significant source of short-term corporate finance.

12.10   The risk involved in accepting bills of exchange is that the debtor may default when the bills mature. As a consequence, the key to running a profitable acceptance activity is being able to evaluate accurately the default risk associated with bills, and to perform this function the British merchant banks have had to acquire considerable information and expertise. As this information and expertise are of use in other areas of activity, the banks have progressively diversified away from acceptances as the main element of their business. The majority now offer a wide range of banking services to corporate customers so that, in addition to taking in deposits and making loans on a wholesale basis and the acceptance activity, the merchant banks as a group now offer:

● Management and underwriting of capital issues by companies;

● Management consulting services, especially with regard to financial aspects;

● Advice on mergers and takeovers;

● Fund management services for pension funds, insurance companies, unit and investment trusts;

● Trading in foreign exchange markets;

● Trading in the bullion (gold and silver) markets;

● Trading in the eurocurrency markets;

● Trading in the derivatives markets.

12.11   Like the retail banks, the British merchant banks have also suffered from increased competition within their spheres of activity. Many have perceived themselves to be too small to withstand this competition, especially from institutions abroad, as their activities become increasingly international in character. In addition, the ability to participate in the capital markets has become increasingly attractive to the retail banks. This has meant that many of the merchant banks have become part of larger banking groups, either UK-based or overseas. For other merchant banks the consequence has been a rethinking of their strategy and the basis of future competition, which has led to some of the smaller banks competing on the basis of expertise within specialist market niches. The larger ones are tending to be known as investment banks, derived from their trading in investments.

Other British banks

12.12 This group comprises a rather disparate range of institutions. Having said that, a significant proportion of the group's activities are overseas, stemming from the fact that many of these banks originated when the UK was a major colonial power and banks were required to service the needs of companies and individuals with dealings in the colonies. These needs have declined, but banking services are still required within the former colonies and the status of London as a major centre of financial activity has meant that it has been appropriate for these banks to retain their base in Britain.

12.13 Other banks in this group include wholesale banks that provide corporate banking services on a regional basis or that specialise in services to particular industries, and former finance houses that have taken on full banking status.

Overseas banks

12.14 The overseas banks represent the largest group of banks within the UK financial system, accounting for around 350 institutions. They exhibited very rapid growth during the 1970s and 1980s, in terms of both assets and numbers of banks.

12.15 The overseas banks came to London originally to meet the business requirements of firms in their own countries. While they still perform that function, they are now important participants within the eurocurrency markets, and as such facilitate the taking-up of deposits from a wide range of sources and the financing of a wide range of different projects, with their activities no longer particularly related to their home countries. London's status as the major centre of eurocurrency market activity has facilitated this development and made it necessary for a bank of any size, wherever it is based in the world, to have a London office.

12.16 In addition to undertaking wholesale banking activities, many overseas banks have moved into other areas of activity. This has in some cases included retail financial services, and in other cases has, as a consequence of the deregulation of the capital markets, included market-making and stockbroking activities. Some of the overseas banks have become major investment banks.

Study Activities 11

1. What is an 'acceptance'? *(Paragraph 12.9)*

2. List the main areas of activity currently undertaken by British merchant banks. *(Paragraph 12.10)*

3. Why have many British merchant banks felt it necessary to reappraise their strategy in recent years? *(Paragraph 12.11)*

4. Outline the activities undertaken by the 'other British banks'? *(Paragraphs 12.12 and 12.13)*

5. How important are overseas banks within the UK financial system?

    (Paragraphs 12.14–12.16)

6. Examine the main types of activities undertaken by the overseas banks in the UK.

    (Paragraphs 12.14–12.16)

13   Building societies

13.1   The primary purpose of building societies is to provide finance for the purchase of residential property. Until the round of building society conversions to bank status and the takeover of building societies by retail banks (which peaked in 1997), building societies dominated the provision of housing finance in the UK. As a consequence of the need to raise funds to do this, they are also major participants in the market for retail savings.

13.2   In more recent years, however, building societies have started to provide a range of other services, to make loans for purposes other than house purchase, and to reduce their dependence on the retail savings market by raising an increasing proportion of their funds from wholesale sources.

Table 2.2 UK building societies: summary balance sheet as at 31 December 1998

Assets	£bn	£bn
Liquid assets		28.4
Notes and coin	0.2	
Sterling bank deposits and foreign currency (including certificates of deposit)	15.0	
Building society CDs	1.3	
British government stocks	0.8	
Other public sector debt	0.4	
Other	10.7	
Commercial assets		122.4
Class 1	103.0	
Class 2	6.4	
Class 3: individuals	0.3	
Class 3: other	12.7	
Other assets		2.2
Total assets		153.0

Liabilities	£bn	£bn
Retail shares and deposits		109.9
Wholesale liabilities		28.4
(of which, foreign currency)	(2.6)	
Certificates of deposit	5.0	
Deposits and commercial paper	15.0	
Bank borrowing	1.3	
Bonds	7.1	
Other liabilities and reserves		14.7
Total liabilities		153.0

Source: *Financial Statistics, Table 4.4*

13.3 With total assets/liabilities of £155bn as at spring of 1999, the building societies in the UK still constitute a sizeable element of the financial system. However, their significance is much diminished from their 1997 peak when their aggregate balance sheet amounted to well over £300bn (approximately one half the size of the aggregate balance sheet of the retail banks).

Assets

13.4 The bulk of the assets of building societies are categorised as 'commercial assets', which are divided into three classes: 1, 2 and 3.

● Class 1 assets are loans secured by a first mortgage on owner-occupied residential property, and as at January 1999 represented 84.2% of all commercial assets.

● Class 2 assets are other loans, secured on property, and these constituted approximately 5.2% of all commercial assets.

● Class 3 assets are loans, both secured and unsecured, that are not covered by Classes 1 and 2, as well as building societies' investments in land and property for residential use and investments in associates. They constituted almost 10.6% of all commercial assets.

13.5 The creation of Class 2 and Class 3 assets by building societies has been allowed only since the relevant provisions of the Building Societies Act 1986 came into force. That Act restricted their creation to the larger building societies (assets of £100m+) and specified that Class 2 assets could not exceed 10%, and Class 3 assets could not exceed 5%, of all commercial assets. These limits were relaxed in 1989 and in 1993 the limit for Class 2 assets was raised to 25% and for Class 3 assets to 15% (with the limit for Classes 2 and 3 together set at 25%). Clearly, the building society sector as a whole is well within the limits that were introduced at the end of 1993. However, the limits may represent a pointer to the way in which building societies are liable to develop in the future: away from sole dependence on mortgage loans and into a more broadly based retail loans portfolio. Furthermore, it is worth noting one implication of the fact that about 84% of all commercial assets are Class 1 assets: building societies are involved in very extensive maturity transformation of funds. Building societies are taking in deposits, mainly from retail sources and mainly repayable on demand, and using them to fund loans with an initial maturity of, normally, 25 years (although the average length of a mortgage loan in practice is about eight to ten years).

13.6   Building societies also hold a significant amount of *liquid assets*. Just over one-half of liquid assets are held in the form of sterling bank deposits. Given that the bulk of building societies' commercial assets (mortgage loans) are highly illiquid, building societies find it necessary to hold substantial liquid assets to meet variations in the volume of funds withdrawn.

Liabilities

13.7   On the liabilities side of the balance sheet, *retail shares and deposits* constitute about 72% of all liabilities, and are clearly the building societies' main source of funds. Prior to the early 1980s, retail shares and deposits constituted the *only* source of funds, since the raising of finance from wholesale sources was not permitted. From 1982 onwards, however, under a series of *ad hoc* arrangements, individual building societies were permitted to raise funds from wholesale sources, and these arrangements were placed on a formal footing by the 1986 Act. As at January 1999, wholesale funds accounted for 18.6% of the total raised. With the limit on wholesale funding being raised in stages to 50%, from the 1986 Act's 20%, the proportion of wholesale funding has scope to rise further, thereby reducing societies' dependence on retail funding.

13.8   The wholesale funding takes place in a variety of forms including, notably, CDs, wholesale deposits, bonds and, most recently, foreign currency. Given the flexibility of wholesale funding, this development is allowing the building societies to operate on lower proportions of liquid assets than previously, and allowing their business to be led by lending opportunities rather than by the availability of retail funds.

13.9   The 'other liabilities and reserves' element of the liabilities of the balance sheet serves to emphasise that building societies, by definition, are *mutual* organisations. They are owned by their borrowing and lending members and not by commercial shareholders. The implication of this is that there are no 'shareholders' funds' within the balance sheet, and building societies cannot raise funds from shareholders. Reserves can only be accumulated by means of making profits, and hence the growth of building societies is constrained by their profitability. More recently, the building societies have been able to issue subordinated debt designed to act as a substitute for accumulated profits, but this facility has tended to be used by only the larger institutions and to a limited extent.

Study Activities 12

1. What is the primary purpose of building societies? *(Paragraph 13.1)*

2. In terms of assets, how has the significance of the building societies sector relative to the retail banks sector altered in recent years? *(Paragraph 13.3)*

3. How are the building societies' assets classified in their accounts?
(Paragraphs 13.4–13.6)

4. What is the most important type of asset held by building societies?
(Paragraph 13.4)

5. Why do building societies find it necessary to hold a significant proportion of their assets in liquid form? *(Paragraph 13.6)*

6. Outline the structure of the liabilities as shown in the building societies' accounts.
(Paragraph 13.7)

7. Why might building societies now be able to operate with lower proportions of liquid assets in their portfolios than was formerly the case? *(Paragraph 13.8)*

The changing environment of the building societies

13.10 Two of the significant changes in the environment facing building societies in recent years – the ability to make loans other than those secured by a first mortgage on residential property, and to make extensive use of wholesale funding – were a consequence of the Building Societies Act 1986. This Act also gave rise to two other significant changes in the societies' environment, the abilities to:

● Convert from being mutual organisations to public limited companies;

● Provide a much wider range of financial services.

13.11 In order to convert to a public limited company, a society requires the permission of its members. This permission is defined as a 75% majority amongst the lending members who vote in the ballot on conversion, where this 75% is achieved from a minimum of 20% of the lending members who are entitled to vote. It also requires a simple majority of the borrowing members who exercise their vote and the approval of the Financial Services Authority. This is designed to ensure that members' interests are protected during the conversion process.

13.12 Since a building society that achieves plc status will have shareholders and will no longer be a *mutual* organisation, it cannot be a building society. In practice, it becomes a *bank*, and therefore authorisation from the Financial Services Authority to become a bank is also a necessary part of the process for conversion to plc status.

13.13 Between 1995 and 1999 a number of the UK's largest building societies (including Halifax, Alliance & Leicester, Woolwich and Northern Rock) converted to plc status. Several others (including Cheltenham & Gloucester, National & Provincial, Bristol & West and Birmingham Midshires) were taken over by banks. Of these institutions only National & Provincial lost its separate identity.

13.14   The major *advantage* of conversion to plc status is considered to be freedom from the restrictions of the legislative framework of the building society industry, the 1986 Act. The restrictions that are often alleged to be particularly harmful to the future prosperity of the building societies are the limits on:

●   Unsecured lending;

●   Lending to corporate and overseas customers;

●   The ability to increase capital only by means of retaining profits;

●   The ability to take over or merge (apart from paying cash) with other financial institutions in order to add to the range of financial services offered;

●   The range of financial services which building societies are permitted to offer;

●   The ability to offer profit-sharing schemes in the form of share distributions to their staff.

13.15   By the mid-1990s, however, there was a new reason for the urge to convert to plc status. A number of the largest societies saw conversion as the only way to continue to grow in size, because the housing market was dormant and the banks were gaining a large market share of new mortgage business. Plc status was the route away from a declining/stagnant mortgage market to the expanding markets of financial services.

13.16   Substantial though these constraints may be, the fact that some building societies strenuously assert their opposition to plc status implies that there are *disadvantages* also. These are seen to include the:

●   Supervisory requirements applied to banking institutions;

●   Need to pay dividends to shareholders and the danger of being pressured into short-term responses to strategic issues;

●   Possible eventual concentration of shareholdings into the hands of a limited number of investors, with the chance of increased shareholder influence on strategy;

●   Possibility of takeover bids;

●   Adverse impact on the image of a building society that its move away from mutual status would bring.

It has also been suggested that the more competitive environment into which a building society would move upon conversion would raise its operating costs as a consequence of having to recruit appropriately qualified staff.

13.17   The 1986 Act allows societies to:

- Provide a much wider range of financial services;

- Take equity stakes in both general and life insurance companies;

- Take equity stakes in stockbroker firms;

- Establish and manage personal equity plans and unit trusts through associated bodies; and

- Undertake fund management.

The Building Societies Act 1997 extended the freedom of societies further in respect of their asset and liability management, strengthened the accountability of societies to their members and removed the five-year take-over protection for converted societies that engage in a contested take-over.

13.18   Thus, building societies are able to offer a much more complete set of retail financial services, although it has been argued that this is still too narrow to allow the building societies to compete with banks on an equal footing. Further powers are available for societies to incorporate in their constitutions, after approval by their members, and these include the ability to establish subsidiaries to lend to small businesses.

The position of building societies relative to retail banks

13.19   The rationale for the 1986 Building Societies Act, which was underlined by the 1997 Act, was that the building societies should be allowed to offer a wider range of financial services, and utilise additional forms of lending and sources of funds. This was perceived as being necessary because if they were restricted to their original activities they would not be able to compete with other financial institutions and hence their share of the retail financial services market would inevitably decline. These legislative changes have caused the majority of building societies to become broader-based retail financial services businesses.

13.20   It must be stressed that restrictions remain on what building societies can do, and some of these – particularly the restrictions on non-traditional lending and whole-sale funding – are seen by some as being prejudicial to the future prosperity of building societies.

13.21   As a consequence of the greater freedom given to building societies there has been a substantial convergence of the retail banks and the building societies in the field of retail financial services for the personal sector. Several of the larger building societies are members of the payments clearing system, and now offer interest-bearing current accounts, personal loans, overdraft facilities and credit cards, as well as several of the permitted non-banking services.

13.22   *Outside* the personal sector, however, this convergence of retail banks and building societies has been very much less. A significant proportion of retail banks' lending is to the corporate sector, compared with only a tiny proportion for building societies. In addition, the retail banks offer a diverse set of services to the corporate sector. The retail banks are also involved in international activities to a substantial degree, whereas the building societies have virtually no involvement.

13.23   Part of the remaining differences between building societies and retail banks is, of course, due to the different regulatory frameworks involved. Given that the convergence of activities of separate institutions over time tends to identify anomalies in the regulatory frameworks, it is likely that increased harmonisation of these frameworks will occur, and that further convergence of activities will result.

Study Activities 13

1. What was the importance of the Building Societies Act 1986 to building societies' operational environment?   *(Paragraph 13.10)*

2. State the advantages to a building society of converting to plc status.
                                                   (Paragraphs 13.14–13.15)

3. Examine the disadvantages to a building society of converting to plc status.
                                                            (Paragraph 13.16)

4. How did the Building Societies Act 1986 affect the range of financial services which building societies are allowed to offer?   *(Paragraph 13.17)*

5. List the ways in which building societies have converged with retail banks in recent years.   *(Paragraph 13.21)*

6. Describe the areas of activity in which building societies and retail banks are still markedly different.   *(Paragraph 13.22)*

14   Finance houses and credit unions

Finance houses

14.1   These are hybrid financial intermediaries, many of them having evolved from hire purchase (HP) companies. Traditionally, HP companies raised finance via issues of share capital, taking deposits from the general public and borrowing from banks. These funds were used to buy assets, effectively on behalf of businesses and individuals borrowing on 'HP'. The ownership of the assets passed to the business or individual concerned once the contracted set of repayments had been made.

14.2   Today, most finance houses do not accept deposits from the public, although some effectively receive deposits channelled to them by parent retail banks. Moreover, they have moved into other areas of business, so that their lending activities comprise:

- Traditional HP business;

- Factoring of book debts;

- Leasing – 'small-ticket' business on machinery and equipment of up to, say, £50,000 per item;

- Second mortgage finance for double glazing, conservatories, kitchens, bathrooms and the like.

Credit unions

14.3 These are savings and lending societies that, in the UK, normally operate on a relatively small scale. Members of credit unions usually share a common bond through location of residence, religion or employment, and members tend to save regular amounts each week. The other main activity is lending, often with a statutory maximum interest rate. There are also limits to the amounts that may be borrowed by members and to the total membership of each union.

15 Investing financial intermediaries

15.1 The foregoing parts of this unit have concentrated upon deposit-taking financial intermediaries that, in general, specialise in taking deposits and on-lending funds, rather than buying and selling assets. The final part of this unit focuses upon intermediaries that raise funds primarily through investment, premium or contribution payments, and then use the funds to purchase a wide range of financial (and sometimes real) assets. Collectively, these financial intermediaries are often referred to as *investment institutions*.

16 Insurance companies

16.1 The central business activity of insurance companies relates to the *evaluation of risk* and the *spreading of risk* over those individuals and institutions facing risk and wishing to protect against it. Insurance business may be divided into two broad categories: *general insurance* and *long-term insurance*.

Table 2.3 Insurance companies' assets – general funds end of 1997

		£bn	%
Short-term assets		5.4	5.6
Gilt-edged securities:		15.7	16.1
Index-linked	0.2		
0–5 years	9.6		
5–15 years	5.2		
Over 15 years and undated	0.7		

	£bn	%
UK company securities	18.4	18.9
Equities	15.0	
Other	3.4	
Overseas securities	14.8	15.2
Unit trusts	0.4	0.4
Loans/mortgages in UK	1.3	1.3
UK land, property etc.	2.8	2.9
Other (incl. £9.4bn for agents' and reinsurance balances)	<u>38.6</u>	<u>39.6</u>
Total assets	97.4	100.0

Source: Financial Statistics Table 5.2A

Table 2.4 Insurance companies' assets – long-term funds end of 1997

	£bn	%
Short-term assets	38.9	5.7
Gilt-edged securities:	107.9	15.9
Index-linked	12.8	
0–5 years	14.5	
5–15 years	44.0	
Over 15 years and undated	36.6	
UK company securities	336.6	49.7
Equities	283.2	
Other	53.4	
Overseas securities	81.9	12.1
Unit trusts	50.2	7.4
Loans/mortgages in UK	8.0	1.2
UK land, property etc	42.3	6.3
Other	<u>12.0</u>	<u>1.7</u>
Total assets	677.8	100.0

Source: Financial Statistics Table 5.1A

16.2   The value of assets held by UK insurance companies as at the end of 1997 amounted to £775.2bn, which was larger than the asset holdings of UK pension funds (£656.9bn) at the same date. These figures illustrate clearly the major significance of these investment institutions in the UK financial system. When added to the value of the assets held by the unit trusts and investment trust companies, the total for the investment institutions at the end of 1997 exceeded £1,640bn.

General Insurance

16.3   This comprises insuring items such as buildings and contents, motor vehicles, ships and aircraft. It also includes insurance to protect against injury to the person. Individuals and institutions purchase cover to protect against specific eventualities such as fire, theft and accident.

16.4   This form of insurance is usually short-term business, with policies renewable annually and often up-rated annually. However, there are two classes of longer-term insurance that are included here, i.e.:

- Permanent health insurance;

- Critical illness insurance.

16.5   Risks in general insurance are spread between individuals and businesses that make premium payments to an insurance company in order to cover the risk of being adversely affected by particular occurrences. If an event covered by an insurance policy should take place, the policyholder may make a claim on the insurance company for compensation as defined by the policy. Claims that arise on such policies are generally met from incoming premiums, but in addition a fund is accumulated from which are met unusually large claims. The time lag that generally occurs between the receipt of a premium by an insurance company and the payment of any claim on the associated policy also ensures that a pool of funds is available for investment. As a consequence, companies involved in general insurance have large funds invested in various assets, especially government securities and equities, and as such are significant participants in financial market activities.

Long-term insurance

16.6   Long-term insurance is often referred to as life assurance, on account of the associated risk being that related to life expectancy, and the fact that death is inevitable! There are four main types of long-term insurance policy:

Whole life assurance

16.7   This type of policy pays out a capital sum upon the death of the person insured, irrespective of when death occurs. Consequently, the insurance company is committed to making a payment against each policy, and the premium payments must reflect this fact. The policy, in effect, provides cover for premature death and a vehicle for long-term saving (the benefits to be enjoyed by someone other than the person insured).

Term assurance

16.8   This provides insurance cover against the risk of death during the period to which the policy relates. If the person insured should survive the specified period, the insurance company will make no payment. A term assurance policy provides financial protection for dependents should the person named in the policy suffer premature death.

Endowment assurance

16.9   This type of policy is issued for a fixed term, often 10, 20 or more years. Life assurance cover is provided during the term of the policy, and if the person named in the policy survives until the policy matures, a capital sum is paid to the policy-holder. The saving/investment value of an endowment policy is clear.

Annuity

16.10   This form of policy entails the purchaser paying a lump sum to the insurance company in exchange for a commitment from the company to pay an agreed income until the death of the policyholder. As with other types of life assurance policy, the calculation of life expectancy is crucial to the income stream provided. For a given lump-sum payment, the older and the poorer is the health of the policyholder, the greater will be the income earned.

With profits policies

16.11   Holders of whole life and endowment policies may share in the profits of the insurance company providing the cover. Traditionally, profits have been declared annually or every three or five years, and added to the sum assured in what are known as reversionary bonuses. These cannot be taken away and so insurance companies adopt a very conservative attitude when announcing them. A second type of bonus is paid on maturity – the terminal bonus – and this fluctuates in line with conditions in the stock and property markets. In the 1990s, many companies reduced their terminal bonuses, while others were unable to declare reversionary bonuses at the level of previous years. The uncertainties of the trend of profits have caused some companies to cease the sale of 'with profits' endowment policies. Instead, they have begun to sell 'unit-linked' endowment policies, which are divided into units whose value fluctuates in line with market trends. In other words, their value can fall, unlike the traditional 'with profits' endowment or whole life policy.

Types of insurance company

16.12   Some companies specialise in life assurance, whilst others concentrate on general insurance. There are also composite insurers, providing both life and general cover from the same business. In addition, there is a very strong 'mutual' element in the industry, with many firms being owned by their policyholders rather than by commercial shareholders.

Asset portfolios of UK insurance companies

16.13 Risk is also an important factor in the decision on where to invest the insurance funds. In general, the more risky are the assets, the greater is the potential return. The greater is the return on the investment portfolio, the greater is the profit for the insurance company and the larger are the bonus payments made to 'with profits' policyholders.

16.14 Insurance companies hold large amounts of gilt-edged securities and other interest-bearing instruments. Careful selection of such instruments allows an insurance company to reduce the investment risk that it faces. Gilt-edged securities in particular are secure, generate a fixed income and have known maturity dates and fixed maturity values. Where possible, holdings of such instruments are matched to the expected pattern of liabilities. In addition, large amounts of equities are held, as over the longer term the return on a diversified portfolio of equities tends to be better than the return on interest-bearing assets, which is necessary to meet the expectations of 'with profits' policyholders. The difference between long-term insurance funds and general insurance funds in terms of the patterns of assets held is easily explained by the nature of their respective liabilities.

Study Activities 14

1. Outline the main functions of finance houses and credit unions.
   (Paragraphs 14.1-14.3)

2. Define the fundamental characteristics of insurance business. *(Paragraph 16.1)*

3. Distinguish between general insurance and life assurance. *(Paragraphs 16.2–16.6)*

4. Describe the main products sold by life insurance companies.
   (Paragraphs 16.7–16.10)

5. Why did 'with profits' life policies become less attractive to insurance companies during the 1990s? *(Paragraph 16.11)*

6. Describe the asset structure of long-term insurance companies in aggregate.
   (Table 2.4)

7. What is the attraction of holding gilt-edged securities as opposed to equities for insurance companies? *(Paragraph 16.14)*

17 Pension funds

17.1   Pensions can be financed in two ways: non-funded or funded.

Non-funded pensions

17.2   Non-funded pensions are, in effect, 'pay as you go' schemes. Examples are the state retirement pension, financed by the National Insurance Contributions of today's workers, and pension schemes for civil servants, school teachers, the police force and the like, in respect of which current contributions from working members pay the pensions of retired members. When current contributions are insufficient to pay current pensions, funds from general taxation will be used to cover the deficit.

Funded pensions

17.3   Funded pensions come in three types:

- Defined benefit schemes;

- Defined contribution schemes; and

- Hybrid schemes.

All have their own funds, with identifiable assets.

Defined benefit schemes

17.4   Contributions are made by employees and (usually) by their employers. Members earn themselves a benefit (a pension, of which part can be taken in a lump sum) of either $\frac{1}{60}$ or $\frac{1}{80}$ of their final salary (or the average of the last three years' salaries) for every year in which contributions are made. Thus, 40 years' service gives a pension of $\frac{2}{3}$ or $\frac{1}{2}$ of final salary if the benefit is $\frac{1}{60}$ or $\frac{1}{80}$ respectively. The assumptions are that employees stay in their jobs for a long time and that salary changes are upwards. However, it is now a fact that job changes are more frequent, so transfers have to be made between funds. Second, the 'upward salary' assumption makes it less desirable for older workers to move to part-time or less remunerative work with their employers as they approach retirement age.

17.5   A severe problem can arise with these schemes if there is a period of substantial inflation because the earlier contributions are unable to finance the higher final salaries caused by the inflation. As a result, the employers are required by the trustees of the schemes to make up the contributions and this can be a drain on their profits and cash flows. Moreover, if inflation then slows, the schemes may become 'over-funded' instead of 'under-funded', so that a 'pensions holiday' is declared. In some funds, the over-funding has allowed employees, as well as employers, to pay lower contribution rates. These 'defined benefit' schemes have been virtually universal in the largest companies and typically are run by trustees advised by merchant banks in their investment decisions. A more common term for them is 'final salary' pensions.

Defined contribution schemes

17.6   With defined contribution schemes (sometimes referred to as 'money purchase' schemes), the contributions are used to build up a fund that is used to buy an annuity when the employee retires. These schemes are typically operated by life assurance companies, and have tended to be popular with smaller firms. As benefits are not linked to inflation or salaries, these schemes cannot suffer the under-funding problems that sometimes inflict defined benefit schemes.

Hybrid schemes

17.7   Hybrid schemes, incorporating features of both the other schemes, have become fairly common in the USA, but have only recently been introduced into the UK in any significant way.

Asset portfolios of pension funds

17.8   The assets of pension funds are distributed in a broadly similar way to those of the long-term funds of insurance companies. The reason is that they are both long-term intermediaries and both operate within the same uncertain financial environment. However, one significant difference is the much larger amount of index-linked gilt-edged securities held by pension funds, when compared to insurance companies. The reason is that pension funds frequently increase their benefits in line with inflation, and the best way of financing this form of liability is, of course, to purchase index-linked assets. Pension funds also hold a larger proportion of their assets in the form of company securities as these have proven to be good hedges against inflation in the longer term, which is helpful given the nature of pension fund liabilities.

Table 2.5 Pension funds' assets end of 1997

		£bn	%
Short-term assets		26.4	4.0
Gilt-edged securities:		80.6	12.3
Index-linked	36.1		
0–5 years	11.3		
5–15 years	19.9		
Over 15 years and undated	13.3		
UK company securities		345.3	52.6
Equities	339.7		
Other	5.6		

	£bn	%
Overseas securities	121.1	18.4
Unit trusts	25.2	3.8
Loans/mortgages in UK	0.2	-
UK land, property etc	24.2	
Other	<u>33.9</u>	<u>5.2</u>
Total assets	656.9	100.0

Source:Financial Statistics Table 5.1B

Study Activities 15

1. Distinguish between the two ways in which pension schemes are financed.
   (Paragraphs 17.1–17.3)

2. Explain what is a defined benefit scheme and why it is often known as a final salary scheme. *(Paragraph 17.4)*

3. Describe how a defined contribution scheme operates. *(Paragraph 17.6)*

4. Why are employees tending to change their pension schemes?
   (Paragraphs 17.4 –17.6)

5. Why do pension funds hold a greater percentage of their assets as index-linked gilt-edged securities than insurance companies? *(Paragraph 17.8)*

18   Unit trusts

18.1   Unit trusts are funds in which individuals and companies may invest in order to obtain a share in the income and capital gains generated by the trusts' assets. They provide a convenient means for investors to obtain a share in a (usually) large and diversified portfolio of assets. Also, they provide a very wide choice of investment opportunities. Managers of unit trusts either are specialist companies, such as M & G or Perpetual, or are banks or insurance companies. The managers play an active role in selling the units to investors, investing the proceeds and finding the cash to repay investors wishing to sell their units back. In addition, there is always a second financial institution involved in a unit trust – acting as trustee and holding the investments (assets) on behalf of the unit-holders. The main advantages of unit trusts for investors are that risks are pooled and that specialist managers should enhance investors' returns.

18.2   Unit trusts are 'open ended' funds. This means that if investors wish to buy more units, the managers must issue more units and buy more assets. If investors sell back their units, the managers have to repay the sellers from their cash balances, cancel the units and, possibly, sell some of trust's long-term investments to top up their short-term assets.

18.3 The buying and selling prices of units are calculated on the basis of the market values of the assets held by a trust. Hence, a fall (rise) in the price of a unit is due to a fall (rise) in the prices of the shares and other assets that the unit trust owns. At present, managers quote two prices – bid and offer – for their units, but it is planned to introduce single pricing soon.

Table 2.6 Unit trusts' assets end of 1997

		£bn
Short term assets (net)		5.0
Short-term assets	5.6	
Liabilities	(0.6)	
Investments		
Gilt-edged securities		3.2
UK equities		86.9
Overseas equities		42.9
Other		11.1
Total assets		149.1

Source: Financial Statistics Table 5.2D

18.4 Unit trusts hold substantial amounts of net short-term assets (mainly in the form of bank deposits), reflecting their commitment to repurchase units on demand and the wish to avoid unnecessary transaction costs. It also makes sense, in certain market conditions for unit trusts to hold liquid funds in readiness for opportunities to purchase investments on attractive terms. However, ordinary shares in both UK and overseas companies dominate most portfolios, recently accounting for around 90% of the aggregate portfolio value. The precise structure for any given trust depends upon its investment objectives

19 Investment trust companies

19.1 Investment trusts are companies that exist to undertake investment mainly in financial assets. They are not trusts proper and they do not operate within the confines of trust deeds. These institutions obtain funds by issuing equity shares, by borrowing (primarily from the banking sector), and from retained income and realised capital gains from assets previously held. They are closed-end funds, meaning that an investor wishing to purchase investment trust shares must either wait until a new trust is launched (or, where appropriate, a rights issue of shares is made) or must find another investor holding such shares and willing to sell.

Shares in quoted investment trust companies may be bought and sold freely on the Stock Exchange. The investor in an investment trust does not buy a share in the underlying assets held by the trust (unlike the investor in a unit trust), but rather, shares in the investment trust company itself are held.

19.2 The value of an investment in an investment trust depends upon the market price of the trust's shares. This price reflects the supply of and demand for the shares on the Stock Exchange, and market conditions are influenced by the performance of the company's investment portfolio. In practice, the share price valuation of an investment trust company is often below the corresponding value of the net assets held. In other words, the share price is often at a discount to the net asset value per share, which reflects investors' perceptions of the risk associated with the investment trust's activities.

Table 2.7 Investment trusts' assets end of 1997

	£bn
Net short-term assets	1.2
Gilt-edged securities	1.1
UK company securities	30.5
Overseas company securities	18.2
Other	2.8
Total assets	53.8

Source: Financial Statistics Table 5.2C

19.3 Ordinary shares in companies dominate the aggregate assets portfolio of investment trust companies. Also, they tend to have a higher proportion of their assets invested in overseas company securities than do unit trusts, reflecting a longer tradition of overseas investment. By contrast, investment trust companies hold smaller amounts of net short-term assets, which hides reasonably large holdings of bank deposits and money market assets balanced by, not quite so large, outstanding short-term liabilities mainly in the form of bank loans.

Study Activities 16

1. Describe the principal features of a unit trust. (Paragraph 18.1)

2. Explain what is meant by 'open ended'. (Paragraph 18.2)

3. Distinguish between the ways in which the values of investments in unit trusts and investment trusts are determined. (Paragraphs 18.3 and 19.2)

4. Outline the principal features of an investment trust. (Paragraphs 19.1 and 19.2)

5. Compare and contrast the assets held by unit trusts and investment trusts. (Tables 2.6 and 2.7)

Summary

Now that you have completed this unit, you should be able to:

- understand the difference between financial institutions and financial intermediaries;

- understand the nature and economic significance of financial intermediaries;

- appreciate the Bank of England's role in liquidity management and monetary policy;

- appreciate the difference between retail and wholesale activities of financial institutions;

- understand the main operations of banks and building societies and appreciate the competitive environment within which they operate;

- describe the activities of the other deposit-taking financial intermediaries;

- compare and contrast deposit-taking and investing financial intermediaries;

- understand the roles and operations of insurance companies and pension funds;

- appreciate the operations of unit trusts and investment trusts.

Self-assessment questions

Short-answer questions

1. What factors are likely to be taken into account by a person contemplating lending money?

2. In what sense might an increase in interest rates bring together borrowers and lenders?

3. A financial intermediary may have liabilities with an average maturity of one month and assets with an average maturity of ten years. How is this institution able to continue in business?

4. List the benefits generated for a borrower by the existence of financial intermediaries.

5. List the main groups of investing financial intermediaries to be found in the UK.

6. In what ways might a financial institution seek to increase the profitability of its financial intermediation business?

7. What is the normal type of distribution system for retail banking services?

8. Why are interest-rate margins for wholesale transactions often finer than interest-rate margins for retail transactions?

9. List the main domestic payments services provided by a typical retail bank.

10. Do retail banks specialise exclusively in the provision of retail banking services?

11. What is the importance of sterling assets and liabilities to the typical retail bank?

12. In what ways have retail banks responded to the competitive threat posed by other financial intermediaries in respect of their personal customer deposit bases?

13. List the dominant characteristics of the financial intermediation activities of UK wholesale banks.

14. Within the context of wholesale banking operations, what is meant by the term 'matching'?

Multiple-choice questions

1. Retail operations of banks normally involve:

    (a) transactions with a minimum size of £500,000

    (b) corporate customers

    (c) primarily personal customers and small businesses

    (d) only sterling-denominated activities

    (e) primarily telephoned-based services.

2. By far the largest single element in the assets portfolio of a typical retail bank is:

    (a) sterling advances to the UK private sector

    (b) money market loans to the UK banking sector

    (c) UK private sector deposits

    (d) foreign currency loans to the overseas sector

    (e) claims under sale and repurchase agreements.

3. An eligible bank bill is:

    (a) a commercial bill of exchange purchased by a bank which is authorised by the Bank of England

    (b) A Treasury bill which has been underwritten by an eligible bank

    (c) a commercial bill of exchange which has been accepted by a bank endowed with eligibility status by the Bank of England

    (d) a commercial bill of exchange which has been issued by the Bank of England

    (e) a certificate of deposit which has been purchased by a commercial or industrial company.

4. In terms of balance sheet size, the wholesale banks' sector in the UK is:

    (a) about the same size as the retail banks sector

    (b) less than half the size of the retail banks sector

    (c) much larger than the retail banks sector

(d) slightly smaller than the size of the European banks based in the UK

(e) much smaller than the size of the Japanese banks based in the UK.

5. The activities of wholesale banks in the UK:

(a) are dominated by foreign currency business

(b) relate purely to customers based overseas

(c) involve no sterling lending to the UK private sector

(d) are dominated by sterling lending to the UK corporate sector

(e) are primarily directed at stock exchange transactions.

6. Overseas banks operating in the UK:

(a) are excluded from participation in capital market activities

(b) undertake no retail activities

(c) are major players in the eurocurrency markets

(d) are a relatively insignificant group as compared to British wholesale banks

(e) are the leading players in the personal savings market.

7. The asset portfolio of the typical long-term insurance company differs from that of the typical pension fund in that the insurance company holds:

(a) a much greater proportion of its assets in the form of equities

(b) no physical assets

(c) no short-term assets

(d) a larger proportion of its assets in the form of gilt-edged securities

(e) most of its gilt-edged securities in index-linked form.

8. An example of financial intermediation is:

(a) the provision of advice on takeover activity by a merchant bank

(b) the purchasing of shares by a stockbroker on behalf of a personal client

(c) the taking of deposits and the making of mortgage loans by a building society

(d) the provision of investment advice by a retail bank

(e) fund management by an investment bank.

9. Financial intermediation benefits retail lenders by:

(a) removing all risk associated with lending

(b) spreading the risk associated with lending over a large number of lenders

(c) ensuring that funds are lent only to individuals and institutions who will not default.

(d) raising the rate of interest which they will receive on their funds

(e) ensuring that all lending decisions are supervised by a regulator.

10. Which group amongst the following comprises investing financial intermediaries?

(a) unit trusts

(b) finance houses

(c) building societies

(d) British merchant (investment) banks

(e) Credit unions

3
Financial Markets

Objectives

After studying this unit you should be able to:

- outline the functions, classifications and interrelationships of financial markets;

- understand the concept of market efficiency;

- appreciate the structure and functions of the UK sterling money markets;

- understand the role of the capital market and be aware of the main functions of the London Stock Exchange;

- distinguish between the equity and fixed-income (debt) markets;

- understand the nature and pricing of eurocurrency transactions and state the reasons for the growth of the eurocurrency markets;

- appreciate the influence of financial innovation on the development of financial markets.

1   Introduction

Functions of financial markets

1.1   Financial markets are where individuals and institutions come together in order to trade financial assets. The three key functions of financial markets are:

- *To provide price information about the financial assets traded on them.* The interaction of buyers and sellers of financial assets generates prices (showing the required returns on the various types of funds involved), which provide signals as to how the available funds should be allocated between competing uses.

- *To offer liquidity* in the broad sense of providing marketability for financial assets, and hence allowing wealth holders to alter their portfolios easily.

- *To reduce the costs of buying and selling financial assets.* This comprises:

  - search costs relating to the expenditure of time and resources associated with finding a suitable trading partner;

- information costs, incurred when assessing the relative merits of a financial asset.

It should also be noted that where new issues of securities (e.g. bonds) are made, new funds are raised for the issuers, perhaps for business investment purposes. This type of operation is known as *primary market activity*. Where existing financial assets are sold, this represents their holders altering their asset portfolios, perhaps in search of better returns, lower risk or greater liquidity. This type of operation is known as *secondary market activity*.

Classification of financial markets

1.2   Financial markets may be grouped according to a range of characteristics:

- Nature of the assets traded – e.g. debt or equity.

- Original maturity of the assets traded– e.g. short-term money market or long-term capital market.

- New assets are created (in primary markets) or existing assets are traded (in secondary markets).

- Immediate or future delivery – cash/spot transactions or derivative transactions.

- Organisation of the market – e.g. auction or over-the-counter markets.

- Wholesale or retail markets – wholesale markets deal with large-scale transactions usually involving large institutions, whereas retail markets deal with small-scale transactions, involving the personal sector and small businesses.

Interrelationships

1.3   Financial markets are not independent entities, but are linked in various ways.

- Although the debt and equity markets are fairly distinct, they are linked by sentiment and economic events, particularly changes in interest rates, as well as by the existence of convertible financial assets. The latter give investors an occasional opportunity to switch from debt to equity of the issuing company.

- There is a continuous gradation of maturity from the money market to the capital market. For example, a medium-term note is a type of financial asset that could be included under either the money market heading or the capital market heading.

- As soon as an asset is issued on the primary market, it becomes eligible for trading in the secondary market. Indeed, unsatisfied investors who did not receive an allotment of the new stock or shares will bid up the price on the secondary market within minutes of the start of trading. This illustrates the way in which primary market activity may disturb the related secondary market.

- The distinction between wholesale and retail is, of course, fairly arbitrary especially when the sizes of the individual retail transactions become very large.

- Cross-relationships are very important – derivatives are to be found in most wholesale markets, such as money, bond and equity markets.

- The effects of changes in economic variables, such as interest rates, may be felt across most, if not all, financial markets almost simultaneously.

Market efficiency

1.4   There are three forms of efficiency relevant to the analysis of financial markets:

- *Efficiency of allocation of funds*, whereby primary markets allocate funds to users according to the signals given by the market prices generated by the factors of supply and demand. The prices of the assets, determining their returns, should reflect the economic value of the funds to the user.

- *Operational efficiency* relates to whether or not the market operates at the lowest cost possible, which means a low buy/sell spread and brokerage charges, when compared to the value of the transaction . The absence of free competition in a market is likely to restrict operational efficiency.

- *Informational efficiency* relates to the extent to which market prices reflect all available information relevant to the decision-making of market participants.

Efficient market hypothesis (EMH)

1.5   EMH states that the general availability of relevant information about companies, borrowers and other issuers of financial securities will lead to a correct valuation (pricing) of such securities, provided that:

- The securities are freely traded in markets.

- These markets are operationally efficient.

1.6   There are three forms of EMH:

- Weak form – the market currently reflects all relevant information implied in historic prices;

- Semi-strong form – the market currently reflects all publicly available relevant information;

- Strong form – the market currently reflects all publicly and privately available relevant information.

1.7   There is debate over EMH amongst academics, who generally support it, and market practitioners, who tend to reject it. Three observations can be made here. First, some investment managers have better track records than others, and have out-performed the market, at least for a time. If the EMH were true, this would not be possible. Second, just because information is available to all does not mean that all investors will incorporate it into their buying and selling decisions. Ignorance, loyalty and memory all play a role when investment decisions are made. Third, some practitioners argue that, although the information is available, the institutions or organisations concerned take a long time to reach their decisions.

Study Activities 1

1. What are the key roles of financial markets?   *(Paragraph 1.1)*

2. Classify the various types of financial markets.   *(Paragraph 1.2)*

3. Examine the links that may exist between the various markets in general terms.
(Paragraph 1.3)

4. In what way can financial markets be regarded as being 'efficient'? *(Paragraph 1.4)*

5. Explain what is meant by the Efficient Market Hypothesis (EMH). *(Paragraph 1.5)*

6. Describe the three forms of EMH.   *(Paragraph 1.6)*

7. What criticisms can be made of the EMH?   *(Paragraph 1.7)*

2 UK money markets

2.1   UK money market transactions involve the *borrowing and lending of short-term wholesale sterling funds*. All the transactions in the UK money markets are denominated in sterling (when in foreign currencies they are classified as transactions in the eurocurrency markets), and 'wholesale' in this context refers to a *minimum* transaction normally set at £50,000, with the *average* size of transaction naturally much higher. It is difficult to be precise about the *short-term* nature of the transactions since this will vary with, amongst other factors, the particular money market under consideration. Nevertheless, the initial maturity ranges from overnight to one year, with the vast majority of the transactions in the UK money markets involving an initial maturity of less than three months. Occasionally, some money market transactions involve assets with an initial maturity of longer than one year. Money market transactions may take the form either of conventional borrowing and lending activities (on a secured or an unsecured basis), or of issues of short-term securities bought or sold for immediate delivery. The integrated structure of the markets involves systems of communications that link the participants. There is no physical marketplace.

2.2   The City of London has been a major *international* centre for money market transactions since the 1950s. This has come about because of:

● The relative stability and sophistication of the UK financial system;

● London's long-established reputation as a centre of financial and trading activities;

● The high concentration of powerful financial institutions in London (with many of these institutions originating from abroad); and

● A level of supervision sufficient to promote confidence but not so much as to stifle innovation.

2.3   More recently, the growth of the money markets has been heavily influenced by the rising demand for increasingly sophisticated financial services. Whereas at first much of the growth of the money markets was associated with circumventing the official restrictions on the more normal banking and credit facilities within the UK, since the early 1970s the growth and development has been associated with demands for new financial services. For example, the:

● Trend towards securitisation of short-term corporate finance needs led to the development of the sterling commercial paper market;

● The evolution of liability management techniques within banks (see Section 6.6 below) led to the further development of the inter-bank market;

● Increasing use of wholesale funding by the building societies led to the further development of the inter-bank market.

2.4   The London money markets may be divided into three parts:

● Primary sterling money market.

● Secondary (or parallel) sterling money markets.

● Open gilt repo market.

The *primary money market* consists of the oldest money market, the *discount market*, which dates back to the early 19th century. The *secondary (parallel) sterling money markets* have only evolved since the 1950s, and in a way that allows the separate identification of six secondary sterling money markets. The open gilt repo market only came into existence at the beginning of 1996, and grew quickly in importance as the Bank of England revised its official money market operations to focus upon this market.

2.5   The full classification of the London sterling money markets is as follows:

● Primary sterling money market: Discount market

● Open gilt repo market

- Parallel sterling money markets: Sterling inter-bank
Sterling certificate of deposit
Sterling commercial paper
Inter-company
Local authority
Finance house.

2.6 These eight money markets will be considered in turn in the following sections. Given the existence of substantial inter-market flows of funds, and given the fact that many institutions operate in several of the money markets simultaneously, care should be taken not to view these eight markets *too* separately.

Study Activities 2

1. What types of transactions take place in money markets? *(Paragraph 2.1)*

2. What are the reasons for London's leading position as an international centre for money market transactions? *(Paragraphs 2.2 and 2.3)*

3. What are the component parts of the London money market? *(Paragraphs 2.4 and 2.5)*

4. Why might it be incorrect to view individual sterling money markets in isolation? *(Paragraph 2.6)*

3   Discount market

3.1 The main functions of the discount market are:

- to make markets for Treasury bills, local authority bills and commercial bills;

- to provide a pool of liquidity for banks;

- to finance short-term public sector debt and trade debt;

- to participate in the Bank of England's money market intervention operations.

3.2 Currently, commercial bills dominate discount market transactions. In summary, companies may raise funds via the drawing of bills of exchange as the counterpart to commercial transactions. When goods are sold on credit, the vendor may draw a bill (effectively a claim on the purchaser of the goods) and then have it 'accepted' by a bank for a fee. This acceptance guarantees payment against the bill to whoever holds the bill at maturity, and hence enhances the prospect of the drawer of the bill being able to sell (discount) it prior to maturity. The difference between the maturity value of the bill and its discounted value measures the implicit interest payment on the funds locked away in the underlying debt.

3.3 It must be emphasised that only instruments of the highest quality are traded and only institutions of the highest calibre participate in the discount market. Major participants include the Bank of England, the main clearing banks and the British merchant banks.

3.4 Until recently, the discount houses (a small group of specialist intermediaries standing between the Bank of England and the commercial banks) gave a commitment to underwrite the weekly Treasury bill tender. The changes in the Bank of England's approach to money market intervention, introduced in March 1997, broadened significantly the group of counter-parties through which the Bank operates and, effectively, removed the discount houses from the long-established pivotal position in the discount market. Today, no underwriting commitment is sought from any counter-party, although all are expected to participate positively in the weekly Treasury bill tender.

3.5 As early as 1987, the discount market's role as a channel for official financial support to the banking system was being weakened by the Bank of England's use of repo agreements with commercial banks. These agreements provide direct help to banks facing short-term liquidity pressures, and hence by-pass the market. The establishment of the open gilt repo market in 1996 and the subsequent official policy changes caused the special status of the market with the UK financial system largely to disappear.

4 Open gilt repo market

4.1 The open gilt repo market began operating at the beginning of January 1996, following the removal of official restrictive controls. For the first time, it would be possible for anyone to borrow or lend gilt-edged securities for any purpose and to transact repo business either directly or via an intermediary.

4.2 For every *repo* there is an equal but opposite *reverse repo*. This means that when a holder of gilt-edged securities enters a repo in exchange for cash, another institution must, by definition, enter a reverse repo involving, in the first instance, the handing over of cash in exchange for the gilt-edged securities. A gilt issue that is not particularly sought by a participant is known as *general collateral*. Where a particular gilt issue is required (for trading or hedging purposes), it is known as a '*specific gilt*'. When the demand for the specific gilt is high, it becomes known as a '*special gilt*'. Clearly, the market status of the gilt will affect its repo price, and hence the interest rate on the cash transfer involved. Gilt-edged securities in heavy demand may allow their holders to obtain cash at an interest rate that is significantly below LIBOR.

4.3 The main participants in the market are banks, but gilt-edged market makers, securities houses, building societies and pension funds are also important players. Institutions may be active in the market for a number of different reasons:

● To borrow cash in order to finance gilt inventory;

- To borrow gilt-edged securities against cash collateral for purposes of trading or to cover failed deals;

- To obtain a competitive return on cash with only low exposure to risk;

- To enhance the yield on a long-term gilt portfolio.

4.4   A holder of gilt-edged securities is likely to prefer to enter into a repo transaction with an institution that has a need for a specific gilt issue, as this will lead to cheaper funding than if the institution was merely seeking to earn a return on cash against any gilt.

4.5   Most repo and stock lending transactions take place on a fixed-term basis, and hence a market participant may find that it has to forgo the opportunity of earning additional returns if the gilt involved trades as a special gilt during the agreement period.

4.6   In order to facilitate the development of the market, a standard repo/reverse repo agreement was drafted by a working party chaired by the Bank of England, and a Code of Conduct was formulated in order to encourage best practice. Counter-party risk is also reduced through the transactions being effectively settled in the Central Gilts Office settlement system, which involves guaranteed payment by the counter-party's settlement bank.

Study Activities 3

1. List the main functions of the discount market. *(Paragraph 3.1)*

2. What is the importance of the acceptance facility to the operation of the discount market? *(Paragraph 3.2)*

3. Why are discount houses no longer the pivotal institutions in discount market operations? *(Paragraph 3.4)*

4. What factors may explain the diminished significance of the discount market in official money market intervention operations? *(Paragraph 3.5)*

5. What is a reverse repo? *(Paragraph 4.2)*

6. What is the difference between a 'specific gilt' and a 'special gilt'? *(Paragraph 4.2)*

7. For what reasons might an institution be active in the gilt repo market? *(Paragraph 4.3)*

8. What is a possible disadvantage to a repo market participant of engaging in a fixed-term repo? *(Paragraph 4.5)*

9. In what ways has the Bank of England worked to facilitate the development of the gilt repo market? *(Paragraph 4.6)*

5 Bank of England sterling money market intervention

5.1   In order to implement its monetary policy, the Bank of England primarily undertakes open-market operations in the sterling money markets. In 1987 the Bank began to take a somewhat more liberal approach to provision of assistance to the markets, interacting with certain institutions beyond the discount houses, which, for many years, had had almost exclusive right of access to the Bank's lending facilities. At certain times of year, the Bank was willing to engage in repo transactions with certain groups of commercial banks in order to help them to manage their liquidity positions. Initially, this process supplemented the traditional lender of last resort facility, which, at that time, largely involved the purchase of bills from the discount market when liquidity shortages became apparent in the financial system. In March 1997 a major shift occurred in the Bank's approach to market intervention, involving an extension of the list of instruments used for open-market operations, and also a broadening of the base of institutions with which the Bank would deal. As stated above, this both elevated the importance of the gilt repo market and removed the special status of the discount houses.

5.2   The purpose of open-market operations is to influence the level of interest rates on instruments with up to 14 days to maturity, and hence, through the money market structure, short-term interest rates in general. In turn, the level of short-term interest rates is believed to have an important influence on the demand for loans and hence on the creation of credit within the economy. Subject to meeting the overriding monetary policy requirements, the Bank's operations are intended to help the banking sector manage its liquidity effectively.

5.3   On any given day, money may be drained from the markets by an excess of government receipts over government expenditure. At such times, in order to avoid destabilisation of the money market due to a shortage of liquidity, the Bank stands ready to provide liquidity to the market. In addition, the assets acquired by the Bank in its money market operations are short-term claims a proportion of which mature on a daily basis, thus creating a natural drain of liquidity from the market. This maturing stream of claims gives the Bank an additional lever on short-term interest rates. If these flows are insufficient to allow the Bank to meet its objectives, it will deliberately drain liquidity from the market via the weekly issue of Treasury bills.

5.4   The fulcrum of the Bank's open-market operations is the accounts of the settlement banks held at the Bank. Final daily cash settlement within the banking sector and between the private sector and the Bank occurs through the settlement banks, which are expected to achieve minimum end-of-day balances with the Bank. The Bank's open-market operations are aimed at ensuring that the settlement banks are able to meet their liquidity requirements.

5.5   On each working day, the Bank monitors the net flows of funds between the public and private sectors, and estimates the overall liquidity position of the market. At 9.45am the Bank publishes an official forecast of the shortage of liquidity for that day and undertakes its first round of open-market operations if required. At 2.30pm, the Bank publishes any revised forecast and undertakes a further round of open-market operations if required. These operations involve the Bank either engaging in repo agreements in respect of gilt-edged securities, marketable HM Government foreign currency debt, Bank of England Euro bills and eligible bills (Treasury bills, eligible local authority bills and eligible bank bills) or purchasing eligible bills outright. The Bank's repo rate, which is also the discount rate for bill purchases, effectively determines the marginal cost of liquidity to the banking system, and hence is a key determinant of short-term interest rates within the economy as a whole.

5.6   The Bank's daily operations involve transactions with approved counter-parties, including banks, building societies and securities institutions that meet the specified criteria in respect of the quality of their market operations and in respect of their willingness to commit themselves to positive participation in market activities.

5.7   The Bank expects counter-parties to have satisfied their needs for liquidity through the 9.45am and 2.30pm operations. However, if necessary, the Bank undertakes a final round of open-market operations at 3.30pm, normally providing liquidity in the form of overnight repos, at a rate set above the Bank's repo rate.

5.8   At 4.20pm, after the markets have closed, the Bank publishes any required final revision to its forecast market liquidity shortage. When this occurs, the Bank also indicates that a facility is to be made available to the settlement banks to allow them to apply for liquidity until 4.30pm. This late assistance facility is normally in the form of overnight repos, with the rate set by the Bank above the repo rate.

5.9   On days when a surplus of liquidity on the market is forecast, the Bank will 'mop' the surplus through the sale of Treasury bills to counter-parties, which are invited to submit bids at an appropriate rate of discount.

Study Activities 4

1. Outline how the Bank of England's approach to money market intervention has altered in recent years.   *(Paragraph 5.1)*

2. What is the purpose of Bank of England open-market operations?   *(Paragraph 5.2)*

3. Why might shortages of liquidity occur in the money market?   *(Paragraph 5.3)*

4. What is the importance of settlement banks to the Bank of England's open-market operations?   *(Paragraph 5.4)*

5. List the instruments that the Bank of England uses in its open-market operations.

   (Paragraph 5.5)

6. Within the context of open-market operations, what are 'approved counter-parties' and what commitments are they expected to make?   *(Paragraph 5.6)*

7. What is the Bank of England's late assistance facility?   *(Paragraph 5.8)*

6   Parallel sterling money markets

6.1   Transactions within the parallel markets are *unsecured*, meaning that the lender has to depend on the 'good name' of the borrower. In addition, there is no lender of last resort facility provided by the Bank of England. Taken together, these differences mean that transactions within the parallel markets are somewhat riskier than comparable transactions within the discount market, and this is reflected in higher interest rates that they generate.

6.2   It should also be noted that the identification of six different parallel markets is primarily for explanatory purposes and in order to highlight the *specialist role* that each market fulfils. In practice, institutions are frequently active in a number of these markets simultaneously, with the result that funds flow very easily between them. Funds may also flow between the parallel and the primary and gilt repo markets for the same reason.

6.3   Although activities in the parallel markets first commenced during the 1950s, the markets are continuing to develop and evolve – most noticeably, in recent times, with the creation of the sterling commercial paper market in 1986 and also the medium-term note market. The development of the parallel markets reflects one of their most important characteristics: their ability to react quickly and flexibly to meet the requirements of participants. In the past, conventional banking channels have often failed to fulfil the requirements of the participants, due to the various official controls and restrictions that have been placed on banking activities. The evolution of the parallel markets has frequently, therefore, been a reflection of these controls and restrictions.

The sterling inter-bank market

6.4   This is the largest, and arguably the most important such market, concerned with the wholesale lending and borrowing of short-term funds between commercial banks. In this context, 'wholesale' would refer to a transaction of at least £0.5m, with many transactions falling within the £5m to £20m range. 'Short-term' refers to a range of periods extending from overnight to five years, although the majority of transactions would be for less than three months. These inter-bank transactions invariably make use of the agency of a broker, known as a money broker.

6.5   Before about 1960, a bank borrowing from another bank was frowned upon, since banks were supposed to be self-sufficient and, if they needed to borrow from another bank, this suggested imprudent policies. Borrowing and lending between banks is now firmly established as acceptable banking practice, and the inter-bank market has become an important means by which the commercial banks may adjust their liquidity positions. A bank that is faced with a shortage of liquidity, or has the possibility of immediate lending opportunities, is able to raise substantial volumes of funds at short notice by using the inter-bank market, and is able to do so at competitive interest rates. Similarly, a bank which has surplus funds is able to lend these out through the inter-bank market to other banks in order to obtain a competitive yield while at the same time retaining a certain amount of liquidity in those funds. For certain wholesale banks in particular which have only a *limited number* of depositors, the inter-bank market is crucial since it allows them to separate their decisions on lending opportunities from their deposit position.

6.6   This has become known as the trend towards *liability management*, meaning that much banking business has now become driven by *lending* opportunities, with banks subsequently arranging the funding of that lending through the use of the inter-bank market. It also means that banks do not need to match their deposits to their lending, in terms of size or in terms of maturity, to the same extent; a withdrawal of a large deposit from a particular bank can be covered by a loan on the inter-bank market. The inter-bank market therefore serves to raise the efficiency of the banking system as a whole, and to provide customers with both deposit and borrowing facilities that would not otherwise be available. Before the early 1960s, *asset management* prevailed: banks took deposits, and then managed the assets which these deposits were used to buy or create. With liability management, banks tend to identify good lending business and then bid for deposits on the inter-bank market to fund the lending.

6.7   The inter-bank market is also important in that it determines the *marginal cost of funds* to a commercial bank. If a bank wishes to obtain additional funds, then the cost of those funds will be determined by the rate ruling in the inter-bank market at the time, with the benchmark interest rate being the three-month London Inter-Bank Offered Rate (LIBOR). Much lending by commercial banks, particularly to the corporate sector, is at rates that are a set margin above LIBOR, and consequently this rate is of importance to borrowers with loans obtained on this basis. In addition, in theory there are links between the *base rates* set by banks and the inter-bank rates, although in practice the links are not straightforward, and it would normally appear that the base rates are, in fact, strongly influenced by the Bank of England's Monetary Policy Committee.

6.8   Although the inter-bank market is believed to be the largest of the parallel money markets, the very nature of the market makes it difficult to establish its precise size. An estimate of its size can, however, be gained from the volume of sterling deposits held by UK banks that originated from *other* UK banks. At the end of March 1999 these stood at £151.2bn.

The sterling certificates of deposit market

6.9   Sterling certificates of deposit (£CDs) are negotiable bearer securities issued by banks and large building societies, usually with a minimum value of £50,000 and a maximum of £1.0m. Their initial term to maturity is normally between 28 days and five years, with a concentration towards the shorter end. £CDs are attractive to their purchasers because no taxation on either interest or capital gains is deducted when the £CD is sold or when it matures. In addition, being bearer securities, for certain purchasers there may be benefits arising from the anonymity they confer. They are attractive to banks since they provide a facility for raising large sums of money for fixed periods of time at fixed interest rates. As such, they provide a very useful alternative to conventional deposits, since £CDs cannot be 'withdrawn' in the same way as conventional deposits and hence the risk associated with portfolio management operations is reduced. £CDs issued by banks amounted to £142.6bn (including other short-term paper) in March 1999.

6.10   Margins on £CDs tend to be very competitive, and banks are able to attract substantial inflows in response to very slight increases in rates offered. Although the banks issuing the £CDs form the *primary* market in these instruments, the success of the market is dependent on the liquidity in the *secondary* market. In practice, the secondary market in £CDs is very liquid, with a wide range of institutions involved including banks, which frequently hold large volumes in their own asset portfolios as an important source of liquidity that also yields a market-related return. In addition holders of £CDs may make capital gains if they sell the £CDs after a fall in market interest rates. They also run the risk of capital losses in the event of having to sell £CDs before their maturity after a *rise* in market interest rates.

Study Activities 5

1. What differences between primary money market and parallel sterling money market activities are likely to make transactions in the parallel markets slightly more risky than those in the primary market?   *(Paragraph 6.1)*

2. In what sense has the evolution of the parallel sterling money markets reflected official controls and restrictions?   *(Paragraph 6.3)*

3. Summarise the key characteristics of sterling inter-bank market transactions.
                                                                              (Paragraph 6.4)

4. What is the relevance of liability management in respect of activities in the inter-bank market?   *(Paragraphs 6.5 and 6.6)*

5. What is LIBOR and what is its relevance for a commercial bank?   *(Paragraph 6.7)*

6. List the attractions of sterling certificates of deposit to an issuing bank or building society.   *(Paragraphs 6.9 and 6.10)*

7. What is the difference between the primary and the secondary market for sterling certificates of deposit?   *(Paragraph 6.10)*

The sterling commercial paper market

6.11   The sterling commercial paper market is one of the newest of the secondary money markets, having commenced operations in May 1986. Prior to that time, the creation of commercial paper within the UK financial system was not permitted; however, the increasing use of euro-commercial paper, and the increasing use of commercial paper in other countries, especially the United States, had made the UK out of line with practice elsewhere. Following alterations to the provisions of the Banking Act 1979 (now the Banking Act 1987) to allow the creation of sterling commercial paper, this market has grown substantially and gained considerable importance to the financing of many corporate enterprises.

6.12   Sterling commercial paper (SCP) has the form of short-term, marketable, unsecured promissory notes with a fixed maturity. The initial maturity is typically between seven days and three months, and hence it is generally shorter-term than many instruments traded on the parallel money markets. Companies issuing SCP must have a net asset value of £25m or more. These companies (or their guarantors that may be banks) must have a listing on the Stock Exchange, and the minimum denomination of such paper is £100,000. SCP is issued in bearer form, at a discount to its maturity value. A good credit rating is a prerequisite for the SCP to be sold readily.

6.13   Unlike commercial bills, SCP does *not* have to be issued as the counterpart to an identifiable commercial transaction. In this respect, it has a substantial advantage over commercial bills, since it can be used as a means of raising short-term finance for any purpose. Issuing SCP can also be a very *cheap* form of raising short-term finance. Due to their high credit ratings, certain companies are better able to raise finance by issuing SCP than by borrowing from a bank. The lower costs of raising finance via an issue of SCP may additionally be accompanied by a higher return for the *purchasers* of the paper. The development of the SCP market, due to the disintermediation that it involves, is therefore of concern to the banks. At the same time, however, banks earn fee income from the management of SCP issues, and there are consequently some offsetting benefits.

6.14   As the majority of SCP is very short-term, figures for the market's outstanding debt tend to understate its importance. Nevertheless, some £8.9bn was outstanding with the non-bank non-building society sector at the end of March 1999.

Study Activities 6

1. What is sterling commercial paper?   *(Paragraph 6.12)*

2. What is the minimum permitted denomination of an issue of sterling commercial paper?   *(Paragraph 6.12)*

3. What is the major advantage of sterling commercial paper over commercial bills from the point of view of the issuer?   *(Paragraph 6.13)*

4. Why might borrowers prefer to raise funds via the issue of sterling commercial paper rather than via a bank loan? *(Paragraph 6.13)*

5. What threat might sterling commercial paper pose to the banks? *(Paragraph 6.13)*

The inter-company market

6.15   The inter-company market originated in 1969 and was a response to the problems faced at the time by companies wishing to raise finance from banks. Restrictions on bank lending caused companies to by-pass the banking sector and, instead, raise funds direct from other companies. The subsequent easing of bank lending restrictions and the development of additional means of raising finance by the issue of securities has meant that the attractions of this market have diminished.

6.16   The difficulties of bringing together two companies, one with funds to lend and the other needing to borrow funds, are considerable. The companies involved need to have compatible objectives with respect to maturity, size and interest rate on any loan, and the level of perceived risk must be deemed acceptable by the lender. The costs involved in overcoming these difficulties explain why the inter-company market is the smallest of the parallel money markets, and why brokers are active in the market to bring about deals.

The local authority market

6.17   The local authority market is the oldest parallel money market, having commenced in 1955. The impetus for the creation of this market was the then restricted access for local authorities to borrowed funds from *central* government, leading the local authorities to seek to raise funds on their own account from the private sector. Furthermore, the implicit guarantee of the Treasury for the debt issued by local authorities has ensured that such debt has had wide acceptance. The result was that the local authorities became important participants in both the bill and the bond markets during the 1960s and 1970s. In more recent years the tighter control over both the expenditure and the borrowing activities of local authorities has meant that its importance has diminished.

The finance house market

6.18   The finance house market is another example of declining importance within the parallel money markets. When finance houses were major providers of credit for both retail and commercial purposes, large volumes of funds were raised within this market. With the relative decline of this means of financing expenditure and the attainment of full banking status by a number of the larger finance houses, the market has declined. Nevertheless, significant sums of money are raised by the finance houses on this market, making use of issues of commercial bills in addition to direct borrowing from a range of institutions, including non-bank financial institutions such as pension funds and insurance companies as well as banks, non-financial organisations and individuals.

7   UK capital markets

7.1   Capital markets are concerned with two activities:

- Raising long-term finance for both private sector companies and for public sector organisations;

- Trading existing securities issued by both private sector companies and public sector organisations to raise long-term finance.

Primary market activity

7.2   The raising of long-term finance (*primary market activity*) is of crucial importance to both private sector companies and public sector organisations. Its importance to the former stems from the fact that it provides the funds for capital investment by industry and commerce, and therefore the means by which companies may develop and grow over time.

7.3   These long-term funds may be raised in the primary market in two different forms, by the issue of:

- *Equity shares*; and

- *Interest-bearing debt instruments*.

7.4   *Equity shares* may be issued in a number of different forms but the owners of those shares (the shareholders) are always the legal owners of the company. As such, the shareholders have the right at general meetings to determine the broad policies of the company and a claim on the profits of the company, with those profits being paid to shareholders in the form of dividends. As owners of the company, the shareholders also have a claim on any residual value of that company in the event of it being liquidated.

7.5   *Interest-bearing debt instruments* may also be issued in a variety of forms, with their distinguishing characteristic being that they are all forms of long-term borrowing. The majority of these instruments therefore normally commit the company to making regular interest payments, with the holders of these securities being creditors (or lenders – not shareholders/owners/investors) of the company concerned. Depending on the circumstances of the company, long-term borrowing by means of issuing interest-bearing debt instruments may give rise to certain advantages and greater flexibility relative to the issue of equity shares. In addition, it offers an alternative to the more conventional forms of borrowing from banks, which would be appropriate in situations where banks would not be prepared to lend in the amounts or for the period of time required by the company.

7.6   The issue of interest-bearing debt instruments in the UK capital market has been an important source of finance for the government to cover any budget deficit between income and expenditure. For the central government this has involved the issue of gilt-edged securities, with the sale of such debt *outside* the bank and building society sector constituting an important element of the control of the money supply. Local authorities were also traditionally significant issuers of debt on the UK capital market to finance any budget deficits they may have or to finance any large-scale projects.

Secondary market activity

7.7   The trading of *existing* long-term securities issued by companies and public sector organisations *(secondary market activity)* is of considerable importance, since it provides the holders with the means of liquidating their investments at very short notice. The significance of this is that the majority of equity shares have no date on which they will be redeemed (that is, they are irredeemable unless the issuing company decides otherwise), and much of the debt issued by both companies and government agencies has a long initial period to maturity. A small amount of government gilt-edged stock (consolidated loan stock) has no maturity date, and it is common for much gilt-edged stock to have a maturity date 25 or more years into the future when issued. Given the irredeemable nature of the majority of equity shares and the long original maturity of many debt instruments, it would be very difficult to find buyers for such securities unless a secondary market for them existed. Few investors would be interested in buying a security that they could never sell or for which they would have to wait decades to mature. In this very real sense, therefore, the existence of a primary market for long-term finance is dependent on the existence of an active secondary market for the securities involved.

7.8   At the centre of the capital market in the UK is the *London Stock Exchange*. Much of the activity on the London Stock Exchange involves the trading of existing securities. This is to some extent a reflection of the need for a liquid secondary market for a primary market to exist, and it must be remembered that the London Stock Exchange is of major importance in the *raising* of long-term finance for both companies and the public sector.

7.9   In addition to providing long-term finance for companies and government agencies within the UK, the London Stock Exchange engages in a substantial volume of trading in securities relating to *overseas* companies and official bodies, and in the trading of Eurobonds. This trading in overseas securities is a reflection of London's reputation as an international financial centre, but also a reflection of the increasing internationalisation of capital markets which, in London's case, has itself been stimulated by the deregulation within the market during the 1980s.

7.10   Although the London Stock Exchange is at the heart of the capital market in the

UK, a significant proportion of the trade in capital-market securities takes place *outside* the London Stock Exchange. There is no *compulsion* for the trading of equity shares or interest-bearing debt instruments to take place within the ambit of the London Stock Exchange. In practice, substantial volumes of overseas securities and Eurobonds are traded outside of the Stock Exchange, much of it by wholesale banks and securities houses based in London but with foreign ownership. Also, certain forms of specialist capital provision (such as venture capital) will not normally involve the trading of securities. The providers of venture capital will generally be investing in a business on a deliberately long-term basis in a way that does not give rise to any marketable securities for a significant period of time. These specialist providers of venture capital may be separate institutions (such as *3i*), or they may be subsidiaries or elements of other investing financial intermediaries able to take a long-term view of investment, such as pension funds or investment trusts.

Study Activities 7

1. What are the two key activities of capital markets?   *(Paragraph 7.1)*

2. What is primary market activity?   *(Paragraph 7.2)*

3. What types of instruments are relevant for capital market activities?
                                                                               (Paragraphs 7.2–7.5)

4. What is secondary market activity?   *(Paragraph 7.7)*

5. In broad terms, what type of activity dominates the operations of the London Stock Exchange?   *(Paragraph 7.8)*

6. What types of capital market activity take place outside the London Stock Exchange?
                                                                               (Paragraph 7.10)

The London Stock Exchange

7.11   The London Stock Exchange comprises two separate markets. The *main market* accounts for the bulk of London Stock Exchange activity, both in terms of the number of securities listed for trading and in terms of turnover. The 'junior' market, known as the *Alternative Investment Market*, trades in the securities of some much smaller companies.

7.12   We have noted that the money markets do not have a tangible, physical presence. The same is increasingly true of the UK capital markets. While the London Stock Exchange has a building in London, the bulk of the space within the building, along with the London Stock Exchange staff, is devoted to the administration and supervision of the capital market. Like the money markets, the capital market essentially comprises a network of communications, making use of computer and telephone links particularly, with participants being geographically dispersed although concentrated in London.

'Big Bang' reforms

7.13   'Big Bang' refers to the major changes in the operations of the London Stock Exchange that came into effect on 27 October 1986. These changes were essentially threefold:

- The system of minimum fixed commissions on London Stock Exchange transactions was ended. After Big Bang, brokers who executed orders on behalf of client investors were given freedom to charge whatever commission rates they wished and were able to negotiate with their clients. This brought London into line with the practice in New York, where the exchange had abandoned fixed commissions in 1975.

- The 'single capacity' system was ended. That is, the distinction between brokers and jobbers (who bought and sold securities on their own account, and formerly could not deal directly with investors) was abolished. Brokers could now buy and sell securities on their own account, and jobbers could deal directly with investors. Hence, a 'dual-capacity' trading system was made available for firms who wished to fulfil both functions. Although a number of firms *did* move into dual capacity trading, often through merger, it was mainly the *larger* firms that did so, and many of the smaller brokers have continued to offer brokerage services only. This is particularly true of those firms that specialise in private client business, since the benefits of offering the jobbing facilities were much less apparent.

- The gilt-edged securities market was freed up to allow greater competition. The gilt-edged securities element of the capital market had not been a particularly competitive part of the capital market prior to Big Bang, with two jobbing firms accounting for 75% of the jobbing activity. After Big Bang, some 27 institutions were authorised by the Bank of England to operate as primary dealers in gilt-edged securities. These 27 institutions were termed gilt-edged market makers, since the dual capacity system was allowed in this part of the capital market also, with participants being able to deal in gilt-edged securities on their own account and to take orders direct from clients.

7.14   The level of competition in the gilt-edged securities market proved to be too great for all 27 participants to operate profitably. At that time public sector borrowing was starting to fall, and eventually a public-sector debt-repayment arose, with the implication that the value of gilt-edged securities in issue was rising only very slowly and subsequently *fell*. Consequently, the number of participants fell, although the return of large borrowing requirements during the mid-1990s gave a major boost to the market.

7.15   Because of dual-capacity in the gilt-edged securities market after Big Bang, the gilt-edged market makers needed to be able to adjust their positions in particular stocks by dealing with *other* gilt-edged market makers. However, no gilt-edged market maker would wish to indicate to other participants that it was short of, or had too much of, a particular stock. Hence, in order to provide anonymity in dealings between gilt-edged market makers, six *inter-dealer brokers* were established. By 1993 only three of these brokers were still active in the market.

7.16   Although these three changes – the ending of minimum commissions, the merging of the brokerage and jobbing functions, and changes in the gilt-edged securities market – were the changes that occurred at Big Bang on 27 October 1986, another far-reaching change occurred prior to this at the beginning of March 1986. From that date, the restrictions on the ownership of London Stock Exchange firms were ended, meaning that member firms could be totally owned by another financial institution, rather than being restricted to a maximum ownership of 29.9% of a firm's equity. With the other changes to the UK capital market in prospect in October 1986, this led to a flurry of merger activity involving London Stock Exchange firms. Much of that activity related to the intention of some financial institutions to become integrated securities houses, providing brokerage and market-making services for a wide range of securities under one roof, alongside comprehensive corporate finance and banking facilities. The widely held view was that this was becoming increasingly necessary for banks in particular in the light of trends towards disintermediation and securitisation in the area of corporate financing. It was argued that only by becoming more heavily involved in the securities markets could the impact of these trends on profitability be offset. Further support for the view that it was necessary to become an integrated securities house was provided by the observation that it was essential to provide corporate customers with a full range of banking and securities services in order to be able to attract their business.

7.17   Not all the institutions that have entered the securities trading business have been successful. The costs of entering the business have been high. The price of jobbing and brokerage firms reflected their attractiveness, while for those institutions setting up their operations from scratch, the costs of acquiring suitable buildings, fitting them out with appropriate communications and computing equipment and recruiting the appropriate personnel have been daunting. It is important to remember that the *profit* earned by any securities trading firm relies on individuals and institutions buying and selling securities – that is to say, it is dependent on *turnover*. For the first 12 months following Big Bang, turnover in the market as a whole was high, and hence the profitability of the majority of securities trading firms or subsidiaries was sufficient to keep them in operation. The Stock Market Crash of October 1987, however, caused turnover to drop substantially, and the inevitable consequence was a fall in profitability with a number of firms withdrawing or scaling down their operations within the UK capital market.

7.18   The impact of the Big Bang reforms of the London Stock Exchange on the *costs* of securities trading and on the services offered to those wishing to raise finance have been more clear-cut. For *institutional investors*, buying and selling blocks of securities of large value, the costs associated with such transactions have fallen substantially. As a consequence of not being bound by the scale of minimum commissions, institutions have been able to negotiate much lower commissions on their deals. Furthermore, the competition in respect of the more actively traded securities within the market has risen, leading to a general narrowing of spreads between bid and offer prices on such occasions. For *private client investors* the outcome is less positive. These investors were, in effect, subsidised by institutional investors under the minimum fixed commissions system and hence, with this subsidy removed, charges were correspondingly increased. However, more recent developments, including the launch of trading via the Internet, are likely to have been to the benefit of these investors. For *companies wishing to raise funds* on the UK capital market, the conclusion is that there is now a wider range of instruments available (and hence also a wider choice for investors to invest in), while the increased competition in the market has raised the quality of service provided.

8   Stock exchange trading systems

8.1   In general, stock exchange trading systems are either:

- order driven, or

- quote driven, or

- a hybrid of quote driven and order driven.

8.2   Order-driven systems involve a broker (or an automated system) matching orders to buy and sell securities at a given price. With this arrangement the broker does not carry the risk that would arise from holding securities as an intermediary. The broker earns a commission on the matched transactions. Automated systems pose a clear threat to brokers' traditional roles, although large orders may cause problems for such systems and may distort market prices. The London Stock Exchange launched a fully electronic order-driven system (SETS) on 20 October 1997.

8.3   Quote-driven systems depend upon the existence of market-makers who, in exchange for certain privileges, are required to quote continuously buy and sell (bid and offer) prices for securities in which they are committed to make markets. The spread between bid and offer prices and the turnover of their businesses determines their gross income. Market makers take on the risk of being left holding securities when their market price is falling or of being short of securities when their price is rising. It is often argued that market makers help to maintain liquidity in the market, although they are often reluctant to deal in small company shares involving little turnover. The main quote driven systems are NASDAQ in the USA and (until recently) the London's SEAQ.

8.4   Hybrid systems involve each security being allocated to a specialist firm that acts as a broker, executing orders from other brokers on a commission basis. These specialists may also act as market makers, holding securities on their own account when it is not possible to find matching trades. The system offers the advantages of the order-driven mechanism, but also the enhanced liquidity found in the quote-driven system. However, it lacks the competitive element found in the pure quote-driven system. The hybrid system is used within the London Stock Exchange's Alternative Trading System (SEATS), and it is also used by the New York and Amsterdam Stock Exchanges.

Study Activities 8

1. List the three main elements of 'Big Bang'.   *(Paragraph 7.13)*

2. How did the environment for the gilt-edged securities market alter after 'Big Bang'?
                                                                  (Paragraph 7.14)

3. What is an 'inter-dealer broker'?   *(Paragraph 7.15)*

4. What regulatory change allowed the flurry of merger activity among London Stock Exchange firms and outside institutions during the mid-1980s?   *(Paragraph 7.16)*

5. Why were banks particularly interested in becoming involved with stock market activities during the mid-1980s?   *(Paragraph 7.16)*

6. What was the general effect of 'Big Bang' on the costs for institutional investors of trading on the stock market?   *(Paragraph 7.18)*

7. Distinguish between order-driven and quote-driven dealing.*(Paragraphs 8.2 and 8.3)*

8. What are the advantages and disadvantages of a quote-driven system?
                                                                  (Paragraph 8.3)

9. Explain the benefits of a hybrid trading system.   *(Paragraph 8.4)*

9   The primary market for equities

9.1   One of the major activities of the London Stock Exchange is reviewing applications from companies for a quotation for their shares to be traded on the Exchange. The Exchange must ensure that companies seeking a quotation satisfy its requirements (the 'Yellow Book'), which involve providing the Exchange (and therefore the investing public) with a broad spread of information about the operations of the company. In order to maintain a quotation, a company is required to supply this information on a continuing basis, with quotations being suspended for those companies that do not comply. However, gaining a quotation does not imply a 'seal of approval' from the London Stock Exchange; rather, it means that sufficient information about the company has been provided for investors to form their own view as to the wisdom of investing in that company. It also enhances the liquidity of the shares.

9.2   When a company first raises capital funds via the London Stock Exchange, the event is referred to as a public flotation of that company. Such events are normally managed by merchant banks and stock brokers, although when the company is relatively small the services of the merchant bank are often dispensed with.

9.3   A flotation may be achieved in one of three ways:

- Offer for sale at a fixed price;
- Offer for sale by tender;
- Placing.

Offer for sale at a fixed price

9.4   An offer for sale may be at a fixed price per share, so that investors have to decide whether, and how many shares they wish to purchase at that price. The difficulty with this approach lies in determining the correct price. Too low a price will result in an over-subscription, which may be exacerbated by 'stagging'. This means that investors will deliberately make applications for more shares than they intend to hold in the long term in the hope of being able to sell some, or all, of their allocation at an immediate profit. Any over-subscription also leads to difficulties in allocating the shares among the investors. Much of the difficulty in determining the appropriate price for a fixed-price offer is caused by movements in the stock market as a whole. What might be considered a 'fair' price relative to the market when the price is set may become very expensive if the market falls substantially, or very cheap if the market rises substantially, during the period in which the offer remains open.

Offer for sale by tenders

9.5   Tenders require investors to specify both the number of shares they wish to buy and the price they are willing to pay for them. Shares are then allocated in descending order of the bid price until all shares are allocated. It is, however, normal market practice to charge all those allotted shares a price that is equal to the price per share offered by the final bid accepted. This price is known as the 'striking price', and those investors bidding below the striking price do not receive an allocation of shares. The advantage of the tender method is that it ensures that the 'right' price is achieved (since all the shares are sold at the highest achievable price). However, it carries the disadvantages that, first, it may lead to a concentrated ownership of shares, and, second, that it tends to deter many investors since they are unsure about the price at which they will need to bid to secure an allocation.

Placing

9.6   A flotation by means of a placing is particularly appropriate for relatively small companies. Under a placing, the merchant bank and/or stockbroker will arrange for the shares to be sold in blocks at agreed prices. These blocks will usually be large, and hence will normally be sold to investing institutions such as insurance companies, pension funds and unit trusts. The London Stock Exchange will usually require that a block is sold to a dealer within the London Stock Exchange in order that there are shares available from which a market in that company's securities can be made. The principal advantage of a placing over an offer is that it is substantially cheaper, but it carries the disadvantage that it necessarily leads to a concentration of shareholdings, since it involves the majority of shares ending up with a limited number of institutions. However, the register of shareholders is smaller and thus cheaper to maintain.

Alternative Investment Market (AIM)

9.7   This opened in June 1995, and replaced the Unlisted Securities Market (USM) at the end of 1996. The latter's companies have, in most cases, joined the main market, whose listing requirements were changed to bring them into line with the EU: The USM, in effect, became an anomaly.

9.8   The requirements for admittance to AIM are fairly simple: companies must be vetted by one of the Stock Exchange's 'nominated advisers', which are member firms approved for this purpose by the Stock Exchange authorities. No minimum number of shares needs to be made available for investors, so the market for some shares in AIM can be illiquid.

Additional finance – rights issues

9.9   When a company is already quoted and wishes to raise additional share capital, London Stock Exchange rules require additional shares must be first offered to existing shareholders. This is known as a 'rights issue' and involves inviting existing shareholders to subscribe to the new shares, usually at a price that represents a discount to the current market price. These 'rights' can be sold in the market. When shareholders receive their rights – usually in a form known as 'allotment letters' – they face several choices, they can:

- Take up all their rights and buy all their shares. If they do not, then they may find that (at least in the shorter-term) future dividends will be smaller, because the profits will have to be divided by a larger number of shares – dilution of the equity, as it is called. However if they take up all of their rights, they must find the cash with which to buy the new shares.

- Sell all their rights and bank the cash.

- Sell some of their rights and use the proceeds to take up only a part of the shares to which they are entitled. In this way, they lessen the impact of dilution and preserve their holdings of cash and other shares.

9.10   To ensure that the new money is raised, a company may arrange for its rights issue to be underwritten by an investment bank, which will buy any shares not purchased with the aid of the rights which have been issued. The fee charged for this underwriting service may be substantial.

Vendor placing

9.11   The shareholders may, however, at a general meeting of the company, waive their rights to be offered the shares first, in which case the company may then sell the shares in blocks (usually) to investing institutions. This process is a vendor placing. A company may also raise additional capital by the issue of interest-bearing debt instruments, as an alternative to further issue of equity shares. Sometimes, the debt is issued together with warrants to subscribe for new shares on certain dates at determined prices. These warrants are, in effect, call options.

Open offer

9.12   Yet another way of raising further equity capital, often used by companies unwilling to pay for the charges for underwriting a rights issue, is to invite existing shareholders to subscribe for new shares in an open offer. This gives no rights to be sold in the market but the offer stays 'open' for several weeks.

Study Activities 9

1. What is a quotation on the London Stock Exchange?   *(Paragraph 9.1)*

2. What is the significance of a quotation on the London Stock Exchange for a potential investor?   *(Paragraph 9.1)*

3. What is a public flotation of a company?   *(Paragraph 9.2)*

4. In which ways may a flotation be achieved?   *(Paragraphs 9.4–9.6)*

5. What is the Alternative Investment Market?   *(Paragraphs 9.7 and 9.8)*

6. What is a rights issue?   *(Paragraph 9.9)*

10   Gilt-edged securities market

The primary market

10.1   In April 1998 responsibility for managing the UK government's debt was transferred from the Bank of England to the newly created Debt Management Office, an agency of the Treasury. The reasons given for changing the long-standing arrangements were related to the Bank of England being granted operational independence in respect of the implementation of monetary policy (in May 1997). It was argued that there could be a possible conflict of interest, with debt management decisions being inappropriately influenced by the needs of monetary policy. Also the relationship between the Bank and the gilt-edged securities market could become strained if it was believed that debt management policy was being influenced by information only available within the Bank on likely future interest rate movements, which, of course, could be detrimental to private investors.

10.2   Gilt-edged securities are issued either as conventional securities or as index-linked securities. Conventional securities pay a fixed coupon (interest payment) per period and have a fixed nominal maturity value and maturity date. Index-linked securities have their nominal coupon payment and maturity value adjusted according to changes in the retail price index. These latter issues provide investors with a hedge against inflation, although during the tenor of a conventional issue, the real return may prove to be better than that received on an index-linked security (as the guaranteed real return tends to be relatively low to correspond with the reduced risk).

10.3   Conventional gilt-edged securities are now issued primarily via sales at auctions, with tap issues being used only as a market management device where there is a temporary excess demand in a particular stock. [Tap issues involve the authorities selling particular issues into the market from their own holdings as a means of stabilising gilt-edged security prices.] During 1997/98, all conventional securities issues were via auctions. By contrast, index-linked issues have traditionally taken place via the tap mechanism. However, the first index-linked issue by auction occurred in November 1998, and it is the government's intention that this will become the primary method of issue in the longer term.

The secondary market

10.4   The secondary market in (second-hand) gilt-edged securities involves a range of players:

- *The holders* – banks, other financial institutions, companies and individuals in the UK and overseas.

- *The Treasury's Debt Management Office* seeks to maintain an orderly and receptive market for gilt-edged securities.

- *Gilt-edged market makers (GEMMs)*, with obligations to make a two-way (buying and selling) market in all the gilt-edged securities that they quote, and to deal at the prices quoted on the screen (some securities are rarely traded, because the amounts outstanding are so small). Until January 1996, only GEMMs could participate in repo transactions.

- *Stock exchange money brokers*, who enable GEMMs to borrow securities from pension funds and insurance companies, for trading purposes. The brokers receive a fee for arranging this borrowing, the GEMMs also paying the lending institutions for the use of the stock.

- *Inter-dealer brokers* act as intermediaries between the GEMMs, so that the transactions between GEMMs are anonymous. This anonymity is vital because the GEMMs are competing with each other for customers (the holders and potential holders) and do not wish to let their rivals know whether or not they have large holdings – or have 'gone short' – in particular stocks.

Gilt repo market

10.5   The establishment of the gilt repo market in January 1996 (discussed in Section 4 of this Unit) has provided a mechanism for increasing the liquidity of the gilt-edged securities market, and in doing so has enhanced the attractiveness of the gilt-edged securities market to investors. It is believed that the success of the gilt repo market should improve the functioning of the gilt-edged securities market and ultimately reduce the cost of government deficit financing.

Gilt strips market

10.6   In December 1997 an official gilt-edged securities stripping facility was introduced. This facility allows the coupon payments on a conventional security to be separated from the repayment of the principal at the maturity date. In effect, conventional gilt-edged securities may be converted into a set of zero coupon bonds, each with a different maturity date (except for the final coupon payment and principal repayment). For example, a five-year security paying a six-monthly coupon would produce eleven gilt strips, comprising the ten coupon payments plus the final principal repayment. The maturity of the first strip would be six months; the second would be one year; and so on. At five years, there would be the final coupon payment and the principal repayment.

10.7   As the gilt strips are direct obligations of the UK Treasury they provide investors with access to default-free assets offering greater flexibility in respect of investment needs than do conventional gilt-edged securities. The difference between what an investor pays for a gilt strip and the amount received at maturity measures the effective interest received on the funds lent. The stripping facility operates through GEMMs and applies only to certain issues of gilt-edged securities.

[Issues relating to the corporate debt market and risk analysis are covered in Unit 10.]

Study Activities 10

1. What reasons have been suggested for the Bank of England losing responsibility for managing the UK government's debt?   *(Paragraph 10.1)*

2. Why might investors be better off holding conventional gilt-edged securities, rather than holding index-linked ones?   *(Paragraph 10.2)*

3. Through what mechanism are gilt-edged securities issued?   *(Paragraph 10.3)*

4. List the main groups of participants in the secondary market for gilt-edged securities and outline their main functions.   *(Paragraph 10.4)*

5. What are gilt strips? (Paragraph 10.6)

6. What are the attractions of gilt strips to investors? (Paragraph 10.7)

11   Eurocurrency markets

Eurocurrency activities

11.1   The term *'eurocurrency'* relates to large-scale foreign-currency-denominated borrowing and lending activities. For example, large-scale US dollar-denominated loans by banks situated outside the USA would be regarded as euro-dollar loans.

11.2   Eurocurrency transactions originated in Europe, so giving them their name. However, the prefix 'euro' tends to cause confusion in that it suggests that the market is confined to Europe or is connected in some way with the European Union's single currency. This is not the case, and although many transactions take place in Europe they can in fact take place in *any country* in the world.

11.3   The main eurocurrencies are the euro-dollar, euro-sterling, euro-deutschmark and euro-yen. The euro-dollar currently accounts for about a half of all eurocurrency transactions.

11.4   Eurocurrency markets deal with the lending and borrowing of eurocurrencies in wholesale amounts. Transactions are normally *for a minimum US$1m equivalent* and are *unsecured*. Many eurocurrency transactions are short-term in nature and mature in one year or less. This short-term activity relates not only to *bank deposits and loans* but also to such instruments as *certificates of deposit*. In viewing the long term, the most popular instrument at present is the *euro-bond*.

Creation and growth of eurocurrency markets

11.5   The first euromarket originated in the early 1950s in eurodollars. Several eastern European banks wanted to disguise their ownership of dollar deposits and consequently placed them with correspondent banks mainly in Britain and France. With this sudden inflow of dollars these banks began to offer dollar loans at interest rates lower than those being offered in the USA. Coupled to this was the existence of direct monetary controls in the USA, which held down US deposit rates but which did not apply to dollars accepted from non-residents by American banks operating outside the USA. This precipitated an increase of overseas branches of US banks, particularly in London, in order to take a share of this new business. European banks also began to compete for this business. Thus, eurocurrency markets were born.

11.6   Other factors which have contributed to the successful expansion of the eurocurrency markets in the past include the:

● *Removal of currency exchange controls* by major Western countries; and

- *Large rises in oil prices* during the 1970s which resulted in a major recycling of funds between the oil-rich nations and those countries which had huge international payments problems.

- The *lack of specific reserve requirements* for either liquidity or capital which meant that banks operating in the eurocurrency markets did not have to hold huge amounts of relatively low-yield liquid assets nor have the capital backing which would be required for similar domestic operations. Some of the financial benefits of this were passed on to the customer in the form of attractive interest rate margins, naturally increasing market activity. (In saying this, it must not be ignored that a higher return on funds will be expected by the ultimate lender due to the higher risk factor that is evident in eurocurrency transactions as opposed to comparable domestic currency business.)

11.7   The major influence that has continued to encourage the growth of the eurocurrency markets is their ability to operate on very fine interest-rate margins. Compared to domestic markets, the eurocurrency markets have been able to offer *lower rates to borrowers* and *higher rates on deposits*. This has been one of the principal reasons for the eurocurrency markets' success. These rates have been achieved by *economies of scale* which have reduced unit administration costs.

11.8   In the latter part of the 1980s the growth of the eurocurrency markets slowed, as steps were taken to *increase regulatory controls on international banking activities*. Of particular significance was the western world's major central banks' agreement to introduce common capital adequacy requirements by the end of 1992. The Third-World debt problem also affected the markets' development. However, even with eurocurrency and domestic markets competing on equal supervisory terms, the eurocurrency markets still have the benefits of *economies of scale* and other operational advantages which should still give them a competitive edge.

11.9   The predominant position that the US dollar enjoys as the main currency of world trade has led to international business maintaining dollar balances in order to meet their commitments. An advantage of doing this is that there is no need to switch into and out of dollars when payments are made and incomes received respectively, thus *negating the effects of any adverse exchange rate movements*. It also obviously *reduces administrative transaction costs*. This situation is naturally linked to the continued provision of funds to the euro-dollar market and the raising of dollar loans against anticipated future dollar earnings.

Study Activities 11

1. Define the term 'eurocurrency'.   *(Paragraph 11.1)*

2. List the main eurocurrencies.   *(Paragraph 11.3)*

3. What are the normal characteristics of eurocurrency market activity?

                                                                               (Paragraph 11.4)

4. What is the connection between regulatory requirements and the growth of the eurocurrency markets? *(Paragraph 11.6)*

5. Why have eurocurrency activities been able to maintain narrow margins? *(Paragraph 11.7)*

6. What has been the impact on eurocurrency market activities of increased regulation of banking activities throughout the western world as a whole? *(Paragraph 11.8)*

7. What is the advantage to a business operating internationally of holding US dollar balances? *(Paragraph 11.9)*

Suppliers and users of eurocurrency funds
Suppliers

11.10 Suppliers can be classified into three categories:

- *Official institutions.* These were prominent providers of funds during the early 1960s and again, particularly, in the mid-1970s when oil monies were recycled through the markets. This category includes international monetary institutions, central banks and public sector bodies.

- *Commercial banks.* Commercial banks have proved to be an important gateway through which *new* funds have been able to flow into the markets, normally being on-lent by the banks on behalf of non-bank customers.

- *Private investors and non-bank private sector institutions.* This group includes wealthy individuals and multinational commercial and industrial companies.

11.11 We have already mentioned why funds have been drawn to the eurocurrency markets at the expense of domestic markets. But obviously some suppliers of funds have additional reasons for using the markets. *Central banks* find it extremely convenient to maintain reserves in interest-bearing liquid assets denominated in internationally accepted currencies. *Commercial banks* have found that participation in the markets has helped in liability and asset-management operations. Added to this, the holding of eurocurrencies helps to minimise exposure to volatile exchange rate movements. This ability to aid the financial management of institutions will undoubtedly keep eurocurrency activity buoyant.

Users

11.12 Users again can be classified into three groups:

- *Official institutions.* Following the Third-World debt problem of the 1980s, there is now much greater emphasis on lending to central governments and other public bodies of the developed countries considered to be of high standing in the international financial markets.

- *Commercial banks.* These raise huge amounts on behalf of their customers in the markets.

● *Non-bank private sector institutions.* This is the main user group. Multinational companies are particularly evident in this area, raising funds through syndicated bank loans, euro-bonds and short-term paper.

11.13 Users of funds are attracted by the general advantages of the market, e.g. fine interest rates, innovative debt instruments and flexibility of terms. However, as with suppliers of funds, users of funds have additional reasons for using the eurocurrency markets. *Central banks* have found them useful for the raising of funds without the unacceptable political ties and strict monetary conditions that often accompany borrowing from official sources. *Corporate borrowers* who are involved in international trade or overseas investment also find it convenient to be able to access huge amounts of internationally acceptable currencies. It also offers them an alternative source of funds when official restraints on borrowing in their home countries are in force.

Study Activities 12

1. What is the particular advantage to a central bank of depositing reserves with the eurocurrency markets?   *(Paragraph 11.11)*

2. Why are the eurocurrency markets popular with the commercial banks?
                                                        (Paragraphs 11.11 and 13)

3. Who are now the main borrowers in the eurocurrency markets?   *(Paragraph 11.12)*

4. What are the advantages for central banks of raising funds through the eurocurrency markets?   *(Paragraph 11.13)*

5. What are the advantages for corporate borrowers of raising funds through the eurocurrency markets?   *(Paragraph 11.13)*

Eurocurrency interest rates
Influences on interest rates

11.14 Basically, interest rates on eurocurrency transactions are determined by the supply of and demand for eurocurrency funds. There are, however, two key influences on those supply and demand conditions. Firstly, the interest rates that apply within the country where the eurocurrency market is based will *not* be reflected in the rates applicable to a eurocurrency transaction. Rather, it is the *interest rates that apply in the country from which the relevant currency originated*. The reason for this is simply that, in order to obtain a foreign currency deposit, a bank must offer rates that are competitive with those quoted for deposits in that currency's country of origin. In addition, market forces and the possibility of arbitrage will guarantee comparability between rates. Hence, whatever factors are influencing the interest rates in the domestic market will also be influencing interest rates in the corresponding eurocurrency market for that currency. (These factors will be those which commonly determine the overall level of interest rates within an economy.)

11.15　Secondly, the size of the transactions involved has enabled economies of scale to be generated, the result of which is that rates paid on eurocurrency deposits tend to be higher and the rates charged on loans lower than on comparable domestic deposits and loans.

11.16　It is sometimes argued that the nature of the eurocurrency market activities means that the depositors of the funds are exposed to *higher levels of risk* than in comparable domestic markets. Although the increased regulation has reduced this extra risk, an element remains, which means that the higher rates paid on eurocurrency deposits are largely justified by the risk premium.

11.17　The existence of *exchange controls* in some form in a number of countries whose currencies are involved in the eurocurrency markets has meant that the differentials between domestic and eurocurrency rates have often been higher than would be justified by economic factors.

The links between foreign exchange rates and eurocurrency interest rates

11.18　Changes in eurocurrency interest rates are likely to have significant effects on the exchange rate of the currency involved. These effects may best be illustrated by following the consequences of a rise in, for example, euro-sterling interest rates. Euro-sterling deposits and loans are based *outside* the UK, and consequently represent foreign currency deposits and loans of banks in countries other than the UK. A rise in the level of euro-sterling interest rates will lead, other things being equal, to a rise in the volume of euro-sterling deposits. However, the sterling will initially have to be obtained in order to make these euro-sterling deposits. Therefore, either bank balances denominated in other currencies will be switched into sterling or assets denominated in other currencies will have to be sold and then switched into sterling. The net result is that an increase in euro-sterling interest rates will give rise to an increased demand for sterling on the spot exchange market, and hence to a *rise in the spot exchange rate*.

11.19　An appreciation of sterling on the spot foreign exchange market will not be the only effect. Other things being equal, there will also be implications for the *forward* foreign exchange markets. The reason for this is that the relationship between spot and forward foreign exchange rates for a particular currency (that is, whether the forward exchange rate stands at a premium or a discount to the spot market) will depend on the relative interest rates for the currencies concerned. Again, the relationship can best be explained by means of an example. Suppose a bank based in the USA undertakes to supply a customer with sterling in three months' time. In order to avoid the risk associated with this commitment to provide sterling in three months' time at a price agreed today, the bank will purchase the necessary sterling *now* on the spot market and then make a euro-sterling deposit with three months to maturity. What the bank has in effect done is convert a quantity of what would have been dollar-denominated interest-bearing assets into interest-bearing sterling assets (the euro-sterling deposit). If the interest rate on the euro-sterling deposit is *higher* than that on the alternative dollar assets, the bank is in an advantageous position – it is earning more on its assets – and hence it will be prepared to supply the sterling at a discount to the current spot price. The interest rate differential will therefore be reflected in the differential between spot and forward exchange rates. Alternatively, if the interest rate on the euro-sterling deposit is *lower* than on the alternative dollar assets, the bank will charge a *premium* on the forward transaction in order to cover the interest rate differential. The existence of competition amongst the banks to supply currencies on a forward basis will ensure that any premiums or discounts are kept in line with interest-rate differentials.

Study Activities 13

1. Broadly, what is the relationship between the rate of interest paid on euro-yen deposits in London and interest rates paid on comparable yen deposits in Japan?
   (Paragraph 11.14)

2. For what reasons are rates of interest paid on eurocurrency deposits often higher than rates paid on comparable deposits in the country from where the currency in question originates? *(Paragraphs 11.15–11.17)*

3. What is likely to be the effect on the spot exchange rate for sterling of an increase in the euro-sterling deposit rate? *(Paragraph 11.18)*

4. What is likely to be the effect on the forward exchange rate for sterling of an increase in the euro-sterling deposit rate? *(Paragraph 11.19)*

Summary

Now that you have completed this unit you should be able to:

● outline the functions, classifications and interrelationships of financial markets;

● understand the concept of market efficiency;

● appreciate the structure and functions of the UK sterling money markets;

● understand the role of the capital market and be aware of the main functions of the London Stock Exchange;

● distinguish between the equity and fixed-income (debt) markets;

● understand the nature and pricing of eurocurrency transactions and state the reasons for the growth of the eurocurrency markets;

- appreciate the influence of financial innovation on the development of financial markets.

Self-assessment questions

Short-answer questions

1. What types of transactions take place within the sterling money markets?

2. List the component parts of the sterling money markets.

3. Which institutions are the major players in the discount market?

4. What are the two broad reasons for Bank of England intervention in the sterling money markets?

5. How does the Bank of England place upward pressure on short-term interest rates through its money market intervention?

6. Why are transactions in the parallel sterling money market likely to be more risky than transactions within the primary money market?

7. What are the attractions of sterling certificates of deposit to an issuing bank?

8. What is the difference between primary and secondary capital market activities?

9. What types of securities are traded on the London Stock Exchange?

10. What must a company do in order to obtain a 'quotation' on the main market of the London Stock Exchange?

11. What is the difference between an offer for sale and a placing, in respect of shares traded on the London Stock Exchange?

12. Why was 'Big Bang' on the London Stock Exchange of such great importance to UK institutional investors?

13. What are eurocurrency bank deposits?

14. What has been the relevance of narrow operating margins to the growth of the eurocurrency markets?

15. What are the particular attractions of eurocurrency bank deposits to companies which operate internationally?

16. Why are interest rate margins on eurocurrency transactions often narrower than margins on comparable domestic transactions?

Multiple-choice questions

1. The London money markets:

    (a) are concerned with the trading of currencies

(b) are under the direct control of the Bank of England

(c) exist via a network of communications linking participants

(d) involve only the participation of banking institutions

(e) involve only the participation of money brokers.

2. An extremely important component of the London sterling money market structure is:

(a) the inter-bank market

(b) the local authority market

(c) the foreign exchange market

(d) the euro-bond market

(e) the gilt-edged securities market.

3. An important function of the discount market is to:

(a) issue Treasury bills on behalf of the government

(b) provide medium-term credit to retail consumers

(c) provide short-term finance for commerce and the public sector

(d) make a market in long-dated gilt-edged securities

(e) link retail banks and building societies.

4. The sterling inter-bank market is of crucial significance to the clearing banks because:

(a) it sets base rates, relative to which all bank on-lending rates are fixed

(b) it determines the marginal cost of funds to the banks

(c) the prices of eligible bank bills are determined within this market

(d) it is through this market that the Bank of England adjusts the amount of liquidity available to the banking system

(e) it is in this market where the Bank of England announces its repo rate to change banks' base rates.

5. The sterling commercial paper market:

(a) involves raising short-term funds which are effectively backed by outstanding debts arising from identifiable commercial transactions

(b) involves the raising of funds with a minimum maturity of three months

(c) poses a threat to the financial intermediation operations of banks by allowing certain companies to raise short-term funds cheaply

(d) allows funds to be raised cheaply, as transactions are effectively underwritten by the Bank of England

(e) is declining, as a result of competition from the medium-term note market.

6. Capital market activity in the UK:

    (a) relates to the raising of short-term funds by private and public sector organisations

    (b) involves the issue of both interest-bearing debt and equity claims on companies

    (c) does not involve transactions in euro-bonds

    (d) relates only to private sector debt instruments

    (e) relates to the raising of short-term and long-term debt.

7. A major difference between the money markets and the capital markets in the UK is that the money markets:

    (a) operate via a communications network, whilst the capital markets involve face-to-face contact on the floor of the Stock Exchange

    (b) involve only private sector participation, whilst the capital markets involve both private and public sector participants

    (c) involve only UK-based organisations whilst the capital markets involve both UK-based and overseas-based organisations

    (d) relate to the raising of short-term finance, whilst the capital markets relate to long-term funding

    (e) are not affected by official market intervention operations, whilst the capital markets are significantly affected.

8. A 'quotation' on the London Stock Exchange:

    (a) means that the company concerned provides the London Stock Exchange regularly with required information about its operations

    (b) is the price set for the company's equity shares at any given time

    (c) is a seal of approval from the London Stock Exchange for the company's activities

    (d) means that the London Stock Exchange guarantees the resale value of the shares of the company concerned

    (e) means that current share prices appear on TV screens in people's homes.

9. 'Big Bang' on the London Stock Exchange:

    (a) involved major changes in the trading framework for gilt-edged securities

    (b) is the term used by the media to describe the London Stock Market collapse of October 1987

    (c) forced all London Stock Market firms to give up their single-capacity status and instead to become broker-dealers

(d) was caused by amendments to the Banking Act 1979 which allowed non-financial companies to issue sterling commercial paper

(e) resulted in the Banking Act 1987.

10. A major implication of the deregulation that occurred on the London Stock Exchange in March 1986 was that:

    (a) it introduced single-capacity dealing as a means of protecting investors

    (b) for the first time euro-bonds could be traded on the London Stock Exchange

    (c) it allowed banking institutions to take full control of London Stock Exchange firms

    (d) foreign companies would in future be allowed to have their shares listed on the London Stock Exchange

    (e) it allowed UK banks to become members of continental stock exchanges.

11. Eurocurrency activity:

    (a) never involves the borrowing and lending of sterling

    (b) always involves short-term borrowing and lending of foreign currencies

    (c) refers to foreign-currency-denominated borrowing and lending of wholesale funds

    (d) is related to the official transactions of the European Commission

    (e) involves the trading of the Euro in exchange for other EU currencies.

12. Transactions in the eurocurrency markets:

    (a) are unsecured and rarely involve amounts of funds less than US$1m equivalent

    (b) are normally secured

    (c) always involve at least one participant based in a European country

    (d) never have an individual value in excess of US$1m

    (e) are all controlled by the Bank for International Settlements.

13. Today the major users of eurocurrency funds are:

    (a) UK local authorities

    (b) non-bank private sector institutions

    (c) central banks of developing countries

    (d) central banks of developed countries

    (e) European central banks.

14. A major cause of the slowdown in the growth of the eurocurrency markets during the 1980s was:

(a) deregulation of banks operating in the USA

(b) rapid fluctuations in the price of crude oil

(c) the implementation of monetarist policies in many western nations

(d) debt repayment problems faced by Third World countries

(e) a change in money market operating techniques by the Bank of England.

15. A reduction in the rate of interest paid on euro-dollar deposits is likely to:

(a) cause the spot exchange rate for dollars to rise

(b) cause an existing premium on forward purchases of dollars to rise

(c) cause an existing discount on forward purchases of dollars to rise

(d) leave the spot exchange rate for dollars unaffected unless other eurocurrency interest rates also alter

(e) leave all exchange rates unaltered, because eurocurrencies are concerned with lending and borrowing and do not involve the foreign exchange market.

4
Derivative Instruments

Objectives

After studying this unit, you should be able to:

- appreciate the significance of the financial derivatives markets;

- explain the role of derivative instruments;

- distinguish between futures and forward contracts;

- be aware of the difference between exchange-based derivatives markets and over-the-counter (OTC) derivatives markets;

- describe the basic features of options;

- understand the risk/reward relationships associated with options;

- understand the operation and usage of interest rate swaps;

- examine the factors which affect the prices of:

  - futures

  - options;

- explain how arbitrage occurs between a derivatives market and the relevant cash market;

- appreciate the nature of very basic models for the pricing of:

  - futures

  - options.

Note: If you have difficulty in understanding the complex nature of some of these derivative instruments, you may wish to postpone further study of this unit until after Units 6 and 8, which cover interest rates and exchange rates respectively. The 'cash markets', to which these Units relate, form the bases from which many derivative instruments are derived.

1   What are derivatives?

1.1   Derivatives are contracts involving rights and obligations relating to purchases and sales of underlying assets, or relating to payments to be made in respect of movements in indices.

1.2 These rights and obligations are related to – or, are derived from – the underlying transactions, so they have been given the general name of *derivatives*. However, they are separate from the underlying transactions. For instance, a person agreeing to buy pigs has to accept delivery of the animals and pay for them. If on the other hand, a right (but not the obligation) is purchased to buy pigs at a fixed price on a particular date one of several things may be done:

- The right may be sold to another trader (for a profit);

- The right may be allowed to lapse if it cannot be sold at a profit;

- The right may be exercised if the market price for pigs is higher than the fixed price under the right.

1.3 These rights and obligations are complex and can smooth out price changes in the underlying assets – on the cash market as it is often termed. However, speculators are very active in derivative markets and unwitting investors can make substantial losses. Barings, the UK's oldest merchant bank, had to cease business as a result of unauthorised derivatives trading by one of its dealers.

1.4 For there to be a derivatives market, the cash market needs to be liquid – easy to trade in without moving the price of an asset (although prices can change for other reasons) – and volatile. By volatile is meant 'changeable in price'. If the price is unmovable then there is no opportunity to make a short-term profit by trading in that asset. Moreover, if a market is illiquid then there will also not be much demand for that asset.

1.5 The major types of derivatives, may be listed as:

- Forwards;

- Futures;

- Options;

- Swaps.

2 Functions of derivatives

2.1 Derivatives give investors a *choice* in respect of altering their portfolios of assets. If there were no derivatives, the only market where these portfolios could be changed would be the cash market. However, investors can chose to alter their holdings of derivatives or underlying assets if *new information* makes them change their opinions of the attraction of certain financial assets relative to others.

2.2 The market in which investors make changes to their portfolios will be the one that is most attractive in terms of cost, other things being equal. As cash market dealings involve settlement of the full transaction including delivery or receipt of the asset in question, it may well be that the rearrangement of a portfolio in the derivatives market will be the cheaper. The derivatives market is also likely to be cheaper for other reasons, such as:

- Liquidity;
- Transaction costs;
- Taxes (stamp duty especially);
- The gearing (leverage) which is possible with derivatives.

2.3   Thus, it is likely that the derivatives market will act as the *price discovery* market, from which signals are sent to the cash market. The derivatives market clarifies investors' opinions about spot prices, i.e. prices in the cash market, in the periods ahead. It also enables investors to protect the values of their portfolios more cheaply.

2.4   The link between the cash market and the derivatives market is a process of buying and selling between the two, known as *arbitrage* – buying in one market and selling in another in order to exploit price differentials. If purchases are made in the lower price market and sales are achieved in the higher price market, then as purchases will tend to raise prices and the sales will tend to lower them, the outcome will be that price differences will diminish.

2.5   Derivatives markets provide opportunities for three different kinds of participants:

- Hedgers;
- Arbitrageurs;
- Speculators.

2.6   *Hedgers* wish to avoid risks by eliminating as much as is possible the impact of price changes. They are prepared to pay to achieve this level of certainty. Obviously, if all traders were hedgers, then the chances of finding counter-parties (people to trade with) would be linked to finding people who had opposite positions in the cash market. Fortunately, derivative markets attract other types of traders, who seek profit rather than price stability or certainty.

2.7   *Arbitrageurs* buy at one price and hope to sell simultaneously at a higher price. Thus, if hedgers were selling, arbitrageurs would become buyers, so long as they could see opportunities for immediate sale at a higher price in a different market. They seek a risk-less profit.

2.8   *Speculators* are attracted to risk, or rather are attracted to the potential gain that may be made by taking on risk. Speculators seek exposure to risk and take up positions, i.e. become over-bought or over-sold, seeking not a small risk-less profit but the chance of a greater profit resulting from the greater risk to which they are exposed. The gearing (leverage) properties of derivatives make them particularly suitable for speculative activities, as for a relatively low initial outlay there will be a much greater profit (or loss) than would occur from the same investment made directly in the underlying asset.

2.9   Speculators, in turn, can be grouped into various categories:

- *Scalpers*, who go short or long (run a position) for no more than a few minutes;

- *Day traders*, running a position during a single day, and not overnight in case the price changes substantially;

- *Position traders*, who hold excess instruments (or go short extensively) for longer periods, in the hope that they will profit from substantial price changes.

Study Activities 1

1. Distinguish between a derivative and the underlying transaction in the cash market.
    (Paragraphs 1.1 and 1.2)

2. Describe the aims of the three types of participants in financial derivatives markets.
    (Paragraphs 2.6–2.9)

3. What determines whether the cash market or the derivatives market is the 'price discovery' market?
    (Paragraph 2.2 and 2.3)

4. Why don't some participants wish to take 'positions'?   *(Paragraphs 2.6 and 2.7)*

3   Derivatives markets

3.1   There are two types of markets in derivative instruments – exchange-based markets, such as LIFFE, and over-the-counter (OTC) markets.

Exchange-based markets and clearing houses

3.2   These were the first markets to be developed and are highly organised and regulated by their owners, who are usually the traders. It is the exchange which decides on the:

- Standard units – currency, size, maturity – to be traded, and the times when trading begins and ceases each day.

- Rules of the *clearing house*, through which all deals are routed, with the result that a deal between (say) X who sells to Y becomes a deal between X selling to Y the clearing house which in turn sells to Y. Conversely, Y pays the clearing house who pays X (irrespective of whether Y pays the clearing house or X delivers to the clearing house). The clearing-house interposes itself between all counter-parties, thereby shouldering the burden of default and lessening the risk. In effect, it standardises the counter-party, just as deals are for standard products; it also facilitates delivery.

- *Margin* requirements, which all members have to deposit with the clearing house, to ensure that default is unlikely. In addition, all investors must maintain margins with their brokers who are, of course, members of the exchange.

3.3   *Marking to market* is a process by which all outstanding deals are revalued daily, because prices may change frequently. In other words, historic pricing/costing is not used because prices may be volatile. Marking to market is done by the clearing-house for all the exchange's members and, again, by the members who act as brokers. The latter 'mark to market' all their transactions with their clients. As margin payments are adjusted according to the price changes in the underlying asset, the exposure to risk experienced by the exchange is limited.

3.4   In London, most derivative exchanges are members of the London Clearing House. They include:

- LIFFE – London International Financial Futures and Options Exchange;

- London Metal Exchange;

- London Commodity Exchange (formerly London FOX – Futures and Options Exchange). On 16 September 1996, this became the Commodity Products Division of LIFFE.

- The International Petroleum Exchange.

OTC markets

3.5   The world's largest OTC market is a cash market – the foreign exchange market. There is no official membership, banks deal with each other by telephone, fax and computer; regulation is undertaken by each country's regulator and co-ordinated by the Bank for International Settlements. It should be noted that there are also large numbers of deals in derivatives in the foreign exchange market.

3.6   OTC markets are characterised by the existence of *quote vendors*, providing real-time price information on computer screens. Firms providing this service include:

- Reuters;

- Bloomberg News Service;

- Knight Ridder.

Quote vendors also link into the exchange markets, so providing a comprehensive price information service. They get their OTC prices from dealers in the markets.

Advantages of OTC markets

3.7   These are that:

- Investors obtain a contract which is tailored exactly to their required quantity and maturity, unlike an exchange's standard contract.

- It is argued that the impact of deals on prices is more gentle than on an exchange where liquidity is said to be more 'concentrated'.

- The supervision by central banks and regulators lessens some of the risk arising from the absence of regulation by an exchange, especially when a highly-rated bank interposes itself as a counter-party in a currency or interest-rate swap.

Disadvantages of OTC markets

3.8   The important ones are that:

- There is no clearing house to eliminate counter-party risk.

- There is no daily margining, which increases the risk of counter-party default.

- Documentation can be more complex than on an exchange.

- Prices can be less transparent than on an exchange, although quote vendors provide as much information as possible – at a price.

Study Activities 2

1. What do standard trading units entail on exchange-based derivative markets?
(*Paragraph 3.2*)

2. What risk is removed by a clearing-house in a market for derivatives?(*Paragraph 3.2*)

3. What is meant by the term 'margining'?   (*Paragraph 3.2*)

4. What is meant by the term 'marking to market'?   (*Paragraph 3.3*)

5 What is an OTC market?   (*Paragraph 3.5*)

6. What are quote vendors?   (*Paragraph 3.6*)

7. What are the advantages of OTC markets?   (*Paragraph 3.7*)

8. What are the disadvantages of OTC markets?   (*Paragraph 3.8*)

4   Forwards and futures

4.1   A forward contract involves the parties agreeing *now* on a price to be paid on a mutually acceptable date for the delivery of an agreed quantity of a commodity or currency on that date. An example from the foreign exchange market might be for A to agree on 31 July 1999 to sell to B £257,000 worth of US dollars on 31 January 2000 at a rate of (say) £1 to $1.67. Both parties will build these amounts into their projected cash flows because they have every intention of honouring their contract. They have bought certainty – the exchange rate – because nobody knows in advance what the spot rate will be. As was explained in Unit 3 (Section 11.19), the forward rate for a currency is not a forecast of the spot rate for the date of delivery. Rather, it is the spot rate on the day the contract was concluded adjusted for the different interest rates associated with the two currencies involved obtaining on that day for the period until settlement.

4.2   *Forward* contracts have a number of distinctive features:

● The *amounts can be tailored to suit the parties' needs*, although contracts for periods in excess of one year may be hard to obtain.

● *There is no secondary market*: contracts are highly illiquid and the parties have very clear commitments.

● The only occasion when cash actually flows is *on delivery*.

● If one party cannot deliver from stock, then it must *buy the commodity or currency* on the spot market in order to fulfil the forward contract.

● As the contract is not guaranteed by a clearing house, there is a *risk flowing from default by the counter-party*.

4.3   Strictly speaking, forward contracts are not derivatives. They resemble cash contracts with very long delivery dates. However, they do contain all the attributes of derivatives contracts, in the sense they can be exploited by hedgers, speculators and arbitrageurs.

4.4   *Futures*, on the other hand, are very different from forwards, because they:

● Have standard terms, which are not negotiable between the parties.

● Can be sold and bought in their own right in a secondary market.

● Are not usually intended to result in the delivery of a commodity or currency.

● Are usually offset, e.g. a purchase by a sale, or vice versa, before delivery.

● Come within the scope of the Financial Services Act 1986 if they are traded:

    ● on a recognised investment exchange

    ● for investment purposes on an OTC market;

● Involve cash flows from the outset, because of margin requirements.

4.5   Most futures deals occur on exchange markets where margin requirements are compulsory. Gearing makes futures trading very attractive to investors. The use of margin requirements limits the amount of cash that has to be spent on the initial transaction. Also, marking to market keeps investors aware of price changes and the clearing-house minimises counter-party risk. Another reason why futures tend to be traded on exchanges is that both parties are obligated to each other, with a symmetrical risk/reward ratio.

4.6   *Forward rate agreements (FRAs)* are effectively forward contracts in interest rates. FRAs relate to the fixing of an interest rate for a specified period of time in advance and independently of the principal sum borrowed. For example, a company may have a long-term bank loan outstanding which attracts a floating rate of interest. Fearing an excessive increase in the market rate of interest, the company may wish to limit the rate of interest that it has to pay over a future period. It may be able to do this by negotiating an FRA with a bank (not necessarily the bank from which the loan has been taken), which will effectively fix the rate on the loan for an agreed period. If the floating rate of interest goes above the agreed rate of interest, the bank entering into the FRA will cover the excess interest payments on behalf of the borrower. If the floating rate falls below the agreed rate, then the borrower will pay the difference to the bank. Therefore, for the period of the FRA, the borrower has certainty in respect of the interest rate to be paid. Of course, if on average the market rate of interest remains below the agreed rate for the period of the FRA, the borrower would have been better off without the FRA.

Study Activities 3

1. Define a forward contract.   *(Paragraphs 4.1 – 4.3)*

2. Define a futures contract.   *(Paragraph 4.4)*

3. Compare and contrast forward and futures contracts under these headings:

    (a) Cash outlay;

    (b) Nature of contract;

    (c) Delivery;

    (d) Trading in a secondary market;

    (e) Liquidity;

    (f) Gearing.   *(Paragraphs 4.2 – 4.5)*

4. What are the attractions of futures for investors?   *(Paragraph 4.5)*

5. Describe the operation of forward rate agreements.   *(Paragraph 4.6)*

5   Futures contracts

5.1   These are two-way contracts, obligating both parties – the buyer has a duty to pay the price and the seller has a duty to deliver the commodity or the asset. Most futures are traded on exchanges, and financial futures can be grouped under four headings:

●   Stock index futures;

●   Interest rate futures (short-term);

- Long-term interest rate (bond) futures;
- Currency futures.

Stock index futures

5.2 In the UK, LIFFE trades the FT-SE 100 index at £10 per full index point. This means that if the index is 6,368 then one contract costs £63,680 (£10 x 6,368). At a 3% margin, the initial cash outlay is £1,910.40. There is always a choice of three delivery months – the nearest following three of March, June, September and December. For example, in May, investors can buy futures expiring in June, September and December. Delivery is the first business day after expiry, and as replicating the 100 company securities of the index in the exact proportion is almost impossible, delivery is in cash. There is also a futures contract on the FT-SE Mid 250 index.

Interest rate futures (short-term)

5.3 LIFFE provides futures in a range of three-month eurocurrency interest rates – including euro-Swiss Francs and euro-yen. The final reference interest rate (on settlement day) is obtained from the British Bankers' Association. Settlement is by cash.

5.4 For sterling there is a three-month LIFFE future available for five quarters ahead, e.g. in May, for June, September, December, March and June. The contract size is £500,000; settlement is by cash and the price is quoted at 100 less the interest rate. The interest rate used is the British Bankers' Association LIBOR for three-month sterling deposits at 11.00am on the Last Trading Day (which is the third Wednesday of the delivery month).

Long-term interest rate (bond) futures

5.5 The LIFFE long-gilt future is based on a notional gilt-edged security with £100,000 nominal value and a 7% coupon. Delivery is physical, from a list of suitable gilt-edged securities published by LIFFE. In addition, there are a number of futures in foreign government bonds. At expiry, the futures price of the bond will equal the cash price, so that futures prices tend to forecast interest rates.

Currency futures

5.6 The leading exchange is the Chicago Mercantile Exchange. Delivery is available in one of the following three months of June, September, December and March.

Open interest and trading volume

5.7 There are two indicators of business traded in futures markets:

- *Open interest* is the number of contracts still open at any one time, i.e. not closed or offset by an opposite trade.

- *Trading volume* is the total of contracts traded over a period, e.g. a day, week or month.

6 Options

Differences between options and futures

6.1 We have mentioned above (paragraph 4.5) that futures have a symmetrical risk/reward ratio. However, options do not, because they are equivalent to 'one-way bets'. Their risk/reward ratio is asymmetrical – which is very useful to investors seeking to hedge either a cash flow and/or an equity shareholding. In effect, the buyer of an option buys a right but not an obligation. The buyer is free to decide what to do with the option – exercise it, sell it or let it lapse.

6.2 The original seller (the writer) of an option is in a very different position. If the buyer exercises the option the writer must honour it. However, irrespective of the buyer's actions, the writer keeps the purchase price of the option (i.e. the option premium). For the buyers of such options, the most they can lose is their purchase price; for the sellers, the most they can gain is that same purchase price (their sales price).

6.3 On the expiry of a future, the contract has to be either honoured or offset by another future expiring on that day. Another difference in the USA between the two forms of derivatives is that margining occurs against futures but not against options. The reason is that cash passes immediately the option is written and sold to the buyer. However, LIFFE does require initial margining from the writer of options.

American and European options

6.4
- American options can be exercised at any time during the life of the option.

- European options can be exercised only at the end of their life; i.e. on the expiry date.

Call options

6.5 These give the buyer of the option the right (not the duty) to buy the asset at a stated price, known as the exercise price or strike price. The price paid for this option – a price that may vary considerably during its life – is the option price (or premium).

Put options

6.6 These give the buyer of the option the right (not the duty) to sell the asset at the exercise price. It too has a changeable option price (premium).

Financial instruments on which options are traded

6.7 Options are available on many cash and derivative financial instruments – on equity share prices, equity indices, swaps and even futures. Options may be purchased that effectively give the right to borrow or to lend (deposit funds) at a specified rate of interest (the striking rate) for an agreed period at a future date, or to purchase/sell currencies at agreed exchange rates at agreed future dates. (See Section 13 of Unit 8 and Section 10 of Unit 10 for further details.)

Equity options

6.8 Once known as 'traded options', the market in these instruments moved from the London Stock Exchange to LIFFE in 1990. At June 1999 these were available for some 74 shares. The exercise prices are determined by LIFFE. Individual equity options may only be dealt in whole contracts that normally represent 1,000 shares, and the options are American-style. The range of exercise prices is also determined by LIFFE, and varies according to the price of the underlying share. For example, a share trading at 500p is likely to have equity options available at 50p intervals – 500 and 550 – whereas a share priced at about 100p is likely to have options with 10p intervals. Each equity option is allocated to a three-monthly cycle – January, April etc., February, May etc. or March, June etc. Delivery is in terms of the actual shares.

Study Activities 4

1. List the main types of financial futures contracts.   *(Paragraph 5.1)*

2. What indicators of trading activity are used in the financial futures market?
   (Paragraph 5.7)

3. In what sense are options riskier than futures?   *(Paragraphs 6.1 – 6.3)*

4. Distinguish between American options and European options.   *(Paragraph 6.4)*

5. Distinguish between 'put' and 'call' options.   *(Paragraphs 6.5 and 6.6)*

7 Interest rate swaps

7.1 An interest rate swap occurs when two borrowers raise funds independently and then exchange the associated streams of interest payments. For example, one party may borrow at a fixed rate and the other at a floating rate of interest, or one may borrow at a rate linked to LIBOR whilst the other borrows at a rate linked to base rate. The two parties then swap their debt servicing commitments. Swaps are used as a risk management instrument whereby a company can change the profile of its interest rate liabilities without disturbing the underlying borrowing. In addition, swaps can be used as a basis for speculation when they are taken out without any matching exposure in the cash market.

7.2   The main features of interest rate swaps are:

- Only interest payments are swapped; there is no exchange of principal;

- Interest payments are swapped at rates and for a term agreed at the outset, based on an agreed notional principal;

- Transactions are usually governed by a standardised swap contract (but the amount and terms are not standardised);

- The rights and obligations under a swap contract are entirely separate from the rights or obligations associated with any underlying borrowing;

- Interest swaps normally cover initial periods of anything from 1 to 10 years or more.

7.3   From the point of view of hedging interest rate risk, interest rate swaps are useful for smaller companies that may not be able to borrow at fixed interest rates. The smaller company borrows at floating rates and the larger company borrows at fixed rates. The resulting interest rate payments may then be swapped, and, in addition, the smaller company may pay a fee to the larger company. As a result, the smaller company has obtained fixed-rate financing which would not normally be available to it, whilst the larger company has obtained floating-rate funds at a lower-than-normal rate of interest, when taking into account the fee.

7.4   In practice swaps are normally arranged through an intermediary bank, with the bank acting as a principal rather than an agent. In this case, the bank guarantees the obligations of the counter-parties, and the standard bank documentation can be used to simplify and clarify the legal position. Normally, the bank makes its return on this activity through the bid-offer spread, rather than by charging a fee for the service offered.

7.5   Interest rate swaps enable financial intermediaries to change the cash flows associated with their assets and liabilities, converting from fixed rate to floating rate and vice versa. This enables the intermediaries to market their loans in the most attractive form desired by their customers (e.g. fixed-rate mortgage loans) and yet preserve their profitability by swapping the cash flows associated with their liabilities from floating rate to fixed rate.

7.6   As an example of using interest rate swaps to take account of anticipated interest rate movements, consider the following:

Company X has fixed-rate borrowing at 7% p.a. with 5 years to maturity. Current swap quotes against 6-month LIBOR for five-year swaps are 5.60 – 5.50. This swap quote is in the form of a bid-offer spread. As the bank counter-party to a swap would be paying the fixed amount against LIBOR, it would wish to pay the lower of the two fixed quotes; i.e. 5.5%. If Company X expects interest rates to fall, it might wish to swap its fixed interest rate commitment for a

LIBOR-linked commitment. Therefore, the following transaction might be entered into:

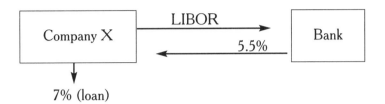

7% (loan)

For Company X the net cost of the loan = LIBOR + (7% – 5.5%) = LIBOR + 1.5%.

7.7   Suppose that one year later interest rates have fallen, but that Company X expects a subsequent rise in interest rates. If 4-year swap quotes were 4.80 – 4.70, and the company used these quotes to fix its interest costs again, the position would be:

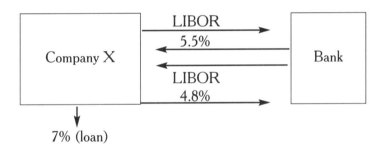

7% (loan)

Following the second swap transaction, for Company X the net cost of the loan = (7% – 5.5% + 4.8%) + LIBOR – LIBOR = 6.3% (i.e. LIBOR is cancelled out).

This example illustrates how a company might switch the profile of its debt interest payments between fixed rate and floating rate commitments, without disturbing the underlying borrowing. The example also shows how the overall cost of the debt servicing might be reduced as a result of the swap transactions.

7.8   A number of reasons have been given for the rapid growth of swap transactions in recent years – credit arbitrage, with some markets preferring certain types of debt instruments and becoming segmented; prudential regulations requiring matching of domestic liabilities in domestic markets; different tax regimes; greater volatility in interest rates.

Primary market

7.9   This is an OTC market comprising the world's leading retail and investment banks, and is regulated by their regulators and the Bank for International Settlements, helped by the International Swap Dealers Association (ISDA). Many banks have moved from being mere intermediaries to becoming principals: in effect, they add their names to deals in this OTC market, in a somewhat similar way in which the clearing house eliminates counter-party risk on a derivatives exchange. The leading banks have their own master agreements, often drafted in consultation with the ISDA, and bringing uniform practice into operation.

Secondary market

7.10   This is a growing OTC market and offers such contracts as:

- Swap reversals, with identical details for the remaining period of the original swap but with a different price and counter-party. The problem is that the 'reversing' party now has two counter-parties and thus greater default risk.

- Swap sales or swap assignments ensure that the new counter-party takes over the seller's liability to the old counter-party, who has to agree to the substitution.

- Buy-backs (close-out sales or cancellations) are where the swap is sold back to the original counter-party.

8   Caps, floors and collars

8.1   *Caps and floors* are effectively types of options. They may be thought of as giving the holder a right to purchase a forward rate agreement (forward contract in interest rates) "with hindsight". *Collars* are hybrid products, being part forward contract and part option.

8.2   *An interest rate cap* may be purchased from a bank in order to protect the holder of an existing floating-rate loan from the interest rate moving upwards beyond the level specified by the cap contract. The borrower is still able to benefit if interest rates fall, but may claim any excess interest charge over the cap level from the seller of the cap.

8.3   *An interest rate floor* has the same characteristics as a cap, except that it protects an investor or depositor against a floating rate of interest falling below the specified floor level. The seller of the floor will pay the purchaser any interest losses below the floor rate. The purchaser is still able to benefit from increases in interest rates.

8.4   *An interest rate collar* is effectively a combination of a cap and a floor. A collar may be purchased by a company wishing to protect itself against the interest rate on outstanding debt going beyond a capped level, but prepared to forgo the gain from the interest rate falling below a lower specified level in exchange for a lower premium on the cap.

Study Activities 5

1. Describe an interest rate swap.   *(Paragraph 7.1)*

2. What are the main features of interest rate swaps?   *(Paragraph 7.2)*

3. Why are interest rate swaps attractive to financial intermediaries? *(Paragraph 7.5)*

4. What is the nature of the primary market for interest rate swaps? *(Paragraph 7.9)*

5. How can parties to an interest rate swap get out of their obligations by trading in the secondary market?   *(Paragraph 7.10)*

6. Define the meaning of caps, floors and collars within the context of interest rates.
                                                          (Paragraphs 8.2 – 8.4)

7. Assess the advantages and disadvantages of caps, floors and collars to a borrower.
                                                          (Paragraphs 8.2 – 8.4)

9 Pricing of futures

9.1   The price of futures contracts is determined by the interaction of supply and demand for such contracts. In order to understand what affects the supply and demand, it is necessary to examine the underlying costs and incomes resulting from trading in these derivatives. Moreover, futures prices converge to the cash price as the delivery date approaches, with the futures contract eventually merging into a cash contract for spot delivery.

9.2   The costs involved in trading are the:

*   Cost of the underlying asset;

*   Cost of borrowing the purchase price of the underlying asset.

9.3   The rewards/incomes involved in trading are the:

*   Proceeds of the sale of the underlying asset;

*   Cash yield (dividends, interest) received by the owner of the asset during the futures contract.

9.4   The next stage of the process is to use what are called 'arbitrage arguments', examining the arbitrage profits (losses) arising from given prices. The equilibrium price is where there is zero profit/loss possible from risk-free arbitrage (buying or selling between the cash and futures markets). The arbitrage strategies are simple.

Either (argument 1):

- Buy the futures contract now;

- Sell the asset now on the cash market;

- Invest the sale proceeds until the futures contract matures;

or (argument 2):

- Sell the futures contract now;

- Buy the asset now on the cash market;

- Borrow the money to finance this cash purchase.

9.5   One way of presenting a simple (ignoring spreads and back-office costs) formula is:

Futures price = Price of asset (cash) + Price of asset (cash) (% cost of finance – % yield from asset)

If the asset costs £100 today and finance is at 6% and the asset yield is 7%, then:

$$Price = 100 + 100(0.06 - 0.07)$$
$$= 100 + 100(-0.01)$$
$$= 100 - 1$$
$$= 99$$

9.6   This formula involves percentages, and can be restated as the 'cost of carry' model which is:

Futures price = Spot price + Carry costs – Carry return

Using the data in the previous example gives (in £):

$$= 100 + 6 - 7$$
$$= 99$$

9.7   It is important to emphasise that this is a simple model, ignoring such factors as:

- The cash flows from dividends and interest payments which are reinvested at varying dates and at unknown rates of interest.

- Transaction costs, including margining.

- Price restrictions imposed by exchanges and markets on selling short.

- The futures contract may give a choice of delivery instruments (as with the LIFFE long gilts future) or a choice of delivery dates.

- There may be a spread of interest rates, so that the arbitrage argument for selling the futures contract involves a higher cost of carry than the carry return yielded by selling the asset now and buying the futures.

- The taxation treatment of futures transactions may be different from cash transactions.

Study Activities 6

1. What are the underlying factors that determine the price of a futures contract?
(Paragraphs 9.2 and 9.3)

2. Explain the two 'arbitrage arguments' used to determine the equilibrium price of a futures contract. *(Paragraph 9.4)*

3. State the futures pricing formula in its two forms: *(Paragraphs 9.5 and 9.6)*

    (a) in percentage terms; and

    (b) in monetary terms.

4. What is meant by the terms 'cost of carry' and 'carry return'? *(Paragraph 9.6)*

5. For what reasons might the actual prices of futures differ from those calculated by using a simple model? *(Paragraph 9.7)*

10 The pricing of options

10.1 This is more complex than the pricing of futures but it does involve 'arbitrage arguments'. However, there are some complicated mathematical models described in more advanced textbooks, and these will be mentioned in the next section.

10.2 The price of an option involves two elements – an intrinsic value, which can be nil or higher, and a time value. The intrinsic value can never be negative, i.e. less than nil.

In the money/out of the money

10.3 These two terms describe the relationship between the current (spot or market) price of the asset and the exercise price. If the market price is higher than the exercise price then a call option is 'in the money'. If the market price is lower than the exercise price then the call option is 'out of the money'. If both prices are equal, then the option is 'at the money'.

Intrinsic value

10.4 For a *call option* the intrinsic value is the current price of the asset (the underlying price) less the strike (or exercise) price. Taking equity options, for example, on 9 June 1999, for a call option at 130 for June on Tarmac (share price of 126) the intrinsic value was 126 less 130 = NIL (not –4). Another example on the same day was a 1,350 December 1999 call on Railtrack (share price 1,301.5). 1,301.5 less 1,350 gives NIL (not –48.5).

10.5 For a *put option*, this is the strike (exercise) price less the underlying price. Again, there are no negative values, so the lowest value is always NIL. On 9 June 1999 a 130 December 1999 put on Tarmac (underlying price 126) had an intrinsic value of 130 less 126 = 4. For Railtrack's 1,350 December 1999 put, the intrinsic value was 1,350 less 1,301.5 = 48.5.

Time value

10.6   This is the extra amount over and above the intrinsic value that a buyer is prepared to pay in order to enjoy the prospect of the underlying price changing and so increasing the option's value. By definition, the time value is obtained by deducting the intrinsic value from the option price.

Option price less intrinsic value = time value.

10.7   The table below uses the two examples from 9 June 1999, with prices being taken from the *Financial Times*. The intrinsic values were calculated earlier in this section.

Tarmac

June Call	130	December Put	130
Price of option	1.5	Price of option	16
Intrinsic value	NIL	Intrinsic value	4
Time value	1.5	Time value	12

Railtrack

December Call	1,350	December Put	1,350
Price of option	108.5	Price of option	152
Intrinsic value	NIL	Intrinsic value	48.5
Time value	108.5	Time value	103.5

10.8   The June 130 call on Tarmac had only a few days to run, so its time value was only 1.5. The underlying price was also close to its high for the year, indicating, perhaps, little immediate scope for further increase. With the December 1,350 call on Railtrack, investors were perhaps looking to the fact that the underlying price was significantly below its high for the year indicating scope for improvement against a generally solid economic performance.

10.9   The two put options are both December 1999. There was little support for Tarmac, with a low intrinsic value. For Railtrack, sentiment was more uncertain, with more support for being able to sell profitably at 1,350, i.e. hoping that the underlying price would fall well below 1,350

10.10   For put options, speculators want the underlying price to fall; for call options they want it to rise.

10.11   It should be noted that extra volatility in the price of the underlying asset is important in option pricing. This is because higher volatility means a greater chance of the option expiring in-the-money by a larger amount, matched by a greater chance of the option expiring out-of-the-money by a larger amount. However, as the holder of the option simply walks away from an out-of-the-money option, the effect of the higher volatility is asymmetrical, benefiting in-the-money option holders without affecting out-of-the-money option holders.

Factors affecting an option's price

10.12 These can be summarised as follows:

- When price of underlying asset changes:

  - call option changes price in same direction; the intrinsic value increases when the asset price rises;

  - put option changes price in opposite direction (because owner's profit diminishes the higher the price that has to be paid for the underlying asset).

- When strike (exercise) price changes:

  - call option price changes in opposite direction because for call options the total from which an unchanged asset price is deducted has risen, so intrinsic value falls.

- Time to expiry:

  - the longer to maturity the greater the time value in the price.

- When price volatility (measured by standard deviation – see Unit 9) increases:

  - the option price rises because there is more likelihood of the underlying price moving to investors' benefit.

- When short-term interest rates increase:

  - call option prices will rise, because call option holders have sold the asset short, and have invested the sales proceeds;

  - put option prices will fall, because assets are financed with borrowed money.

- Expected cash receipts for asset-holders increase:

  - call option prices will fall, because these cash distributions make it more attractive to hold the asset than the option;

  - put option prices will rise because the distributions increase the value derived from holding the asset.

11 Option pricing models

11.1 Although the discussion in the preceding section seems almost as elementary as the section on the pricing of futures, a theoretical model for the pricing of options is much more complex because of the inherent price instability of the underlying asset.

11.2   The basic aim of all option pricing models is to attempt to create a portfolio comprising the underlying asset (of the option), borrowed money and own funds, which will give the same pay-off as the option would give for the same price movements in the underlying asset.

11.3   The first options pricing model was devised in 1973 by Black and Scholes, who were mathematicians working on European call option prices. The complexity of options pricing models is illustrated by consideration of the main assumptions upon which the Black and Scholes model is based. The assumptions are that:

● There are no transaction costs or taxes.

● All securities are perfectly divisible.

● The interest rate has no spread and is risk-less, constant and the same irrespective of the asset maturity.

● The spot price behaves as if it is log-normally distributed with constant mean and standard deviation.

● Trading is continuous and markets are always open.

● Short selling of securities is permitted (that is, it is possible for an investor to sell assets that he/she does not own with a view to future purchase and delivery).

11.4   An alternative model is the binomial options pricing model, using a hedged portfolio comprising:

● A long position in the asset; protected by

● A short call position in it.

This portfolio is protected, i.e. it is risk-free, so that the price of the option is equal to the risk-free interest rate on the value of the portfolio.

12   Categorisation of derivative instruments

12.1   The derivative instruments examined in this Unit may be divided into two categories according to the type of risk incurred by the user. These categories apply equally to all derivative instruments, including those aimed at interest rate risk management and at exchange rate risk management (to be covered in Unit 8).

12.2   Using the example of interest rate risk management:

● The first category relates to derivative instruments that deny the user the opportunity to benefit from favourable interest rate movements and/or create an additional exposure to risk if the underlying borrowing is paid off early or is not required. Financial futures, interest rate swaps, collars and forward rate agreements fall into this category.

● The second category relates to derivative instruments that allow the user to benefit from favourable interest rate movements with the initial fee or premium payment effectively buying insurance cover against risk. The buying of options, caps and floors fall into this category.

12.3   In general terms, the first category of derivative instruments involves an obligation for the user, but with the major benefit that normally there is no up-front fee or premium to be paid by the user. The second category involves the payment of a fee or premium up-front (for the insurance cover), but there is no obligation placed on the buyer. Viewed in this way, the selling of an option would fall into the first category, given the acceptance of an obligation by the seller.

12.4   As implied above, risk can never be totally eliminated. For example, hedging against a rise in interest rates may prove to be expensive if market rates subsequently fall. Nevertheless when used as hedging devices, forwards, futures and swaps may reduce risk, so long as the hedger's underlying cash market position materialises. If the underlying cash market position does not materialise, a liability is created for the hedger, as the instruments effectively become speculative. By contrast, options are inherently speculative, as they involve no obligation for the buyer but a clear obligation for the seller (which may be very costly if excessive movements in market prices occur). However, for a hedger, options fix the 'worst case' position, but leave scope for unlimited gain if the market moves to the hedger's advantage.

12.5   The above categorisation of derivative instruments should help potential users to choose between instruments. A particularly important factor is the certainty of the cash market exposure. There is also the ever-present risk of counter-party default, which may result in uncovered exposures. However, by undertaking transactions with major banks (acting as principals) or through recognised exchanges, this problem is minimised.

Study Activities 7

1. Separate the price of an option into its two component elements.   *(Paragraph 10.2)*

2. Outline how the intrinsic value of a call option is calculated.   *(Paragraph 10.4)*

3. Why is extra volatility in the price of the underlying asset important in option pricing?
   (Paragraph 10.11)

4. List the main factors affecting an option's price and indicate how each factor affects the prices of call options and put options.   *(Paragraph 10.12)*

5. State the assumptions underlying the Black and Scholes model.   *(Paragraph 11.2)*

6. Describe the binomial option-pricing model.   *(Paragraph 11.3)*

7. Categorise derivative instruments in terms of the obligations that they entail for their users. *(Paragraphs 12.2 and 12.3)*

8. In what sense may forwards, futures and swaps reduce risk for their user? *(Paragraph 12.4)*

Summary

Now that you have completed this unit, you should be able to:

- appreciate the significance of the financial derivatives markets;

- explain the role of derivative instruments;

- distinguish between futures and forward contracts;

- be aware of the difference between exchange-based derivatives markets and over-the-counter (OTC) derivatives markets;

- describe the basic features of options;

- understand the risk/reward relationships associated with options;

- understand the operation and usage of interest rate swaps;

- examine the factors which affect the prices of:

  - futures

  - options;

- explain how arbitrage occurs between a derivatives market and the relevant cash market;

- appreciate the nature of very basic models for the pricing of:

  - futures

  - options.

Self-assessment questions

Short-answer questions

1. What are the economic functions of derivative markets? Need they attract speculators?

2. Distinguish between the two main types of derivative markets.

3. Indicate how the use of financial derivatives can indirectly help a person in the UK who has:

   (a) a floating-rate mortgage

   (b) a defined contributions pension

(c) an endowment policy for £40,000 with profits

(d) an elderly relative in Canada, and who he/she supports by making regular remittances.

4. Distinguish between the primary markets in gilt-edged securities and interest rate swaps.

5. Distinguish between a forward rate agreement and an interest rate swap.

Multiple-choice questions

1. Within the context of derivatives trading, scalpers are speculators who:

    (a) run a position for no longer than a few minutes

    (b) run a position until the next day

    (c) seek to buy cheaply in one market and sell at a higher price in another market

    (d) seek maximum profit at minimum risk

    (e) seek maximum profit from long-term price changes.

2. The price of a futures contract is largely determined by:

    (a) margin requirements enforced by LIFFE

    (b) the interaction of the spot price of the relevant asset, the carry costs and the carry return

    (c) the sum of the carry cost and the carry return associated with the relevant asset

    (d) the spot price of the relevant asset and the forward exchange rate for the currency in which the asset is denominated

    (e) the supply of such contracts on the London Stock Exchange.

3. In the London financial futures market, margins are imposed by:

    (a) LIFFE

    (b) London Clearing House

    (c) Bank of England

    (d) Financial Services Authority

    (e) Securities and Futures Authority.

4. Which of the following financial products have a symmetrical risk/reward ratio?

    (a) all derivatives traded on a secondary market

    (b) all products traded on a derivatives exchange

    (c) futures and options

(d) options

(e) futures.

5. A call option at 200p is available for a share with a current price of 193p. The price of the option is 8p.

    (a) The intrinsic value of the option is 192p

    (b) The time value of the option is nil.

    (c) There is insufficient information to calculate the time value of the option

    (d) No rational investor would purchase the call option at the price specified

    (e) The intrinsic value of the option is nil.

6. Interest rate swaps:

    (a) normally involve standardised amounts and terms

    (b) can be reversed in the secondary market, but with the possibility that the risk incurred by the reversing party will be increased

    (c) are normally traded on LIFFE

    (d) create rights but no obligations for the parties involved

    (e) alter the profile of interest rate liabilities by allowing borrowers to swap borrowed funds.

5

Regulation of Financial Institutions and Financial Markets

Objectives

After studying this unit, you should be able to:

- appreciate the purpose of governmental regulation of financial institutions and financial markets;

- describe the different ways in which governments regulate financial institutions and markets;

- appreciate the economic risks of over-regulation of financial institutions and markets;

- describe the structure of the regulatory framework within the UK;

- understand the rationale for the recent changes in the financial regulatory framework;

- analyse the commercial banks' and building societies' needs for liquidity and capital adequacy;

- assess the general impact of the major requirements of the EU Banking Directives on the operations of UK banks;

- discuss the influence of international institutions (e.g. Bank for International Settlements) and the EU on the framework for supervising and regulating the financial system;

- outline the implementation of regulation in the world's major economies;

- understand the causes of reform, including financial crises, financial innovation and globalisation.

1   The need for regulation and the way it is implemented

1.1   Modern financial systems are so complex and so important to the economic well-being of nations that it is generally agreed that regulations are required to:

- Protect the users and providers of financial services;

- Promote the stability of financial institutions;

- Promote competition and fairness in financial markets;

- Ensure that issuers of securities do not conceal relevant information.

Protecting the users and providers of financial services

1.2   A major purpose of financial regulation is the protection of the user of financial services from unscrupulous or incompetent providers of services. The emphasis of regulation is often placed upon protecting the small, unsophisticated investor or saver, rather than the experienced professional operator. In addition, it may be felt necessary to offer protection to the providers of financial services against their own greed or ineptitude.

Protecting the stability of financial institutions

1.3   An equally important function of financial regulation is to contribute to maintaining the stability of the financial system. The failure of financial intermediaries can not only cause the liquidation of firms and unemployment to those directly involved, but also may undermine confidence in the financial system as a whole, leading to possible runs on banks and damaging withdrawals of funds from other institutions that are otherwise sound. The need for stability applies not only to deposit-taking financial intermediaries but also to investing ones. The failure of motor insurance companies in the 1970s and the collapse of some of the Maxwell companies' pension funds in the early 1990s show the distress that can be caused when regulation is inadequate. This type of control is often called 'prudential regulation' to distinguish it from the implementation of economic policy and to emphasise its aim of preventing reckless or imprudent business practices.

Promoting competition and fairness in financial markets

1.4   Many examples could be cited, some of which are as follows:

- Preventing insider dealing, e.g. employees and managers dealing in their company's securities or their client companies' securities before market-sensitive news is published.

- Disclosing charges made by insurance companies, unit trusts and investment trusts, so that the full costs of financial transactions are made clear.

- Reducing the complexity of financial contracts so that the parties involved may be fully aware of their commitments and rights.

- Creating a 'level playing field' in international financial markets. Without equity of treatment, countries with less stringent regulations could gain a competitive advantage, but the result may be hidden risks for market participants.

Ensuring that issuers of securities do not conceal relevant information

1.5   In general, there is an asymmetry of information in financial markets because the users of funds almost invariably have a greater knowledge of their affairs than have their potential lenders and investors. If the latter are professionals, then they will ascertain as much as possible by research, taking references or going to credit rating agencies (as with commercial paper). However, if the potential lenders and investors are private individuals, there is a far greater chance of their being enticed into dealing with such companies without making the necessary inquiries. Moreover, they may not be able to make such inquiries, so the market regulator will often require such information, e.g. contracts between a company and its directors, to be published before a company's security can be issued.

Implementation of financial regulation

1.6   The activities of financial institutions and markets may be regulated through a wide range of bodies, with differing degrees of power and legal status. In the UK, for example, all of the following have, at least until recently, been involved in the regulation of financial activities:

- Government departments; e.g. the Department of Trade and Industry and the Treasury.
- Statutory bodies; e.g. the Building Societies Commission.
- Non-governmental public sector bodies; e.g. the Bank of England.
- Professional bodies and trade associations; e.g. the accountancy institutes.
- Private sector institutions; e.g. the London Stock Exchange Council.

1.7   In the UK, until the 1980s, the emphasis of financial regulation and supervision was placed upon the honesty of the provider of financial services, rather than upon his or her technical competence. Since the early 1980s, the authorities have been attempting to:

- strengthen the regulatory framework;
- formalise and standardise regulation wherever possible;
- make the system of control more equitable;
- remove restrictive practices and encourage competition;
- recognise the competence of providers of financial services.

1.8   Major problems faced by the authorities have related to the increased sophistication of financial instruments, the greater complexity of financial transactions and the diversification of activities of financial institutions. These developments have made effective regulation more difficult to achieve. One outcome has been the shift towards regulation based upon types of activity, rather than types of institutions. Another outcome has been the increased technicality of the regulations. This trend has raised the costs of compliance for those regulated. It has also led to concerns about the reduced supervisory recognition of institutions as a whole.

Study Activities 1

1. What are the fundamental reasons for regulating financial institutions and markets?

   (Paragraph 1.1)

2. In what ways does financial regulation promote economic stability? *(Paragraph 1.3)*

3. How might financial regulation ensure fair competition? *(Paragraph 1.4)*

4. What is meant by the 'asymmetry of information' within the context of financial regulation? *(Paragraph 1.5)*

5. List the different types of body that might be responsible for the implementation of financial regulation. *(Paragraph 1.6)*

6. In the UK, how has the emphasis of financial regulation altered in recent years?

   (Paragraph 1.7)

7. In what ways has financial regulation become harder to implement in recent years?

   (Paragraph 1.8)

2 The framework for banking regulation and supervision in the UK

2.1 On 1 June 1998, the Financial Services Authority took over responsibility from the Bank of England for the regulation and supervision of banking activity within the UK. The Banking Act 1987 was amended by the Bank of England Act 1998 to enable this transfer of responsibility to occur, but the Banking Act 1987 still provides the legal framework for banking regulation and supervision. Initially, at least, the Financial Services Authority is carrying forward the practical implementation of its duties in this regard largely as would have the Bank of England. Therefore, reference to the Financial Services Authority in the following description of banking regulation and supervision could easily be replaced by reference to the Bank of England to describe the situation prior to June 1998.

The Banking Act 1987

2.2 The activities of the Financial Services Authority in supervising the domestic banking system may appear to relate to individual banks within the system. However, the overall thrust of the supervisory efforts is directed towards maintaining the integrity of the banking sector, since only in such circumstances can the general public's confidence in its stability be maintained.

2.3   Traditionally, the supervision of commercial banks by the Bank of England was on an informal basis, with the Bank seeking to ensure, on a case-by-case basis, that individual banks were not over-exposed to risk in their lending portfolios, that they had an appropriate level of liquidity, and so on. Since the enactment of the Banking Act 1979, however, the supervision of the domestic banking system has had a formal legal basis, with these legal aspects being extended by the Banking Act 1987 (which repealed almost all the 1979 Act).

2.4   The Banking Act of 1987 was intended to make the supervision of banks within the UK more rigorous following the failure of the Johnson Matthey Bank in 1984, and to introduce a unified system of regulation for banking institutions. As a consequence, under this Act there is just one category of authorised banking institutions, with all banks required to operate within the same statutory supervisory requirements. The 1987 Act made two significant changes to the supervisory framework. It increased the:

● Volume and frequency of the data concerning a bank's activities to be provided to the regulator, thereby allowing a closer monitoring to be made; and

● Powers – including discretionary powers – of the regulator for the supervision of banking activities.

2.5   Under the Banking Act 1987, a bank must satisfy certain minimum criteria before it can receive authorisation. These criteria require, in particular, that:

● The bank's directors, controllers and managers are 'fit and proper' persons to hold such positions;

● The bank is effectively directed by at least two individuals;

● For banks incorporated within the UK, there must be as many non-executive directors as the Financial Services Authority considers appropriate;

● The business be conducted prudently, with regard to liquidity, capital adequacy, foreign currency exposure, provisions for bad and doubtful debts, accounting and other records, and internal management controls;

● The institution has a minimum value of net assets when authorisation is granted (set at Euro [formerly ECU] 5m since the beginning of 1993).

2.6   In respect of the 'fit and proper' test, the Financial Services Authority has substantial discretionary powers. Also, within the provisions of the Banking Act 1987 the Financial Services Authority:

● Retains the discretion to set prudential standards on a case-by-case basis; and

● Has the power to object to proposed takeovers and mergers involving UK banking institutions.

2.7   Also, under the Act:

- The provision of false or misleading information to the Financial Services Authority is a criminal offence;

- The auditors of a bank are expected to pay close attention to the Financial Services Authority's supervisory information requirements as a further check on the provision of adequate information to the Financial Services Authority; and

- Banks are required to give notice to the Financial Services Authority when their exposure to individual borrowers is expected to exceed 25% of their capital, and to report exposures of 10–25% to the Financial Services Authority.

2.8   In order to buttress the ability of the Bank of England to fulfil its supervisory responsibilities, the 1987 Act established a Board of Banking Supervision, which was to advise the Governor of the Bank of England on matters relating to the:

- Supervision of authorised institutions;

- Development and evolution of supervisory practice;

- Administration of banking supervisory legislation; and the

- Structure and staffing of the Banking Supervision Division of the Bank of England.

This Board has been carried over to the Financial Services Authority, but with some important changes in its structure.

2.9   Currently, there are two *ex officio* members, namely the Chairperson of the Financial Services Authority and another officer of the Authority chosen by the Chairperson. The other six members of the Board are independent, in the sense that they have no executive responsibilities in the Authority. However, these members are appointed jointly by the Chancellor of the Exchequer and the Chairperson of the Authority, and are chosen on the basis of their legal, accounting or banking backgrounds. The Chairperson of the Board of Banking Supervision is one of the independent members chosen by those members.

2.10   The independent members of the Board of Banking Supervision are to advise the *ex officio* members on the operation and administration of banking regulation and supervision and the formulation of policy. However, the *ex officio* members may ignore the advice, but must give written notice to the Chancellor of the Exchequer that this is being done, in which case the independent members will be entitled to put before the Chancellor the reasons for their advice. Hence, it may be argued that, except in extreme circumstances, ultimate authority for supervision remains firmly with the Financial Services Authority, which could lead to the criticism that there is too little independent scrutiny of regulatory and supervisory practices. This type of arrangement is less problematic than when the Bank of

England was responsible for banking regulation and supervision, given its interest in supporting the development of the City and, in particular, the banking sector.

Study Activities 2

1. What was the broad intention of the Banking Act 1987? *(Paragraph 2.4)*

2. List the minimum criteria that a bank must satisfy in order to gain authorisation from the Financial Services Authority. *(Paragraph 2.5)*

3. What requirements does the Banking Act 1987 place upon authorised banks in relation to their exposure to individual borrowers? *(Paragraph 2.7)*

4. What were the original functions of the Board of Banking Supervision? *(Paragraph 2.8)*

5. In what respects have the recent changes in banking regulatory arrangements affected the independence of the regulatory process? *(Paragraphs 2.9 and 2.10)*

The supervision of bank liquidity

2.11 An important component of the supervision of banking institutions by the Financial Services Authority is with regard to their *liquidity positions*. In broad terms, the objective here is to ensure that all banks will be able to meet their obligations when they fall due. The major obligations relate to:

- the repayment of both sight deposits and time deposits;
- commitments in the form of unutilised overdraft facilities;
- commitments to lend to particular customers at a specific date in the future.

The maturity transformation of funds by banks will result in the average maturity of their deposits being significantly shorter than the average maturity of their advances (which constitute the major element of a bank's assets). Therefore, the problem of ensuring that a bank is able to meet its obligations when they fall due is a significant one.

2.12 In principle, a bank is able to ensure that it can meet its obligations by means of one or more of the following methods. The bank may:

- Hold cash or other liquid assets, recognising that the value of many liquid assets will be variable due to fluctuations in market prices.
- Attempt to match the maturity characteristics of its assets with the maturity characteristics of its deposit base, so that (after allowing for defaults on loans) there is an appropriate cash flow from maturing assets.
- Seek to maintain a diversified deposit base and an appropriately high standing in the money markets such that it is able to attract deposits as and when required, without having to pay excessive interest rates.

2.13   Although there has been some discussion about the possibility of introducing a standardised requirement for all banks to hold a similar stock of liquid assets as a 'safety net', the basic principle of liquidity control remains one of self-regulation. The Financial Services Authority sets the broad guidelines for evaluating the quality of assets and for classifying liabilities, and then leaves the institutions to select that combination of assets and liabilities they consider appropriate to their commercial objectives. Furthermore, the Financial Services Authority does not specify which, or what combination, of the three approaches to ensuring adequate liquidity identified above should be utilised. The only exception to this general rule relates to the position of large UK retail banks. That is, in January 1996, a new system for measuring the sterling liquidity of large UK retail banks was implemented (by the Bank of England). Whilst being quite compatible with the then existing framework, it has introduced a common minimum standard. This is designed to ensure that, at all times, a bank maintains a stock of highly liquid assets that can be mobilised quickly and discreetly to replace funding that has been withdrawn because of a perceived problem in the institution. Liquid assets that are acceptable for meeting the minimum requirements include:

- cash;

- operational balances at the Bank of England;

- UK Treasury bills;

- gilt-edged securities;

- UK eligible bank bills;

- UK eligible local authority bills;

- secured overnight and callable deposits with Stock Exchange Money Brokers and with Gilt-edged Market Makers.

2.14   It should also be remembered that banks are required to provide to the Financial Services Authority with a continual flow of confidential information regarding the nature of their assets and liabilities. This information, together with the regular meetings that senior managers are required to hold with Financial Services Authority supervisors, ensures that the Financial Services Authority is kept informed of the liquidity position of all banks. Should the Financial Services Authority consider that the policies being followed by a bank are not giving rise to an adequate level of liquidity, it will issue a warning, and failure by the bank concerned to act on such a warning is likely to lead to the suspension of authorisation. In general terms, it is the intention of the authorities to provide encouragement for banking institutions to follow prudent policies with regard to their overall liquidity positions. Also, banks are expected to ensure that their internal management systems are capable of monitoring their liquidity positions and dealing with unanticipated liquidity problems.

Study Activities 3

1. In relation to liquidity controls, what are a bank's major obligations?
   (Paragraph 2.11)

2. What is the overall objective of liquidity controls? *(Paragraph 2.11)*

3. List the ways in which a bank may meet its liquidity commitments. *(Paragraph 2.12)*

4. To what extent does the Financial Services Authority dictate the liquidity management policy to be pursued by individual banks? *(Paragraph 2.13)*

5. How does the Financial Services Authority maintain the effectiveness of its supervision of bank's liquidity? *(Paragraph 2.14)*

The supervision of capital adequacy

2.15 The capital that a bank has is an important consideration since it is a measure of the bank's ability to absorb losses that can arise from bad debts or trading losses on investments. It is also a source of finance for investment in technology and acquisitions of other financial institutions. An adequate level of capital in relation to a bank's lending is therefore, along with an adequate level of liquidity, an essential requirement for the maintenance of a sound banking system and the maintenance of confidence in that system.

2.16 The Bank of England was given a legal duty to regulate the capital adequacy of banking institutions with the enactment of the Banking Act 1979, and that duty was strengthened by the Banking Act 1987. The Financial Services Authority has now taken over this responsibility. Despite that legal duty to regulate the banks' capital adequacy, during the 1980s there was no common minimum level of capital adequacy applied to banks in the UK, and the requirement imposed on any bank was the result of the Bank of England's assessment of that bank's position and capabilities.

2.17 Different assets in a bank's portfolio carry different levels of risk, and given that the characteristics of a portfolio will vary widely from one bank to another, it is inappropriate to require a bank to hold capital equal to a particular proportion of its assets. A necessary first step, therefore, was for an assessment to be made of the risk attached to the various items in a bank's asset portfolio and then to weight that portfolio according to the associated risk. The outcome was that the greater the level of risk in a bank's asset portfolio, the greater the amount of capital required in order to maintain a given degree of capital adequacy. There was a clear recognition, therefore, that a particular level of protection for depositors would have to take account of the risk associated with the bank's lending activities.

2.18 The Bank of England, in addition to setting down the parameters for assessing risk in the asset portfolio, also set down a clear definition of what could be regarded as the 'capital' of a bank for the purposes of specifying capital adequacy ratios.

However, the Bank retained the flexibility to specify the ratio of capital to the risk-weighted assets that any individual bank would be required to hold. This ratio was set to take account of the Bank of England's assessment of the bank's managerial capacity with regard to its risk position, its profitability and its overall prospects. The Bank of England, therefore, set a *minimum* ratio (termed the 'trigger' ratio) below which it would be likely to intervene, with the expectation that in normal circumstances the bank would maintain a 'target' ratio which included a margin over the value of the trigger ratio.

The Basle Accord

2.19   Moves at an international level to harmonise the capital adequacy ratios of banks in different countries have led to some change in the nature of the capital adequacy regime facing banks in the UK, towards a more rigorously defined framework. *The Committee on Banking Regulations and Supervisory Practices* of the Bank for International Settlements (BIS) put forward a framework in July 1988 for the harmonisation of standards of capital adequacy. The objective of this framework was to strengthen the world's banking system and place it in a better position to withstand any future problems in world financial markets. In addition, the requirements are intended to provide a more equal basis for competition between banks in different countries and to remove the incentive for a bank to relocate activities in another country in order to take advantage of its relatively lax regulatory requirements. The BIS is located in Basle, and hence the requirements are known as the Basle Accord.

2.20   The majority of western central banks undertook to implement the BIS proposals by the end of 1992. Although in strict terms they only relate to banks that are internationally active, the Bank of England applied them as a common standard to all authorised banks in the UK. Furthermore, the Bank of England announced that it would make use of the discretionary powers allowed under the proposals for individual central banks to set capital adequacy requirements *above* the minimum level specified, and that it would continue to set 'trigger' and 'target' ratios. These latter ratios are confidential and very important in day-to-day supervision.

2.21   On the *risk* side of the capital adequacy proposals, and along the lines of the system for weighting the risk characteristics of different assets used by the Bank of England, the BIS proposals specify risk weightings for the various categories of assets. These include:

- Cash: 0%
- Call money at the discount houses: 10%
- Fixed interest securities issued by OECD central governments: 20%
- Mortgage loans to owner-occupiers: 50%
- Commercial loans: 100%

2.22 In addition, account is also taken of off-balance-sheet risks, i.e. risk-carrying activities with which a bank might be involved which do not need to appear on the bank's balance sheet, such as forward currency exchange contracts, underwriting commitments and guarantees. Such items are included in the calculations by means of 'credit conversion factors' that are designed to provide a measure of their value weighted for credit risk.

2.23 On the *capital* side of the proposals of the BIS, capital is split into two types:

- Tier 1 capital (core capital), which comprises shareholders' equity and disclosed reserves; and

- Tier 2 capital (supplementary capital) which consists of revaluation reserves, general provisions, hidden reserves, subordinated debt and certain other approved capital instruments.

2.24 The requirement of the BIS proposals is that banks should have capital equal in value to *at least 8% of total risk-weighted assets*, and that within this ratio at least half of the capital should be Tier 1 capital.

Prudential controls on foreign currency exposure

2.25 A further important aspect of the Financial Services Authority's supervisory responsibilities relates to the control of banks' exposures to foreign currency risks. As movements in currency exchange rates may have adverse effects on a bank's net worth, if its assets and liabilities are not balanced in terms of their currencies of denomination, the Financial Services Authority seeks to measure, monitor and discuss with banks their foreign currency exposures. It also sets out guidelines for the maximum desirable exposures in individual currencies and for total net positions in all currencies. These controls relating to foreign currency risk are separate from and additional to the monitoring of each bank's overall risk position in respect of large exposures to individual borrowers or types of assets.

Study Activities 4

1. Why is an adequate level of capital vital for a bank's financial stability?
(Paragraph 2.15)

2. Why is the evaluation of the risk associated with assets of importance to the determination of a bank's desired capital base? *(Paragraph 2.17)*

3. In relation to the Financial Services Authority's supervision of capital adequacy, what are a bank's trigger and target ratios? *(Paragraph 2.18)*

4. What is the relevance of the BIS requirements for the way in which the Financial Services Authority supervises UK banks' capital adequacy? *(Paragraphs 2.19–2.24)*

5. What is the Financial Services Authority's role in respect of foreign currency exposure of banks? *(Paragraph 2.25)*

BCCI/Barings and banking supervision in the 1990s

2.26   In July 1991 the Bank of England moved to close down the UK operations of the Bank of Credit and Commerce International (BCCI), a major international bank incorporated in Luxembourg. At the same time, or shortly afterwards, in a coordinated operation, banking supervisors in a number of other countries took similar action in respect of BCCI operations falling within their jurisdiction. The reason for this extraordinary action was the discovery of overwhelming evidence of gross banking irregularities and suspicion that BCCI employees had undertaken fraudulent transactions on a huge scale.

2.27   Whilst the closure of BCCI had extremely serious implications for many of its depositors and borrowers, the immediate impact on banking markets as a whole was muted. The major effect of the BCCI affair came some time later through its influence on the way in which international banks are supervised.

2.28   Following the closure of BCCI there was widespread criticism of the failure of banking supervisors to act sooner to protect the interests of depositors. The Bank of England was a particular target for criticism because of the importance of UK-based operations for BCCI. Consequently, amid allegations that the Bank had been made aware of improper activities at BCCI several years before its closure, the UK Government appointed Lord Justice Bingham to undertake an official independent enquiry into the supervision of BCCI.

2.29   The Bingham Report was published in October 1992. Whilst the report was not unduly critical of the Bank of England's actions or of the basic system of banking supervision used in the UK, it nevertheless questioned the emphasis and rigour of the Bank's supervisory activities, and put forward suggestions and recommendations for improving the supervisory regime. The outcome of the enquiry was a reinforcement of changes that the Bank had already begun to make in respect of its approach to banking supervision.

2.30   The UK responses to the Bingham Report were directed largely toward the identification of potentially troublesome banks before their activities are able to cause problems for their depositors or for the banking sector. In addition, the EU Commission and the Bank for International Settlements have also taken actions to strengthen the basis of banking supervision on an international level. *The Directive to Reinforce Prudential Supervision within the EU following the collapse of BCCI* was implemented in July 1996. This piece of EU legislation (which also covers investment firms and insurance companies) gives powers to supervisors to refuse authorisation where a group or ownership link prevents effective supervision. It also requires institutions to have their head office and their registered office in the same EU country, and it allows greater exchange of information between supervisors and bodies responsible for the detection and investigation of breaches of company law. Duties are also placed on auditors to provide the supervisory authorities with relevant information (which was already required in the UK).

2.31   In February 1995, it became apparent that Barings Bank, the UK's oldest merchant bank, was unable to continue in business. The reason was that most of its capital and reserves had been transferred to a subsidiary in Singapore to finance losses incurred by a trader in derivatives. No other banks would help and the Chancellor of the Exchequer refused to sanction taxpayers' money being used to support a failed merchant or investment bank. Thus, Barings ceased trading momentarily and was bought shortly afterwards by a Dutch bank (ING Bank) for a nominal sum. It now operates as Barings ING Bank.

2.32   Naturally, there was an outcry and the Board of Banking Supervision was asked to inquire into the bank's collapse. For the purposes of this enquiry, the Bank of England members of the Board did not take part. A Bank of England manager who had exceeded his discretion in 'authorising' the transfers of funds from Barings in London to Singapore later resigned. However, the episode and the report highlight two problem areas:

● The relations between the Bank of England and the Singapore Monetary Authority, its counterpart in that offshore banking centre;

● The fact that a central bank is more used to supervising lending, deposit-taking and foreign exchange trading than the buying and selling of securities and derivatives.

2.33   In July 1996, two documents were published in the aftermath of the Baring collapse. One was a paper prepared by Arthur Andersen, the chartered accountants, on its review of the Bank's supervision and surveillance procedures, and the second was the Bank's Review of Supervision. Basically, more human and financial resources were to be devoted to supervision, a more systematic model of a risk assessment was to be developed and quality assurance was to be given a higher profile.

2.34   With the transfer of responsibility for banking supervision to the Financial Services Authority, there is no reason to believe that the work set in train by the Bank of England to enhance supervisory practices will not be carried forward. Indeed, it is expected that once the various aspects of the Financial Services Authority's responsibilities have been drawn together, the opportunity will be taken to review the structure of regulation and supervision. Any review is likely to take full account of the relationships between the various types of financial services operations that banks (and other institutions) may now undertake.

Study Activities 5

1. Why did the Bank of England close down BCCI in July 1991? *(Paragraph 2.26)*

2. Why was the Bank of England criticised following the closure of BCCI?
   (Paragraph 2.28)

3. The Bingham enquiry was set up in order to examine the quality of banking supervision in the light of BCCI. What was the broad tenor of the Bingham Report?
   (Paragraph 2.29)

4. What was the impact of the BCCI closure on banking regulation at an international level? *(Paragraph 2.30)*

5. Why did Barings Bank collapse in 1995? *(Paragraph 2.31)*

6. What major problems were brought to light by the inquiry into the collapse of Barings Bank? *(Paragraph 2.32)*

3 Banking regulation within the EU

3.1   The EU's internal markets initiative set the end of 1992 as the target date for the completion of a Single European Market. This Single Market means that there should now be completely free movement of goods, services, labour and capital between EU member states. Since services are included in the Single Market initiative, the relevance of EU legislation to banking activities within the UK has been given a major boost.

3.2   In January 1993 the Second Banking Co-ordination Directive came into force. This legislation has crucial implications for the future of banking activities within the EU. Its two major elements are that:

- It has introduced a *Single European Banking License* which will ensure that EU-incorporated banks which are authorised within their own country's regulations (e.g. UK banks authorised by the Financial Services Authority under the terms of the Banking Act 1987) are automatically recognised as banks in any part of the EU by virtue of their home country recognition.

- *Home country supervisors* are now responsible for the supervision of all operations within the EU of banks incorporated in the home country. However, the local monetary authorities retain exclusive responsibility for measures imposed upon banks in respect of monetary policy. In addition, for the time being host countries have primary responsibility for the supervision of liquidity and position risk. (Position risk relates to risks which banks run if their assets and liabilities are not matched, particularly in respect of currency and interest rates. For instance, if a UK bank had large amounts of Euro deposits which had been used to fund sterling lending, that bank would be at risk if the Euro strengthened against the pound, assuming no action had been taken beforehand to hedge this risk.)

3.3 Thus, a bank that is authorised within the UK by the Financial Services Authority is now able to set up branches in any other EU member state. Also, it is allowed to provide a wide range of cross-border banking services without the need for separate authorisation by the authorities of the host country.

3.4 Clearly, it is necessary for banking authorities in the various EU countries to *harmonise* their banking authorisation regulations if there is to be mutual recognition of each other's banks. Thus, the Second Banking Co-ordination Directive sets out:

● Minimum levels of capital (now set at Euro 5m) required before authorisation can be granted;

● Supervisory requirements in relation to major shareholders and banks' participation in the non-banking sector;

● Accounting and internal control mechanisms.

3.5 In December 1990, the Bank of England implemented the *Solvency Ratio Directive* (relating to credit risk and capital ratios) and the *Own Funds Directive* (defining capital for supervisory purposes). On 1 January 1996 the EU *Capital Adequacy Directive* became effective, setting out minimum capital requirements for market risks in the trading books of banks and investment firms. The Financial Services Authority has now implemented an up-dated version of this Directive, which is compatible with the amended *Basle Accord on Capital Adequacy*, implemented at the same time. An interesting aspect of this development is that the authorities have agreed, subject to certain conditions, to allow banks to use their own in-house "value-at-risk" models as the determinant of supervisory capital for market risks.

3.6 In addition to the above-mentioned directives, which are of direct relevance to banking activities, there are several other directives relevant to banks wishing to offer a range of financial services. Examples are the:

● *Capital Liberalisation Directive*, which aims to make illegal the imposition of exchange controls on movements of capital within the EU;

● *Admissions Directive* on the requirements to be fulfilled before a company can have its shares listed on any EU Stock Exchange;

● *UCITS Directive* (Undertaking for Collective Investment in Transferable Securities) which relates to investments such as unit trusts.

3.7 There has been a flood of EU legislation over the past few years. Even banks wishing to concentrate on their traditional domestic markets will feel the effects of free competition and harmonisation of banking regulations within the EU. Many institutions have already found that the EU legislation has had an effect on operating procedures and internal management structures.

3.8   Some banks have adopted an aggressive strategy to try to take advantage of the harmonisation of EU supervision and regulation. A number of major UK financial institutions have formed alliances with institutions based in other EU countries to take advantage of new business opportunities as they arise.

Study Activities 6

1. What was the ultimate objective of the EU's 1992 initiative?   *(Paragraph 3.1)*

2. What are the two major elements of the Second Banking Co-ordination Directive?
                                                                                    (Paragraph 3.2)

3. Why is it important that the minimum regulatory standards applied to banks should be harmonised within the EU?   *(Paragraph 3.4)*

4. List some of the aspects of harmonisation of regulations to which the Second Banking Co-ordination Directive refers.   *(Paragraph 3.4)*

5. What important innovation is included within the EU's 1996 Capital Adequacy Directive?   *(Paragraph 3.5)*

6. Identify some of the EU directives that affect the provision of financial services by banks.   *(Paragraph 3.6)*

7. Even when a UK bank wishes to restrict its activities to the UK, it is still likely to be affected by the EU's 1992 initiative. Why?   *(Paragraph 3.7)*

4   The changing structure of UK financial services regulation

4.1   Since the mid-1980s, the regulatory framework of the UK financial system has undergone a number of very significant changes. These include the implementation of the Financial Services Act 1986, which, at the time, was widely regarded as the most important piece of UK legislation in respect of investor protection.

4.2   The ongoing restructuring of the UK financial services sector, the requirement for conformity within the EU and the visible inadequacies of the current regulatory system, would seem to indicate that the regulation and supervision of UK financial institutions and markets will be far from static during the foreseeable future.

4.3   In May 1997, the new Labour Government announced its intention to introduce legislation to put the regulation and supervision of financial services and banking into a single framework, which would be the responsibility of an enhanced Securities and Investments Board (subsequently renamed the Financial Services Authority) with full statutory powers. In addition to the passage of legislation through Parliament, a great deal of preparatory work has to be done to bring together the responsibilities of the current wide range of regulatory authorities. Consequently, the full effects of the proposed changes are unlikely to be felt before 2000. However, some measures, especially in respect of the management and staffing of the Financial Services Authority and the transfer of responsibility for the regulation of banks (from the Bank of England) have already been introduced.

4.4　The key elements of banking supervision and regulation in the UK have already been explained in Sections 2 and 3 of this Unit. The following sections examine the evolution and nature of the supervision and regulation of investment business and, more briefly, aspects of the supervision and regulation of other important sectors of the UK financial system.

5　Supervision and regulation of investment business

5.1　The Gower Report (1984) concluded that the supervision and regulation of investment business in the UK was excessively complex, inequitable and inefficient. As a result of the Gower Report, the Financial Services Act 1986 was enacted in order to lay down a comprehensive framework for the regulation of investment business and for investor protection. It established the Securities and Investments Board (SIB) to oversee the regulation of investment businesses primarily via self-regulatory organisations (SROs) and recognised professional bodies (RPBs).

The Financial Services Act 1986
Allocation of responsibilities

5.2　The Financial Services Act made the DTI responsible for the regulation of investment business in the UK. In turn the Secretary of State for Trade and Industry delegated operational powers to the SIB. In June 1992, the DTI's responsibilities in respect of the Financial Services Act were transferred to the Treasury, in order to consolidate a wide range of financial regulations under one ministry.

5.3　It must be emphasised that the SIB system did not cover all activities that might be included under the heading of investment business. Its scope of responsibility included:

- Securities markets (other than gilt-edged securities, which were the responsibility of the Bank of England);

- Futures and options;

- Unit trust management;

- Insurance brokerage;

- Fund management;

- Investment advice;

- Corporate finance.

5.4   The Financial Services Act explicitly made the Bank of England responsible for the regulation of the gilt-edged securities market, the bullion markets, the wholesale money markets, and the foreign exchange market. Also, the DTI maintained considerable power in respect of the operations of insurance companies and unit trusts, despite responsibility for their marketing activities resting ultimately with the Treasury.

SIB/SRO structure

5.5   An initial function of the SIB was to formulate a rulebook embodying codes of conduct and regulations for institutions and individuals involved in investment business. As all regulations tend to reduce competition and may lead to restrictive practices, this rulebook had to be approved by the Director General of Fair Trading. Once it had also been approved by the Secretary of State at the DTI, formal powers were transferred to the SIB (in April 1987), which was then able to set about the job of delegating specific responsibilities to a number of SROs. Between them, the SROs covered the bulk of activities as prescribed by the Financial Services Act. In order to obtain their own delegated powers, each SRO had to produce its own rule book, which had to be approved by both the SIB and the Director General of Fair Trading. The rulebooks were intended to give investors equivalent protection to that implicit in the SIB's own rulebook.

5.6   Initially, there were five SROs, but this was subsequently reduced to three by merger:

- Securities and Futures Authority;

- Personal Investment Authority;

- Investment Management Regulatory Organisation.

These three bodies remained in existence at October 1999, but their function and responsibilities were by that time being absorbed by the Financial Services Authority.

5.7   *The Securities and Futures Authority (SFA).* This was formed in 1991 from the merger of The Securities Association (TSA) and the Association of Futures Brokers and Dealers (AFBD). The overlap in the responsibilities of these two SROs made their amalgamation a logical development. TSA supervised the activities of the members of the London Stock Exchange, whilst the AFBD supervised the trade and broking in financial and commodities futures and options. The SFA assumed these responsibilities for the securities and derivative markets.

5.8   *The Personal Investment Authority (PIA).* This body became responsible for supervising the marketing and management of unit trusts and life assurance businesses and the activities of independent financial advisers who deal with the general public in respect of investments such as unit trusts and life assurance. It also covers the activities of licensed dealers and those providing investment management services for retail clients. The PIA resulted from the merger of two of the original five SROs, LAUTRO and FIMBRA, creating a single self-regulatory body for those individuals and institutions involved directly in the provision of investment services to the general public.

5.9   *The Investment Management Regulatory Organisation (IMRO).* This became responsible for the activities of independent investment managers and advisers, especially those managing institutional funds, collective investment schemes and in-house pension funds.

5.10   A major criticism of the formal basis of the SIB/SRO structure was that it was excessively legalistic and detailed in its requirements, and hence potentially damaging to investors' interests, by restricting choice and increasing costs. As a result of this criticism, the SIB simplified its operating procedures and requirements. Since 1990 investment firms have been expected to operate in line with 10 broad principles laid down by the SIB and in 1991 a series of 'core rules' were published by the SIB which now form the basis for the production of simplified rule books by the individual SROs. Less than half of these core rules apply to dealings between professional investors.

5.11   Within the SIB structure, which is currently being operated by its successor, the Financial Services Authority, there are also:

- *Recognised Professional Bodies* (RPBs), e.g. the Law Societies; the institutes of Chartered Accountants. Where an individual undertakes investment business as a minor element of his or her professional activities, then so long as certification is obtained from one of the RPBs, there is no need for full authorisation from the Financial Services Authority or an SRO. A professional body will only be granted RPB status if its standards and codes of practice are compatible with those of the Financial Services Authority.

- *Recognised Investment Exchanges*, e.g. the London Stock Exchange, the London Metals Exchange, Tradepoint, and *Recognised Clearing Houses*, e.g. CRESTCo. These institutions are responsible for the regulation of specific financial markets and transactions, and via recognition from the Financial Services Authority they escape direct supervision of their activities.

Study Activities 7

1. What did the *Gower Report* conclude about the supervision and regulation of investment business in the UK? *(Paragraph 5.1)*

2. Which government departments have had responsibility for the implementation of the Financial Services Act 1986? *(Paragraph 5.2)*

3. For which areas of investment business regulation was the SIB responsible? *(Paragraph 5.3)*

4. For which areas of financial supervision was the Bank of England made responsible by the Financial Services Act? *(Paragraph 5.4)*

5. What was the relevance of rule books within the SIB regulatory framework? *(Paragraph 5.5)*

6. List the three SROs still existing in 1999 together with their areas of responsibility. *(Paragraphs 5.6–5.9)*

7. What action did the SIB take in order to counter the criticism that its regulatory framework restricted choice and increased costs for investors? *(Paragraph 5.10)*

8. What are Recognised Professional Bodies and Recognised Investment Exchanges? *(Paragraph 5.11)*

Authorisation of investment businesses

5.12   Under the Financial Services Act 1986, a person is deemed to be carrying on an investment business if he/she:

- buys or sells investments (unless acting in purely a personal capacity); or
- arranges for others to buy or sell investments; or
- manages investments on the behalf of others; or
- advises others on their investments; or
- operates a collective investment scheme.

Unless exempt under the Act, it is a criminal offence for any person to operate an investment business within the UK without prior authorisation.

5.13   As at October 1999, individuals and institutions may obtain authorisation in one of four ways:

- Through membership of an SRO. As the scope of responsibility of each SRO is limited, an individual or institution offering a wide range of investment services may require membership of more than one SRO.
- Certification by an RPB, where the investment business is only a minor part of a person's activities.

- From the Financial Services Authority in respect of endowment and unit-linked insurance policies and unit trust management.

- From the relevant regulatory body of another EU state, where the level of investor protection given is comparable to that in force in the UK, and where the business does not have a permanent place of residence within the UK. At the beginning of January 1996, the EU's *Investment Services Directive* became effective. This directive, which amended the Financial Services Act, introduced a single European 'passport' for investment firms, along similar lines to the European single banking licence. Firms authorised for business in one EU country are given appropriate access to the markets of other EU countries, upon the basis of mutual recognition of authorisation.

5.14   In order to obtain authorisation from an SRO, individuals or organisations proposing to set up an investment business must satisfy certain criteria which establish that it is 'fit and proper' to run an investment business. These criteria relate to:

- Capital adequacy;

- Previous business record;

- Compliance arrangements in respect of supervision;

- The good character of the firm's owners, directors and employees.

The firm must also produce a business plan that sets the approved limits of the investment business that may be undertaken.

5.15   To maintain authorised status, an investment firm must comply with the conduct of business rules laid down by its regulator. These rules relate to:

- Advertising;

- Disclosure of commissions;

- Making unsolicited calls;

- Fair treatment of clients;

- Provision of customer agreements;

- Maintenance of records to be produced if complaints are made.

Sanctions against investment firms and individuals

5.16   The relevant SRO may investigate an investment firm that is believed to be in violation of the conduct of business rules. The SRO may take action to protect the firm's clients. It may issue private or public warnings, limit the scope of the firm's activities, or suspend or withdraw authorisation.

5.17   The Financial Services Authority may investigate any authorised firm, and any other business suspected of undertaking investment activities without authorisation. It may seize documents and require people to give evidence. Its powers override those of the SROs, and in addition to the sanctions available to the SROs, SIB may also apply to court for a winding-up order and may undertake criminal prosecutions.

Compensation fund

5.18   The Financial Services Act established a compensation fund to provide compensation to investors with authorised firms which go into liquidation or which are involved with fraudulent operations. The fund gives 100% cover for the first £30,000 of individual investments, and 90% cover for the next £20,000, i.e. a total of £48,000.

5.19   The fund is financed by a levy on the SROs, which recoup their contribution via levies on their individual members. The initial burden of compensation falls upon the SRO that authorised the firm in respect of which claims are made. If claims exceed a preset sum, the other SROs must also contribute. There has been some criticism of the fund, both in terms of the cover given, and on account of the levies not reflecting the inherent risk associated with the activities of the different authorised firms.

The cost of regulation

5.20   As suggested above, there has been some criticism of the costs associated with the regulation process. In particular, costs arise in respect of:

- Gaining authorisation;
- Annual membership fees;
- Compliance arrangements;
- Auditing of accounts;
- Production of financial statements;
- Contribution to the compensation fund.

5.21   Whilst some cost is unavoidable, the question arises as to whether the investor is getting value for money as, ultimately, it is the investor who pays for the regulation via lower returns and higher fees. If the quality of protection, and hence the stability of the markets is improved, then all parties involved may benefit substantially. However, if the associated costs are seen as being excessive, firms may be forced out of business and activities may be pushed to more lightly regulated markets overseas.

Study Activities 8

1. In what circumstances is an individual deemed to be undertaking an investment business? *(Paragraph 5.12)*

2. In what ways may individuals and institutions obtain authorisation within the provisions of the Financial Services Act 1986? *(Paragraph 5.13)*

3. What factors are covered by the criteria for authorisation within the provisions of the Financial Services Act 1986? *(Paragraph 5.14)*

4. To what issues do the conduct of business rules relate? *(Paragraph 5.15)*

5. What sanctions may be applied to an investment business found to be in violation of the conduct of business rules? *(Paragraphs 5.16 and 5.17)*

6. What compensation is available to investors with authorised firms that go into liquidation? *(Paragraph 5.18)*

7. How is the investors' compensation scheme financed? *(Paragraph 5.19)*

8. In what ways do costs arise in respect of investor protection, and what problems do they cause for investors and investment firms? *(Paragraphs 5.20 and 5.21)*

6 Supervision and regulation of building societies

The main functions of the Building Societies Commission

6.1 The Building Societies Commission was established within the provisions of the Building Societies Act 1986 as the regulatory body for building societies in the UK. The responsibilities of the Commission are being taken over by the Financial Services Authority, and no doubt this will lead to greater convergence with the regulation applying to banks. However, the broad functions of the Commission are likely to be carried forward within the new regime.

6.2 The Building Societies Commission is responsible for:

- *Supervision and regulation* of all building societies in accordance with the provisions of the Building Societies Act 1986, as amended by the Building Societies Act 1997. Such societies are exempt from the provisions of the Banking Act 1987, unless they apply to convert to plc status. Such conversion requires the approval of the Commission and the Financial Services Authority.

- *Providing an official channel* for the building societies to appropriate government departments on matters relevant to the operations of building societies.

- Safeguarding the *financial stability* of building societies.

- Promoting the *protection of shareholders'* funds and *depositors'* funds in building societies.

- Promoting the *principal purpose* of building societies, which is to raise funds from members to enable them to grant mortgage loans for the purchase of residential property by members.

- Ensuring that societies exercise *prudently* the powers granted to them under the Building Societies Acts 1986 and 1997.

The powers of the Building Societies Commission

6.3 The Commission has considerable powers to restrict the activities of individual building societies and to interfere with their operations. The Commission:

- Is responsible for the *authorisation* of building societies and has the power to revoke such authorisation if a society fails to meet the criteria for prudent management set down in the Building Societies Act 1986. These criteria relate to:

  - the maintenance of adequate reserves, adequate liquid assets and adequate capital resources;

  - provision of effective accounting records and internal controls; and the use of suitable arrangements for assessment of the adequacy of securities for advances.

  In addition, the directors and officers of a society must be fit and proper persons to hold office, and they are expected to conduct business with appropriate professional skills, prudence and integrity.

- May *issue a directive* requiring a society to submit an appropriate restructuring plan where the society has breached the limits for wholesale funding, deposit liabilities, commercial assets or liquid assets. The society must then either submit a restructuring plan or, alternatively, seek the approval of its members to convert to plc status. If the society fails to comply with a restructuring plan or if it fails to apply for plc status, the Commission may apply for a court order to wind up the society.

- May *issue a prohibition order* if it decides that a particular activity of a society is beyond its powers.

- May direct that any *advertising* which it considers to be misleading or unsuitable be withdrawn.

7 Supervision and regulation of insurance companies

7.1   The major legislation affecting UK insurance companies is the Insurance Companies Act 1982, which consolidated existing UK legislation and incorporated EU directives on insurance business.

7.2   The *objectives* of this legislation are to protect:

● Policyholders from the insolvency of an insurance company;

● Individuals from being sold insurance which is unsuitable for their needs.

7.3   In 1999 the Financial Services Authority took over responsibility from the Treasury for the implementation of the Act's provisions. The Financial Services Authority has powers to grant or revoke authorisation of insurance companies, to stipulate solvency margins for insurance companies, to monitor insurance companies and to intervene in their operation if necessary.

7.4   Under the Act, there are three classifications of ownership of insurance companies:

● UK companies, supervised by the Financial Services Authority;

● EU companies, supervised by the authorities of the EU country where their head office is located;

● External companies, based in non-EU countries are supervised by the Financial Services Authority if they operate in the UK. They must appoint a UK agent, whose executives and underwriters must be 'fit and proper' persons under the Act.

7.5   It is a criminal offence to undertake insurance business in the UK without prior authorisation of the Financial Services Authority, and authority will be granted only if the applicant is deemed to be fit and proper to undertake such business.

7.6   The Financial Services Authority maintains regular surveillance of insurance businesses through the various returns that the companies must submit. If the Financial Services Authority is not satisfied that the business is properly conducted it may revoke authorisation. Alternatively, some less severe sanction may be adopted, such as a directive forbidding the issue of new policies or ordering a restructuring of the assets of the insurance company.

7.7   Other legislation affecting insurance business includes the Lloyd's of London Act 1982 (which deals exclusively with this unique insurance institution) and the Financial Services Act 1986 (which involves mainly the marketing of insurance and the provision of advice on insurance products).

7.8   In July 1994, the EU's *Third Life Assurance Directive* came into force. With temporary exemptions for certain EU states, the directive allows life companies to sell their products in other EU states on the basis of home regulation. However, the complexity of the insurance market means that EU legislation on the single market has a much longer time horizon for harmonisation than that found for most other financial services, and consequently the impact on the UK market is likely to be slower in materialising. As with other elements of the UK financial services sector, the insurance market will undoubtedly be affected by the introduction of the Financial Services Authority's regulatory regime.

Study Activities 9

1. What are the main functions of the Building Societies Commission? *(Paragraph 6.2)*

2. When considering the authorisation of a building society, what criteria are taken into account under the Building Societies Act 1986?   *(Paragraph 6.3)*

3. List the ways in which the Building Societies Commission may restrict the activities of building societies.   *(Paragraph 6.3)*

4. What are the key objectives of the Insurance Companies Act 1982? *(Paragraph 7.2)*

5. Outline the broad functions of the Financial Services Authority in respect of the regulation of insurance companies?   *(Paragraph 7.3–7.6)*

8   Reform of financial services and banking regulation and supervision

The changing regulatory framework

8.1   The proposed fundamental changes to the regulatory and supervisory framework for financial services and banking have been put forward against the background of widespread dissatisfaction with the quality of the supervision and investor protection in the UK. A number of recent high-profile cases, including the Maxwell pension scandal, personal pension mis-selling, the inappropriateness of home income plans for some of their elderly purchasers, and so on, have drawn widespread attention to the problems of financial regulation. Also, a general confusion in respect of responsibilities within the existing structure makes attractive the proposal for a single regulator with statutory powers.

8.2   The proposed changes also recognise the increasingly complex nature of financial services business, both domestically and internationally, and the trend towards diversified financial institutions offering services and products that transcend the traditional boundaries of the financial services sector. In this context, the inclusion of banking, building societies and insurance regulation within a single financial-services framework is a logical step. There would appear to be important potential gains both in terms of ensuring a consistent and all-embracing approach to regulation and supervision, with recognition of the full set of activities undertaken by each institution, and in terms of simplicity, cost and effectiveness. Whilst the significance of the shift to a statutory base for regulation should not be under-estimated, the Chancellor of the Exchequer has noted that the benefits of practitioner involvement in regulation and the differential needs of retail and wholesale activities should not be forgotten.

The Financial Services Authority

8.3   In July 1998 the Government published the draft *Financial Services and Markets bill*. This bill proposed giving wide-ranging powers to the Financial Services Authority. Included in the bill was confirmation of the Government's desire to bring under a single authority the regulation and supervision of virtually all banking and financial services activities and products in the UK. The bill also proposed reserve powers to allow the Government to bring other financial services and products under the control of the Financial Services Authority without further recourse to Parliament.

8.4   The powers to be endowed upon the Financial Services Authority include all of those currently available to the existing regulatory bodies, plus additional powers designed to deal more effectively with market abuse. For example, it is proposed that the Financial Services Authority will have powers to compel the providers of financial services and products to answer its questions, to initiate civil court actions and to levy unlimited fines. Indeed, the extent of the proposed powers has already led to concerns being voiced in respect of the fairness of the proposed arrangements and the protection of the rights of the market participants. Anticipating these concerns, the bill includes provision for the establishment of a *Financial Services and Markets Appeals Tribunal*, run as part of the court service.

8.5   The *Financial Services and Markets bill* also specifies a set of statutory objectives for the Financial Services Authority, including:

- Maintaining confidence in the financial system.

- Promoting public understanding of the financial system, including awareness of the risks and benefits of different kinds of investment.

- Securing the appropriate degree of protection for consumers.

- Reducing financial crime.

In the light of these objectives, the Financial Services Authority itself specifies its 'high level aims' quite simply as being:

- To protect consumers of financial services.

- To promote clean and orderly markets.

- To maintain confidence in the financial system.

8.6   In pursuit of its aims, the Financial Services Authority applies broad principles that recognise the inherent risks that exist in competitive financial markets within which firms will fail. The Financial Services Authority emphasises that regulation does not absolve consumers of responsibility for their own decisions on their financial affairs, although it also recognises that the level of knowledge and expertise that it is reasonable to expect consumers to possess. In this context the Financial Services Authority states that it will ensure that appropriate distinctions are made between retail and wholesale business, whilst adopting a risk-based approach to regulation and supervision reflecting the nature of the business activities concerned. The Financial Services Authority has also stated that it will place great weight upon senior management responsibility for ensuring that financial services firms are run in accordance with regulatory requirements. In addition, it will seek to promote a commitment to high standards against a background of consistency in authorisation, but underlining its willingness to enforce standards through intervention and discipline when this is felt to be required.

8.7   The Financial Services Authority has committed itself to being open and accountable, not merely through the statutory requirements involving Government and Parliament, but also in terms of consultation with, and accessibility for, those affected by its extensive powers. Taking on board criticisms of the previous regime, the Financial Services Authority has stated that it will seek to operate in a way that recognises the benefit generated by financial innovation and free competition, and will involve practitioners and consumers in the policy formulation and decision-making processes. The cost effectiveness of regulation is also recognised.

8.8   The position taken publicly by the Financial Services Authority, so far at least, has provided some reassurance to those who fear that the Government is creating a regulatory monster, that will become overwhelmed by its own complexity and powers. Nevertheless, the scope of the task facing the Financial Services Authority should not be underestimated. Once the proposals embedded in the *Financial Services and Markets bill* become law the Financial Services Authority will have responsibilities unequalled by any other financial services regulatory body in the world. This is both in terms of the financial services and banking activities covered, and the nature of the regulatory and supervisory powers envisaged.

8.9   The phased establishment of the Financial Services Authority, over what is likely to amount to a three-year period, clearly acknowledges the work that has to be done. The *Bank of England Act 1998* has already transferred responsibility for banking regulation and supervision to the Financial Services Authority. Responsibility for the work of the Building Societies Commission, the Friendly Societies Commission and the insurance supervisors at the Treasury has also been transferred. It is unlikely that the Financial Services Authority will assume statutory powers in respect of investment business until 2000. Consequently, in the meantime, the existing self-regulatory organisations and recognised bodies will continue to undertake their regulatory and supervisory duties, working closely with, and drawing upon the staff of, the Financial Services Authority.

Study Activities 10

1. What factors contributed to the decision to undertake a fundamental restructuring of UK financial services and banking regulation? *(Paragraphs 8.1 and 8.2)*

2. What will be the ultimate scope of responsibility of the Financial Services Authority? *(Paragraph 8.3)*

3. Why was a proposal for a *Financial Services and Markets Appeals Tribunal* included in the *Financial Services and Markets bill*? *(Paragraph 8.4)*

4. What are the proposed statutory objectives of the Financial Services Authority? *(Paragraph 8.5)*

5. What are the 'high level aims' that the Financial Services Authority has itself specified? *(Paragraph 8.5)*

6. Outline the broad principles that will guide the Financial Services Authority's activities. *(Paragraph 8.6)*

7. In what ways does the Financial Services Authority intend to take on board the criticisms of the previous financial services regulatory regime? *(Paragraph 8.7)*

9   Regulation overseas

USA

9.1   In the USA, the financial regulatory structure has been heavily influenced by financial and economic crises, especially the Great Depression of the 1930s and the earlier stock market crash of October 1929. The two statutory pillars are the Securities Act 1933 and the Securities Exchange Act 1934. Both of these Acts require substantial detail to be disclosed by companies seeking to make new debt and equity issues. The 1934 Act also created the Securities and Exchange Commission (a federal agency) to enforce the two Acts.

9.2   The Banking Act 1933 created the Federal Deposit Insurance Corporation for bank deposits and separated commercial banking from investment banking operations. However, since the 1980s, there has been some relaxation in this rigid distinction.

9.3   A range of bodies (including the New York Stock Exchange and the National Association of Securities Dealers) undertake self-regulation of financial activities.

9.4   The US Federal Government takes responsibility for the supervision of financial markets. Monetary policy is the responsibility of the Federal Reserve System. However, some banks are 'chartered' by individual states. Regulation in respect of the scope of commercial banking is being relaxed gradually, from the earlier restrictions that largely limited individual banks to operate within a single state.

Japan

9.5 Japan, like the UK, is a unitary state and operates a highly centralised regulatory framework. The Securities Bureau of the Ministry of Finance is responsible for the supervision of securities markets. Commercial banks are permitted to operate on a national level.

Germany

9.6 Germany, like the USA is a federal state, and the individual states (known as Länder) are responsible for the regulation of their own stock exchanges. However, the central bank (Bundesbank) supervises the bond market, which tends to be dominated by government, bank and mortgage bonds.

9.7 Like the USA, Germany has a central bank that has traditionally been very independent of governmental political interference, although its discretion in the determination of exchange rates has been minimal. This independence has recently been transformed with the establishment of the European Central Bank and the introduction of the Euro. In many key aspects of central bank functions, the German Central Bank now has little discretion, with major decisions being taken at an EU-level.

10 Causes of regulatory change

10.1 Three major causes of change in regulatory regimes can be identified:

- Crises;
- Innovation;
- Globalisation.

Of these, perhaps crises have been the most important.

Crises

10.2 The Great Depression of 1929–1934 resulted in the US legislation of 1933 and 1934 (as mentioned above) and, also, in the creation of the *Bank for International Settlements* (BIS) in 1930. The BIS was created as a sort of 'central bank for central banks' to monitor the German World War 1 debt repayments which had caused so many problems in the 1920s. Located in Basle, Switzerland, it survived World War 2 when its shareholding central banks were on opposing sides and then took on a new lease of life administering European Iron and Steel Community loans. The BIS now:

- Provides an important focus for debate on the regulation and stability of international banking and derivatives markets.

- Publishes extensive statistical surveys on a wide range of financial activities.

- Plays a major role in the drafting of global capital adequacy requirements, contributing to the creation of a 'level playing field' for global banking.

- Monitors over-the-counter markets in financial derivatives.

10.3   In the UK, the failure of a number of insurance companies in the 1960s and 1970s prompted the enactment of the Insurance Companies Act 1974, the Policyholders Protection Act 1975 and, ultimately, the Insurance Companies Act 1982. In February 1981 the failure of Norton Warburg, an investment firm, together with an ongoing investigation into the activities of Halliday Simpson (a regional stockbroker) resulted in the appointment of Professor Jim Gower to consider the problem of regulating investment business. This, in turn, led to the Financial Services Act 1986. The fate of members of pension schemes associated with Maxwell companies caused a public outcry during the early 1990s. The result was the Goode Report and the Pensions Act 1995.

10.4   In banking, cause and effect can be listed in a similar fashion. The 'secondary banking crisis' of 1973–74 recorded gaps in regulation between the Bank of England and the DTI, resulting in the Banking Act 1979. However, the Act was also prompted by the need to have a statutory regulatory framework to harmonise with that on most of mainland Europe. In 1984, the failure of Johnson Matthey Bankers (a full bank under the 1979 Act and not a mere 'licensed deposit-taker') led to the Banking Act 1987. As we have seen, the BCCI and Barings crises led to administrative changes rather than new primary legislation.

10.5   Lugano is a word that triggers a knee-jerk reaction in many bankers. It is a town in Switzerland where Lloyds Bank Europe (as it then was) had established a small branch to buy 'suitcase money' coming across the border from Italy. Collusion occurred between the management and the only foreign exchange dealer, who blatantly exceeded his limits. When the deception was discovered, both lost their jobs, and Lloyds Bank incurred substantial losses. As a result, there developed the practice of separating dealers (traders) in the 'front office' or dealing room from the clerks and supervisors in the 'back office'.

Innovation

10.6   In many respects, financial innovation has run ahead of the regulatory frameworks designed to protect users of financial services and the stability of the financial system. New products and services have been introduced, and individual institutions have diversified in pursuit of profit to such an extent that regulatory requirements have increasingly been in need of revision and, in some cases, fundamental restructuring. Of course, it may be argued that innovations have arisen as a result of institutions seeking to by-pass restrictions and take a competitive advantage.

10.7   A well-known example of financial innovation relates to how UK banks began to move into the mortgage market in the early 1980s, designing new products to increase their share of what is perceived to be a low-risk area of lending. Building societies responded by seeking powers to challenge the banks on current accounts – powers that they received in the Building Societies Act 1986. Meanwhile, they had been granted access to the sterling wholesale money markets as the pressures to compete and diversify grew.

10.8   The two great market developments in the second half of the twentieth century were the growth of the eurocurrency markets and the growth in the use of financial derivatives. The response of the financial regulators has included the assumption of a regulatory role by the Bank for International Settlements. There have also been many other initiatives from both official and trading bodies attempting to bring order to increasingly complex relationships, where the potential for the creation of risk goes hand-in-hand with profitable opportunities.

Globalisation

10.9   To some extent, the concept of globalisation dovetails into 'innovation' and has resulted in a need for regulators to consult with their opposite numbers in other countries. In many markets there is now 24-hour trading five days a week, so that no single authority can regulate all the deals occurring within its territory, because so many of them involve an overseas counter-party. Regulation has, therefore, become increasingly complex and the requirement for international co-operation is without question. Again the BIS initiatives provide good examples of a global response, as do more *ad hoc* responses to global crises arising from a number of bodies including the G7 Economic Summits. There are now also many influential international groups of regulators that work to support consistent and robust regulation of international financial activities. For example, in the field of securities and futures trading there is *The International Organisation of Securities Commissions*. In relation to corporate governance there is *The International Accounting Standards Committee*, and so on.

Study Activities 11

1. In the broadest terms, compare and contrast financial regulation in the USA with that in Japan and Germany.   *(Paragraphs 9.1–9.7)*

2. Outline the role of crises in the evolution of financial regulation.
                                                                       (Paragraphs 10.2–10.5)

3. What key events influenced the development of banking regulation in the UK?
                                                                       (Paragraph 10.4)

4. 'Financial innovation both drives and is driven by financial regulation.' Explain.
(Paragraph 10.6)

5. To what extent is globalisation an underlying cause of changes in financial regulation?
(Paragraph 10.9)

Summary

Now that you have completed this unit, you should be able to:

● appreciate the purpose of governmental regulation of financial institutions and markets;

● describe the different ways in which governments regulate financial institutions and markets;

● appreciate the economic risks of over-regulation of financial institutions and markets;

● describe the structure of the regulatory framework within the UK;

● understand the rationale for the recent changes in the UK financial regulatory framework;

● analyse the commercial banks' and building societies' needs for liquidity and capital adequacy;

● assess the general impact of the major requirements of the EU Banking Directives on the operations of UK banks;

● discuss the influence of international institutions (e.g. Bank for International Settlements) and the EU on the framework for supervising and regulating the financial system;

● outline the implementation of regulation in the world's major economies;

● understand the causes of reform, including financial crises, financial innovation and globalisation.

Self-assessment questions

Short-answer questions

1. What are the basic criteria that must be satisfied by a bank in order to obtain authorisation from the Financial Services Authority?

2. In what ways may a bank seek to ensure its ability to cover its obligations when they fall due?

3. In what way did the acceptance of the Basle Accord affect the Bank of England's approach to the supervision of capital adequacy?

4. In what way did the closure of BCCI influence the development of international banking supervision?

5. What was the SIB?

6. Did the SIB framework cover all investment businesses?

7. In what ways has the Building Societies Commission been able to restrict the activities of individual building societies?

8. What role has now been taken over by the Financial Services Authority from the Treasury in respect of the regulation of insurance companies?

Multiple-choice questions

1. As a result of the Banking Act 1987

   (a) a bank's auditors must be deemed to be 'fit and proper' by the Financial Services Authority

   (b) it is a criminal offence for a bank to lend funds equal to more than 25% of its capital base to a single borrower

   (c) the Financial Services Authority is required to set uniform reserve ratios for all banking institutions in respect of their liquidity and capital adequacy

   (d) it is a criminal offence for a bank to provide false or misleading information to the Financial Services Authority

   (e) the regulation of banks has been harmonised with that of building societies.

2. In relation to the supervision of banks' liquidity

   (a) the Financial Services Authority sets minimum required ratios of liquid assets to deposit liabilities for all banks

   (b) the Financial Services Authority sets broad guidelines for evaluating the quality of assets and for classifying liabilities, but leaves policy on liquidity management to the discretion of the banks themselves

   (c) the overriding principle of self-regulation means that the Financial Services Authority does not interfere in any way with individual banks' liquidity policies

   (d) all banks are required to hold minimum amounts of high-quality liquid assets on the approval of the Financial Services Authority

   (e) all banks are required to hold cash deposits with the Bank of England equal to a set percentage of their total assets.

3. Under the provisions of the Banking Act 1987, an authorised banking institution must

   (a) inform the Financial Services Authority when any single borrower accounts for more than 25% of its total loans

(b) return an annual report on its liquidity position to the Board of Banking Supervision

(c) have owners, controllers and managers who are deemed to be fit and proper persons by the Financial Services Authority

(d) hold liquid assets equal to at least 8% of its risk-weighted asset base

(e) hold sufficient liquid assets to cover all short-term sterling deposits.

4. Under the BIS capital adequacy requirements, all banks are required to

(a) hold designated types of capital equal to at least 8% of a risk-weighted asset base

(b) hold risk-weighted assets which are equal in value to at least 8% of total asset holdings

(c) hold designated types of capital equal to at least 8% of a risk-weighted liabilities base

(d) make quarterly returns to the BIS demonstrating the adequacy of their capital holdings

(e) balance their risk-weighted assets with their risk-weighted liabilities during each accounting period.

5. The Second Banking Co-ordination Directive

(a) is the only piece of EU legislation to be of direct relevance to UK banking institutions

(b) specifies minimum capital adequacy requirements for all the western world's banking institutions

(c) lays down regulations on the maximum amount of capital which an EU bank may hold

(d) sets out guidelines for the harmonisation of bank supervision within the EU

(e) requires that all EU banks must be authorised separately in each EU country in which they operate.

6. The Financial Services Authority:

(a) co-ordinates the advertising of building societies

(b) was established to protect the interests of insurance companies by lobbying government on their behalf

(c) is a private company established by the Financial Services Act in order to oversee the activities of building societies

(d) is the trade body to which all mortgage lenders belong

(e) has recently absorbed the responsibilities of the Building Societies Commission for the regulation and supervision of building societies.

6

The Analysis of Interest Rates

Objectives

After studying this unit, you should be able to:

- understand the general nature of interest rates;

- distinguish between nominal and real rates of interest;

- examine the basic theories concerning the determination of interest rates and their structures;

- outline the causes of changes in interest rates;

- calculate the yield to maturity of a bond;

- identify and draw yield curves, and explain the significance of their shapes and slopes;

- appreciate the factors which affect the yield spread between two bonds;

- understand why there are so many rates of interest;

- appreciate the relationship between domestic, international and eurocurrency interest rates.

1   Introduction

1.1   Interest rates have been mentioned extensively in the foregoing units, for example in relation to how they influence certain financial flows in the economy or how they influence the profitability of particular groups of financial institutions. This repeated reference to interest rates underlines their crucial role within the financial system. The primary purpose of this unit is to examine the process by which interest rates are determined and to consider relationships between interest rates. Monetary policy aspects of interest rates are dealt with in Unit 7.

1.2   Reference is frequently made in the media to *the* rate of interest, as if there was one single interest rate throughout the economy. Even the most casual observation reveals, however, that there is a multitude of interest rates. Hence, an additional purpose of this unit is to consider the *range* of interest rates that exists within the economy and to examine the determinants of the pattern of interest rates that apply at any one time.

Definitions

1.3   It is important to appreciate that an interest rate is a *price*, and that the price relates to *present* claims on resources relative to *future* claims on resources. An interest rate is therefore the price that a *borrower pays* in order to be able to consume resources now rather than at a point in time in the future. Correspondingly, it is therefore the price that a *lender receives* to forgo current consumption in order to take advantage of consumption of resources at some point in the future. Like all prices in free markets, interest rates are established by the interaction of supply and demand; in this context, it is the supply of future claims on resources interacting with the demand for future claims on resources. We may therefore adopt as our definition of an interest rate that it is *a price established by the interaction of the supply of, and the demand for, future claims on resources*. That price will usually be expressed as a proportion of the sum borrowed or lent over a given time period. Hence, an interest rate of 10% p.a. on a loan states that the price of that loan will be 10% of the value of the loan for each year that the loan remains outstanding.

1.4   The importance of *time* to the concept of interest rates should be noted. Thus, many interest rates are calculated on an annual basis – 'per annum' is usually understood. However, rates may be charged on a daily, weekly or monthly basis, with annualised equivalents being specified. This is often a cause of misunderstanding of interest rates and complaints by borrowers.

1.5   'Interest on interest', or compounding, can have substantial effect on the value of debt where the interest payments are not made by the borrower. Such compounding may be calculated over any period agreed by the parties concerned. To give two arithmetical examples: 1% per calendar month becomes 12.7% p.a.; 10% a year, if unpaid, increases the total debt by 21% after two years and by 33% in three years. Compound interest can be a boon to savers, but a curse to borrowers.

Real and nominal interest rates

1.6   An important distinction is made between *real* and *nominal* interest rates. A *nominal* interest rate is what is normally observed and quoted and represents the actual money paid by the borrower to the lender, expressed as a percentage of the sum borrowed over a stated period of time. A *real* rate of interest, on the other hand, is a nominal rate that is adjusted to take account of the impact of inflation on the real value of the loan.

1.7   A bank might, for example, pay an interest rate of 4% p.a. on deposits. The 4% rate is the *nominal* interest rate and represents the nominal price that the investor receives in return for delaying his/her consumption of resources for a year. However, that investor will only be able to purchase an additional 4% of goods and services with his/her funds at the end of the year if the price level of those goods and services *remains constant* over that year. If the price level is *not* constant, but rises by, say, 3% over that year, then while the nominal interest rate is 4% the *real* interest rate is only 1%. This is because the investor can only purchase additional goods and services equivalent to 1% of the loan when the loan matures, due to their increase in price. Thus, the real interest rate will always be less than the nominal interest rate when inflation occurs (when the purchasing power of money is falling). If, with a nominal interest rate on deposits of 4% p.a., the inflation rate were to be 6% p.a., then the real interest rate would be minus 2%. That is, the real rate of interest would be negative, since the nominal interest payments would be insufficient to maintain the purchasing power of the capital as a result of the inflation of 6% p.a.

Measuring the real interest rate

1.8 One of the major problems surrounding the concept of the real interest rate lies in its *measurement*. For a period of time *in the past*, calculation of the real interest rate involves deflating the nominal interest paid by an appropriate price index. There is no 'perfect' price index and, in principle, each individual within an economy is likely to have had their own price index based on the unique combination of goods and services that they purchased. Hence, any real interest rate calculated for a previous period is necessarily an approximation to some degree, although the choice of an appropriate price index will usually bring this approximation to within acceptable limits.

1.9 For a period of time into the *future*, the calculation of the real interest rate to be paid by the borrower (and received by the lender) is considerably more problematic. In addition, although the calculation of the real interest rate that applied for a *previous* period may be of some use, the calculation of the real interest rate that will apply in the *future* is of much greater use. It is with regard to future interest rates that decisions will be made on the allocation of funds for investment purposes.

1.10 The calculation of the future real rate of interest involves deflating the future nominal rate of interest by the future rate of inflation. The difficulty surrounding the future rate of inflation is not only that it involves the problem of choosing an appropriate price index, as explained in the previous paragraph but, also, given that future rates of inflation are not known with certainty, it can only be an *expected* rate of inflation. By extension, therefore, any future real interest rate can only be an *expected* real interest rate. Given that future rates of inflation, especially for anything but a short period into the future, are extremely difficult to forecast accurately, the actual real interest rate paid and received will often vary substantially from what was expected.

1.11 A particular real interest rate can be achieved on a loan extending into the future, with both the borrower and lender protected from unanticipated changes in the rate of inflation, through the use of *indexation*. The principle of indexation is that, in order to protect the capital value of the loan, that capital value would be linked to an appropriate price index. This would have the effect of ensuring that the real purchasing power of the capital at the end of the period of the loan would be the same as it was at the start. In order to protect the value of interest payments, these would be paid as a proportion of the index-linked capital sum, which would have the effect of guaranteeing the agreed real rate of return on the loan. The overall effect, therefore, is to make the real rate of return on the loan totally independent of the rate of inflation. Despite the attractions of such an agreement, index-linked loans are comparatively uncommon in the UK. The only major borrower in this form is the government through the issue of index-linked savings certificates and gilt-edged securities.

1.12   The main alternative to index-linking loans is for funds to be lent at market-related (i.e. not fixed) rates of interest. The basis for this arrangement is that market rates of interest tend to move in line with the rate of inflation. Consequently, if there is an unexpectedly high rate of inflation during the life of the loan, this will be compensated for by an increase in the rate of interest payable on the loan.

1.13   While historical experience tends to show that market rates of interest do indeed move in line with inflation, two points should be noted:

● The movement of interest rates has often occurred some time *after* the rise in inflation, with the result that loans maturing within that time lag are not protected.

● The adjustment has often been much less than total. In other words, while the movement in interest rates is usually in the right *direction*, it has frequently not been of a sufficient *amount* to protect fully the value of the loan from the effects of inflation.

1.14   The reason for the incomplete adjustment of market interest rates to inflation rates is simply that, as we shall see later in this unit, there are other influences on market interest rates in addition to the level of inflation. While use of market-related interest rates therefore represents an imperfect means of protecting a loan from inflation, its widespread use would indicate that it offers sufficient protection for many borrowers and lenders, and it should be remembered that it avoids the complexities associated with the use of a price index.

Positive and negative interest rates

1.15   We can see that if the rate of inflation over the period of a loan is greater than the nominal interest rate paid, the *real* rate of interest on that loan will be negative as it was on many occasions in the 1970s. It is equally possible for *expected* real interest rates to be negative. In these circumstances, lenders expect the inflation rate to be greater than the nominal interest rate and thus expect a negative real return, but they may choose to accept this if it constitutes the best use of their funds at that time.

1.16 *Nominal* interest rates, however, should normally be positive (subject to the exceptions in paragraph 1.22) for the following reasons.

Hoarding becomes attractive

1.17 The self-evident reason that nominal interest rates will never be less than zero is that no rational individual is going to lend out £100 now to get back, say, £95 in a year's time. The lender would clearly do better simply by putting the £100 under the mattress or in a safe so that they would still have £100 at the end of the year.

1.18 There are three additional and closely related reasons for nominal interest rates being positive (rather than just zero), however:

- Compensation for risk
- Compensation for loss of liquidity; and
- Compensation for delayed consumption.

Compensation for risk

1.19 Any loan involves some risk of default of either interest or principal. In some instances, such as the purchase of government securities, the risk is negligible, but in other instances it will plainly be considerable. For a financial intermediary making a number of loans at the same time, the risk of default on any one loan will be reflected in the interest rate being higher, for all loans made, than it would have been in the absence of any risk.

Compensation for loss of liquidity

1.20 Lending a sum of money will generally involve a loss of liquidity. Very few loans are subject to repayment on demand. For most lenders, therefore, there is a loss of the immediate purchasing power associated with holding money. Consequently, the lender will require compensation for this loss of liquidity, which will be reflected in the interest rate paid on the loan, with higher interest rates (other things being equal) being paid on less liquid loans.

Compensation for delayed consumption

1.21 Lending funds involves forgoing consumption in the current period in favour of consumption in a future period. Given that individuals prefer consumption now to consumption in the future (while recognising that the *rate* of time preference will vary between individuals), it is inevitable that compensation will be required by lenders for their delayed consumption. Once again, this compensation will be reflected in the interest rate. For individuals who have a very strong preference for consumption now rather than at a point in the future, the interest rate will need to be correspondingly high to persuade them to forgo current consumption. Note, however, that some individuals will not so much be forgoing current consumption as taking the opportunity to accumulate sufficient funds (in the form of financial claims) with which to make a larger purchase in the future than they can at present.

Negative interest rates

1.22 There are, however, occasions when the nominal rate of interest becomes negative, although banks and building societies describe the negative nominal rate of interest as a 'maintenance charge'. For instance, the Swiss banking laws have provided secrecy for many depositors, who are quite willing to pay a fee for such a service, guaranteeing the safety of their funds denominated in a strong currency and free from prying eyes of regulators and other official bodies. Another example occurs in the UK where some institutions, eager to see adequate balances maintained in small accounts, have on occasion levied a quarterly fee should the balance fall below the stipulated balance.

Study Activities 1

1. State the general definition of an interest rate. *(Paragraph 1.3)*

2. What is a nominal rate of interest? *(Paragraphs 1.6 and 1.7)*

3. What is a real rate of interest? *(Paragraphs 1.6 and 1.7)*

4. Why can a past real rate of interest only be measured approximately? *(Paragraph 1.8)*

5. Why can a future real rate of interest only be an expected rate when the nominal rate paid on an asset is fixed? *(Paragraphs 1.9 and 1.10)*

6. How does indexation make the real rate of return on a loan independent of the rate of inflation? *(Paragraph 1.11)*

7. List the reasons for nominal interest rates normally being positive. *(Paragraphs 1.17–1.21)*

2   The overall level of interest rates

2.1 Two major theories have been advanced to explain the overall level of interest rates in an economy: the Classical theory (otherwise known as the loanable funds theory and based on Fisher's theory) and the Keynesian theory. These two theories take radically different approaches to the explanation of the overall level of interest rates but they can in practice be reconciled quite easily by making use of the differing time horizons to which they are intended to apply. Thus, while they are in a sense alternatives, it is more useful to regard them as being two halves of a more complete explanation than either theory could provide on its own. It should also be noted that both these theories seek only to explain the *overall level of interest rates* and do not seek to explain the distribution of interest rates that may apply at any particular point in time. Explanations of the distribution of interest rates at a point in time are considered in Section 5 of this unit.

2.2 The *Classical theory* focuses upon what might be termed the real economic variables. The theory argues that the level of *real* interest rates is determined by the level of saving (which provides a flow of loanable funds) and the level of investment in capital equipment and so on (which provides a demand for loanable funds). The more that people wish to save, the lower will be the level of interest rates, as the supply of loanable funds rises relatively to demand. Conversely, the more that people wish to invest, the greater will be the demand for borrowed funds and, other things being equal, the higher will be the rate of interest.

2.3 The Classical theory dismisses the relevance of money, arguing that its use is merely to determine the absolute price level and does not influence the real amounts of saving and investment. By contrast, the *Keynesian theory* emphasises the supply of and demand for money, arguing that it is the interaction of these two variables that determines the rate of interest. Basically, the more money (or liquidity) that people wish to hold, other things being equal, the higher will be its price (the rate of interest); the greater the supply of money, the lower the price, and so on.

The reconciliation of the Classical and Keynesian theories

2.4 The two theories can in practice be reconciled by making reference to the *time period* over which they are intended to apply. The Keynesian approach is essentially concerned with the causes of *short-term* changes in interest rates. Thus, it is argued that in the short-term an increase in the money supply would exert downward pressure on the interest rate, without spilling over into increased prices in the rest of the economy. However, in the longer term any increases in the money supply *would* cause increased prices, which should in turn raise the demand for money in order to meet the costs of transactions at these higher prices, and hence would bring about a return to the original level of interest rates.

2.5 The Classical theory, on the other hand, is primarily concerned with *longer-term* changes in interest rates. While the Classical theory maintains that an increase in the money supply will only have an impact on the price level in the longer term, it accepts that due to imperfections within the economic system this will not occur over shorter time periods. In the short term, an increase in the money supply, the Classical theorists accept, will probably increase the supply of loanable funds and hence bring about a fall in interest rates. In the longer term, as the effects of the increased money supply feed through into the general price level, the interest rate will return to its previous level since all the additional liquidity will have been absorbed into increased prices.

2.6   Thus, we are left with the position that while the Keynesian theory seeks primarily to explain short-term changes in interest rates, it is not inconsistent with the explanation for the longer-term changes in interest rates proposed by the Classical theory. Equally, while the Classical theory is primarily concerned with explaining longer-term changes, it is not, in turn, inconsistent with the explanation of short-term changes in interest rates put forward by the Keynesian theory.

Summary of causes of changes in the overall level of interest rates

2.7   Having examined the Classical and Keynesian theories of the determination of interest rates, we turn next to the use of these theories in summarising the major causes of changes in interest rates within the real world. For this purpose we must look separately at the factors giving rise to changes in *nominal* interest rates on the one hand and *real* interest rates on the other.

Nominal rates

2.8   The causes of *increases* in nominal interest rates are as follows.

- *A reduction in the money supply*, or the introduction by the authorities of policies to reduce the rate of growth of the money supply, would generally result in higher nominal rates of interest. The techniques for controlling the money supply that are considered in Unit 7 may all be utilised, and in this respect the attainment of a higher level of interest rates might constitute a deliberate target in order to curb the demand for borrowed funds within the economy.

- *Increased actual or expected rates of inflation* are likely to give rise to increases in interest rates, as lenders within the economy, in the absence of index-linking, seek to protect the real purchasing power of their financial assets.

- *Increases in the level of economic activity* will cause increases in nominal interest rates, since with an increasing number of transactions to be financed by a given stock of money a shortage of liquidity will become apparent at the original level of interest rates.

- *Increases in interest rates in overseas financial markets* are likely to cause an increase in interest rates in the domestic economy. The increasingly international nature of financial markets means that higher interest rates overseas will cause a relocation of funds towards those overseas markets to benefit from the higher rates. To limit the loss of deposits, domestic financial intermediaries are likely to increase their rates, or else the monetary authorities in order to avoid a large outflow of funds and an associated drop in the exchange rate may initiate an increase in interest rates.

2.9   These sources of upward pressure on interest rates will, when operating in reverse, cause decreases in nominal interest rates. In addition, note that all these factors will operate to increase nominal interest rates on an 'other things being equal' basis. It should be recognised, however, that other things will frequently *not* be equal, and certain factors will be operating in opposite directions. For example, while an increase in the expected rate of inflation may be acting to raise nominal interest rates, increases in the money supply (which may itself be the cause of the raised expectations of inflation) may be operating to keep nominal interest rates low.

Real interest rates

2.10   Factors likely to cause a rise in *real* interest rates include:

- *Factors causing increases in nominal interest rates which are not accompanied by equal increases in inflation* will, by definition, give rise to increases in real interest rates. For example, an increase in the demand for money with the supply of money held constant. Alternatively, any factor reducing the inflation rate while leaving nominal interest rates unchanged would raise the real interest rate. The majority of influences on the inflation rate will, in practice, also cause changes in nominal interest rates (indeed, many of the counter-inflation policies deliberately make use of higher nominal interest rates). However the operation of a prices and incomes policy by the government, if successful and unaccompanied by any changes in monetary or fiscal policy instruments, would reduce inflation whilst leaving nominal interest rates unchanged. By extension, of course, any factor causing a proportionately greater reduction in inflation than in nominal interest rates would also raise the real interest rate.

- *Increases in the desired level of investment or reductions in the desired level of saving* would, in terms of the Classical theory, increase the real interest rate. Given the emphasis of the Classical theory, this will be a longer-term influence with increases in the desired level of investment originating perhaps from technological developments.

- *Monetary policy*, designed to reduce the rate of growth of the money supply, may require increases in the *real* interest rate. The monetary authorities may need to raise nominal interest rates substantially above either the current or the expected inflation rate in order to bring down the rate of growth of the money supply to target rates.

- *The fiscal policy* of the government may have implications for real interest rates. If the government is running a large budget deficit, the financing of this deficit in a non-inflationary manner may give rise to a high level of real interest rates due to the increased demand within the economy for borrowed funds.

● A *high level of uncertainty* will generate higher real interest rates through an increase in the perceived risk associated with lending in financial markets. The increased level of uncertainty could have a number of causes, both short-term and long-term, which would include social and political changes either within the country itself or in major overseas countries, given the international nature of financial markets.

All these five factors will operate in reverse to bring about a fall in real interest rates. In addition, we have again assumed that they operate on an 'other things being equal' basis, whereas in practice they may operate together either to offset or to reinforce the direction of change of real interest rates.

Study Activities 2

1. What is the 'Classical theory' of the level of interest rates? *(Paragraphs 2.2 and 2.3)*

2. What is the 'Keynesian theory' of the level of interest rates? *(Paragraph 2.3)*

3. In what sense are the Classical theory and the Keynesian theory of interest rates complementary? *(Paragraphs 2.4–2.6)*

4. Summarise the factors that may cause nominal rates of interest to rise.
   (Paragraphs 2.8 and 2.9)

5. Examine the factors that may cause real rates of interest to rise. *(Paragraph 2.10)*

3 Interest rates and yields

Introduction

3.1 The par (or nominal) value of a marketable financial asset is the amount which the investor will receive when the asset matures. The yield on the financial asset measures the return to the investor over a given period of time (usually a year). If a fixed interest marketable asset is purchased at its par value, and it maintains this market value over time, the yield on the asset is equal to the interest payment that it attracts. For example, for a £100 par value asset giving a £7 p.a. interest payment, the interest rate measured against par value would be 7% p.a. and the yield would also be 7% p.a. However, the interest rate and the yield will differ if the market price of the asset is not equal to the par value.

3.2 If market rates of interest have risen since the asset was first issued, the attraction of the asset will be reduced for investors, and hence the market price of the asset will fall below the issue price. Conversely, lower market rates of interest will cause the market price of the asset to rise, as its fixed interest payment will be more attractive to investors. The inverse relationship between market rates of interest and market prices of fixed interest assets gives rise to the divergence of interest rates and yields on any particular asset.

3.3 Three types of yields on fixed-interest securities may be identified:

- Interest yield

- Redemption yield

- Performance yield

Interest yield

3.4 This yield may also be referred to as the simple yield, the flat yield, the running yield, the income yield, the earnings yield or the annual yield.

3.5 The yield is calculated by dividing the annual interest payment by the current market price of the asset.

For example, if an asset has a par value of £100, a market price of £95 and pays an annual interest (or coupon) of £7, The interest rate on par value will be 7%p.a. and the interest yield will be (7/95) x 100% = 7.37%p.a.

Where the investor is subject to tax, an appropriate deduction must be made from the gross interest yield to obtain the net interest yield.

3.6 The above calculations are simple ratios, and do not have to take into account the length of time to maturity for the asset. In other words, the same calculation is done irrespective of the stock's maturity date.

Redemption yield

3.7 Although they appear daily in the financial press, redemption yields are very difficult to calculate without the aid of a computer. The reason is that they contain two components, both of which are discounted to today's value and then added. One is the stream of income to be received and the other is the capital gain or loss on redemption. The formula is:

$$P = C_1/(1 + i) + C_2/(1 + i)^2 + C_3/(1 + i)^3 + ... + C_n/(1 + i)^n + R/(1 + i)^n$$

Where:

P is the market price
C is the coupon payment (say 7%)
R is the redemption value
n is the number of years to maturity
i is the yield (which is unknown and to be determined from the formula)
$C_1/(1 + i)$ is the present value of the first dividend to be received
$C_2/(1 + i)^2$ is the present value of the next dividend to be received

and so on ...

Solving this equation is a complex process involving algorithms and using iteration – in ordinary language, trial and error.

3.8 Although there is an answer to such an equation, its accuracy does depend on the assumption – which many people may make instinctively – that interest rates remain unchanged. In other words, when the interest received is reinvested then that reinvested money receives a constant rate of interest. When phrased like that, the response is obvious – interest rates change.

Performance yield

3.9   This type of yield is not used so frequently, but it resembles the redemption yield except that it is looking forward only to a date of sale rather than the maturity of the security. Once the stock has been sold the value P is certain (not an unknown) and so the performance yield can be calculated exactly. However, when looking to a prospective sale, the future price can be only an estimate based on forecasts of the yields and on possible dates.

Study Activities 3

1. In general terms, when are the interest rate and the yield on an asset the same and when are they different?   *(Paragraphs 3.1 and 3.2)*

2. What is an interest yield?   *(Paragraph 3.5)*

3. State the formula for the redemption yield on a fixed interest security.   *(Paragraph 3.7)*

4. What assumption is required in order to be able to calculate redemption yield?   *(Paragraph 3.8)*

5. What is a performance yield?   *(Paragraph 3.9)*

6. Explain why performance yields are not published on a regular basis in the financial press.   *(Paragraph 3.9)*

4   Term structure of interest rates

Introduction

4.1   This unit has concentrated so far on explaining the *overall level* of interest rates – either nominal or real – that will apply within an economy at a point in time. In this section, we turn to considering the *distribution* of interest rates at a point in time, specifically the *term structure* of interest rates. The term structure of interest rates may be defined as *the spread of interest rates that are paid on the same type of assets with different terms to maturity.*

4.2   This concept of the term structure of interest rates is only of relevance in the case of those assets that have a fixed term to maturity and pay a fixed interest at specified periods. The major group of such assets in the UK is gilt-edged securities issued by the government, although other groups, such as sterling certificates of deposit, also satisfy the requirements and the general principles involved can be applied to financial assets more widely.

4.3   Examination of the list of 'British funds' (gilt-edged securities) in the *Financial Times* will reveal that there are a number of different gilt-edged securities with the same coupon rate (for example, 7%) but with differing periods to maturity. The list also reveals that the *yield* on these gilt-edged securities – which differ only in terms of the period to maturity –often varies quite markedly. It is this *spread* of yields paid on the same type of assets (in this case gilt-edged securities) with different terms to maturity that theories of the term structure of interest rates seek to explain.

The yield curve

4.4   The term structure of interest rates on a particular type of asset may be represented diagrammatically in the *yield curve*. Strictly speaking, the yield on an asset includes not only the interest income from that asset but also any capital appreciation (due to the current price being less than the sum paid on maturity) or capital depreciation (due to the current price being greater than the sum paid on maturity). In the list of gilt-edged securities in the *Financial Times*, the return that includes any capital appreciation or depreciation is termed the *redemption yield*, while the return that only takes account of the interest income is termed the *interest yield* (as described in Section 3 of this Unit).

Figure 6.1 Normal yield curve

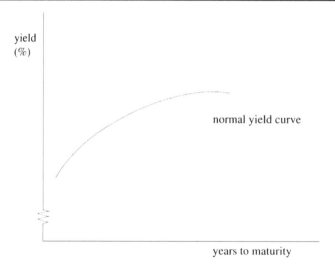

4.5   The curve depicted in Fig. 6.1 is referred to as the 'normal' yield curve because it is constructed on the assumption that within the market there is no specific expectation of interest rate movements in either direction. It is furthermore assumed that there exists some element of uncertainty within the financial environment. Given those two assumptions, the characteristic upward slope of the normal yield curve is attributable to *liquidity preference* and to *risk*.

4.6   With regard to *liquidity preference*, note first that any lending involves a loss of immediate purchasing power. When lending for a short period of time, this loss of immediate purchasing power may be relatively slight and so the lender may not require much compensation. When lending for longer periods of time, however, the lender would generally require a higher level of compensation. This compensation is, of course, reflected in the interest rate and so is one explanation why, under 'normal' conditions, interest rates on long-dated loans will be higher than on short-dated loans. It is important to appreciate that this principle applies just as strongly to marketable securities as to non-marketable loans. The reason for this is that while with marketable securities the lender can sell the security, there is a risk of capital loss associated with a premature sale, and the possibility of premature sale increases with the maturity of the security.

4.7   The overall *risks* associated with lending increase over time, because other risks increase. These are the risks of:

- *Default*, of either interest or principal, which will generally increase with the length of the loan;

- *Real capital loss due to inflation*, which increases with the length of the loan;

- *Capital loss on marketable securities* which, if they have to be sold prior to maturity, increases with the length of the loan;

- *Changes in the lender's circumstances* which, making a particular loan within a portfolio inappropriate to new circumstances, will increase with the length of the loan.

4.8   For all these four reasons, lenders will seek compensation, in the form of higher interest rates, for loans of long maturity compared with loans of short maturity. When taken in conjunction with the liquidity preference principle, it is clear to see why the normal yield curve slopes upward. The strength of the attitude towards liquidity preference and towards risk will determine the slope of the curve. As the maturity becomes longer, there is a tendency for the curve to rise more gently. This reflects the fact that it becomes difficult to evaluate the compensation required for the increased risk and for the loss of liquidity associated with, say, an extra year to maturity when a loan already has several years to maturity.

The influence of interest rate expectations on the yield curve

4.9   Having considered the determinants of the shape of the 'normal' yield curve (i.e. when there are no specific expectations of changes in interest rates), the next issue to address is the impact on the shape of the yield curve *if there are specific expectations of changes in interest rates*.

Expectations of a fall in interest rates

4.10   When there is a general expectation of a fall in interest rates, the effect is for long-term rates to be depressed relative to short-term rates. The reason for this is that lenders prefer to make longer-term loans now at the higher rate; they want to avoid lending short-term now because they will only be able to re-lend the funds at low interest rates after those short-term loans have matured. Hence, there will be an increased supply of long-term funds to the market and a reduced supply of short-term funds, which will serve to lower long-term rates and raise short-term rates. These effects will be *reinforced* by the preferences of borrowers; expecting a fall in interest rates, borrowers will wish to borrow short-term in order to be able to rollover their loans at the new, lower rates when those short-term loans mature. Equally, they will seek to avoid borrowing long-term until the fall in interest rates materialises. Hence, there will be an *increased demand* for short-term loans which, in conjunction with the reduced supply from lenders, will serve to increase short-term interest rates. There will also be a reduced demand for long-term loans which, in conjunction with the increased supply from lenders, will serve to lower long-term interest rates. The impact on the yield curve is to make it flatter, as shown in Fig. 6.2.

Figure 6.2 Effect on yield curve of expectations of an interest rate fall

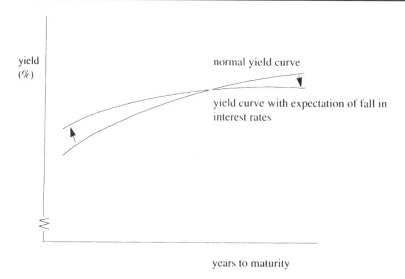

4.11   If the expectations of falls in interest rates are particularly strong, then it may be the case that the influence of these outweighs the influences of risk and of liquidity preference that give rise to the upward-sloping 'normal' yield curve. In such circumstances, the yield curve will become *downward* sloping, with interest rates on long maturity securities being *lower* than those on short maturity securities.

4.12   Downward-sloping yield curves were clearly visible in the UK gilt-edged securities market and in several other UK securities markets in a number of periods between the early 1980s and autumn 1992. As we have just discussed, for downward-sloping yield curves to be observed, the expectations of lower interest rates have to be sufficient to swamp the normal risk- and liquidity-preference influences. Within the UK markets, this in turn was a reflection of the very high nominal interest rates observed periodically, when combined with the expectation that inflation-reducing policies would prove successful, thus leading to reductions in interest rates in due course. Frequently, these expectations were for falls in interest rates in the *medium* term, with the result that the yield curve was upward-sloping over the span of shorter maturities and only became downward-sloping over the longer maturities (Curve 1 in Fig. 6.3). Only on those occasions when interest rates were particularly high and were seen as a short-term expedient, expected to last only a short period of time, was the yield curve downward-sloping throughout (Curve 2 in Fig. 6.3).

Figure 6.3 Downward-sloping yield curve

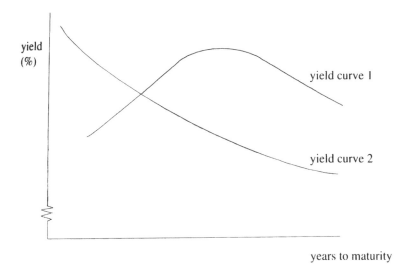

Expectations of a rise in interest rates

4.13   When a rise in interest rates is generally expected, the impact will be for long-term rates to be increased relative to short-term rates. The reasons for this are largely the reverse of the reasons for a rise in short-term rates relative to long-term rates when a fall in interest rates is expected. If there are generalised expectations of a rise in interest rates, borrowers will seek to borrow long-term in order to lock in at the current low rates, and will seek to avoid borrowing short-term since this may involve rolling-over loans at higher interest rates. Hence, there will be an increased demand for long-term loans and a reduced demand for short-term loans. Lenders, on the other hand, will be unwilling to lend long-term if rates are expected to rise, and will instead seek to lend only short-term in order to profit from the high rates when they materialise. The combination of a reduced demand from borrowers and an increased supply from lenders of short-term loans means that short-term rates will fall, while the increased demand from borrowers and reduced supply from lenders of long-term loans means that long-term rates will increase. The effect will be for the yield curve to become more steeply upward sloping than the 'normal' yield curve, as is shown in Fig. 6.4.

4.14   In practice, the yield curves that are observed will frequently *not* be smooth curves; they invariably display humps or dips. We have already considered why the yield curve might initially be upward-sloping and subsequently downward-sloping when there are expectations of falls in the interest rate in the medium term, but the patterns are often considerably more complicated than this. The reason is that the precise shape of any yield curve will be influenced by the particular format of the expectations about interest rate changes. We have only taken a general form here, in terms of a rise or fall in interest rates. In practice, for example, rates might be expected to fall in nine months' time and then to rise in two years' time. These expectations would be reflected in the shape of the yield curve.

Figure 6.4 Effect on yield curve of expectations of interest rate increases

---

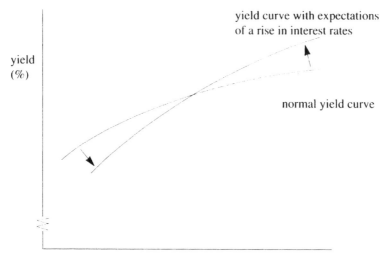

Study Activities 4

1. Define the 'term structure of interest rates'.   *(Paragraphs 4.1 and 4.2)*

2. To what type of assets is the 'term structure analysis' relevant?
                                                                      (Paragraphs 4.2 and 4.3)

3. What is a yield curve?   *(Paragraphs 4.4 and 4.5)*

4. Why does the 'normal' yield curve slope upward from left to right?

(Paragraphs 4.5–4.8)

5. In what way do expectations of a fall in interest rates affect the shape of the yield curve?

(Paragraphs 4.10–4.12)

6. In what way do expectations of a rise in interest rates affect the shape of the yield curve?

(Paragraph 4.13)

The underlying theory on yield curves

4.15   A great deal of work has been done to establish the theoretical underpinnings of yield curves and to explain the various shapes which may be observed in practice. None of the established theories is wholly satisfactory, and many economists believe that the assumptions required by the theories undermine their practical value. Nevertheless it is worthwhile to summarise the key features of these theories as a basis for more advanced study of yield curves.

4.16   Two main theories seek to explain the shapes of yield curves. These are:

- The expectations theory, which is subdivided into:

  - pure expectations

  - liquidity-biased expectations

  - preferred habitat-biased expectations

- The market segmentation theory, which disallows large-scale arbitrage between the various segments of the market.

Pure expectations

4.17   The basis of this theory is that the shape of yield curves is determined by market expectations of future short-term interest rates. If lenders and borrowers expect short-term interest rates to rise, then lenders would wish to invest at the short end of the market, profiting when bond prices had fallen by enjoying higher yields. This would push up short-term bond prices (force down the yield curve for short maturity bonds). Borrowers would, of course, want to borrow for much longer periods, forcing up the yield for long maturity bonds. These actions will tilt the curve in an anti-clockwise direction, making it steeper (rising from left to right). However, the theory fails to consider the risks involved, as nobody knows future bond prices (price risk) or future rates of interest (reinvestment risk).

Liquidity

4.18   This theory assumes that the risk associated with investment in bonds increases with their term to maturity. It is argued that this increasing risk will lead investors to require a progressively larger liquidity premium for investing in bonds with a progressively longer maturity. Investors require a premium for not being liquid, e.g. buying long-dated bonds, and this urge to be compensated for holding il-liquid assets may be more important than the expectations which may result in a downward-sloping curve. This premium has an upward bias on the curve. This theory fits very closely with the intuitive explanation for the shape of yield curves given above in Sections 4.4 to 4.14.

Preferred habitat

4.19   This theory argues that investors prefer to match their assets with known liabilities and borrowers will seek to raise funds for a time period that matches their needs. Also, investment institutions may try to match the maturity of their assets and liabilities.

4.20   In order to be encouraged to shift out of their preferred habitats, lenders and borrowers will require a premium on the yield to cover the risk that they feel they are being asked to accept. The premium will vary according to the extent that the investor or borrower has to shift from their preferred habitat. Therefore, as there is no reason to believe that the premium will rise uniformly with maturity, the theory is able to explain any shape of yield curve.

Market segmentation

4.21   A lay person might describe this theory as 'a highly structured and inflexible version of the preferred habitat theory'. It assumes that neither investors nor borrowers are able or willing to move along the yield curve to take advantage of arbitrage opportunities.

4.22   The reason for this highly inflexible segmentation of the market might be because regulators and/or the investing institutions' own rules require them to keep certain strict percentages of their assets in each of the market's maturity sectors.

4.23   Under this theory, the yield curve is constructed from the yield curves of the various segments of the fixed-interest securities market. Some economists regard this theory as unsustainable because it presupposes that there is absolute risk aversion, whereas evidence shows that investors are willing to take risks and arbitrage along the yield curve.

5   Yield spreads on bonds

Definition of a yield spread

5.1   The difference in yield on any two different bond issues is called the *yield spread* (and this is normally reported in basis points; i.e. in one-hundredths of a percentage point). Yield spreads may relate to:

- Two issues from within a single bond market sector – *intra-market sector spread*.

● Issues from two different bond market sectors – *inter-market sector spread*.

5.2   Yield spreads may be defined for:

● Different types of bonds with the same maturity.

● Comparable bonds with different maturity (to generate a term structure of interest rates).

Benchmarks

5.3   A common benchmark for the analysis of yield spreads is an appropriate issue of British Government gilt-edged securities. In the USA Treasury securities perform the same function. These securities effectively carry no default (credit) risk, and provide investors with a floor to the yields that they are normally willing to accept on other bonds of comparable maturity.

5.4   The most recent issue of gilt-edged securities (known as 'current coupon' or 'on-the-run' issues) are used for this benchmarking purpose. Yields may be expressed as the spread over this risk-free rate.

The creditworthiness of the issuers of bonds

5.5   The yield spread between bonds reflects the relative creditworthiness of the issuers of the bonds. When considering the spread between a bond and the comparable risk-free rate (which is sometimes referred to as the *quality or credit spread*), the relevant factor is clearly the default risk associated with the issuer of the bond. In this context, credit-rating agencies provide a valuable service. The best-known credit-rating agencies are *Moody's* and *Standard and Poors*. The highest rated companies (given AAA or Aaa ratings) are able to raise funds at very narrow margins above the yield on the comparable gilt-edged security or Treasury security.

Other factors affecting the yield spread

5.6   Whilst the risk differential between any two bonds is crucial to the determination of their yield spread, other factors may also have a significant influence on the spread, and, in certain circumstances, may swamp the effect of differential risk on yields. The main factors to consider are:

● The term to maturity on a given type of asset.

● Options which might be attached to bonds.

● The tax position of holders and potential holders of bonds.

● The expected liquidity of specific issues of bonds (in terms of their general marketability).

Study Activities 5

1. Outline the 'pure expectations' theory of the shape of yield curves. *(Paragraph 4.17)*

2. What is thought to be the main weakness of the 'pure expectations' theory of the shape of yield curves? *(Paragraph 4.17)*

3. What are the particular attractions of the 'liquidity' theory of the shape of yield curves? *(Paragraph 4.18)*

4. Distinguish between the 'preferred habitat' and the 'market segmentation' theories of the shape of yield curves. *(Paragraphs 4.19–4.23)*

5. Define a yield spread. *(Paragraph 5.1)*

6. What is the difference between 'intra-market sector spread' and 'inter-market sector spread'? *(Paragraph 5.1)*

7. What is a benchmark security within the context of yield spreads? *(Paragraph 5.3)*

8. What is the importance of credit-rating agencies in relation to the calculation of yield spreads? *(Paragraph 5.5)*

9. List the main factors that may influence the yield spread on two bonds. *(Paragraph 5.6)*

6 Differentials between interest rates on different types of assets

6.1   There is a danger in regarding loans as being somehow uniform, varying only in terms of maturity. In practice, every loan – whether or not it involves the issuance of a security – is unique since it represents a composite of characteristics that are particular to that loan (asset), and the interest rate on that loan is only one characteristic. It is the combination of these various characteristics that influences the demand for and supply of that asset, and hence determines the price – which here means the interest rate. The extent to which the various characteristics underlying each asset are demanded or supplied determines the pattern, and any changes in the pattern, of interest rates across different assets within the economy.

6.2   This section seeks to draw together some of the characteristics involved in loans that have already been identified, at the same time as identifying others that have not been considered so far. Given that every loan involves a *combination* of characteristics, remember that these will vary in importance; and indeed some will not figure at all in particular loans. It is the particular combinations that do, indeed, generate the spread of interest rates applying at any one time.

Characteristics of borrowing and lending transactions

Term to maturity

6.3 As we discussed in the context of the term structure of interest rates, the longer the term to maturity of a fixed interest rate loan the higher will be the interest rate which is sought by the lender as compensation for the loss of liquidity. This, of course, assumes that any expectations of future interest rate reductions do not outweigh the underlying risk and liquidity preference factors. Moreover, the longer this period of a loan, the greater is the chance that the other characteristics – such as government policy – may change.

Risk

6.4 The default risk associated with the payment of either interest or principal on a loan was identified above. The higher the perceived risk involved in lending to a particular borrower, the larger will be any risk premium charged by the lender, in the form of a higher interest rate. With large financial intermediaries this may be formalised by means of charging a borrower a certain margin, over a reference interest rate such as LIBOR, according to the perceived risk.

Expectations of changes in interest rates

6.5 As we also saw above, in the discussion of the term structure of interest rates, an expectation of a rise in interest rates would induce lenders to seek higher interest rates for any long-term loan. Equally, an expectation of lower interest rates would induce lenders to accept lower interest rates than would otherwise be the case. However, expectations of interest rate movements will not be identical across all borrowers and lenders. Hence, at any one time the interest rate that a borrower and a lender are prepared to pay and accept for a transaction may well be different from that for a comparable transaction elsewhere in the economy. To avoid becoming locked in to interest rates which bear little relation to market interest rates after the loan has commenced, both borrowers and lenders may be inclined to agree loans on a floating interest rate basis at times of high interest rate volatility.

Size of the loan

6.6 The existence of economies of scale on both the borrowing and the lending sides means that a large-scale loan may attract preferential interest rates. From the point of view of a financial intermediary, a large deposit would attract lower administration costs (per £1 deposited) and hence the financial intermediary would be prepared to offer a higher interest rate to attract such deposits. Similarly, large-scale loans may justify a lower interest rate charged by the financial intermediary because lower administration costs are associated with servicing that loan. However, large-scale deposits and large-scale loans may involve an increase in *portfolio risk* for the financial intermediary – the withdrawal of a large-scale deposit may pose problems and a large-scale loan may involve an undesirable concentration of risk due to inadequate diversification. Both these aspects of increased portfolio risk may serve to offset – in some cases, more than offset – the benefits of enhanced economies of scale.

Interest rates elsewhere

6.7   The high level of international interdependence of financial markets means that most domestic interest rates will be influenced by changes in interest rates in other financial markets, particularly in the USA.

Expectations of inflation

6.8   These will cause lenders to seek higher rates of interest, and borrowers to be prepared to pay higher interest rates than if price stability were anticipated. As with expectations of interest-rate changes, however, expectations of inflation will vary across the participants in borrowing and lending transactions. The borrower and lender in one transaction in which both parties have relatively low expectations of inflation would result in a lower interest rate on that transaction than one in which the parties have higher expectations of inflation. In this way, another cause of a *spread* of interest rates is established.

Tax considerations

6.9   The taxation regime applicable to particular assets and the taxation position of the borrower and of the lender is likely to affect the interest rate applicable to one asset compared with others. By way of example, examination of the list of gilt-edged securities in the *Financial Times* will often reveal short-dated gilt-edged securities with a redemption yield somewhat higher than fixed rate National Savings Certificates. This is due to the different tax treatment of capital gains and interest income from a gilt-edged security and the complete exemption of National Savings Certificates from these two taxes.

Marketability of an asset

6.10   Where a loan transaction results in the issue of a security, the marketability of that security will influence the interest rate, with higher marketability being associated with lower interest rates.

Business strategy of the financial intermediary

6.11   A particular financial intermediary may decide to follow a strategy of maximising its short-term profits, in which case we might expect to see low rates for depositors and high rates for borrowers, depending upon the elasticity of supply of deposits and the elasticity of demand for loans. Whereas another intermediary may be following a strategy for short-term growth by squeezing its margins and offering relatively high rates for depositors and low rates to borrowers. The effect, along with other alternative strategies, is for financial intermediaries to be offering a spread of lending and borrowing rates at any one point in time.

Type of interest rate

6.12   The extent to which the interest rate on a loan is fixed (both in terms of the range within which it is fixed and the time period over which it is fixed) will influence the rate that the lender is willing to accept. Also, the terms for negotiating 'rolling over' the loan will affect the rate agreed. Facilities for index linking of a loan may reduce the *real* interest rate that a lender requires in order for a loan to be made.

Type of loan

6.13   Term loans offered by a financial intermediary will generally attract a lower interest rate than an overdraft facility. This is because interest is paid on the whole of the term loan regardless of whether or not the money is used, whereas interest is paid only on the overdraft funds used by the borrower.

Official intervention

6.14   This is likely to influence the spread of interest rates at a point in time in a number of ways. The various methods of financial regulation established by the authorities will influence the cost structures, and hence the interest rates paid and required by financial intermediaries, to different extents. The policies pursued by the authorities to control monetary conditions may also influence the structure of interest rates, through the use of open-market operations, restrictions on hire-purchase agreements, interest rate ceilings and officially administered rates. The form of control chosen may well have an impact on the interest rate structure according to the type of security traded and the institutions or individuals involved.

Market imperfections

6.15   Finally, it is important to recognise that sizeable participants in a financial market, in addition to the government, may distort the interest rate structure. Legal constraints on the participation of certain groups of institutions in particular markets may also give rise to a distorted pattern of interest rates. The interest rate cartel operated by the building societies until the early 1980s, buttressed by restrictions on the ability of banks to enter the housing finance market, resulted in mortgage rates being out of line with rates elsewhere for long periods of time.

6.16   Taken together, the above-listed 13 factors provide ample explanation for a spread of interest rates observed within the economy at any one point in time. They do not, however, cover variations between interest rates in domestic and eurocurrency markets. These interest rate relationships are examined below.

Study Activities 6

1. Why might each type of loan be thought of as being unique?

   (Paragraphs 6.1 and 6.2)

2. In what way might the size of a loan affect the rate of interest charged?

   (Paragraph 6.6)

3. What is the relevance of expectations of inflation to the pattern of interest rates established?

   (Paragraph 6.8)

4. What is the importance of a financial intermediary's business strategy to the pattern of interest rates established?

   (Paragraph 6.11)

5. How may market imperfections affect the pattern of interest rates established?

   (Paragraph 6.15)

7 Key UK interest rates

Money market rates

7.1   The London sterling money market interest rates are crucial for the financial system of the UK. The reason for this is that they determine the cost of acquiring funds for many financial institutions and the *marginal* cost of funds for many more. As a consequence, they influence the interest rates applied to every loan transaction within the economy.

7.2   As regards the *level* of money market interest rates, since the maximum maturity of the transactions to which these interest rates apply is one year, the Keynesian (liquidity preference) theory of the determination of interest rates is relevant. In this context it is important to remember the influence of the *Bank of England* on these rates. The Bank seeks to influence interest rates by intervention in the gilt repo market and the discount market (the 'primary' money market). In recent years the emphasis has been on the manipulation of very short-term rates (up to 14 days to maturity), and hence for these rates the influence of the Bank of England is crucial. However, given the portfolio adjustment that occurs if interest rates of any particular maturity are affected, in practice the influence of the Bank of England will spread outwards across the maturity spectrum. If the Bank engineers a rise in very short-term rates, for example, then rates for slightly longer-dated assets will become more attractive to borrowers and less attractive to lenders, thereby giving upward pressure to those slightly longer-term rates.

7.3   The *term structure* of the interest rates within the money market may be explained by the theory of the term structure of interest rates which makes use of risk, liquidity preference and interest-rate expectation characteristics. If the term structure generates a yield curve which is generally upward-sloping throughout, this implies that there are no expectations of future falls in interest rates sufficient to offset the normal upward-sloping tendency associated with risk and liquidity preference.

7.4 Finally, the *spread* of interest rates between different money market assets will be determined by the *particular set* of characteristics of each asset. The instruments with the lowest rates (often Treasury bills and bank bills) are those associated with the primary market; those with the higher rates are associated with the secondary markets and reflect the higher risk and, in some instances, reduced marketability.

7.5 Day-to-day variations in the supply and demand in respect of particular instruments help to explain both absolute movements in associated interest rates and changes in their bid-offer spread.

Bank base rates

7.6 Bank base rates are another important set of interest rates. Whereas money market interest rates attract little attention from the media, changes in bank base rates are very widely reported because they are usually initiated by official policy actions – today, decisions made by the Bank of England's Monetary Policy Committee. Partly as a consequence of their prominence within the media, bank base rates have become an indicator of the health of the economy. Before the Bank of England was granted independence in respect of the implementation of monetary policy, changes in bank base rates also had acquired political importance.

7.7 It is important to bear in mind that bank base rates are indeed *base* rates. They are used as a *starting point* from which a bank determines its lending rates and, to some extent, its deposit rates also. Lending rates are calculated as a percentage above the bank's base rate, with loans regarded as being low-risk charged at a small margin above base rate and loans of higher risk charged at a much greater margin above base rate.

7.8 A proportion of term loans provided by banks are at rates linked directly to money market rates, and so bypass the base rate calculation altogether. This is not to say, however, that the principles involved in the calculation of base rates are overlooked. The money market rates will generally represent the interest cost to a bank of acquiring *additional* funds, and the margin over money market rates will reflect the perceived risk and the administration costs associated with loans. Lending at rates linked to money market rates does, of course, have the advantage of reducing the interest rate risk associated with lending.

7.9 Finally, although bank base rates are the starting point for determining the lending rates charged by banks, many other lending rates are linked to bank base rates and acquire an increased importance as a result. Since base rates are an important competitive tool, differences of any size between the base rates of competing banks would lead to large switches of loans and deposits between them. Consequently, bank base rates tend to be very similar, if not identical, at least for the larger banks. Furthermore, any *changes* in bank base rates will all tend to be announced at the same time for the same reasons.

Study Activities 7

1. Why are the London sterling money market rates of such crucial importance for the operation of the UK financial system? *(Paragraph 7.1)*

2. Which theory is relevant to the explanation of the level of sterling money market interest rates? *(Paragraph 7.2)*

3. What factor is crucial to the level of bank base rates? *(Paragraph 7.6)*

4. What is the advantage to a bank of making loans at rates linked to market rates? *(Paragraph 7.8)*

The relationship between sterling money market rates and commercial bank lending rates

7.10　We have noted that both interest rates generated in the sterling money market and bank base rates represent very important sets of interest rates within the financial system. In this section we look more closely at the relationship between sterling money market rates and bank base rates, emphasising particularly the link between sterling money market rates and the lending rates charged by commercial banks.

7.11　The commercial banks are important participants in the sterling money markets, both in lending funds and in borrowing funds. In this respect, the markets are crucial to the adjustment of the banks' liquidity positions since it is virtually impossible for a bank to increase its funds at short notice through increasing its retail deposits (in response to profitable lending opportunities). Equally, it is virtually impossible for a bank to *reduce*, at short notice, its funds obtained through retail deposits when it has excess funds due to a shortage of lending opportunities. Retail deposits generally take a long time to respond to any changes in interest rates. Furthermore, any changes in rates will have to be applied to *all* the funds to which those rates apply – a bank cannot just pay a higher rate on the *additional* retail deposits that it attracts to a particular type of account.

7.12　The *marginal* cost of raising additional funds from retail sources is therefore very high and sufficient to encourage substantial use by the banks of the wholesale money markets for liquidity adjustment purposes. The wholesale markets are relatively sensitive to small changes in rates, and transactions are negotiated individually and quickly. The short-term inter-bank interest rates therefore provide a good indicator of the marginal cost of funds to a bank, and it is the three-month LIBOR (London Inter-Bank Offered Rate) and three-month LIBID (London Inter-Bank Bid Rate) that have become the benchmark interest rates in this respect. (Three-month rates are used due to their stability relative to shorter-term rates, and due to the widespread use of three-month maturity in many money market instruments and transactions.)

7.13   The impact of changes in short-term inter-bank interest rates on the rates charged by commercial banks on their lending depends upon the basis on which the loan has been agreed. There are three alternative bases relevant here. These are at:

- a fixed margin above an inter-bank rate (for example, LIBOR);
- a fixed margin above the bank's base rate;
- a fixed rate.

At a fixed margin above an inter-bank rate

7.14   The relationship between the inter-bank rate and the rate charged on a commercial bank loan is straightforward here, since if a loan has been made at, say, 3% above three-month LIBOR, a rise in LIBOR will give rise to an immediate rise in the rate charged by the bank.

At a fixed margin above the bank's base rate

7.15   The relationship is somewhat more complicated here, since it depends on the link between a bank's base rate and the inter-bank rates. Base rates tend to follow the general trend in short-term inter-bank rates over the longer term, due to the fact (considered above) that the short-term inter-bank rates represent the marginal cost of funds to a bank. For some banks, where a significant proportion of their lending is funded from these wholesale sources, these short-term inter-bank rates come close to representing the *average* cost of funds in addition to the marginal cost. However, over the short term, inter-bank rates will tend to diverge from bank base rates due to the cost and perhaps the loss of customer goodwill associated with frequent changes in base rates. Accordingly, banks will tend to adjust their base rates when the change in inter-bank rates is expected to be long-lasting, when it is a relatively large change, and when the proportion of a bank's funding at these inter-bank rates is relatively high. The result is that adjustment tends to take place with a lag, and in relatively large steps when it does occur, but in certain cases a very narrow profit margin on lending activities may cause a bank to change its base rates quickly.

7.16   Banks will not wish to let the divergence – in either direction – between base rates and inter-bank rates become too large, since this will encourage *arbitrage* at the bank's expense. Arbitrage involves, for example, borrowing from the banks when base rates are low in order to on-lend in the wholesale markets. In this instance, it is the divergence between very *short-term* wholesale rates and base rates that is important, since arbitrageurs will generally only wish to lend short-term in case base rates rise when they will find themselves locked into an arbitrage transaction at rates that lose them money. If money lent on the wholesale markets can be regained quickly in order to end the borrowing from the banks, the risk is naturally reduced.

At fixed rates

7.17   Some bank lending is undertaken on a fixed-rate basis. Clearly, changes in inter-bank rates will have no impact on existing fixed rate loans, but as they mature and new loans are negotiated, the new fixed rates are likely to reflect the altered cost of funds to the bank.

The relationship between mortgage rates and short-term interest rates

7.18   Given that mortgage repayments constitute a substantial element of the total expenditure of many households, changes in mortgage rates have become an important and politically sensitive issue. The UK housing finance system is dominated by *variable rate mortgages* (which are by no means universal in other countries), which means that while the mortgage loan may be for an initial maturity of 25 years, this is of little importance in determining the interest rate charged. Typically, the provider of the housing finance has to obtain funds on a short-term basis, and hence the rate charged will necessarily reflect changes in the cost of these funds. If the cost of funds rises, the need to maintain profitability will ensure that borrowers are charged a higher rate, and if the cost falls, competitive pressures will ensure that this change is also reflected in mortgage loan rates.

7.19   Short-term money market rates will clearly be important in the determination of mortgage rates where mortgage providers obtain their funds from the money markets. An increasing proportion of mortgage funds has been obtained from the money markets in recent years. Where a mortgage provider does obtain a significant proportion of funds from the wholesale markets, any change in short-term money market interest rates will be reflected that much more fully and quickly in changes in the mortgage rate. Even where a mortgage provider obtains all the funds from retail sources, however, changes in short-term rates will still have an impact. Changes in money market rates filter through to change rates in the rest of the financial system relatively quickly. Borrowers and lenders of all types adjust their portfolio positions to reflect the changed structure of interest rates, causing changes in the rates that have to be paid to attract retail deposits. Nevertheless, there is likely to be a time lag involved here and the movement may not be of the same amount. A consequence of this is that different mortgage providers may be charging different mortgage rates at any one point in time, because the composition of their sources of funds gives rise to a varying cost of funds, rather than because of any differences in competitive strategy. The relative cost positions of mortgage providers will, of course, vary over time with changing money market and retail rates.

7.20   Although short-term interest rates will therefore have an impact on mortgage rates, other factors, especially in the longer term, will exert their influence also. The overall profile of the demand for and supply of long-term mortgage funds will be a significant factor in the establishment of rates, alongside the shorter-term influences from the money market. In this regard, those factors that affect the overall level of interest rates, as discussed in Section 2, are relevant. In addition, there may be particular considerations that apply to the demand for and supply of mortgage funds, such as the extent to which housing is seen as a tax-efficient and profitable investment, and demographic changes in the population. Such considerations and other market imperfections may lead to a differential between rates on mortgage funds and those elsewhere.

7.21   As with commercial bank lending, mortgage providers will seek to avoid very frequent changes in rates due to the administrative cost and lost goodwill associated with such changes. Some mortgage providers now only change the repayments due from borrowers once a year (although the rates charged on the loan may be changed more frequently). Overall, mortgage rates do not adjust particularly quickly to changes in short-term rates. Fixed-rate mortgages, at least over a limited number of years, are becoming more familiar within the UK system.

The relationship between domestic and international interest rates

7.22   Section 2 above noted that one of the influences on the overall level of interest rates in an economy would be the level of interest rates that applied in other financial centres in the world. This influence will be greater the more open is the financial system of the economy and it is notable that the UK possesses one of the most open financial systems. Given that openness, the links between interest rates in the UK and interest rates elsewhere in the world are likely to be very complex. Nevertheless, three broad influences linking interest rates in one country with those elsewhere in the world may be identified:

● The economic environment;

● Expectations of movements in exchange rates;

● Actual and expected inflation rates relative to other countries.

The economic environment

7.23   A robust economy that is experiencing, and is expected to continue to experience, a high growth rate normally generates considerable confidence. In the current context, that high level of confidence will be reflected in a low rate of expected defaults on loans. With that low-risk premium incorporated into the interest rates, we would expect such economies, other things being equal, to have low interest rates relative to other economies. Conversely, of course, countries where investments are perceived to carry greater risk – due to doubts about economic prospects or about political or social stability – would see higher interest rates than elsewhere.

Expectations of movements in exchange rates

7.24 Expectations that the value of a currency is going to depreciate relative to other currencies will lead investors to require a premium to compensate for any loss in international purchasing power resulting from such depreciation. This premium will naturally make interest rates higher in that country than elsewhere. Conversely, in circumstances where there are general expectations of an appreciation of a currency, interest rates on assets denominated in that currency will tend to be lower than elsewhere. When an expectation of an appreciation or a depreciation of a currency develops, unless there is a sufficient differential in interest rates, funds are likely to be moved between currencies in order to obtain the best expected returns. Funds will tend to move towards currencies that are expected to appreciate in value, other things being equal. By definition, the funds will be moving from currencies that are expected to depreciate in value. These expectations may, of course, become self-fulfilling, unless interest rate differentials adjust accordingly under the pressure of market forces.

Actual and expected inflation rates relative to other countries

7.25 A country with a high rate of inflation relative to those in other countries will carry a higher (nominal) interest rate since investors will require a premium in terms of interest rates to compensate for the loss in purchasing power that the high rate of inflation involves. A higher expected rate of inflation would have a corresponding implication for the term structure of interest rates relative to other countries.

7.26 These three broad influences on a country's interest rates relative to those elsewhere may also be the source of pressure for *changes* in interest rates. As was implied in paragraph 7.24, expectations of a depreciation of the exchange rate may induce the authorities to raise interest rates in order to prevent these expectations being borne out. These expectations may also induce financial intermediaries to raise their deposit rates in order to avoid the outflow of funds that would otherwise occur.

Study Activities 8

1. Why do banks use money markets to adjust their liquidity positions rather than retail deposit markets? *(Paragraph 7.11)*

2. Examine the ways in which an increase in money market rates may affect banks' on-lending rates. *(Paragraphs 7.12–7.17)*

3. Other than money market interest rates, what factors are likely to affect the rate of interest charged on mortgage loans? *(Paragraph 7.20)*

4. In what way is the general condition of a country's economy likely to affect the level of its interest rates relative to those existing in other countries? *(Paragraph 7.23)*

5. What is the relevance of expected exchange rate movements for the determination of domestic interest rates? *(Paragraph 7.24)*

8 Recent trends in UK interest rates

8.1 While real interest rates on the majority of retail, and frequently wholesale, financial assets were *negative* during the 1970s, since the early 1980s the position has changed significantly. Since 1981 real interest rates have been positive for the majority of both retail and wholesale financial assets and in several years, furthermore, have been historically *high*. The UK has not been unique in this respect; most industrialised countries have experienced similar trends.

8.2 It is useful to identify some of the causes of this trend in real interest rates. Note that the emphasis here is on explaining the trend rather than the more detailed changes and levels that have applied at particular points in time.

Inflation

8.3 Given that real interest rates are nominal rates adjusted for inflation, the inflation rate is an important influence on real interest rates. With nominal interest rates remaining at high levels, the fall in average inflation rates experienced during the 1980s saw real interest rates rise. In addition, it appears that nominal rates adjusted more quickly to the increase in inflation during the early 1980s, perhaps due to learning from experience in the 1970s. It has also been suggested that expectations of inflation were very slow to fall, with the result that nominal interest rates lagged well behind the fall in inflation. More recently nominal interest rates have fallen substantially but so too has the rate of inflation, thereby having only a limited impact on real interest rates.

Monetary policy

8.4 The monetary authorities have a major influence over nominal interest rates through monetary policy, and it is notable that the UK government has made extensive use of monetary policy in order to control inflation. Tight monetary controls have periodically pushed up interest rates which, in so far as the controls led to a fall in inflation, thereby pushed up real interest rates.

Sterling exchange rate

8.5 During the latter half of the 1980s, the government became more acutely aware of the implications of depreciation in the value of sterling on the international exchanges, particularly for the inflation rate in the UK. As a result, monetary policy increasingly took into account the sterling exchange rate, with high interest rates being used to sustain the value of sterling when depreciation looked likely. Since Autumn 1992, policy has been more relaxed in this context, with the result that interest rates have been set to reflect the strengths and weaknesses of the domestic economy, with special emphasis on the outlook for underlying inflation over a time horizon of around two years ahead.

Economic policy in the USA

8.6   The US dollar dominates the international financial system, with the consequence that the economic policies followed by the US government impinge upon all other countries in the system. During much of the 1980s, large fiscal expansion in the USA was accompanied by a relatively tight monetary policy, leading to high nominal interest rates. Since inflation rates were relatively low in the USA, this implied high real rates. The ease of movement of funds between the UK and the USA meant that the rates offered to attract deposits within the UK had to be high to offset the competition from the USA.

Problems within the international financial system

8.7   A major influence here was the Third-World debt crisis that pushed up the risk premium and therefore the interest rate charged by financial institutions on international lending. The relatively severe world recessions of the early 1980s and early 1990s also served to increase the default risk associated with much commercial lending, leading once again to upward pressure on interest rates.

Increasing financial sophistication

8.8   It has been suggested that the lenders of funds within the private sector are now much more sensitive to the real interest rate as a consequence of their experience of the 1970s. Funds are no longer deposited at low or zero nominal interest rates to the extent that they were, and a greater readiness to search out and shift money to assets with higher interest rates has put upward pressure on rates.

Competition between financial institutions

8.9   The growth of competition between financial institutions (a notable example being that between banks and building societies) has also put upward and downward pressure on rates. At least until the recession at the beginning of the 1990s, the high level of demand for credit – especially within the housing market – allowed higher rates to be charged. Afterwards, competition in the mid 1990s caused interest rates to fall as a number of banks and building societies competed for market share in a stagnant market.

Long-term trend in interest rates

8.10 It has been argued that the *normal* pattern for interest rates is for real rates to be positive. On this basis, the negative real interest rates seen in the 1970s were a deviation from the norm that requires explaining, and the situation since the early 1980s should be seen as being the normal situation. The negative real rates of interest during the 1970s were probably the result of rapid monetary growth and slow adjustment of inflationary expectations. However, real interest rates were, on a historical basis, 'above trend' in the 1980s and early 1990s; these can, though, be attributed to the combination of the other seven influences identified here. It can be said that the high real rates of interest hurt over-borrowed companies and individuals during these periods.

Study Activities 9

1. Examine how inflation and monetary policy are believed to have influenced the level of interest rates in the UK in recent years. *(Paragraphs 8.3 and 8.4)*

2. How dependent is the UK on world interest rates? *(Paragraph 8.6)*

3. Compare and contrast the general effect on the level of interest rates of competition between banks and building societies in the late 1980s and in the mid 1990s. *(Paragraph 8.9)*

4. What was likely to have been the impact on interest rates of a number of large building societies converting to banks during the middle to late 1990s? *(Paragraph 8.9)*

5. Are real interest rates in the UK ever likely to become negative again? *(Paragraph 8.10)*

Summary

Now that you have completed this unit you should be able to:

- understand the general nature of interest rates;
- distinguish between nominal and real rates of interest;
- examine the basic theories concerning the determination of interest rates and their structures;
- outline the causes of changes in interest rates;
- calculate the yield to maturity of a bond;
- identify and draw yield curves, and explain the significance of their shapes and slopes;
- appreciate the factors which affect the yield spread between two bonds;
- understand why there are so many rates of interest;
- appreciate the relationship between domestic, international and eurocurrency interest rates.

Self-assessment questions

Short-answer questions

1. Real rates of interest can only be measured approximately even when nominal rates of interest are absolutely fixed. Why?

2. What is the relevance of money to the Classical theory of interest rates?

3. What is shown by a term structure of interest rates?

4. Why are there so many different rates of interest in a modern economy?

5. List the major characteristics of a borrowing and lending transaction relevant to the determination of its interest rate.

6. What factors will tend to speed up the response of a retail bank's lending rates to an increase in sterling money market rates?

7. List the three broad influences that tend to link one country's interest rates to those of other countries.

Multiple-choice questions

1. Indexation:

   (a) guarantees to the lender a minimum nominal return on funds lent

   (b) means that the borrower is uncertain of the nominal amount of interest to be paid until the time it is due for payment

   (c) removes all risk for the lender associated with lending

   (d) provides the borrower with a ceiling to the amount of interest which will have to be paid on a loan in nominal terms

   (e) spreads the risk associated with lending between all lenders equally.

2. Which of the following is most likely to cause nominal rates of interest to rise?

   (a) reduced levels of inflation and expected inflation

   (b) a slump in the domestic economy

   (c) a fall in the level of real interest rates required by lenders

   (d) a tightening of official monetary controls

   (e) a reduction in the general level of interest rates in overseas financial markets.

3. The real rate of interest:

   (a) will rise if the rate of inflation falls more quickly than the level of nominal interest rates

   (b) will fall if the rate of inflation rises more slowly than the level of nominal interest rates

(c) depends entirely upon the position of the authorities' monetary policy

(d) will tend to fall over time as the desired level of capital investment in the economy rises, other things being equal

(e) is only relevant to saving decisions in times of rapid inflation.

4. If there are general expectations that interest rates are to fall, yield curves for gilt-edged securities:

   (a) will always slope downward from left to right

   (b) will slope downward from left to right as long as the expectation effect outweighs the underlying risk and liquidity preference effects

   (c) will only slope downward from left to right when there is felt to be no risk attached to lending

   (d) will always slope upward from left to right because of the underlying risk and liquidity preference effects

   (e) will never slope upward from left to right.

5. Bank base rates:

   (a) will always rise when sterling money market rates rise

   (b) are the rates which banks charge on their loans (other than those linked directly to market rates)

   (c) form the starting point only for the calculation of interest rates charged to some borrowers

   (d) tend to differ quite significantly between banks due to the high degree of competition which now exists

   (e) set the upper limit to the rates charged by banks on mortgage loans.

6. Higher real rates of interest will tend to:

   (a) reduce the 'endowment' effect which retail banks experience

   (b) cause bank turnover to increase as it is much easier for them to attract deposits

   (c) cause banks to narrow their profit margins in order to remain competitive

   (d) have adverse effects on banks' profitability due to ensuing reduced demands for loans and increased provisions for bad debts

   (e) cause the monetary authorities to raise nominal rates of interest to counteract the associate threat from inflation.

7
Monetary Policy

Objectives

After studying this unit, you should be able to:

- state the objectives of monetary policy and relate monetary policy to the other types of economic policy;

- understand the need for intermediate targets, with stable relationships between them and the goals of economic policy, within the monetary control framework;

- describe in detail the instruments of monetary policy;

- appreciate the role of the Bank of England's Monetary Policy Committee in meeting the UK's inflation target;

- analyse the impact of monetary policy on financial intermediaries;

- assess the effectiveness of the UK's monetary policy since 1980;

- appreciate the differing goals and targets of monetary policy in the UK, the USA, Germany and the Euro Area.

1   Monetary policy in context

1.1   An emphasis on monetary policy is appropriate for two reasons:

- Since the beginning of the 1980s the UK authorities – along with governments and central banks in many other industrialised nations – have attached considerable importance to monetary policy within the overall framework of economic policy.

- The granting of independence to the Bank of England in respect of the implementation of monetary policy has highlighted the significance of monetary policy matters in general, and has raised questions on the political accountability for monetary control and the policy priorities of government.

1.2   It should be remembered that monetary policy constitutes only one possible element of an economic (strictly, macroeconomic) policy package. The emphasis placed upon monetary policy in recent years is not the historical norm. For much of the post-war period, macroeconomic policy packages tended to comprise a balance of alternative policies, and monetary policy was not seen as being of any particular importance.

Economic policy objectives

1.3   Although it may seem obvious, it is important to emphasise that the purpose of economic policy is to attain *economic policy objectives*. In addition, only if those objectives are clearly identified can the *design*, *implementation* and *evaluation* of economic policy take place. Conventionally, the four objectives of economic policy are held to be:

- A *high and stable level of employment*. This does, of course, have its equivalent in a low and stable level of *unemployment*. It does not, however, imply zero unemployment. A certain level of unemployment is appropriate for the efficient operation of a dynamic economy, since, for example, it will take people a period of time to switch between jobs, or to retrain for a new job, and so on.

- A *low and stable rate of inflation*, which is considered a necessary objective of economic policy, in order to try to avoid the costs associated with inflation. In particular, many economists (but by no means all) argue that low inflation is a necessary prerequisite for achieving sustainable economic growth.

- A *high rate of economic growth*, since economic growth provides for the increases over time in the living standards of the population. This rate of economic growth should be at least comparable to the rates experienced by similar nations.

- A *satisfactory balance of payments*, which is usually taken to mean an equilibrium, or a modest surplus, over the longer term. A long-term equilibrium on the current account of the balance of payments implies that a country is able to pay its way in international terms and to purchase imports, while a surplus would imply that its stock of overseas net assets is, in addition, increasing.

1.4   Whilst the above-listed objectives are generally regarded as the main objectives of economic policy, other objectives should not be overlooked. For example, a *satisfactory distribution of income and wealth* may be put forward as a fifth objective. This distribution of income and wealth can be held to refer to either *individuals* or *regions*; i.e. it may be argued that there should not be particularly rich and particularly poor regions in the country.

Conflicts between economic policy objectives

1.5   A serious problem surrounding the attainment of the four major economic policy objectives identified above is the existence of *conflicts* between those objectives. In other words, the attainment of any one objective is often at the expense of the attainment of one or more of the other objectives.

1.6   The major conflicts are between full employment and economic growth on the one hand, and inflation and balance of payments equilibrium on the other. In more detail, policies to raise the level of employment (and hence reduce unemployment) will generally involve raising the overall level of demand for goods and services within the economy (the level of 'aggregate demand'). This will encourage producers to produce more and perhaps to invest in new production facilities, and will generally lead to an improved rate of economic growth. However, policies that raise the level of aggregate demand will tend to *raise prices* (and hence be inconsistent with the low inflation objective). In addition a high level of aggregate demand will frequently spill over into a raised level of *imported* products (which has often been a particular problem for the UK) with the consequence that the *balance of payments worsens*.

1.7   A further illustration of the potential inconsistency between the two pairs of objectives can be seen when the aim is to control inflation and the balance of payments. A policy to achieve a low rate of inflation may be consistent with balance of payments equilibrium since it may involve a low demand for imported goods. However, as it may involve a generally low demand for goods and services, it may be *inconsistent* with low unemployment and high economic growth objectives.

1.8   In practice, much of the debate about how economic policy should be operated is ultimately concerned with how a *package* of policies may be put together. Ideally, the policy package should allow the attainment of all four objectives at once – or, at least, the attainment of two or three while maintaining the remaining one or two within 'acceptable' ranges. Invariably, however, the government is left with the need to make choices and to trade off one policy objective against another, in order to identify an appropriate balance between the objectives. Into this problem enters the additional consideration of the *time scale* involved. For example, most economists would agree that an increase in employment and economic growth could be achieved by means of pursuing expansionary policy. Monetarists, however, would maintain that this increase in employment and economic growth would be only *temporary*, and that the expansionary policies would lead to an increase in inflation in the longer term, concurrent with falls in employment and economic growth. Monetarists see low inflation as a prerequisite for longer-term economic growth and employment and therefore advocate policies to reduce inflation – which would generally involve policies aimed at producing an *economic contraction and reduction in employment and growth in the short term*. In this context, therefore, the importance is that not only does the government have to decide on the trade-off between different objectives, it has also to decide over what *time period* it wishes to pursue those objectives.

1.9   Since the beginning of the 1980s, governments of many industrialised countries have allocated priority to containing inflation, with economic growth being given second priority. Of course, conflict can occur in international relations when governments of important countries have different priorities in respect of economic policy objectives.

Study Activities 1

1. What are the four objectives normally listed in respect of a government's economic policy? *(Paragraph 1.3)*

2. Give some examples of the ways in which economic policy objectives may conflict. *(Paragraphs 1.6 and 1.7)*

3. Why is it generally accepted that governments require a 'package' of economic policies? *(Paragraph 1.8)*

4. Why is it important for a government to be clear over the time period for which a policy objective is to be pursued? *(Paragraph 1.8)*

2   Forms of economic policy

2.1   Bearing in mind our concentration on macroeconomic policy, the five major forms of economic policy are:

- Monetary policy;

- Fiscal policy;

- Exchange rate policy;

- Prices and incomes policy; and

- National debt management policy.

This section will look briefly at what each of these forms of economic policy involves. In doing so, it must be remembered that any one policy will normally form part of a policy *package*, and that the way in which that policy is employed will be dependent upon the other components of that package.

Monetary policy

2.2   Monetary policy relates to the control of some measure (or measures) of the money supply and/or the level and structure of interest rates. The importance attached to monetary policy within a government's policy package will depend not only upon its view of the operation of the economy (monetarist/Keynesian) but also upon the decision it has reached regarding the priority given to different objectives. For example, if the attainment of low inflation is seen as being the major objective and the government is of a monetarist persuasion, considerable importance will be attached to monetary policy. If, on the other hand, inflation is the major objective but the government is of a Keynesian persuasion, different policies such as a prices and incomes policy or fiscal policy are likely to be emphasised, with monetary policy being allocated a supporting role.

Fiscal policy

2.3   Fiscal policy is concerned with decisions regarding the level and structure of government expenditure and taxation. Given the importance of the levels of government expenditure and taxation in determining the size of the Public Sector Borrowing Requirement (PSBR) or the Public Sector Debt Repayment (PSDR), fiscal policy therefore also involves decisions regarding the size of the PSBR/PSDR.

2.4   As with monetary policy, the importance of fiscal policy within an economic policy package is dependent upon the prioritisation of objectives and of the view taken of the operation of the economy. Fiscal policy has traditionally been regarded as having its impact through its influence on the level of aggregate demand within the economy.

● An *expansionary* fiscal policy would involve increasing government expenditure relative to taxation in order to boost the level of spending within the economy and thereby bringing more people into employment and enhancing economic growth.

● Alternatively, a *contractionary* fiscal policy would involve raising taxation relative to government expenditure, with the purpose of reducing aggregate demand and lowering inflation and the demand for imports – though with the possible side-effects of lowering employment and growth.

Exchange rate policy

2.5   Exchange rate policy involves the targeting of a particular value of the exchange rate. While the exchange rate relative to any one currency may carry particular weight (for example US$, Euro), the value of the currency relative to the country's major trading partners in general is more likely to be the objective. A major purpose of exchange rate policy is to influence the flows within the balance of payments, and may be used by some countries in conjunction with other measures such as exchange controls, import tariffs and quotas. However, the latter three practices are restricted or forbidden under a number of trade agreements (such as those implemented by the EU and the World Trade Organisation), so their use is generally confined to smaller countries with particularly difficult economic problems to address.

Prices and incomes policy

2.6   A prices and incomes policy is intended to influence the rate of inflation by means of either statutory or voluntary restrictions upon increases in wages, dividends and/or prices. The range of prices and incomes over which such a policy may prevail, and the degree of statutory control involved, is subject to considerable variation. Since 1979 the UK government has not used prices and incomes policies, although extensive use was made of them, in various formats, during the 1960s and 1970s.

National Debt management policy

2.7 *National debt management policy* is concerned with the manipulation of the outstanding stock of government debt instruments held by the domestic private sector with the objective of influencing the level and structure of interest rates and/or the availability of reserve assets to the banking system. Given that fiscal policy involves decisions regarding the issue of new government securities and that monetary policy has as one of its concerns the level of interest rates, it is inevitable that national debt management policy is closely related to both fiscal policy and monetary policy.

2.8 From this brief discussion of the different forms of economic policy, it should be clear why a *package* of economic policies will be required. Any one particular policy may have a beneficial impact upon one – or perhaps more than one – of the economic policy objectives. However, it may also often have a *detrimental* impact on one or more of the other objectives, and hence *additional* economic policies may be required in order to offset those detrimental impacts. By juggling the form and severity of the different economic policies – and taking into account the expected future trends within the economy – a package of policies may be put together to achieve the objectives identified.

2.9 By way of illustration, consider an example where the economy has high unemployment, moderate inflation and an approximate equilibrium on the balance of payments. In order to cure the high unemployment, an expansionary fiscal policy may be advocated. Such a policy may, however, initiate a rise in inflation and an increased volume of imports giving rise to a balance of payments deficit. Accordingly, a prices and incomes policy may be instituted in order to prevent inflation rising, along with an exchange rate policy to maintain a low exchange rate to deter imports and maintain the competitiveness of exports.

2.10 It is important to appreciate that, in the context of the formation of a package of economic policy measures, the government *has* to make a decision about the position of most components of such a package. While the decision regarding a prices and incomes policy is (at least initially) an either/or decision, this does not apply, for example, to fiscal policy; the government is forced to take decisions about expenditure and taxation, and hence a stance on fiscal policy is automatic. Similar considerations apply to monetary policy and to exchange rate policy; even a decision to 'do nothing' to interest rates and the exchange rate is a conscious decision with corresponding policy implications.

Study Activities 2

1. What determines the importance of monetary policy in the government's economic policy package? *(Paragraph 2.2)*

2. What does fiscal policy involve? *(Paragraph 2.3)*

3. What are prices and incomes policies? *(Paragraph 2.6)*

4. In what ways is debt management policy closely related to monetary and fiscal policies? *(Paragraph 2.7)*

5. Explain how a package on economic policies may be formulated to deal with a set of economic policy objectives. *(Paragraphs 2.8 and 2.9)*

3 Objectives, targets and instruments

3.1 We have, so far, been assuming that a particular economic policy – say, monetary policy – will have a direct impact upon one of the objectives of economic policy, such as inflation. This is not, in practice, the case. In reality, there will be a *chain* that links policies to objectives, with policies having their impact through instruments and intermediate targets.

- *Economic policies* are the group of five policies, such as monetary policy and fiscal policy, identified in paragraph 2.1. Each of the policies may have a number of associated instruments, intermediate targets and policy objectives.

- *Instruments* are those variables over which the authorities have some control, and through which they hope to influence the intermediate targets.

- *Intermediate targets* are, in turn, those variables through which the authorities attempt to achieve their objectives.

- *Objectives* are the ultimate goals of economic policy.

The relationship between policies, instruments, intermediate targets and objectives may perhaps best be illustrated by means of some examples.

3.2 Taking *monetary policy* as an example – open-market operations, which involve official sales and purchases of government debt, are one of the associated *instruments*. Open-market operations may be regarded as an instrument since they constitute a variable over which the authorities have some control. They have no particular purpose of their own, however; rather, they may be used to facilitate the attainment of one or more *intermediate targets*, which in this case would constitute the level of short-term interest rates and the rate of growth of a measure of the money supply. Those intermediate targets, rather than constituting ends in themselves, are the variables through which the authorities attempt to achieve the *objective*, which in this case could be the rate of inflation.

3.3 As another example consider *fiscal policy* as the economic policy. The *instrument* might be income tax rates, with the *intermediate targets* being the level of disposable income (since a rise in tax rates reduces disposable income) and the level of aggregate demand (since a lowering of disposable income will lower aggregate demand). The ultimate *objective* may be to attain a satisfactory balance of payments through a lowering of imports. Alternatively, with fiscal policy remaining as the economic policy, the *instrument* might be government expenditure plans; the *intermediate targets* the *actual* level of government expenditure and the level of aggregate demand; and the *ultimate objective* the level of employment.

3.4   The particular policy–instrument–intermediate target–objective chain will depend upon the way in which policy is perceived to work in practice. Consequently, a range of intermediate targets would be consistent with a particular instrument of economic policy according to the perception of the operation of economic policy taken.

3.5   In conclusion, we stress that the chain of causation is instrument → intermediate target → objective. It is also vital that the relationship between the intermediate target and the objective is stable and predictable. In the case of monetary aggregates, such as M0 and M4, this is not the case (see Section 7). The ratio between money supply and output does vary over time.

4   Problems in the implementation of economic policy

4.1   Even when a chain linking economic policy to instrument, intermediate targets and ultimate objective has been identified, there will frequently be additional complications in the implementation of that economic policy. Some of the major ones are discussed below.

4.2   It may be the case that the *intermediate target may not be effectively controlled by the instrument chosen*. For example, one of the problems associated with ceilings on bank lending when used as an instrument of monetary policy is that the money markets could bypass this restriction by means of various forms of lending (so-called disintermediation). Therefore, the level of purchasing power within the economy may not be curtailed as effectively as might have been intended.

4.3   The *intermediate target variables may be difficult to define*. For example, open-market operations may be the instrument used to control the rate of growth of the money supply but there are many different measures of the money supply which do not grow at identical rates, and the choice of measure is problematic.

4.4   The *relationship between an instrument and a target variable may be subject to change over time*. For example, the reaction of the private sector to calls for restraint in wage demands may well differ from one period of prices and incomes policy to another. Experience of a prices and incomes policy may cause people to ignore calls for 'voluntary restraint' or to seek out more quickly alternative means of receiving increases in wages. As we noted in paragraph 3.5, there is no long-term stable relationship between the monetary aggregates and output.

4.5   The *wrong instrument to achieve a particular variable may be chosen*. The instrument that is appropriate at one time may well *not* be the instrument appropriate at another. For example, if an increase in investment expenditures is the intermediate target, reducing interest rates will not boost investment if there is a large surplus of productive capacity at that time. Instead, an increase in the level of aggregate demand would first be required.

4.6   The *links between an intermediate target and the final objective may not be known with precision*. Of particular note has been the long-running debate regarding the relative importance of aggregate demand on the one hand and the money supply on the other in the determination of the rate of inflation. Clearly, the operation of economic policy will inevitably be a hit-and-miss affair unless such links are reasonably well established.

4.7   *Timing considerations may be important*. Changing the value of an instrument will not have an *immediate* impact on the policy objective, even if the links in the policy chain are well established. For example, the decision to raise government expenditure takes some time to put into effect, since money cannot be spent immediately (hospitals, for example, take time to design and build). When government expenditure does rise, it will take some time to have its full impact on aggregate demand; and there will be a further lag before employers recruit the labour to cope with that raised aggregate demand. Hence it may take a considerable time before the unemployment rate falls.

4.8   A *government has to anticipate the way the economy is heading*, for which purpose forecasting is crucial. However, remember that the collection of statistics about the state of the economy occurs only after a time lag, and hence policy-makers also have to estimate where the economy *currently is*. In addition, they have to forecast where unemployment will be, on present policies, at some point in the future in order to implement policies *now* to move that level of unemployment towards its target level. If the estimate of the time lags is wrong (and there is evidence that many time lags are *variable*), such policies may end up doing more harm than good by moving the economy *further away* from the intended position.

4.9   It is for this reason that managing economic policy has been compared to driving a car that only has a rear window and where the accelerator and brake pedals only operate with a variable time lag. It is like a car with only a rear window because we only know with accuracy where the economy *has been*, not where it is and still less where it is going. It is like a car where the brake and accelerator pedals only operate with a variable lag since any expansionary or contractionary policies take a variable amount of time to impact on the economy. If driving such a car would prove difficult, then insofar as the comparison is valid, so too is the management of economic policy!

4.10 These problems of implementation – particularly that associated with time lags – has led some economists to put forward the view that the government should not attempt discretionary economic policies, since there is a very real danger that more harm than good will be done. Instead, they advocate that economic policy should be guided by policy 'rules', with the intention of creating a stable background against which free market forces can operate.

5 The interrelationship of monetary and fiscal policy

5.1 So far we have assumed that the various instruments of economic policy will be independent of each other, whereas in practice this will not always be so. The major area where one set of instruments will be dependent upon another set lies in the link between monetary and fiscal policy. Consider the following example.

5.2 Suppose that the government wishes to lower the level of unemployment and that it seeks to do this by raising government expenditure and/or lowering taxation. Such a policy is clearly an act of fiscal policy, intended to have its effect by altering the level of aggregate demand. *But* raising government expenditure and/or lowering taxation will *also* either raise the PSBR or lower the PSDR, which will have *monetary* implications. It *may* be that these monetary implications fit what the government had planned for monetary policy anyway, but it is more likely that they will not. The essential point, however, is that monetary and fiscal policy are not independent, and policy-makers will have to ensure that the stance they take with regard to the one is consistent with that taken for the other.

Study Activities 3

1. Define policy instruments, intermediate targets and objectives.   *(Paragraph 3.1)*

2. Give an example from either monetary policy or fiscal policy of a chain of instrument, target and objective.   *(Paragraphs 3.2 and 3.3)*

3. List the main types of problems which governments may face in the implementation of their economic policies.   *(Paragraphs 4.2–4.9)*

4. Why do some economists argue that governments should not tinker with the operation of the economy, but rather should set policy 'rules'?   *(Paragraph 4.10)*

5. Give an example of how monetary and fiscal policy may be interrelated.
      (Paragraph 5.2)

6 The basics of monetary policy

6.1 The money supply within the economy is the outcome of a wide array of different forces. These forces can, in broad terms, be split into two: the 'free market' forces and the influence of the monetary authorities. The 'free market' forces would generate a specific quantity of money on their own account. This would be determined by factors such as the prudential reserve ratios operated by banks, the propensity of the general public to hold cash relative to bank money, the demand from the private sector for loans and so on. The actions of the authorities (that is, in the UK, the Treasury and particularly the Bank of England) with regard to monetary controls are, in effect, *in addition to* these free market forces. The primary reason for such intervention is that the money supply and/or the level and structure of interest rates implied by the free market forces are not consistent with the economic policy objectives.

6.2 Monetary policy is concerned with the attempts of the authorities to influence some measure (or measures) of the money supply or the level and/or structure of interest rates. In a free market financial system, at any one point in time the authorities are only able to control *either* the money supply *or* the rate of interest; what they are unable to do is to control both simultaneously. The reason for this is straightforward. The interest rate is the *price* of borrowed money and seeking to control the interest rate therefore implies seeking to control the price of money. The money supply is the quantity of money potentially available for lending. Therefore control of both the interest rate and the money supply implies controlling both price and quantity of borrowed funds simultaneously, which is not feasible in a free market financial system.

6.3 The situation may be illustrated in terms of a supply and demand diagram relating to the money market (Fig. 7.1). It is assumed that the authorities are, to some extent at least, able to control the supply curve. If they choose to fix the quantity of money (say at M^*) then they have to accept whatever interest rate results from the interaction of that supply with the private sector demand for money. In this case the interest rate generated is i^*. From the alternative viewpoint, if the authorities decide to fix the interest rate at i^*, then they have to adjust the money supply in order to maintain that interest rate (in the figure that is M^*). If the demand for money should increase (and the curve shift to the right) the authorities will have to *expand* the money supply in order to retain the interest rate of i^*.

6.4 The *caveat* to the authorities' inability to control the interest rate and the money supply simultaneously is that they may be able to do so in the short term through the use of very restrictive monetary controls. For example, the authorities might institute very tight controls, including specific requirements on banks and building societies to limit the extent of credit creation, and thus fix the money supply within narrow limits. *On top of* those controls limits could be imposed (by means of directives) on the interest rate that could be charged on loans by banks and

Figure 7.1 Relationship between interest rate and quantity of money

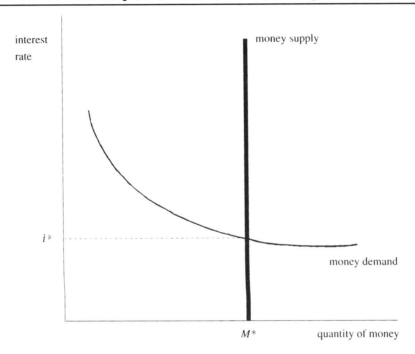

building societies. If that interest rate was below the market clearing rate, these institutions would have to initiate some form of rationing procedure – which might, in practice, be solved for them as a result of further directives from the authorities stipulating the preference to be given to particular categories of borrowers. Clearly, the authorities will have achieved control of both the interest rate and the money supply.

6.5   However, it should be recognised that the authorities will have achieved control of both the money supply and interest rates by means of *suspending* the operation of free market adjustments. In particular, the interest rate would not be allowed to adjust in response to market forces within the financial system. Within any market that is controlled in this way there will be suppliers (the potential lenders of funds) and those with a demand for the product or service (potential borrowers) whose needs are not being satisfied, and this will lead to transactions taking place *outside* the regulated market.

6.6   What is likely to happen here is that there will be a process of *disintermediation* as prospective borrowers find lenders of funds outside the controlled institutions. The borrowers involved in this disintermediation process will in all likelihood be prepared to pay higher interest rates than those determined by the authorities. Lenders will also be likely to receive more than the banks and building societies would be permitted to pay. Hence, there is a strong commercial incentive for such disintermediation activity to take place. The rise of the inter-company market in the late 1960s provides a classic example of disintermediation resulting from restrictive bank lending controls.

6.7 The result is that the volume of borrowing and lending within the economy will continue to rise, which then calls into question the appropriateness of the measure of the money supply being controlled. With an increasing proportion of borrowing and lending activity taking place *outside* that measure, it is likely to become inappropriate, for policy purposes, to continue to seek to control it. Equally, with the interest rates being paid and received on this disintermediation activity being *higher* than the officially determined rate, that rate will become increasingly meaningless. Thus, while the authorities are able to control both the interest rate and the money supply simultaneously in the short term, the bypassing of the required restrictive controls means that it will be impossible for them to do this in any meaningful sense in the longer term.

7 The intermediate targets of monetary policy

7.1 Traditionally, the two intermediate targets of monetary policy have been regarded as the:

- Rate of growth of the money supply; and

- Level and/or structure of interest rates.

Rate of growth of the money supply

7.2 This intermediate target was widely employed during the 1980s in the UK because of its perceived link with the rate of inflation. The immediate problem raised by its use is, however, in identifying the measure of the money supply to be utilised. Also, there is the fear that targeting any particular measure, even if the target is achieved, is likely to lead to distortions with the effect that other measures of the money supply grow at different rates than they would otherwise, and affect the real economy accordingly.

7.3 A further problem is that the ratios of the main money supply measures to Gross Domestic Product (GDP) have varied over time. For example, M0 grew less rapidly than GDP, at a stable rate until recently, largely as a result of the growth of 'the banking habit'. The market for banking services is saturated at present, and this could be the prime reason for the new stability in the ratio. Other suggested causes are low interest rates and the rise of the 'informal economy' with its preference for cash.

7.4 The ratio of M4 to GDP shows great swings, largely as a result of changes in bank and building society lending policies. In turn, these depend on the stance of monetary policy, e.g. tight in the early 1990s, resulting in a stabilisation of the ratio.

Level and/or structure of interest rates

7.5   Although less widely employed than the money supply during most of the 1980s, interest rates have in the past been important intermediate targets. In 1989, the Chancellor used to repeat 'interest rates will stay as high as is required for as long as is required to bring down the rate of inflation'. The essential rationale for employing interest rates as a target is that interest-sensitive expenditure (for example investment expenditure and credit-based consumer expenditure) will be altered as a consequence of changes in interest rates initiated by the authorities. In addition, however, there may be important supplementary rationales:

●   Since international currency flows are influenced by interest rates, they will have an impact on the balance of payments.

●   Interest rates may be used as a means of attaining other intermediate targets, most notably the rate of growth of the money supply. By raising interest rates the authorities may be able to reduce the demand for bank and building society credit and hence reduce the rate of growth of the money supply.

Additional intermediate targets

7.6   While control of the money supply and of interest rates are the two major intermediate targets of monetary policy, there may from time to time be additional intermediate targets. These include:

●   Exchange rates;

●   Projected inflation rates;

●   Credit creation by banks and building societies;

●   Nominal domestic expenditure (or nominal national income).

Exchange rates

7.7   Exchange rates may constitute an intermediate target, since by affecting the relative prices of imports and exports, trade flows will be influenced. Altered trade flows will obviously have an impact on the attainment of the balance of payments objective, but they will also impact upon the level of domestic output and hence employment, and upon the rate of inflation.

Projected inflation rates

7.8   When the actual inflation rate is the policy objective, it may be appropriate to use some measure of projected inflation rates in future periods as the intermediate target. The precise measure to be used is problematic, as is the time horizon over which the measure is to be targeted. However, market expectations of inflation are likely to provide a reasonable indication of inflationary pressures within the economy, and hence should give broad direction to the adjustment of policy.

Credit creation by banks and building societies.

7.9 Credit creation by banks and building societies may be an intermediate target for the straightforward reason that it constitutes an important element of any growth in the money supply, and may be, in this respect, one of a chain of intermediate targets. However, such credit creation may also constitute an intermediate target of monetary policy because of a perceived direct link between credit provided by banks and building societies on the one hand and private sector expenditures on the other. The authorities may seek to influence such expenditures, and hence the overall level of aggregate demand, through some form of control on bank and building society credit creation.

Nominal domestic expenditure (or nominal national income)

7.10 The primary rationale for having the nominal level of domestic expenditure as an intermediate target is that this variable would be expected to be a determinant of the rate of inflation, and the levels of output and employment. Monetary policy would then be designed so as to achieve a particular growth rate of nominal domestic expenditure, taking into account the prevailing rate of inflation. The advantage of using this variable as an intermediate target is its close relationship to the ultimate objectives of inflation and employment, but there is the corresponding disadvantage in that the links between the instruments of monetary policy and this intermediate target are rather weak.

Choice of intermediate target

7.11 The main influence on the choice of intermediate target will be the policy-makers' perception of the economic determinants of the ultimate policy objectives. Hence they will be concerned with the reliability of the relationships between the ultimate objectives and the intermediate targets used to attain them. If the policy-makers hold monetarist views, we would expect to see an emphasis on control of the money supply (in view of the importance placed on money as the major determinant of inflation, particularly in the longer term). Also they would pay attention to the growth of nominal domestic expenditure because of difficulties with the appropriate measurement of the money supply. Policy-makers of a more Keynesian/demand management persuasion might be expected to pay more attention to the level and structure of interest rates, with correspondingly less attention to the money supply.

7.12 There has been considerable debate as to whether policy targets should be publicised in advance. This is particularly so in respect of the use of the money supply as an intermediate target.

7.13 The major argument *in favour* of such announcements is that, if the private sector believes that the authorities are intent on achieving their intermediate target, the *expectations* of inflation or other policy variable will be favourably affected.

For example, if expectations of inflation are reduced, then wage settlements in particular are likely to be pushed downward, bringing about a lowering of inflation. Thus, inflation will have been lowered quickly and relatively painlessly through the lowering of expectations.

7.14   There are disadvantages however.

- The non-achievement of the intermediate target may lead to an element of political embarrassment and give rise to a suspicion and disbelief about *future* announcements, so that their beneficial impact on the lowering of expectations is reduced.

- The announcement of intermediate targets may lock the authorities into a particular path for economic policy and reduce their flexibility to respond to developments – though it has to be recognised that this is also seen as an *advantage* since it reduces the ability of the authorities to initiate *destabilising* economic policy.

- It has been argued that as soon as any particular variable is targeted publicly it starts to react in an unpredictable fashion because the private sector makes use of alternative channels to avoid the restrictions implied by the targeting of the one variable.

Study Activities 4

1. Except in the short term, the authorities are able to control either the growth of the money supply or interest rates, but not both. Why?   *(Paragraph 6.3)*

2. What is the relevance of disintermediation to the authorities' attempts to control both the money supply and interest rates?   *(Paragraphs 6.6 and 6.7)*

3. Why might the rate of interest be used as an intermediate target of monetary policy?   *(Paragraph 7.5)*

4. In addition to the growth of the money supply and the level/structure of interest rates, what other variables might be set as intermediate targets of monetary policy?   *(Paragraph 7.6)*

5. What is likely to determine the choice of intermediate target variable for monetary policy?   *(Paragraph 7.11)*

6. List the advantages and disadvantages of announcing publicly the intermediate target variable for economic policy.   *(Paragraphs 7.13 and 7.14)*

8   Methods of monetary control

8.1   Monetary policy involves the control of some measure (or measures) of the money supply and/or the level and structure of interest rates in order to attain a particular policy objective. Also, unless the authorities are prepared to use directives to control interest rates, interest rates are influenced by means of controlling at least some element of the money supply. The authorities therefore have the choice of controlling the money supply as an end in itself, because of the link with inflation, or manipulating the money supply in order to influence interest rates and hence aggregate demand, output, employment and so on. In any event, it is clear that monetary policy is crucially dependent upon controlling the money supply or some element thereof.

The targets of monetary control

8.2   The components of the money supply that will be the targets of monetary policy will be dependent upon the particular measure of the money supply that is selected. Nevertheless, there are essentially two elements to any widely accepted measure of the money supply:

- Notes and coin;

- Bank and building society deposits.

8.3   Although notes and coin constitute only a small element of the money supply in the UK, it is a very important element because it forms a vital part of the reserve base that is the prerequisite for the credit creation process by banks and building societies. Control of the cash base of the financial system may therefore be a desirable target of the authorities since it constitutes a means of controlling the broader money supply measures. The quantity of notes and coin within the financial system may be controlled within quite fine limits by the authorities. However, their willingness to do so will be countered by the possibility of a loss of confidence in the stability of the financial system if any decline in the availability of cash is too sharp. In practice, the total of notes and coin is loosely controlled, being largely demand determined by the growth of output (nominal GDP).

8.4   For the most part, however, monetary control is targeted towards deposits with banks and building societies, as these deposits constitute a large proportion of most measures of the money supply. The control here can take one of two forms:

- It can be directed towards limiting the *supply* side – by limiting the ability of banks and building societies to supply credit; *or*

- It can be directed towards the *demand* side – by limiting the willingness of the non-bank, non-building society private sector to borrow funds.

8.5   The *instruments* used to limit either the demand or supply of credit are considered below, but note that they are likely to influence the holdings of other liquid assets in addition to bank and building society deposits.

Monetary control instruments

8.6   It is useful to place the instruments through which monetary control is achieved into three groups:

- Instruments of market intervention;

- Instruments of portfolio constraint;

- Longer-term control mechanisms.

Instruments of market intervention

8.7   As the title suggests, the instruments of market intervention are designed to achieve the intermediate targets of monetary policy by means of the authorities intervening in the operation of the money markets. Within the UK financial system, this involves the setting of the *official repo (discount) rate* and the use of *open-market operations*.

8.8   *The repo (discount) rate* is the rate at which the Bank of England is prepared to engage in repo transactions with the private sector or to make outright purchases of bills in cases where there is a shortage of liquidity within the financial system. The Bank of England is able to engineer a shortage of liquidity in order to force the market to raise funds from it at its repo (discount) rate. This action then has a knock-on effect throughout the whole structure of interest rates within the economy since the repo (discount) rate is representative of the marginal cost of funds to the banking system as a whole.

8.9   *Bank of England open-market operations* involve the buying and selling of securities and the use of repo agreements. The aim is to influence interest rates on instruments with up to 14 days to maturity, and hence, through the money market structure, short-term rates of interest in general. The level of short-term interest rates is felt to have an important influence on the demand for loans, and hence on the growth of credit creation within the economy. Open-market operations may also affect the reserve bases of banks and building societies, and hence the ability of those institutions to lend. Subject to meeting the overriding monetary policy requirements, the Bank's operations are intended to help the banking system manage its liquidity effectively.

8.10   One of the advantages of changes in the repo (discount) rate and the use of open-market operations over other methods of monetary control is that they impinge upon financial institutions in general rather than on banking institutions in particular. While the initial impact is centred upon the Bank of England's counter-parties in the repo and discount markets, the effects will quickly filter through to affect all institutions through the changed interest rates prevailing in the markets.

Instruments of portfolio constraint

8.11   Instruments of portfolio constraint refer to those controls that may be imposed by the authorities on the portfolio structure of financial institutions, with the purpose of influencing either the volume and/or the type of lending and hence credit creation. In contrast to the market intervention instruments discussed above, the problem is that these instruments of portfolio constraint tend to have a narrow and therefore distorting impact. Although in principle they could be applied to a wide range of financial institutions, in the past in the UK they have been applied only to banking institutions. The result of this is that the banks have, in effect, been discriminated against. It should also be noted that disintermediation has tended to occur as those institutions not subject to the controls have taken over unfulfilled opportunities. As a consequence, less use has been made of these instruments in recent years. Nevertheless, the instruments are potentially available for use, with the major components being:

- Reserve requirements;
- Special deposits;
- Supplementary special deposits;
- 'Moral suasion'; and
- Direct controls.

8.12   *Reserve requirements.* Banks and building societies need to hold a base of reserve assets for prudential purposes. If and when a bank or building society falls to its minimum desired reserve asset ratio it will have to turn away any incoming demands for loans or else seek to acquire additional reserve assets from which to expand its lending. The result in either case will generally be a rise in interest rates that will serve to reduce the demand for loans. The purpose of any imposed reserve requirements is, in effect, to duplicate this process. If the authorities impose a reserve requirement in excess of the desired reserve ratio (or else reduce the availability of reserve assets) the consequence will be that the institutions involved will have to curtail their lending and/or acquire additional reserve assets. This will result in higher interest rates and a reduced demand for loans, which, in turn, will curb the rate of growth of the money supply.

8.13   *Special deposits.* Special deposits are deposits that the Bank of England may require certain banking institutions to deposit with it. These deposits, equal to a specified proportion of certain elements of their deposit liabilities, are then 'frozen' at the Bank of England and may not be used as part of the reserve asset base for lending purposes. While they are particularly discriminatory as regards the institutions to which they apply, they do have a very rapid impact upon the ability of these institutions to create credit and are useful for drawing off any excess reserve assets within the system. At present, they are not used.

8.14   *Supplementary special deposits.* Supplementary special deposits are additional deposits that banking institutions had to make at the Bank of England if and when a category of their deposit liabilities exceeded an upper limit set by the Bank of England. This mechanism, referred to as the 'corset', was operated on a periodic basis by the Bank of England between 1973 and 1980 and was phrased in terms of a *growth rate* for certain interest-bearing eligible liabilities. Institutions exceeding the specified growth rate of these liabilities were required to make supplementary special deposits with the Bank of England on a scale dependent upon the extent of the overshoot. The penalty involved was not only that, like ordinary special deposits, they could not be used as part of the reserve asset base when required but also that (unlike ordinary special deposits) they attracted no interest payment.

8.15   The *advantages* of this supplementary special deposit mechanism are that it can be adjusted quickly in the light of developments and the requirements of monetary policy and that it allows very direct control over a major element of the money supply. The corresponding *disadvantage* is that it constitutes a distortion of the banking mechanism and hence is once again liable to lead to disintermediation.

8.16   'Moral suasion'. This refers to the range of informal requests and pressure that the Bank of England may exert over banking institutions. The extent to which this is a real power of the Bank relative to direct controls is open to question, since much of the pressure that the Bank would exert would involve the institutions taking actions that were not in their commercial interest. However, the position and potential power of the Bank of England probably provides it with some power with regard to 'moral suasion' which may perhaps be utilised most effectively in the context of establishing lending priorities rather than absolute levels.

8.17   *Direct controls*. Direct controls involve the Bank of England in issuing directives in order to attain particular intermediate targets. Thus, for example, the Bank of England might impose controls on interest rates payable upon deposits, impose limits on the volume of credit creation or direct banks to prioritise lending according to type of customer. Although these direct controls have the benefits of speed of implementation and precision, they are discriminating towards the institutions involved and are likely to lead to disintermediation as both potential borrowers and potential lenders seek to pursue their best interests. Their use, therefore, is perhaps best reserved for short-term requirements, not least since their effectiveness will decline the longer they are applied.

Reasons for the decline of portfolio constraints

8.18   Since 1980, there have been few portfolio constraints in use for monetary policy purposes. The reasons have been summarised from time to time in official speeches and papers and are as follows:

● Prior to 1980, banks and building societies operated in separate markets in the personal sector and did not compete on product range. That has now changed, so that *constraints on banks would have to be replicated not only on building societies but also on the remaining specialised mortgage lenders*. Also, although the Bank of England keeps accounts for some building societies, the majority of building societies do not have such accounts.

- *Disintermediation*, largely by companies, is a 'knee-jerk' reaction to portfolio constraints and this became conspicuous in the late 1970s. 'Interest rates reach those parts of the economy which portfolio constraints don't reach' is one description of why credit is controlled by price rather than quantity.

- Throughout the 1950s, 1960s and 1970s, when portfolio constraints were used by both major political parties when in government, the UK maintained a system of *exchange control*. This restriction on the movement of funds to and from abroad prevented borrowers from seeking finance from overseas when UK monetary policy was restrictive. Moreover, most European countries had similar restrictions preventing their banks and investors from moving funds outside their countries. These exchange controls had the effect of supporting the portfolio constraints but they now no longer exist, with the result that UK borrowers can ask banks overseas for loans in sterling.

- Portfolio constraints are regarded as *inimical to competition* because they place ceilings – of one kind or another – on the growth of banks and other deposit-taking intermediaries.

Longer-term control mechanisms

8.19 A major influence on the longer-term growth of the money supply is the size of the public sector's borrowing requirement (PSBR). A *reduction in the size of the PSBR* through altering levels of taxation and/or government expenditure will have a direct influence by reducing the demand for borrowed funds within the economy and will therefore serve to lower interest rates relative to what they otherwise would have been.

8.20 The *financing method* of any PSBR is also important because any financing through the sale of short-term government debt instruments will alter the availability of potential reserve assets to the banking system. In addition, the larger the proportion of any PSBR that is financed by sales of gilt-edged securities and National Savings instruments to the non-bank, non-building society private sector, the smaller the impact upon the money supply.

8.21 A policy of *funding* the national debt in order to reduce the availability of liquid assets to the banking system may also assist in the control of the money supply in the longer term. The use of the surplus funds arising from the existence of a PSDR will also have an impact on the money supply, since a PSDR results in a withdrawal of funds from the non-bank non-building society private sector, unless those funds are used to repay debt held by that sector. In addition, of course, the greater the PSDR the greater the scope for reducing money supply growth. On the *demand* side, it is possible that the use of taxation penalties or other disincentives to borrowing may serve to slow down any increase in the demand for credit and hence to slow the growth of the money supply.

The effectiveness of monetary controls

8.22   We have concentrated on what monetary controls can achieve in principle. The practice is often far removed from the principle, however, and in countries where there have been strenuous attempts to use monetary policy (emphasising the control of money supply growth rather than the control of interest rates) the success in attaining the money supply growth targets has been generally modest.

8.23   The reason for the limited ability to reach money supply growth targets is essentially twofold.

●   The instruments of monetary control have proved to be inadequate to achieve the desired precision of control over money supply growth.

●   There exists only a limited understanding of how the participants within the financial system will react to changes in the values of the instruments and targets used to implement monetary policy.

Taken together it is clear that monetary policy will remain a difficult policy to use for the attainment of the ultimate policy objectives.

8.24   In addition, even when money supply and interest rate variables can be controlled, this will only have the desired effects on economic policy objectives where the economic behaviour of individuals and organisations within the private sector is influenced in a consistent manner by the relevant intermediate target variables.

Study Activities 5

1. Why might it be thought desirable for the authorities to control the cash base of the financial system?   *(Paragraph 8.3)*

2. Why, for the most part, are monetary controls targeted towards bank and building society deposits?   *(Paragraph 8.4)*

3. What is the nature of the impact of instruments of market intervention in respect of monetary control?   *(Paragraphs 8.7–8.10)*

4. List the instruments of portfolio constraint in respect of monetary control.   *(Paragraph 8.11)*

5. Why do instruments of portfolio constraint tend to distort the operation of the financial system?   *(Paragraph 8.18)*

6. List the ways in which the authorities might seek to influence money supply growth in the longer term.   *(Paragraph 8.19–8.21)*

7. What are the basic reasons for monetary authorities being unable to achieve money supply growth targets?   *(Paragraph 8.23)*

8. Even when monetary target variables can be controlled precisely, the effect on policy objectives may be disappointing. Why?   *(Paragraph 8.24)*

9   The operation of monetary controls in the UK

9.1   The operation of monetary controls in the UK has seen considerable change over time, partly as a consequence of the increased importance attached to monetary policy in recent years but also as a consequence of developments within the financial system. Up to 1980 the emphasis was upon the use of portfolio constraints for the purposes of monetary control. The instruments used included special deposits, supplementary special deposits and various direct controls on both lending and interest rates. As we have seen, the problem with such portfolio constraints is that they tend to distort financial activities and lead to disintermediation. In addition, in the UK, they appear not to have worked very well.

9.2   The introduction of new monetary control provisions in August 1981 resulted in a switch of emphasis towards market intervention, combined with measures to ensure longer-term control of the money supply. The key element of this market intervention has been the manipulation of short-term interest rates, achieved through the use of open-market operations and use of the Bank of England's repo (discount) rate. One result of this policy, at least until the mid-1990s, was the prevalence of high *real* interest rates in the UK as the inflation rate fell relative to nominal interest rates. Longer-term policies to restrain the growth of the money supply have centred around the PSBR, with the stated objective of the government being to attain a balanced budget (that is, a zero PSBR) on average over the longer term. The reduced need for borrowing from banks given by a lower PSBR will, it is intended, lead to a lower rate of credit creation combined with lower interest rates.

9.3   Periodically, use has also been made of *funding policy* to try to limit the supply of liquid assets available within the financial system. A strategy of over-funding of the PSBR during the early to mid-1980s involved sales of gilt-edged securities and National Savings instruments to the non-bank, non-building society private sector often exceeding the PSBR. This resulted in there being a *negative* impact on the money supply arising from public sector financing. During the years 1987/88 to 1990/91 a PSDR existed, and the strategy was to fund fully such surpluses by means of debt repurchases from the non-bank, non-building society private sector in order to neutralise the contractionary impact on the money supply that a PSDR would otherwise have.

9.4   Comparisons of the actual growth of the money supply over various periods since 1980 relative to the target rates demonstrate that the authorities in the UK have achieved only limited success in meeting their targets. The early years of the 1980s (when the rate of growth of the money supply was seen as being a major target for economic policy) showed persistent overshoots of targets. It may be argued, of course, that the growth of the money supply itself is of little importance and it is the ultimate objectives of economic policy that are of primary concern. As Section 11 demonstrates, however, over the longer term the success of the UK in meeting the policy objectives has, at best, been mixed.

Developments in the framework of economic policy

9.5 Prior to the late 1970s, economic policy in the UK focused primarily on aggregate demand management. Successive governments therefore paid attention to managing the level of aggregate demand with the intention of 'fine tuning' the economy to keep the level of employment, the balance of payments and the rate of inflation on their appropriate paths. This management of the level of aggregate demand was achieved primarily by the use of fiscal policy, with monetary policy given the supporting role of stabilising the interest rate. In consequence the money supply was permitted to accommodate the money demand.

9.6 The need to borrow substantial sums of money from the International Monetary Fund in 1976 (occasioned by the marked international payments problems experienced at the time) led – under additional pressure from the IMF – to a reappraisal of the framework within which economic policy was to operate in the UK. The significant shift that resulted was towards greater attention being paid to the role of monetary policy and to the targeting of the growth rate of the money supply in particular, in order to curb inflation. This shift of emphasis towards the control of the money supply and towards the lowering of inflation as a policy objective was strengthened by the change of government in 1979. The commitment of the incoming Conservative government towards monetarism installed monetary policy as the major element of economic policy; but a parallel commitment of that government to the free operation of market forces also gave rise to a number of other changes in the framework of economic policy.

9.7 The overriding policy objective of the post-1979 government was the control of inflation, which stood in contrast to the full-employment objective of all previous postwar governments. However, it should be noted that one of the underlying precepts of the monetarist philosophy is that the economy is inherently self-regulating. It is argued that any intervention by the government in the form of active macroeconomic policies would be likely merely to create distortions and to move the economy *away* from its optimal employment position and economic growth path. Furthermore, the attainment of a low rate of inflation is necessary for the free market forces to operate satisfactorily to bring about full employment in the longer term. Thus, the adoption of monetarist policies may be seen as consistent with the objective of full employment, but only on a longer time scale than that associated with demand management policies.

The Medium-Term Financial Strategy (MTFS)

9.8 The Medium-Term Financial Strategy (MTFS) is the title given to the broad approach to the implementation of economic policy by the successive

Conservative governments between 1979 and the mid-1990s. However, it is important to avoid equating the MTFS too closely with monetarism and with the aim of controlling inflation. Although one of the main aims of the MTFS was indeed to reduce inflation by means of tight monetary control, the strategy also included other important aims. These were to reduce the burden of taxation on the working population (in order to boost incentives and thereby raise the rate of economic growth) and to reduce the proportion of national resources that are absorbed by the public sector.

9.9   The MTFS had the purpose of mapping out in broad terms how the government intended to achieve its longer-term objectives of low inflation, sustainable economic growth and low unemployment consistent with broad equilibrium of the balance of payments. Targets and projections were subsequently added to those broad aims of the MTFS. The targets and projections were formulated for four years ahead on a rolling basis, with the figures being updated each year. The intention was for the targets relating to money supply growth, PSBR and so on to be progressively reduced over time. The purpose was to inform the private sector exactly what the government's intentions were regarding the management of the economy, in the hope of influencing expectations, and therefore behaviour, in critical areas such as the setting of wages. The practice did not go entirely as planned and the targeted reductions in money supply growth were not consistent from one year to the next, with the consequence that the potential benefits from reducing inflation expectations were less than hoped.

9.10   By March 1987, the only monetary measure for which a policy target value remained was M0, and this target was itself abandoned in March 1993. The abandonment of specific targets for money supply growth may be seen as a reflection of a shift towards a less rigid application of the MTFS. Indeed, even before this time, the authorities had been placing increasing emphasis upon the need for policy instruments to be set in the light of a range of indicators of monetary conditions, and not simply on the basis of the growth rates of precisely defined monetary aggregates. In this context, the authorities looked increasingly towards movements in sterling exchange rates during the second half of the 1980s. The ultimate step in this regard was the placing of sterling into the European Union's (then European Community's) Exchange Rate Mechanism (ERM) in October 1990. This action undoubtedly constrained the extent to which monetary policy instruments could be directed towards controlling the growth of the domestic money supply, and hence modified further the practical operation of the MTFS.

Economic policy since September 1992

9.11   The most fundamental turning point for government economic policy in the UK in recent years came with the withdrawal of sterling from the EU's ERM in September 1992. This event followed an apparent widespread loss of confidence in the authorities' ability to maintain the exchange value of sterling within its parity bands relative to other ERM currencies. The withdrawal from the ERM led to a substantial reduction in the exchange rate of sterling, and allowed the authorities to sanction significant reductions in interest rates (on the grounds that the recessionary forces prevalent in the UK economy were sufficient to counteract any ensuing inflationary pressures). In February 1994 base rates were reduced to 5.25% (their lowest level since 1977). The lower rates of interest, the reduced exchange value for sterling and subdued inflation rates during 1993 undoubtedly contributed to an improvement in business conditions in the UK, with unemployment falling marginally as output began to rise.

9.12   Base rates were subsequently increased and peaked at 7.5% in June 1998. More recently, they have once again fallen, and at August 1999 they stood at just 5%. However, despite the extreme change of policy introduced in September 1992, the overall approach to implementing policy continued to be couched in terms of the MTFS, although it was regarded more simply as providing a framework for achieving sustainable economic growth based on permanently low inflation. An important development of the strategy was the introduction of the *inflation target* in October 1992. Strictly, this inflation target is the *objective* of policy. Therefore, it may be more appropriate to think of the real target (in the sense defined earlier in this unit) as being *expected inflation*, with policy instruments being adjusted according to expectations of inflation. Nevertheless, despite this potential point of confusion, this target effectively committed the government to directing its economic policy instruments to the maintenance of the underlying rate of inflation within the range of 1% to 4% p.a. In order to support this policy, the Bank of England began to provide a quarterly report on the progress being made towards the achievement of the inflation target. Also, the Treasury began to be more open on policy matters via the publication of the minutes of meetings between the Chancellor of the Exchequer and the Governor of the Bank of England some six weeks later. The idea here was that debate on policy would be better informed, and the government would find it more difficult to take actions that were not consistent with its stated policy objectives.

9.13   Choosing to target the (expected) rate of inflation directly meant that the government bypassed all the conventional targets of monetary policy. Thus, the monitoring ranges announced for M0 (0–4% p.a.) and M4 (3–9% p.a.), along with monitoring the exchange rate for sterling and changes in asset prices, effectively provided early warning devices to indicate when policy was running off course. Such variables would in future be taken into account in the setting of monetary controls (interest rates). The authorities also made clear that they would look beyond the more traditional monetary and financial variables when setting policy. Therefore, in addition, indicators of activity (including measures of spare capacity, retail sales growth and labour shortages) and the overall stance of fiscal policy were to be taken into account, as were indicators of costs, in particular wage costs and material input prices (including commodity prices).

9.14 The new approach to policy still recognised the importance of fiscal policy. In particular, considerable concern was expressed in respect of the need to reduce the huge PSBR, which was approximately £46bn during 1993/94. Measures introduced in Budgets during the mid-1990s were aimed at raising additional revenue and holding back the growth of government expenditure. It is only recently that the PSBR has fallen to relatively modest levels, partly as a result of the natural improvement in government finances that follows recovery in the economy. The broad priorities and general balance of policy were carried over by the new Labour government, which came to power in May 1997. Continuity, stability and prudence in economic management were billed as being key aspects of the new government's policy agenda.

The monetary policy framework since May 1997

9.15 In May 1997 a fundamental shift took place in the approach taken to the implementation of monetary policy in the UK. The new Labour government announced that it was giving, with immediate effect, independence to the Bank of England in respect of the implementation of monetary policy. The legal basis for the new framework for monetary policy was eventually provided by the *Bank of England Act 1998*, which formally gave the Bank of England operational responsibility for the setting of interest rates. Under these new arrangements the Bank of England's monetary policy objective is to deliver price stability as defined by the Government's inflation target and, subject to that objective, to support the Government's economic policy, including its objectives for economic growth and employment.

9.16 The Government's inflation target (objective) has been set at 2.5% p.a. for retail price inflation, excluding mortgage interest payments. This target for this preferred measure of the rate of underlying inflation is to be confirmed each year in the Chancellor of the Exchequer's Budget Statement. Furthermore, the Governor of the Bank of England will be required to provide a written explanation to the Chancellor, in the form of an open letter, if the actual rate of inflation deviates by more than 1% on either side of the 2.5% target. Therefore, in practice, the Bank will aim to keep the rate of inflation within the 1.5% to 3.5% band, which should help to avoid a deflationary bias being built into Bank of England policy actions. If the rate of inflation does go outside of the band, the Governor must also explain what the Bank intends to do to rectify the situation. The *Bank of England Act 1998* allows the Treasury to give instructions to the Bank of England in respect of the implementation of monetary policy. These powers, which can only be applied for a limited period of time, can only be used if the Treasury believes that they are necessary in the public interest in the face of 'extreme economic circumstances'.

9.17 Within the Bank of England, the Monetary Policy Committee (MPC) has responsibility for deciding upon the Bank's repo rate, which effectively determines the level of short-term money market interest rates and bank base rates. The MPC was given a formal legal status by the *Bank of England Act 1998*. Its membership comprises the Governor and two Deputy Governors of the Bank, two members appointed by the Bank after consultation with the Chancellor of the Exchequer, and four members appointed by the Chancellor of the Exchequer. A representative of the Treasury attends meetings of the MPC in a non-voting capacity. The MPC meets monthly and its decisions are announced immediately after the meeting. Minutes of meetings are normally published two weeks after the meeting, although publication of details on market intervention may be delayed.

9.18   The powers given to the Bank of England in respect of the implementation of monetary policy have been balanced by increased accountability to Parliament and the public. This comes about through:

- The publication of the minutes of the meetings of the MPC.

- The publication of the Bank's quarterly *Inflation Report.*

- Appearances by MPC members before the Treasury Select Committee of Parliament.

- A debate in Parliament on the Bank's *Annual Report.*

9.19   Throughout the 1990s, the main intermediate target of monetary policy remained short-term interest rates. However, as explained in Unit 3 (Section 5), the Bank has moved progressively towards the use of repo transactions in the gilt repo market and in the discount market as the key instrument of policy. Nevertheless, the Bank still engages in outright purchases and sales of securities to assist liquidity management in the sterling money market. Eligible bank bills remain an important instrument in this regard.

9.20   Important aspects of the transmission mechanism of monetary policy, from changes in the Bank's repo rate through to the major economic variables of inflation, output and employment, are implicit in the explanation of the effects of monetary policy on financial intermediaries in Section 10 of this unit.

Study Activities 6

1. What have been the main instruments of control used by the UK monetary authorities since the early 1980s?   *(Paragraph 9.2)*

2. What was the success of the UK authorities in meeting their money supply growth targets during the early 1980s?   *(Paragraph 9.4)*

3. In what fundamental way did the economic policy objectives of the Conservative government, which came to power in 1979, differ from those of the previous postwar governments in the UK?   *(Paragraph 9.7)*

4. Within the context of recent UK economic policy, what was the Medium-Term Financial Strategy? *(Paragraphs 9.8–9.10)*

5. What economic policy changes were precipitated by the withdrawal of sterling from the ERM in September 1992? *(Paragraphs 9.11 and 9.12)*

6. In what way did the UK's approach to monetary targeting alter in October 1992? *(Paragraph 9.12)*

7. What have been the objectives of Bank of England monetary policy since May 1997? *(Paragraph 9.15)*

8. What aspect of the new monetary policy arrangements in the UK should help to avoid deflationary bias? *(Paragraph 9.16)*

9. What is the composition and role of the Bank of England's Monetary Policy Committee? *(Paragraph 9.17)*

10. In what ways is the Monetary Policy Committee accountable for its actions? *(Paragraph 9.18)*

11. How have the instruments of monetary policy as used by the Bank of England altered in recent years? *(Paragraph 9.19)*

10 Effects of monetary policy on financial intermediaries

10.1 The *direct* effects of monetary policy on financial intermediaries are felt primarily through changes in the level of short-term interest rates. In the longer term the whole term structure of interest rates may be affected, depending upon expectations of the impact of policy on future inflation rates. In addition, to the extent that changes in monetary policy affect real economic activity (national income, employment and so on), financial intermediaries may be affected *indirectly* through changes in the demand for their products and services and the general levels of prosperity in the economy. Taking the example of monetary policy being altered so as to reduce interest rates, the effects on banks in particular may be analysed as follows:

10.2 For all banks lower rates of interest will reduce interest income on floating rate loans and will reduce interest payments on floating rate deposits. For wholesale banking activity, an important effect is likely to be felt via an increase in the demand for loans, whilst perhaps the flow of deposits may be reduced. If the operating margin remains unaltered, then a higher level of turnover will probably lead to an increase in profits. If the margin has to be narrowed, then profitability may be adversely affected.

10.3 For retail banking activity, the situation is somewhat more complex. To the extent that banks have use of funds deposited in non-interest-bearing sight accounts, a lower rate of interest reduces the *endowment effect*. Of course, lower interest rates may stimulate turnover, so pulling in the opposite direction in relation to profitability levels. Furthermore, base rates tend to move only periodically, whilst an increasing proportion of funds is raised at market-related rates. Therefore, in the shorter-term at least, margins may rise as interest rates fall.

10.4   For all banks lower rates of interest are likely to generate capital gains on holdings of fixed interest securities. Banks may also benefit in that the value of some assets charged as security for loans may be increased. In addition, lower rates of interest are likely to take pressure off borrowers, and hence reduce the chances of default on loans. Coupled with the possible boost to economic activity, banks may feel able to reduce provisions for bad debt.

10.5   If the lower rates of interest lead to a weakening in the exchange value of sterling, foreign currency profits will translate into a larger amount of sterling profits. Of course, to the extent that a bank carries foreign currency liabilities in excess of foreign currency assets, the impact on the balance sheet is likely to be detrimental.

10.6   It should be recognised that expectations of future inflation rates may be crucial in determining the actual outcome of a reduction in nominal interest rates. Banks and their customers may not be impressed if a reduction in nominal interest rates is seen merely to compensate for expected reductions in the rate of inflation.

10.7   Financial intermediaries in general will experience some of the effects of a reduction in interest rates (which would be reversed for an increase in interest rates). For example, changes in the capital value of fixed interest assets or exchange rate effects on foreign currency asset values will be universal. So too would be any effects on business volumes in general resulting from changes in the broader economic variables. Of course, the nature of the asset portfolios held will determine the precise impact felt.

Study Activities 7

1. In general terms, how might monetary policy affect financial intermediaries both directly and indirectly? *(Paragraph 10.1)*

2. What is the importance of the operating margin for wholesale banks responding to changes in monetary policy? *(Paragraph 10.2)*

3. Outline the direct impact of lower rates of interest on retail banks' intermediation activities. *(Paragraph 10.3)*

4. Why might banks feel able to reduce provisions for bad debts in the face of lower interest rates? *(Paragraph 10.4)*

5. How might changes in monetary policy impact upon banks via the exchange rate? *(Paragraph 10.5)*

6. How might expectations of future inflation rates affect banks' responses to monetary policy initiatives? *(Paragraph 10.6)*

11   The success of economic policy

11.1   The success of the government's economic policy, and by implication the monetary policy element, can only really be assessed in terms of the main objectives of economic policy. It was stated above that these are normally regarded as being:

- High and stable level of employment;

- Low and stable rate of inflation,

- High rate of economic growth; and

- Satisfactory balance of payments.

A high and stable level of employment

11.2   This objective is usually evaluated in terms of *unemployment* rather than employment. The evidence demonstrates that the objective of achieving a low and stable unemployment rate has not been achieved, although the general trend since 1993 has been downward. Unemployment rose from 5.8% of the total workforce in 1980 (a high figure in post-war terms) to 11.1% in 1986, before falling back to 5.8% in 1990. Unemployment rose again, and stood at 10.3% in 1993; after which it fell steadily to average 4.6% in 1998. This level, which equates to around 1.3m unemployed, remained fairly steady well into 1999. These figures do, furthermore, relate to the official unemployment statistics. There have been a number of changes in the basis of collection, which have served, overall, to depress the figures. This unemployment record is not, however, markedly worse than that of many other industrialised nations, and in recent years has been better than that experienced by many comparable countries. Nevertheless, it was not until 1998 that the unemployment rate fell below that experienced in 1980, although it has to be recognised that the attainment of low unemployment was always regarded as a longer-term objective which would be facilitated by reductions in the rate of inflation. The government also points to the fact that a large number of new jobs have been created – that is to say, the growth in *employment* that has been achieved – as a better indicator of its success in achieving this particular objective of economic policy.

A low and stable rate of inflation

11.3   This has been the government's major economic policy objective, but even here fortunes have been mixed. During 1983–88 inflation was on average lower than it had been at any time since the 1960s, and remained significantly lower than the rates experienced during the 1970s and at the beginning of the 1980s. Between 1988–91, the rate of inflation once again gave cause for concern, and in the autumn of 1990 reached almost 11% p.a. (as measured by changes in the retail price index). More recently the rate has fallen substantially. In June 1993 it reached a 30-year low of 1.2% p.a., although it touched 3.9% p.a. in September 1995. By May 1996 it had fallen to 2.2% p.a. and since that time it has not risen above 3.5% p.a. However, it should be noted that throughout much of the past decade the UK's inflation rate has generally remained higher than the rates experienced by most of the UK's major trading partners. Therefore, it is not possible to conclude without qualification that the major objective of economic policy has been achieved in recent years.

A high rate of economic growth

11.4   The success of the government's economic policy in achieving a high rate of economic growth since 1980 is more difficult to evaluate, due to the substantial variation in experience. Over the decade 1980–89, economic growth at an annual average rate of 2.3% was slightly higher than that achieved during the 1970–79 period and *lower* than that achieved in the period 1960–69 (2.9%) and 1950–59 (2.6%). However, the evidence reveals that between 1983 and 1988, economic growth was significantly higher than the average of preceding years and comparable to, if not exceeding, that achieved by many of the UK's major trading partners. The experiences of 1980–82 and 1990–92 may then be attributed to the world recessions at the time although, in terms of economic growth, the recessions in the UK were markedly more severe than in the many other countries, and this requires some explanation. More recently performance in respect of the rate of growth has remained variable. The relaxation of economic policy following 'Black Wednesday' in September 1992 (when sterling was withdrawn from the EU's Exchange Rate Mechanism) was followed by a relatively sustained period of strong economic growth (reflected in the unemployment statistics). However, 1998 saw a rapid slowdown of activity, particularly in the manufacturing sector (hit by a strong exchange value for sterling in very competitive international markets). By mid-1999, it appeared that a complete halt to growth had only been narrowly avoided.

A satisfactory balance of payment

11.5   The *current account* of the balance of payments, reflecting the value of goods and services imported relative to the value of those exported, has displayed very marked fluctuations since the early 1980s. In the first half of the 1980s large oil surpluses contributed to a series of large current account surpluses. In the second half of the 1980s there was a succession of very large deficits on the current account, culminating in a deficit of almost £23bn in 1989. Closer examination of the figures reveals that there was a steady worsening of the non-oil component of the current account over the decade, giving rise to concerns about the ability of the UK to pay its way in international terms. More recently the position has improved, with a surplus of £6.3bn being recorded in 1997. Subsequent competitive pressures resulting form the strengthening of sterling eroded this value, although a surplus of £1.5bn remained in 1998.

11.6   The former division of the current account into its *visible* and *invisible* components reveals some additional worrying trends. Traditionally, the invisible component of the balance of payments (relating to services, current transfers, interest, profits and dividends) has generated strong surpluses that have to a large extent offset any deficits on the visible (tangible goods trade) component. During the early 1990s, however, the surplus on invisible items became less reliable and when combined with the massive deficit on the visible component, contributed to the huge current account deficit. More recently, earnings from services and interest, profits and dividends have reasserted their strength.

11.7   On the *capital account* of the balance of payments, the flows involved have been volatile since the early 1980s. This is partly attributable to the high real rates of interest that applied at times, leading to large inflows of short-term investment funds (the so-called 'hot money') which has in turn contributed to the instability of exchange rates.

11.8   Overall, it is clear that while the government has achieved some success in attaining its economic policy objectives, there remain areas where its success has been very limited. It is also clear that the *conflicts* between economic policy objectives identified earlier remain, and that the government has experienced considerable difficulty in reconciling the objectives of high economic growth and low unemployment on the one hand with low inflation and a stable balance of payments on the other.

12 Monetary policy in the USA, Germany and the Euro Area

12.1   Most of the world's major economies pursue similar economic policy objectives, with stable prices having a somewhat greater priority than economic growth. However, not all of these countries are at the same stage of the economic cycle at any particular time, so that conflicts can occur if one country is contracting aggregate monetary demand at a time when others are seeking to expand it. Moreover, although the political leaders have exchanged views at their regular G7 summits (held between the USA, Japan, Germany, France, UK, Italy and Canada) and, more recently, G8 summits (G7 + Russia), they are answerable only to their electorates at different times and in different ways. In addition, the independence of most of these leading countries' central banks may augur well for the control of inflation, but may sometimes be politically inconvenient for governments seeking to contribute to agreements on global economic stabilisation.

USA

12.2   In the USA, goals of economic policy are similar to those of the UK, except that greater priority may be given to interest rate stability, possibly in view of the importance of bond markets in the American financial system. The USA operates an independently floating exchange rate regime for the dollar, with any official intervention being aimed at moderating the rate of change of the exchange rate rather than attempting to determine the rate. In conducting its monetary policy the USA has no explicitly stated target variable. Instead it monitors a range of monetary indicators.

12.3   The Federal Reserve uses the full range of traditional methods in implementing monetary policy, but it does use one that is not found in the UK. This is to operate on the reserve assets of commercial banks, i.e. the balances that they keep with the 12 regional reserve banks. If a bank has more reserves in its account than it is required to keep then it can increase its lending – with the inevitable result that these reserves will gradually fall to the minimum level. Alternatively, that bank can lend its excess reserves to banks that are below their minima, or it can buy government securities. In its open market operations, the Federal Reserve will be seeking to contain the growth of the money supply, stabilise interest rates and adjust the level of the banks' total reserves. An important instrument of monetary policy used in the USA is the sale and repurchase agreement (or 'repo'). Using these instruments, the central bank provides liquidity for a stated period or may remove liquidity from the money markets in order to put pressure on interest rates.

Germany

12.4   On 1 January 1999 Germany became a founder member of the European single currency arrangement. In consequence it lost its hitherto jealously guarded freedom to operate an independent monetary policy. Prior to that time the goals of monetary policy in Germany were similar to those in the UK and USA, except that there was a greater consensus over the overwhelming priority of low inflation. This arose as a result two brief period of hyperinflation this century: the first in 1922–23, the second in 1947–48. It was no coincidence that both occurred shortly after the end of each of the two world wars. The German central bank had great independence in setting interest rates but little discretion over exchange rates. This asymmetrical distribution of discretion was the cause of problems, because exchange rates and interest rates are closely connected.

12.5   German monetary policy was, in consequence, very cautious and there was great reluctance to reduce interest rates in case the reduction caused a rise in retail prices. In midsummer 1996, Germany had four million people unemployed and the pressure to make cuts in interest rates was substantial.

12.6   Germany, like the USA, did not have a target for inflation but it did have a target for the growth of a broad measure of money: M3, as the Germans term it. The target was for a calendar year, being announced each December. Quite often the target was breached rather than observed. Instruments of monetary policy were largely three interest rates and ample use of 'repos'. The interest rates were the repo rate, usually posted for one month, the Lombard rate for loans from the central bank, and the discount rate for special advances.

Euro Area

12.7 Since 1 January 1999 Germany (along with Austria, Belgium, Finland, France, Ireland, Italy, Luxembourg, Netherlands, Portugal and Spain) has been a part of the Euro Area and has only been able to influence monetary policy indirectly via its participation in the European Central Bank (ECB). The currencies of the individual members of the Euro Area are now rigidly locked together, and in July 2002 are due to be replaced entirely by the Euro.

12.8 The ECB would appear to be allowing the Euro to float against other currencies without intervention. Also, it has no explicitly stated monetary policy target, but, as for the UK and the USA, monitors a range of monetary indicators to inform the setting of short-term interest rates. The individual central banks of the Euro Area countries utilise the standard range of open market operations and repo arrangements (as described for Germany) to implement monetary policy actions on behalf of the ECB. The ECB is legally independent of the Euro Area member states, but has been given the policy objective of achieving monetary stability. This objective is taken to mean stability of prices, interest rates and exchange rates.

12.9 Within the ECB, the Governing Council is responsible for the formulation of monetary policy, and the Executive Board implements monetary policy. The ECB uses three main instruments of monetary policy:

- Open market operations – these are normally in the form of repo transactions or secured loans. The 'main refinancing operation' (as it is called) takes place weekly with transactions having a 14-day maturity. This provides the bulk of liquidity to meet market requirements. The 'longer-term refinancing operation' is conducted monthly with transactions having a three-month maturity. The ECB may also undertake fine-tuning operations to adjust market liquidity for short periods at short notice as required.

- Standing facilities – these are used to provide or to absorb overnight liquidity and hence to limit fluctuations in the overnight rates of interest. Funds are provided in the form of secured loans to institutions eligible to take part in ECB operations. Institutions with excess funds may make use of the overnight deposit facility.

- Minimum reserve requirement – institutions eligible to take part in ECB operations are required to hold balances in a reserve account at the ECB. These balances must average 2% of each institution's eligible liabilities over the 'maintenance period' (which is usually one month). Required reserves attract an interest payment equal to the main refinancing rate, but there is no payment for excess reserves. However, there are penalties imposed on institutions failing to meet the reserve requirement at the end of the maintenance period. The ECB uses the minimum reserve requirement as a means of creating or enlarging the structural shortage of liquidity within the Euro Area. This reinforces the ECB's ability to implement its desired monetary policy.

Study Activities 8

1. What has been the success in recent years of UK economic policy measured in terms of achieving a low level of unemployment? *(Paragraph 11.2)*

2. What has been the UK's record in inflation since the early 1980s?
(Paragraph 11.3)

3. To what extent has the UK succeeded in achieving its objective in respect of economic growth in recent years? *(Paragraph 11.4)*

4. How has the UK's current account on the balance of payments fared in recent years? *(Paragraph 11.5)*

5. In what sense might central banks hinder the achievement of international economic stabilisation objectives? *(Paragraph 12.1)*

6. In what way are the goals and targets of US monetary policy different from the goals and targets of UK monetary policy? *(Paragraph 12.2)*

7. Describe and explain the key characteristics of German monetary policy for much of the post-war period. *(Paragraphs 12.4–12.6)*

8. In what way has German monetary policy changed since the beginning of 1999?
(Paragraph 12.4)

9. Compare and contrast the goals and targets of the European Central Bank's monetary policy with the goals and targets of the Bank of England's monetary policy.
(Paragraphs 9.16, 12.7 and 12.8)

10. Which parts of the ECB are responsible, respectively, for the formulation and the implementation of monetary policy? *(Paragraph 12.9)*

11. Explain the operation of the main instruments of monetary policy used by the ECB.
(Paragraph 12.9)

Summary

Now that you have completed this unit, you should be able to:

- state the objectives of monetary policy and relate monetary policy to the other types of economic policy;

- understand the need for intermediate targets, with stable relationships between them and the goals of economic policy, within the monetary control framework;

- describe in detail the instruments of monetary policy;

- appreciate the role of the Bank of England's Monetary Policy Committee in securing the UK's inflation target;

- analyse the impact of monetary policy on financial intermediaries;

- assess the effectiveness of the UK's monetary policy since 1980;

- appreciate the differing goals and targets of monetary policy in the UK, the USA, Germany and the Euro Area.

Self-assessment questions

Short-answer questions

1. List the objectives normally specified for government economic policy.

2. Why is it often argued that governments require a package of economic policies in order to achieve their policy objectives?

3. What factors are likely to affect the importance attached to monetary policy by a government?

4. The occurrence of disintermediation means that the authorities are unable to control both the money supply and interest rates simultaneously. Why?

5. List the possible intermediate targets of monetary policy.

6. Cash is only a minor element of the money supply in the modern economy. Why, therefore, might control of the cash base be seen as a desirable target for monetary policy?

7. To what extent has the UK government achieved its major economic policy objectives since the early 1980s?

Multiple-choice questions

1. An intermediate target of monetary policy is

   (a) a variable over which the authorities have some control and through which they hope to influence a policy instrument

   (b) the ultimate objective of the policy

(c) a variable through which the authorities attempt to achieve a policy objective

(d) a concept which is only relevant in respect of inflation objectives

(e) not required when the monetary policy objective is the control of inflation.

2. The Bank of England's Monetary Policy Committee

   (a) has responsibility for deciding upon the Bank's repo rate

   (b) is required to keep inflation below 2.5%

   (c) is accountable solely to the Governor of the Bank of England

   (d) was established within the provisions of the Banking Act 1987

   (e) is charged with stabilising the value of sterling against the Euro.

3. Within the Euro Area, monetary policy

   (a) is directed toward maximising the level of employment

   (b) focuses upon achieving a specified inflation target

   (c) has the objective of achieving monetary stability

   (d) is aimed at stabilising the value of the Euro against the US dollar

   (e) is under the direct control of the European Commission.

4. Within the context of monetary control, instruments of portfolio constraint

   (a) have a generalised effect on all borrowing and lending activities within financial markets

   (b) include the use of the Bank of England's repo rate

   (c) tend to distort the financial system the longer the term for which they are applied, and hence lead to disintermediation

   (d) involve the setting of targets for the size of the PSBR/PSDR

   (e) dominated UK monetary policy implementation during the 1990s.

5. Since the early 1980s the UK monetary authorities have

   (a) placed emphasis on the use of portfolio constraints in order to control the money supply

   (b) used instruments of market intervention backed by prudent public financing in order to control monetary variables

   (c) relied solely on reducing the PSBR in order to control interest rates

   (d) attempted to control money supply growth by a mixture of reserve asset requirements, special deposits and intervention on the foreign exchange market

   (e) concentrated upon stabilising short-term interest rates at a low level.

6. In recent years the UK authorities' monetary policy has

   (a) adhered strictly to the original framework of the Medium Term Financial Strategy

   (b) concentrated less heavily on money supply growth, and now takes into account a range of variables affecting monetary conditions

   (c) relied heavily on the setting of targets for the growth of broad measures of the money supply

   (d) been explicitly directed towards the reduction of unemployment

   (e) has aimed to peg the value of sterling relative to other major EU currencies.

8

The Analysis of Exchange Rates

Objectives

After studying this unit, you should be able to:

- define foreign exchange rates and cross rates;

- calculate a theoretical cross rate;

- describe the structure of the foreign exchange market;

- discuss the fundamental determinants of exchange rates;

- explain how a forward exchange rate is determined using the concept of covered interest parity;

- describe the structure of a country's balance of payments and its terms of trade;

- analyse how changes in the terms of trade affect a country's balance of trade and balance of payments;

- appreciate how changes in a country's balance of payments affect its currency's exchange rate;

- identify and understand the operation of the different types of exchange rate system;

- identify the types of foreign exchange risk, and the various financial derivatives which have been devised to manage such risk.

1   Exchange rates

Basic definitions

1.1   An exchange rate is the price of one currency in terms of another. For example, on 5 January 1999:

- One pound sterling was trading for 1.6556 US dollars;

- One US dollar was trading for 111.61 Japanese yen;

- One Euro was trading for 1.6116 Swiss francs; and so on.

1.2   When an exchange rate is quoted in terms of the number of units of the local currency exchangeable for one unit of the foreign currency, this is referred to as a *direct quote*. In the UK a direct quote would be £0.7118 for 1 Euro. An *indirect quote* is the number of foreign currency units that are required to purchase one unit of local currency. For example, in the UK an indirect quote would be 1.405 Euro for £1. An indirect quote is quite simply the reciprocal of the corresponding direct quote.

1.3 A currency is said to strengthen against a foreign currency if less is required to purchase each unit of the foreign currency. This is exactly the same as saying that more of the foreign currency is required to purchase each unit of the domestic currency. This inverse relationship between each pair of currencies means that if one strengthens, by definition, the other must have weakened. By the same token it is logically impossible for *all* currencies to strengthen (or *all* currencies to weaken) relative to all other currencies at any given time. Of course, an individual currency may strengthen relative to all others. It may also strengthen relative some currencies, whilst at the same time weakening against other currencies.

1.4 Given the importance of the US dollar in international trade and finance, it is not surprising that most currencies are quoted relative to the US dollar. In many respects the US dollar provides a convenient benchmark for currency trading. If a quote is made in terms of US dollars per unit of the other currency, this is often referred to as quoting in *American terms*. A quote specified as the number of units of the other currency per US dollar is referred to as *European terms*. By convention, currency dealers have tended to use European terms except for sterling, the Australian dollar and the New Zealand dollar.

Cross rates

1.5 The *theoretical exchange rate* between any two currencies excluding the US dollar may be calculated from their quoted exchange rates with the US dollar. The calculation gives rise to what is known as the *theoretical cross rate* for the currencies, which is effectively the quote on European terms for currency X divided by the quote in European terms for currency Y. For example, if x units of currency X buys one US dollar, and y units of currency Y also buys one US dollar, the theoretical cross rate must be:

x units of currency X = y units of currency Y,

which may be specified as:

one unit of currency X = y/x units of currency Y.

1.6 In practice, the cross rates quoted by dealers rarely differ from the corresponding theoretical cross rates due to the opportunity for *risk-free arbitrage*. That is, so long as transaction costs do not outweigh any anticipate gain from trading currencies, it would be worthwhile for a dealer to buy the currency that appeared to be cheap and sell the currency that appeared to be expensive relative to their theoretical cross rate. For example, if one US dollar trades for 2 units of currency Y or for 4 units of currency X, the theoretical cross rate is $2Y = 4X$ or $Y = 2X$. If the actual rate quoted between the two currencies is $Y = 3X$, then relative to the theoretical cross rate, currency X is cheap and currency Y is expensive. Holders of currency Y may gain by selling it for currency X, because every unit of Y will only purchase $0.5 directly, whereas a unit of Y may be traded for 3 units of X which may then be traded for $0.75. Indeed, dealers could use dollars to purchase Y (at $0.5 per Y), then exchange the Y for X (at 3X per Y), and then exchange the 3X for dollars at a rate of $0.25 per X (i.e. at $0.75 for 3X). The gains are clear. However, the resulting changes in supplies and demands for the currencies would tend to push up the price of X in terms of Y, and possibly cause the dollar value of Y to rise and the dollar value of X to fall. The overall outcome would be to push the actual exchange rate toward the theoretical cross rate. The adjustment would continue until all arbitrage gains had been exhausted. Needless to say, these so-called *triangular arbitrage opportunities* are normally short-lived, and any inconsistency in theoretical and actual cross rates can usually be explained in terms of transaction costs outweighing potential arbitrage gains.

2   Currency baskets

2.1   Currency baskets are combinations of foreign currencies, devised as artificial currencies that do not fluctuate in value as much as individual currencies. The best-known currency baskets to have been created are the Special Drawing Right (SDR) and the European Currency Unit (ECU).

Origins

2.2   As explained in Unit 1, one of the functions of money is to act as a unit of account and one of the characteristics needed by an asset used as money is that it must be stable in its value (purchasing power). In the past, gold was a very popular money asset. Gold had its heyday in the 19th century, when the gold standard ensured that foreign exchange rates linked to gold did not fluctuate significantly. Effectively, all gold standard currencies were given a fixed value in terms of an amount of gold, and the domestic money supplies could only alter if the gold holdings of the monetary authorities altered. Hence, domestic price adjustments were viewed as taking the strain of international payments imbalances.

2.3   In 1944 the allied powers decided at Bretton Woods (in the USA) to revert to stable exchange rates, linking their currencies to the US dollar, and thus indirectly to gold. These Bretton Woods 'parities' worked well until the strains of international payments problems in the 1970s put too much pressure on them, and they were widened from one per cent either side of parity to 2.25%. Soon afterwards the Bretton Woods system collapsed, with fundamental implications for exchange rate arrangements (and the volatility of exchange rates).

Special drawing rights

2.4   In the mid-1960s, agreement was reached on a new form of international money, called the Special Drawing Right (SDR), with an exchange rate of 1 SDR to 1 US dollar. However, in the early 1970s, the US dollar itself was devalued against gold and in 1973 the currencies of most leading countries began to float against each other. This caused the SDR to float exactly in line with the US dollar, so the link was broken.

2.5   From 1974 to 1980, the SDR was calculated as a weighted-average of the world's most important currencies – defined as the currencies of all countries with more than 1% of the world's total trade in goods and services for the years 1968–1972. This gave a basket of 16 currencies that proved to be unwieldy.

2.6   Since January 1981, the SDR has comprised a basket of five leading currencies – US dollar, DM, yen, sterling and the French franc – with their weights changed every five years. The International Monetary Fund publishes exchange rates for the SDR one day in arrears, as will be seen from the data on the 'Currencies and Money' page of the *Financial Times*.

2.7   As well as being a unit of account, the SDR is a form of money, and allocations of SDRs have been made to member nations of the International Monetary Fund. In this role it functions as an international 'reserve asset', i.e. as a liquid store of value.

European Currency Unit

2.8   The ECU originated in the early 1970s as a bookkeeping mechanism for the budget of the European Community (as it then was). The ECU comprised a basket of the currencies of the first 12 members of the EU, with the currency weights being revised in 1984 and, for the final time, in 1989.

2.9   In 1979, this European Monetary System was launched with the creation of the Exchange Rate Mechanism (ERM). Effectively, EU member states choosing to do so were able to peg their currency values to each other, within a 'parity grid' arrangement. There was also an 'ECU indicator' whereby the broad strength of individual ERM currencies would be measured against a basket of all EU currencies. Furthermore, EU member nations agreed to swap 20% of their official holdings of gold and US dollars for ECU. Thus, ECU reserves were created by the exchange of existing money.

2.10   The ECU gave way to the Euro on 1 January 1999. This EU single currency is expected to replace the individual currencies of EU member states that elect to join European Monetary Union. The key date here is 1 July 2002 when the individual EU currencies participating in the arrangement cease to be legal tender. In effect, the exchange rates of the participating currencies are already immutably fixed.

Study Activities 1

1. Explain what is meant by the terms 'direct quote' and 'indirect quote' in relation to exchange rates. *(Paragraph 1.2)*

2. Why is it impossible for all countries to have strong currencies? *(Paragraph 1.3)*

3. Define 'American terms' and 'European terms' within the context of exchange rate quotations. *(Paragraph 1.4)*

4. In general terms, what is the theoretical cross rate for two currencies? *(Paragraph 1.5)*

5. Why do cross rates quoted by dealers rarely differ from the corresponding theoretical cross rates? *(Paragraph 1.6)*

6. What is an important attraction of a currency basket? *(Paragraph 2.1)*

7. What were the key elements of the gold standard? *(Paragraph 2.2)*

8. In what ways has the SDR been valued? *(Paragraphs 2.4–2.6)*

9. What was the ECU? *(Paragraph 2.8)*

10. What were the key elements of the EMS? *(Paragraph 2.9)*

3 Foreign exchange markets

3.1 Within a country's domestic economy, inter-party transactions can normally be settled by the transfer of domestic currency from one party to the other by cash, cheque or other funds-transfer mechanism. However, once trade between different countries or currency areas is instigated the situation becomes more complex. The parties to the trade need to decide in which currency the transactions will be denominated – seller's currency, buyer's currency or that of another country? For example, oil exports from Saudi Arabia to Japan could be invoiced in Saudi riyals or Japanese yen. In fact, trading practice in the oil industry means that most oil shipments are invoiced in US dollars so that would be the most likely currency of the transaction. Whatever method is chosen, one party (or possibly both) will be faced with the prospect of paying or receiving payment in a currency other than its own. *Currencies will have to be traded*, and to meet this need a network of foreign currency exchange markets has evolved, inter-linked today by a sophisticated communications network. There is no central marketplace as such; groups of dealers around the world communicate with each other by telephone, telex, facsimile and computers, trying to match the supply of and demand for various currencies, according to the needs of governments, commerce, industry and individuals. It is, in effect, a global OTC market.

3.2   According to a survey undertaken by the Bank for International Settlements, as at April 1998, the leading centres for foreign exchange market activity as measured by turnover per day were:

- United Kingdom – US$637bn

- United States – US$351bn

- Japan – US$149bn

- Singapore – US$139bn.

The UK has held the leading position for many years, and as shown above the volume of business now amounts to almost the same as that undertaken by the next three largest centres combined.

Who are the players?

3.3   The actual market participants operate either as dealers or as principals or as both. A *dealer* buys or sells currencies for third parties, selling at a margin above the market rate and buying at a margin below. The difference between the buying and selling rate is called the 'turn', in addition to which the dealer may well charge a service fee or commission. The commercial banks are the main dealers, acting for the whole spectrum of their customers from tourists to multinational investors.

3.4   *Principals* buy and sell currencies on their own account, speculating on favourable exchange-rate movements to enable them to profit from dealing. Principals are prepared to hold currency for short periods in the hope that its exchange rate will improve so that it can be sold at a profit. Many dealers will also act as principals in the market to try to enhance their profitability. Indeed, most of the banks acting as dealers have now designated their foreign exchange market operations as profit centres, so the dealers have an incentive to act as principals if they believe that they can read the market trends correctly.

3.5   Often a country's *official monetary authorities* will enter the foreign exchange market, usually in order to reduce undesired short-term fluctuations in exchange rates. By buying or selling currencies they can raise or lower currency exchange rates, funding transactions from official reserves or loans from international institutions. Currency swap arrangements with overseas monetary authorities are sometimes utilised in order to support these operations.

The 'commodity'

3.6   This market is where bank deposits denominated in various currencies are bought and sold; it must be distinguished from the market in bank notes of different countries, which is separate. The size of the bank deposits is large, because this is a wholesale market. The usual minimum size of an individual transaction is US$1m equivalent for most currencies.

3.7 It is a global financial market, operating around the clock for five days a week. The week really begins (about 10.30pm on Sunday London time) when the foreign exchange dealing rooms open in Tokyo (Monday morning there), although the market is already open in New Zealand. Soon afterwards dealers join them in Sydney, Hong Kong and Singapore. By 6.30am in London, the markets are opening in Frankfurt and Paris, but the Far East markets are about to close. Normally, the Continent is one hour ahead of London, except for one month in the autumn, when the continental countries have reverted to mean time one month earlier than the UK. At 2.00pm London time, New York opens, to be followed in the early evening by California, to be followed in the late evening by Tokyo … The market is highly automated and deals are executed by pressing the appropriate buy or sell button on the keyboard.

Study Activities 2

1. Why are foreign exchange markets required? *(Paragraph 3.1)*

2. What form do foreign exchange markets take? *(Paragraph 3.1)*

3. In 1998 where were the world's four main foreign exchange markets located? *(Paragraph 3.2)*

4. What is the role of a dealer in the foreign exchange market? *(Paragraph 3.3)*

5. What is the role of a principal in the foreign exchange market? *(Paragraph 3.4)*

6. Why do national monetary authorities become involved with foreign exchange activities? *(Paragraph 3.5)*

7. Outline the daily operating cycle of the global foreign exchange market. *(Paragraph 3.7)*

4   Types of foreign exchange transactions

4.1 *Spot* currency transactions are those for which settlement must be completed within two business days. *Forward* currency transactions involve a price being agreed for currency to be delivered at a future date with settlement being more than two business days after dealing. Forward currency transactions may relate to an exchange rate being booked at which currency will be delivered on a fixed future date or on a day between two future dates. In the first instance, a *fixed forward currency contract* is arranged between buyer and seller, and in the second, an *option forward currency contract* is written, the 'option' being *when* to deliver between the agreed dates not *whether* to deliver. Delivery of agreed currencies *must* be made by the final date of the contract.

4.2   Forward contracts are useful to importers or exporters who are carrying out transactions denominated in, what is to them, foreign currency. At the time of quoting for or agreeing their trading deal, they can crystallise the domestic currency value of the expected future foreign currency invoice, and hence ensure that the profitability of the deal is not eroded by adverse future movements in foreign exchange rates. This is known as 'hedging' exchange rate risk, and forward currency contracts are one of several hedging tools used by international traders.

How are rates for forward transactions determined?

4.3   When quoting forward currency rates dealers will add a premium or deduct a discount from the spot rate to reflect the differential between interest rates prevailing for the two currencies concerned. If, for example, interest rates on sterling funds are higher than interest rates on US dollar funds, then the forward dollar will be quoted at a premium against sterling. This is in order to compensate for the loss by the writer of the forward contract (usually a bank) of interest earned on dollars compared with what would have been earned on sterling for the contract period involved. This interest rate differential is used to calculate *forward* exchange premiums and discounts from the spot rate and which dealers quote to clients according to the length of the contract required. Forward exchange rates are not forecasts of the spot rate on future dates, they are today's spot rate adjusted for interest rate differentials.

4.4   The relationship between the spot exchange rate, the interest rate differential and the forward exchange rate is called the *interest rate parity*. This means that by hedging in the forward currency exchange market an investor will realise the same return irrespective of whether investing domestically or in the country from which the foreign currency originates. The market mechanism that will bring about interest rate parity is called *covered interest arbitrage*. This process exploits inconsistencies that occur from time to time in the spot/forward relationship given the interest rate structures pertaining to the two currencies.

4.5   On a practical level, if investors see interest rates rise in one country then they may wish to buy that currency in order to benefit from the higher rate of interest. However, there is one unknown – how much will that foreign currency be worth when they come to sell? The forward exchange market gives them the chance to sell that currency now for settlement in (say) six months' time, so that they know now what the profit on the whole transaction will be. Thus, the investors buy the spot currency, with the result that the spot rate rises, but they sell the forward currency, so that the forward rate falls.

Study Activities 3

1. What are 'spot' foreign exchange transactions'?   *(Paragraph 4.1)*

2. What is a fixed forward exchange contract?   *(Paragraph 4.1)*

3. What is an option forward exchange contract?   *(Paragraph 4.1)*

4. What use are forward exchange contracts to importers and exporters?
   (Paragraph 4.2)

5. What determines the premium or discount on forward exchange rates?
   (Paragraph 4.3)

6. What is meant by interest rate parity within the context of the relationship between spot and forward exchange rate?   *(Paragraph 4.4)*

7. What is likely to be the impact on spot and forward foreign exchange market transactions of an increase in interest rates on a particular currency?   *(Paragraph 4.5)*

5   The balance of payments and the terms of trade

Basic concepts

5.1   The balance of payments accounts are effectively a systematic record of all transactions between domestic residents of a country, such as the UK, and residents of foreign nations, over a given time period. All UK transactions are recorded in sterling. *Credit items* are given a positive sign and *debit items* a negative sign. Credit items include exports of goods and services and earnings of interest from overseas and investment from overseas. Debit items include imports of goods and services, dividend payments made to overseas residents and domestic investment made overseas.

Structure of the balance of payments accounts

5.2   The accounts can be split into three parts, the:

● Current account;

● Capital and financial account;

● Balancing item.

Current account

5.3   The current account is now subdivided into four sections:

● Trade in goods;

● Trade in services;

● Income from investment and as compensation of employees;

● Current transfers.

5.4   *Trade in goods* relates to the export and import of tangible items, e.g. basic raw materials, manufactured goods, fuels, and so on. The balance of trade in goods is often referred to as the *visible balance*.

5.5   *Trade in services* includes:

- Earnings from and payments for private sector services (such as financial services, tourism, transport);

- Government sector services, e.g. running overseas embassies.

5.6   *Investment income* includes:

- Interest, profits and dividends arising from international financial activities.

5.7   *Current transfers* include:

- Private-sector current transfers (such as gifts overseas, private pensions and remittances of private pensions); and

- Government sector current transfer payments, e.g. official overseas aid, payments relating to the EU budget, and retirement and war pensions paid to overseas residents who have emigrated from the UK.

5.8   The aggregation of trade in goods and services, investment income, compensation of employees and current transfers yields the *current account balance*. This is considered the most important component of the balance of payments accounts because of its implications for other major macroeconomic variables such as output and employment.

Capital and financial account

5.9   The main components of the capital and financial account (formerly termed 'transactions in external assets and liabilities') are:

- Overseas investment in the UK – divided into direct investment (investment in physical assets) and portfolio investment (involving financial instruments).

- UK private-sector investment overseas (divided as above).

- Foreign currency and sterling borrowing/lending by UK banks.

- Deposits with and borrowing from banks overseas by the UK non-bank private sector and public sector.

- Changes in official reserves.

- Transactions in other external assets and liabilities, e.g. borrowing from or repaying of funds to the IMF.

Balancing item

5.11 The balancing item is included to deal with errors and omissions in the accounts. If more currency flows into the country (in net terms) than is recorded in real transactions the balancing item will be positive. If the opposite outcome occurs, then the balancing item will be negative.

Study Activities 4

1. What do the balance of payments accounts show? *(Paragraph 5.1)*

2. Give some examples of credit items in the current account of the balance of payments. *(Paragraphs 5.3–5.7)*

3. What is the difference between the balance of trade in goods and services and the current account balance? *(Paragraph 5.8)*

4. What types of items are included in the capital and financial account of the balance of payments? *(Paragraph 5.9)*

5. What is the balancing item in the balance of payments? *(Paragraph 5.10)*

Official financing

5.11 Should the sum of the current account, the private sector elements of the capital and financial account and the balancing item be negative, there is said to be a balance of payments deficit. This means that *official financing* (changes in official reserves and net official borrowing) has to be positive. The reverse case applies if the sum is positive and a balance of payments surplus occurs. Possession of official reserves is vital to finance balance of payments deficits (and hence for the authorities to be able to influence currency exchange rates). Reserves are made up of the following assets:

- *Convertible currencies* – normally the major component of reserves.

- *Gold* – used as a 'second line of defence' rather than on a day-to-day basis.

- *Special Drawing Rights* – a reserve asset created by the IMF and available to member countries.

- *Reserve positions at the IMF* – effectively overdraft facilities in foreign currencies.

5.12 The sum of these items provides a *narrow* definition of a country's international liquidity. Recently, however, more attention has been focused on a broader definition that includes borrowing facilities made available to sovereign states from the IMF, commercial banks and central banks of other countries. The broader definition is a better guide to the liquidity available to a 'creditworthy' country but is far more difficult to calculate than the narrow definition.

Accounting equality and economic equilibrium

5.13   The balance of payments accounts are compiled using *double entry bookkeeping*, and hence always balance in accounting terms. Effectively, every international transaction must be financed by international payments. If the sum of the current account, private sector capital account and the balancing item is −£x, this will be balanced by +£x of official financing, making the accounts sum to zero.

5.14   *Economic equilibrium* occurs only when official financing is zero. When a balance of payments deficit or surplus occurs, there is economic disequilibrium. If disequilibrium persists in the long run a fundamental disequilibrium is said to exist and has important implications for the level of official reserves and overseas official borrowing. In recent years the focus has been on the current account. This is because it reflects a country's ability to pay its way internationally. Hence it may be argued that the balance of payments is only in equilibrium when there is a zero balance on the current account.

5.15   Ignoring the balancing item, if the current account is in deficit this must be balanced by a surplus of equal size on the private sector capital and financial account, otherwise official financing has to be used and reserves are run down or overseas debt is increased.

5.16   If exchange rates are clean floating rates, the balance of payments will always be in equilibrium as by definition there is no official intervention in the currency markets. Problems may exist, however, if a large capital account surplus is balanced by a large current account deficit due to the latter's implications for the export of goods and services and hence domestic employment.

Terms of trade

5.17   The terms of (visible) trade for any particular country relative to the rest of the world are defined as:

$$\frac{\text{Index of export prices}}{\text{Index of import prices}} \times (100)$$

5.18   Initially both price indices are set at 100 and therefore the terms of trade are also 100. Now, if export prices rise while import prices remain constant, the terms of trade rises above 100 and is said to have improved. This means that for every unit of goods exported the country will obtain a larger quantity of imports. The converse is true for deterioration in the terms of trade.

5.19   Care must be taken when interpreting a change in the terms of trade. An improvement in the terms of trade will be beneficial if the price of a country's exports has increased due to increased demand. This will have a favourable effect on the balance of trade. If the price of exports has risen due to rising domestic production costs then the improvement in the terms of trade will be beneficial only if the demand for that country's exports is price inelastic (that is, demand falls by a proportionately smaller amount than prices rise). If the converse case is true (demand is price elastic), then the balance of trade is likely to deteriorate.

5.20 If the terms of trade deteriorate due to rising import prices, whether this is beneficial to the balance of trade and hence to the economy as a whole, again depends on the elasticity of demand for imports. If the imported goods are seen as necessities (that is, low price elasticity of demand) the balance of trade will deteriorate.

5.21 Due to the importance of the terms of trade and their implications for a country's economy, a government may want to influence their value. The government will have a limited influence on the terms of trade because the relative prices of imports and exports are at the mercy of world supply and demand. Despite this, there are a number of ways in which the government can influence the terms of trade: first, by influencing the exchange rate; secondly, by trying to reduce domestic price inflation through tight monetary or fiscal policy and so causing the terms of trade to deteriorate. If we assume an elastic demand for the country's exports, this will then improve the balance of trade. It is unlikely that the government would use the reverse of the above policy to improve the terms of trade. Instead, it would try to encourage the production of high-quality goods thereby stimulating higher demand and pushing the prices of the goods upwards.

Study Activities 5

1. Under what circumstances will official financing be positive?   *(Paragraph 5.11)*

2. List the main components of the official reserves.   *(Paragraph 5.11)*

3. What is the difference between the narrow definition and the broad definition of international liquidity?   *(Paragraph 5.12)*

4. Why must balance of payments accounts always balance?   *(Paragraph 5.13)*

5. In what circumstances does economic equilibrium occur on the balance of payments?   *(Paragraph 5.14)*

6. In what sense does a clean floating exchange rate imply a permanent equilibrium position for the balance of payments?   *(Paragraph 5.16)*

7. Define the terms of trade.   *(Paragraph 5.17)*

8. What happens to the terms of trade if export prices rise, other things being equal?   *(Paragraph 5.19)*

9. In what circumstances is an improvement in the terms of trade good for the balance of trade?   *(Paragraph 5.19)*

10. Why is the influence of a government on the terms of trade likely to be limited?   *(Paragraph 5.21)*

11. What actions might be taken by a government to influence the terms of trade?   *(Paragraph 5.21)*

6 The economic significance of the balance of payments

The current account

Deficits

6.1 As we mentioned earlier, a current account deficit means that a country is not covering its current overseas expenditures with its current overseas income. Of course, the deficit must be financed by a surplus on the capital and financial account, assuming a zero balancing item.

6.2 The extent to which a deficit on the current account is regarded as being unfavourable depends, first, on its size and, second, on its persistence. The underlying economic and financial strength of the country is also important. Hence, a short-term deficit may not be looked on as being too harmful, as long as it is easily financed by running down reserves or by capital inflows. It may even lead to an increased standard of living.

6.3 If it is believed that a current account deficit will persist into the future, the implications become more serious. The longer a deficit has to be financed the more the (finite) official reserves will be run down or the more the foreign borrowing will have to increase. The larger the deficit, the worse this situation will become.

6.4 Clearly, the larger the size of debt that is amassed the progressively more onerous the servicing requirements will be. This may lead to a loss of confidence in the debtor nation and therefore, to prevent investment funds flowing out of the country, interest rates may have to be raised. This is clearly at odds with trying to correct the current account deficit through a low exchange rate.

6.5 The international debt problem of the early 1980s came about due to less-developed countries borrowing heavily to finance current account deficits. Unfortunately, the advent of high real interest rates and the strengthening of currencies in which debt was denominated led to unmanageable debt repayments. Only major rescheduling exercises and the provision of extra funds prevented a global financial crisis.

Surpluses

6.6 A persistent surplus is seen as a favourable situation for a country to be in, as it can use the surplus either to build up overseas investments, to increase official reserves or to repay overseas debt (or a combination of all three).

6.7 A country may come under political pressure to reduce its surplus, if it is excessively large, due to it being matched by a current account deficit in at least one other country. A more attractive solution to curing a country's deficit on the current account is for the surplus country to increase its imports rather than for the deficit country to depress demand for goods and services in its economy or to introduce tariffs. The surplus country may also benefit from a higher standard of living without increasing its international indebtedness.

The capital and financial account

6.8   Due to the rather varied nature of the components of the capital and financial account, great care must be taken when interpreting capital and financial flows. Even if a country has a balanced capital and financial account it may be relying on short-run capital inflows which are extremely volatile and likely to flow out of the country in response to a small change in relative interest rates.

Deficits

6.9   A deficit means there is a net outflow of funds. The implications here are far less disturbing than for a current account deficit. For instance, the deficit may be due to heavy investment in capital goods by that country in a foreign country, and may therefore lead to inflows of profit in the current account in future years. In addition, capital account outflows are likely to hold down the domestic currency's exchange rate, and hence help to improve the competitiveness of exports.

6.10   Capital outflows may be detrimental if output is raised and jobs created abroad at the expense of the domestic economy. It may also have detrimental effects on the demand for exports produced by the domestic economy.

Surpluses

6.11   If the capital and financial account surplus involves long-term capital investment from foreigners in domestic industry this will encourage the production of more goods domestically, perhaps increasing visible exports and decreasing imports. On the other hand, the capital may be withdrawn in the future and also generate interest, profits and dividends that flow abroad, worsening the balance on the current account.

6.12   Problems may also occur if capital inflows consisting of 'hot money' (that is, short-term investments that flow in due to relatively high domestic interest rates) takes up a considerable part of the capital account. Large flows of hot money tend to destabilise the domestic currency's exchange rate and may contribute towards a current account deficit by raising outflows of interest payments.

Study Activities 6

1. What factors will influence the extent to which a current account deficit on the balance of payments is seen as unfavourable?   *(Paragraph 6.2)*

2. Why might a current account deficit eventually lead to a loss of confidence in the country?   *(Paragraph 6.4)*

3. Why might a country see a persistent current account surplus as a good thing?   *(Paragraph 6.6)*

4. Give some reasons for a country seeking to reduce its current account surplus.

(Paragraph 6.7)

5. In what sense may a deficit on the capital and financial account of the balance of payments be detrimental for the economy? *(Paragraph 6.10)*

6. How might a surplus on the capital and financial account be a good thing for the current account? *(Paragraph 6.11)*

7 Correction of a balance of payments imbalance

The basic payments problem

7.1 Above we discussed how certain imbalances within components of the balance of payments might cause problems for a country's economy. Sometimes, however, these problems may be self-correcting over time. For example, a current account deficit reduces demand for domestic goods and therefore puts downward pressure on domestic inflation, increasing competitiveness of exports and therefore improving the current account position.

7.2 However, these natural mechanisms may be too slow, necessitating government intervention to deal with such imbalances. Care must be taken with timing when implementing these policies, and the government will also have to make sure such policies do not conflict with other economic objectives.

A current account imbalance
Deficits

7.3 The following policies may help to reduce a current account deficit:

- Reduce the sterling exchange rate.

- Demand management policies.

- Direct controls.

- Exchange controls.

- Quality improvement.

7.4 *Reducing the sterling exchange rate* reduces the foreign currency price of exports and raises the sterling price of imports. This will be successful as long as 'the sum of the price elasticity of demand for imports plus that for exports is greater than one' (the Marshall-Lerner condition). Hence the above policy is most successful when the demand for exports and imports is highly price elastic. The result is that eventually total receipts from exports rise and total payments for imports fall.

7.5 One short-run problem this policy has to contend with is the 'J-curve effect'. In the short run, before demand for exports has had time to increase, revenue from exports will decrease due to a fall in price, while expenditure on imports will increase – worsening the current account. As demand for exports increases and for imports decreases over time the current account will start to improve. The bottom of the 'J' shows the deficit worsening at first and then improving.

7.6   *Demand management policies* aim to improve the current account by reducing the volume of imports bought. The authorities may tighten monetary policy (but note the problems of higher interest rates), reduce government spending or increase taxation. This approach to policy may also create spare capacity to service export markets.

The above policies are the only two *seriously viable policy options*. The policies mentioned below are theoretically possible but run into problems in practice:

7.7   *Direct controls* include tariffs (taxes on imports) and quotas (quantity restrictions on imports). Both these may result in retaliation from other countries.

7.8   *Exchange controls* limit the use of foreign currency by UK residents.

7.9   *Quality improvement* of exports enhances their competitive position, and hence the current account of the balance of payments will also be enhanced.

Surpluses

7.10 A current account surplus may also be undesirable and therefore governments may want to eradicate such a surplus. Using the reverse of the policies just outlined does this:

- *Raising the sterling exchange rate* may be done by buying sterling and selling foreign currency. Alternatively, the government may try to attract foreign currency capital inflows. Again, this policy will only be successful if the Marshall-Lerner criterion holds.

- *Raising domestic demand* by expansionary monetary and/or fiscal policy, hence drawing in more imports. Both of these policies also fuel inflation, decreasing the competitiveness of exports. These policies are successful as long as the demand for imports/exports is elastic.

- *Abolition of import controls*; alternatively *export controls* may be introduced.

- The government may *encourage foreign holidays for its residents*, or encourage students to study overseas and so on.

Capital and financial account imbalance
Deficits

7.11 Inflows of capital funds or the stemming of outflows of such funds are aided by the implementation of the following policies:

- *The raising of domestic interest rates* through tight monetary policy. This makes domestic financial instruments more attractive to overseas investors.

- *Stabilising the exchange rate* in order to discourage speculative outflows.

- *Government incentives* for foreign investment in the domestic economy, via grants, subsidies or tax-free allowances.

- Reduction of government capital expenditure outflows.

7.12   The above policies do have their drawbacks. The magnitude and timing of such policies may be hard to judge. Also, if too much capital is attracted this may put the current account under pressure due to an appreciating exchange rate and the need to meet interest and dividend payments on the overseas capital flows.

Surpluses

7.13   The policies to deal with a capital account surplus are basically the *reverse* of those outlined above. These policies will be pursued if a large capital account surplus is sustained at the expense of a current account deficit.

Study Activities 7

1. Give an example of how a balance of payments problem may be self-correcting.
   (Paragraph 7.1)

2. What condition is required for a reduction in a country's exchange rate to have a positive effect on the current account of its balance of payments?   *(Paragraph 7.4)*

3. What is the 'J-curve effect'?   *(Paragraph 7.5)*

4. How might demand management policies be used to influence a country's current account on the balance of payments?   *(Paragraph 7.6)*

5. List the policies that might be implemented to reduce a surplus on the current account of the balance of payments.   *(Paragraph 7.10)*

6. State the policies that might be implemented to reduce a deficit on the capital and financial account of the balance of payments.   *(Paragraph 7.11)*

8   Determinants of exchange rate movements

Long-term trends in exchange rates

8.1   In the longer term, the relative economic performances of different countries determine the broad structure of exchange rates. The major contributory factors are usually referred to as the 'economic fundamentals', and are:

- Relative inflation rates (purchasing power parity)

- Relative interest rates (interest rate parity)

- The position of the balance of payments.

Relative inflation rates

8.2   One theory linking exchange rates and differing inflation rates between countries is the *purchasing power parity* (PPP) theory, which claims that the equilibrium exchange rate between currencies will be the rate at which the domestic purchasing powers of these currencies is equalised. For example, if a basket of goods costs £1 in the UK and $1.50 in the USA, then the equilibrium exchange rate would be £1 = $1.50. If this is not the case, people will in theory import goods from the 'cheaper' country, which will experience a trade surplus tending to force up the value of that country's currency.

8.3   This theory might work if all goods and services were traded internationally and international capital flows were zero or equal between the two countries concerned. As this is rarely the case, the PPP theory is too simplistic for the real world and, in any case, ignores transport and other trading costs. The PPP theory does help to explain, however, why the exchange rate of a country with high inflation will tend to fall relative to a country with a lower rate of inflation. The high-inflation country's export prices will rise but its imports will be relatively cheaper. In time, balance of payments problems will arise and official policy actions may be needed to correct the imbalance.

Relative interest rates

8.4   The level of *real* domestic interest rates (that is, nominal rates adjusted for the effects of expected domestic inflation) compared with those abroad is usually thought to have a strong influence on international capital flows, particularly in the short term. High interest rates attract capital funds from overseas and also add to investor confidence, since they suggest that the authorities have strong policies to control domestic inflation. Capital inflows from abroad create an increased demand for the domestic currency, thus pushing its exchange rate higher, all other things being equal. As official monetary policy determines inflation rates to a large extent, it can be seen that it has a strong knock-on influence on the level of exchange rates and the state of the balance of payments capital and financial account.

The position of the balance of payments

8.5   The balance of payments accounts reflect the actual flow of currencies related to international trade and capital movement, and the longer-term trends in these accounts influence exchange rate patterns. The current account shows the ability of a country to finance current overseas expenditure with current overseas earnings. A persistent *current account surplus* will tend to put *upward pressure* on the domestic currency's exchange rate – current account deficits will have the opposite effect. However, *capital and financial account flows* can counteract the effects of current account deficits or surpluses, but to the extent that balance of payments accounts are out of balance overall there will be an effect on long-term exchange-rate trends.

Other influences

8.6 In addition to the above three key economic variables, the following factors can have some influence on exchange rates:

- *Changes* in consumers' tastes, real income levels and productive capacities.

- *Expectations* concerning future economic conditions or government policies.

- Actual or expected changes in the *political and social environment*.

- Effects of *government policies* on the economy and investor confidence, inflation, investment, import controls and so on.

Short-term movements in exchange rates

8.7 In addition to the long-term effects of the above variables, they can also cause short-term changes in exchange rates. For example, a sharp reduction in interest rates could trigger an outflow of short-term international capital. This outflow added to the domestic effects of lower interest rates (such as cheaper credit taken to purchase imports) can only serve to undermine the domestic currency's exchange rate. If interest rates rise, it is likely that short-term investment will be attracted from abroad. If all other conditions remain unchanged the extra demand for sterling for this inward investment will strengthen the exchange rate.

8.8 More important, however, in the short term is the effect of *official currency market intervention* by the monetary authorities both at home and abroad. Large-scale purchases or sales of currencies by a central bank, *if unanticipated by the market*, can have a substantial effect on the exchange rates. Changes in *government economic policies* on trade or investment, if not previously anticipated and discounted by the market, are also likely to alter exchange rates if they are thought to be of serious intent.

8.9 There are many other short-term factors influencing the foreign exchange markets, including speculative activities, industrial unrest (particularly in vital sectors of the economy), forthcoming general elections, the health of influential leaders and bad weather.

Spot and forward exchange rates

8.10 As we have seen above, it is difficult to quantify a *direct* relationship between interest rates and *spot* exchange rates because of the many other factors affecting the equation. However, it is possible to show a direct relationship between interest rates and forward exchange rates, or at least the margin between spot and forward rates. The basic rules for calculating forward rates relate directly to the interest rate differential between the two countries involved. A currency with a higher interest rate will be quoted at a *discount* on the forward exchange market (that is, cheaper than spot). A currency with a lower interest rate will be quoted at a *premium* (more expensive than spot). The premiums and discounts quoted are calculated directly on an annualised basis by using the differences between the eurocurrency interest rates of the two currencies involved. This means that an investor will not gain by buying foreign currency for investment abroad and booking a forward exchange rate for repatriation of the funds on completion of the investment.

Study Activities 8

1. What is the purchasing power parity theory, and what is its relevance for exchange rate determination?   *(Paragraphs 8.2 and 8.3)*

2. What is the relevance of the level of real domestic interest rates for the determination of a country's exchange rates?   *(Paragraph 8.4)*

3. Why is the occurrence of a current account deficit or surplus on the balance of payments regarded as being important for the determination of exchange rates?
                                    (Paragraph 8.5)

4. What is the relevance of official exchange market intervention for exchange rate determination?   *(Paragraph 8.8)*

5. List the types of factors that are likely to influence exchange rates in the short run.
                                    (Paragraphs 8.7–8.9)

6. Other things being equal, what is likely to be the effect on a country's spot exchange rate of an increase in domestic interest rates?   *(Paragraph 8.7)*

7. What determines the discount or premium on a forward exchange transaction relative to a corresponding spot transaction?   *(Paragraph 8.10)*

8. Why will investors not gain simply by buying foreign currency for investment abroad, and then booking a forward exchange rate for repatriation of the funds on completion of the investment?   *(Paragraph 8.10)*

9   Exchange rate regimes

Clean floating exchange rates

9.1   If exchange rates are left purely to market determination, with no direct or deliberate intervention from the monetary authorities, then there is said to be a *clean floating* exchange rate regime in force. Exchange rates will be determined solely by the interaction of the supply of currencies and the demand for currencies on the open market.

9.2   As far as the UK is concerned, credits to the balance of payments accounts represent a supply of foreign currencies (that is, a demand for sterling) from foreigners buying UK exports, investing or making other payments in the UK. Debits to the accounts represent a demand for foreign currencies (that is, a supply of sterling) from UK residents wishing to purchase imports, to invest or make other payments overseas. The interaction of this supply and demand, and supplies of and demands for foreign currencies, will determine sterling's exchange rate against other currencies. Hence, any factor which increases (or decreases) the supply of sterling relative to demand is likely to push the value of sterling downward (or upward) in terms of other currencies.

9.3   The *advantages of clean floating* may be summarised as follows:

●   In theory it provides an automatic mechanism for dealing with balance of payments problems. A current account deficit will lead to foreign currency borrowing to cover current expenditure. Foreign holders of sterling assets will seek higher interest rates to compensate them for holding weak assets or will sell them. This will depress the exchange value of sterling as supply exceeds demand. If the price elasticity of demand for traded goods is high enough the current account balance should improve.

●   Official international currency reserves are not required as government exchange market intervention does not take place.

●   Market forces determine the exchange rate, thus relieving the government of making economically and politically difficult decisions.

●   The government's economic policy may therefore be directed towards domestic problems, e.g. unemployment, inflation and slow economic growth.

9.4   The *disadvantages of clean floating* may be summarised as follows:

●   With no official intervention to stabilise short-term exchange rate fluctuations, markets may become unstable, caused perhaps by pure currency speculation.

●   If price elasticity of demand for internationally traded goods is low, then an ongoing balance of payments problem may result in persistent pressure on exchange rates.

●   A continuing depreciating exchange rate, leading to higher prices for imported raw materials and consumer goods, may generate inflationary pressures within the domestic economy. These pressures may well offset the competitive advantage to exporters given by the depreciating exchange rate.

Managed floating exchange rates

9.5   The above disadvantages of clean floating tend to undermine its attractiveness in practice, particularly in view of the economic instability and financial uncertainty that could arise. However, the *principle* of allowing exchange rates to move broadly in line with market forces, producing a gradual adjustment of exchange rates to reflect underlying real economic factors, is sound enough. A compromise would appear to be a system in which market forces are permitted to determine the longer-term trend in exchange rates with the authorities taking discretionary action to control short-term fluctuations. This system has been used by the UK for most of the period since 1972–3 (except for the 23 months when sterling was admitted to the EU's ERM).

9.6 Within such a system, normally referred to as a *managed floating* regime, the authorities intervene by *buying and selling currencies* on the foreign exchange markets, using the official reserves or official borrowing from overseas. For example, they can sell domestic currency (increase supply) to depress the domestic currency's exchange rate, or buy it (increase demand) to give the exchange rate an upward push. Alternatively, the authorities may *adjust short-term domestic interest rates* to alter net inflows of short-term capital funds from abroad, and increase or reduce demand for domestic currency relative to its supply. One problem with this regime is in deciding when and by how much to intervene; and there are limits to which the authorities are able to intervene.

9.7 It should be recognised that, irrespective of the degree of official intervention to smooth exchange rate fluctuations, there is no guarantee that balance of payments problems will be automatically solved. In fact, experience has shown that substantial deficits and surpluses may persist, as it takes time for trade flows to adjust, and speculative capital flows may cause further problems. However, it is generally agreed that managed floating rates have helped the world economy to adjust to various disturbances, such as the massive oil price rises of the 1970s.

9.8 A variant of managed floating is the *crawling peg* regime. Within this arrangement official intervention takes place in order to achieve specific objectives in relation to the controlled adjustment of the exchange rate. Intervention may be on a continuous basis. This type of arrangement can only be sustained if the market is in broad agreement with the adjustment path chosen by the monetary authorities. The adjustments may be made in accordance with a view on relative inflation rates of competing countries or, perhaps, with reference to a basket of currencies.

Study Activities 9

1. What is meant by a clean floating exchange rate regime?   *(Paragraph 9.1)*

2. What determines exchange rates in a clean floating regime?   *(Paragraph 9.2)*

3. List the key *advantages* of clean floating exchange rates.   *(Paragraph 9.3)*

4. List the main *disadvantages* of clean floating exchange rates.   *(Paragraph 9.4)*

5. What is a managed floating exchange rate regime?   *(Paragraph 9.5)*

6. What instruments do the authorities use in order to operate a managed floating exchange rate regime?   *(Paragraph 9.6)*

7. Describe the crawling peg exchange rate regime.   *(Paragraph 9.8)*

8. What fundamental condition is required for a crawling peg exchange rate regime to be sustainable? *(Paragraph 9.8)*

Fixed exchange rates

9.9   A fixed exchange rate system is one where the authorities attempt to hold the exchange rate of their currency at a fixed rate, or within a narrow margin of a pre-determined value, against other currencies. Extensive exchange market intervention is usually needed by all parties, but there will often be some facility for the adjustment of fixed currency parities if economic pressures demand it. The difference between this system and managed floating is that there is an *overriding commitment to the stability of exchange rates within agreed, narrowly defined margins.* Adjustments to currency parities are not expected to be commonplace, and will usually be countenanced only after extensive negotiations between the countries involved in order to accommodate *fundamental* shifts in their relative economic performances.

9.10   A past example of a fixed exchange rate system, the Bretton Woods adjustable peg system, operated between 1945 and 1972 with each of the major western currencies being pegged to within a plus/minus 1% margin of a fixed US dollar par value. Central banks were obliged to intervene on a day-to-day basis to hold their currencies within the accepted range. Devaluation or revaluation of the currency was allowed only when a country experienced serious balance of payments difficulties, and then only with the permission of the International Monetary Fund if a change in parities of more than 10% was needed. The Bretton Woods system collapsed because the USA ran huge balance of payments deficits in the late 1960s but refused to devalue the US dollar against gold (suspending the gold convertibility of the US dollar instead). In addition, nations with large balance of payments surpluses (particularly Japan and West Germany) refused to revalue.

9.11   Obviously, there are many advantages for countries that are able to achieve stable exchange rates. Business confidence is much higher when international traders and investors can easily assess the value of foreign currency transactions without resorting to currency hedging tools, which are sometimes expensive. Of course, domestic inflation in one country may make devaluation of its currency essential if it is to maintain international competitiveness. Therefore, fixed-rate systems incorporate 'safety valves' which enable such actions to be taken, albeit after appropriate negotiations with other members of the system.

9.12   However, fixed exchange-rate systems suffer from certain disadvantages:

- Authorities must hold sufficient reserves for foreign exchange market intervention purposes to fend off speculative pressures.

- Governments must define exactly how far they are prepared to intervene to protect their exchange rate against market pressures, before they resort to domestic deflationary policies.

● The authorities face the difficult problem of deciding when and by how much fixed exchange rates should be altered if intervention policies do not succeed.

● Sudden alterations in fixed parities under fixed-rate schemes cause periodic destabilisation in financial markets and are also slow to take effect, as trade takes time to adjust to the new exchange rate structure. In the short term, therefore, the underlying problems may well persist.

● Unless the economic performances of the parties to a fixed exchange-rate mechanism converge (particularly with respect to inflation rates), then fixed parities will continuously come under pressure. If they can converge, however, the benefits can be substantial.

● If the parties have differing economic objectives, e.g. growth is espoused by one party, and price stability by the other – then the system will be difficult if not impossible to maintain.

9.13 An extreme version of the fixed exchange rate regime is the *currency board (or gold standard)*. Within this arrangement a country's base money (currency plus bankers' balances at the central bank) must be fully backed by foreign currency (or gold) at a fixed rate. The exchange rate for the domestic currency, therefore, moves with the exchange rate of the currency used as the anchor (or with the value of gold in the case of a gold standard base). Whilst there are clear advantages arising from the automatic discipline enforced on the domestic economy, the regime may also create pressures which may lead to the desire to alter the fixed exchange rate or to abandon the regime.

Study Activities 10

1. In modern usage, what is meant by a 'fixed exchange-rate regime'? *(Paragraph 9.9)*

2. Under what circumstances is it thought to be appropriate for the authorities to alter 'fixed' exchange rates? *(Paragraph 9.9)*

3. What is the major *advantage* of a fixed exchange-rate system? *(Paragraph 9.11)*

4. What are the main *disadvantages* of a fixed exchange-rate system? *(Paragraph 9.12)*

5. What basic economic condition is required for a system of fixed exchange rates to be successful? *(Paragraph 9.12)*

6. How does a currency board exchange-rate regime operate? *(Paragraph 9.13)*

7. Why might a currency board cause problems for the domestic economy?
(Paragraph 9.13)

10 The European Monetary System (EMS)

Background

10.1   On 1 January 1999 a major step was taken on the road to European economic integration. On that date the currencies of EU member states meeting certain criteria for economic performance became eligible to join a single currency arrangement. Consequently, the mutual exchange rates of most major EU currencies (with the notable exception of sterling) became immutably fixed, as did their value relative to the newly launched single currency, the Euro. In order to understand the true significance of this development, it is necessary to have some appreciation of the evolution of the monetary arrangements within the EU (and its predecessor, the EC). Consideration of this evolution also makes an excellent case study of the development of exchange rate regimes in recent years.

10.2   For many years there has been much debate on the view that the EU (formerly the EC) should move towards full economic and monetary union (EMU). At the extreme, EMU may imply the introduction of a single EU currency, with monetary controls being implemented by a European Central Bank, and with substantial power over economic policy being vested with EU institutions. However, as might be expected, there have often been major reservations expressed about such objectives, and in particular a number of EU governments have resisted strongly any proposal which would undermine their sovereign powers in respect of economic policy.

10.3   In 1970 the Werner Report put forward the first comprehensive plan for a movement towards EMU. This plan was accepted in principle, but due to adverse economic conditions during the first half of the 1970s, and with a general lack of practical support from several EC member states, the plan only had a limited impact on exchange rate arrangements within the EC.

10.4   An important step forward was taken at the Bremen Summit of EC Heads of Government in July 1978, when proposals for the formulation of the European Monetary System (EMS) were accepted. The objectives of the EMS were far more limited than those of full EMU, and related primarily to the stabilisation of EU currency exchange rates and mutual financial support for member states. Its overall objective might be summarised as being to achieve a 'zone of monetary stability' (with emphasis on exchange rates, interest rates and prices). The successful operation of the EMS was generally seen as being an important first step on the road towards EMU, and the requirements for its operation were intended to force the necessary economic convergence between EC member states.

The European Monetary System (EMS)

10.5   The European Monetary System was launched in March 1979, although not all
EC member states joined all aspects of its operation. In particular, a number of
member states remained outside of the Exchange Rate Mechanism.

The Exchange Rate Mechanism (ERM)

10.6   This mechanism operated on the basis of two criteria:

● A 'parity grid' arrangement set upper and lower intervention rates for each
pair of currencies. Initially, the grid allowed a maximum of +/– 2.25% relative movement (with +/– 6% for a small number of currencies). However,
following extreme turbulence on the currency exchanges, in July 1993 the
band was widened to +/– 15% for most currencies (officially a temporary
expedient). Once any two currencies reached their relative value limits the
central bank of the country with the weak currency was required to sell the
other country's currency on the currency exchanges, whilst the central bank
of the country with the strong currency was required to buy the weaker currency. These purchases and sales, with supporting currency swaps among
central banks if required, continued until pressure was taken off the currencies' values and they were pushed away from their parity limits.

● *The European Currency Unit Divergence Indicator* provided early warning of
exchange rate pressures. The ECU was used as the basis for calculating a
central rate for each member's currency. Each currency was allocated divergence limits against its ECU central rate. In the event of a currency's value
moving beyond 75% of the maximum deviation permitted, it was expected
that the relevant government would take some form of remedial action. For a
country with a weak currency this might involve the raising of domestic interest rates or perhaps a tightening of fiscal policy. For a strong currency country, some form of expansionary policy might be expected. Thus, the ECU
indicator related to the broad position of a currency relative to all other EC
currencies taken as a group.

10.7   The values of individual currencies could be realigned within the parity grid and
in terms of the ECU central rate if the fundamental economic relationships
underlying the exchange rates altered.

The European Monetary Co-operation Fund

10.8   The European Monetary Co-operation Fund (EMCF) provided financial support to EMS members with international payment problems. It issued ECU to
EU central banks in exchange for deposits of 20% of their gold and dollar
reserves. These swaps were renewed every three months; gold and dollar reserves
did not actually change hands so central banks continued to manage and earn
interest on their dollar deposits. The 'official' ECU created by these swaps could

only be used for transactions between EMS central banks and certain other monetary institutions, e.g. for settling debts incurred in operating the ERM. All EMS members participated in the EMCF swap arrangements, although non-members of the ERM were not obliged to.

The Very Short-term Financing Facility (VSTFF)

10.9   Under the EMS scheme central banks which were members of the ERM opened to each other short-term credit facilities in their own currencies in unlimited amounts to finance intervention when currencies threatened to breach ERM margins. The facilities were short-term in nature, but repayment could be deferred if the borrower's international payments position deemed this necessary.

Study Activities 11

1. Why has the plan for Economic and Monetary Union often generated opposition from individual EU states?   *(Paragraph 10.2)*

2. What were the main objectives of the European Monetary System? *(Paragraph 10.4)*

3. Describe the ERM.   *(Paragraph 10.6)*

4. What was the function of the European Monetary Co-operation Fund?
    (Paragraph 10.8)

5. What were 'Very Short-term Financing Facilities' within the context of the EMS?
    (Paragraph 10.9)

The objectives of the EMS

10.10   The long-term aim of the EMS was to *promote full EMU*, but in the medium term it was intended to create *a zone of monetary stability* within the EU, providing a sound base for trade and payment between members.

10.11   To achieve these objectives, as with any fixed exchange-rate regime, it was essential that the economic performances of all members should be broadly similar. The successful operation of the EMS therefore required a high level of economic policy co-ordination between EC governments to this end. Their policies were required to provide:

● Similarly low levels of inflation in each country;

● A narrowing of interest rate differentials between members;

● Tight limits on balance of payments imbalances.

Failure to achieve these policy objectives would have resulted eventually in exchange rate adjustments having to be made, thus undermining the objectives of the system.

Operation of the EMS and recent developments

10.12   Between its establishment in March 1979 and September 1992, the EMS appears to have operated reasonably successfully, although it was necessary to realign currency exchange values on a number of occasions. Despite these realignments, the exchange rates of ERM participants' currencies were more stable than the exchange rates of the other main Western currencies, and to the extent that this helps to support business confidence this is clearly a positive outcome. However, it must also be recognised that some critics of the ERM have argued that its operation tended to undermine economic growth within the participating countries. Indeed, it must never be forgotten that in order to achieve exchange rate stability in the longer term, it is necessary that the economic performances of the countries involved should be broadly similar. In consequence, the successful operation of the EMS required the subordination of domestic policies within individual countries to this purpose.

10.13   It is the implied loss of sovereignty over economic policy decisions which was often used by the British government to justify sterling being kept out of the ERM. When sterling was put into the mechanism, in October 1990, there was much controversy over the parity chosen. In addition, the fears proved to be well founded that because of sterling's importance in international trade and investment, it might generate instability within the ERM (especially relative to the DM), thereby requiring excessive exchange market intervention. As events turned out, excessive speculation against sterling caused it to be withdrawn from the ERM in September 1992.

10.14   Despite the possible difficulties that might have arisen with the UK's full membership of the EMS, it is important to recognise that there would have been several substantial benefits. In particular, as the EU has for some time accounted for over a half of all the UK's overseas trade, a more stable relationship between sterling and other EU currencies could help both exporters and importers in their business planning and pricing decisions. Also, if UK producers were no longer able to rely upon a depreciating value for sterling in order to maintain their international competitiveness, they would be under greater pressure to hold down wage and price rises, in the face of generally modest inflation rates within the rest of the EU. Failure to hold down UK inflation rates relative to other ERM members could have had dire consequences for UK output and jobs, assuming that devaluation of sterling was not seen as an acceptable option. Finally, the political advantage of full membership of the EMS could not be ignored, especially in the light of the Maastricht Treaty, which saw full participation of all EU members in the EMS as a vital part of the first stage for achieving EMU.

10.15   The ratification of the Maastricht Treaty in July 1993 did little to quell the debate on the future shape of EU monetary arrangements. The Treaty envisaged that by as early as 1997 (a date put back to 1999) there could be the irrevocable fixing of exchange rates within the EU, as the precursor to the introduction of a single EU currency. This development would be subject to a qualified majority of EU states being in favour, meaning that no one member state could veto the move. In addition, at least seven member states would have to meet the economic convergence criteria relating to the long-term determinants of exchange rates, such as inflation and interest rate differentials. However, not only did the UK Government reserve the right to decide nearer the time whether or not the UK would proceed to join a single currency arrangement, but also the EU currency crisis of July 1993 raised doubts as to whether a single EU currency would be viable. Following the crisis (caused by intense speculation against the French franc), most EU currencies within the ERM operated within fluctuation bands of +/– 15%, which could hardly be regarded as a rigid framework for currency stability. The dangers in attempting to force economic convergence through the implementation of an inflexible exchange rate regime between EU currencies were clearly demonstrated through the events of the summer of 1993.

10.16   An important aspect of the Maastricht Treaty was the proposal that a European Central Bank (ECB) should be established, to take up its full powers with the introduction of a single EU currency. It was proposed that the ECB would be politically independent, and would have as its main objective the maintenance of price stability within the EU. In addition, it was agreed that each member state's own central bank would be maintained as part of the European System of Central Banks, and would be expected to support the ECB in the implementation of agreed policy. Each individual central bank would also be required to be politically independent of its own country's government. The responsibilities of the ECB were billed as being the conduct of EU monetary policy and control, foreign exchange market operations, the holding and management of member states' foreign exchange reserves, and the promotion of the smooth operation of EU payments systems.

Study Activities 12

1. What was the long-term aim of the EMS?   *(Paragraph 10.10)*

2. What was the medium-term aim of the EMS?   *(Paragraph 10.10)*

3. What economic conditions were required for the EMS to achieve its desired objectives?   *(Paragraph 10.11)*

4. How successful was the operation of the EMS, at least until the autumn of 1992?   *(Paragraph 10.12)*

5. Why did the ratification of the Maastricht Treaty not signal the end of the controversy over the EU's movement towards EMU?   *(Paragraph 10.15)*

6. What was the role proposed for the European Central Bank by the Maastricht Treaty?   *(Paragraph 10.16)*

11 The Single European Currency

11.1   The single European currency, the Euro, was introduced on 1 January 1999. The EU member states meeting the convergence criteria and choosing to join the single currency at its launch were Austria, Belgium, Finland, France, Germany, Ireland, Italy, Luxembourg, Netherlands, Portugal and Spain. These countries' currency exchange rates are now irreversibly fixed relative to each other and in terms of the Euro. All new public debt issues of these countries are now denominated in Euro, as are all their open-market operations in money markets. General use of the Euro in these countries is still voluntary, but dual pricing will become increasingly common. The changeover period for notes and coin is scheduled for the first half of 2002. From 1 July 2002 the currencies of the EU states listed above will cease to be legal tender.

11.2   Arguments for and against a single currency are complex and divisive. As a single currency means a single form of money and a single monetary policy for the EU, the decision on membership is political as well as economic and commercial. It also affects taxation and public expenditure, because changes in government borrowing affect the money supply and monetary policy.

Arguments in favour

11.3   The following is a summary of the arguments in favour of the UK joining the single currency arrangement:

- There will be a substantial saving in costs. There will no foreign currency exchange costs for businesses exporting to and importing from other participating countries.

- Businesses operating within the single currency zone will avoid translation risk and economic risk (see Section 12 below) that might otherwise arise from exchange rate movements involving the currencies of other participating countries.

- The ECB's major policy goal will be monetary stability, with particular emphasis upon achieving a low rate of inflation.

- There would be a clear political signal given in respect of the UK's commitment to Europe, and its status and influence would be raised within the EU.

- UK interest rates have often been higher than those in the EU. If the UK joins, then UK interest rates could fall.

- A fall in interest rates would help consumers and firms and also reduce the budget deficit.

- Economic growth will be higher because lower interest rates mean more purchases of new plant and machinery.

Arguments against

11.4   Arguments against include:

- The UK loses control of monetary and fiscal policy, although some people argue that in practice it has already lost it before joining a single currency and that independence of action is illusory.

- There could be a requirement for huge budget transfers from richer to poorer EU regions. Supporters of the single currency counter this argument by stating that private capital flows and the market mechanism can perform this redistribution role.

- Europe is not 'an optimal currency area' because:

    - all its regions are not subject to common real economic change with common effects; in particular, labour productivity varies greatly;

    - labour is not mobile between its regions (this latter point is countered by arguments that capital is mobile).

    [It may be argued that Canada and the USA have all the characteristics needed for a single currency, except the desire for one!]

- The costs of conversion far exceed the benefits, especially when much of the required new machinery will be imported.

- The UK will lose the possibility of devaluing to overcome the external demand shocks which are likely to lead to unemployment. Supporters argue that devaluation is not a remedy because inflation is an inherent result and price rises eliminate the temporary benefits brought by devaluation.

Study Activities 13

1. Outline the transition arrangements for the introduction of the single European currency.   *(Paragraph 11.1)*

2. Summarise the arguments in favour of the UK joining a single European currency arrangement.   *(Paragraph 11.3)*

3. Why might the EU not be regarded as 'an optimal single currency area'?
                                                                                                                          (Paragraph 11.4)

4. Summarise the arguments again the UK joining a single European currency arrangement.   *(Paragraph 11.4)*

12   Foreign exchange risks

12.1   Foreign exchange risks can be conveniently classified under three main headings:

- Transaction risk;

- Translation risk;
- Economic risk.

Transaction risk

12.2 Transaction exposure arises from normal trading activities when goods and services are invoiced in a foreign currency. Exporters will gain if the foreign currency appreciates in value between the time of invoicing and the time of settlement of the obligation, whereas importers will lose in such a situation. The converse applies if the foreign currency depreciates in value between invoice date and settlement.

12.3 Since exchange rates are volatile and often unpredictable, it is difficult for a business to anticipate the effect on its earnings of changes in foreign exchange rates.

Translation risk

12.4 Translation exposure arises when there is a mismatch between the currencies of denomination of the assets and liabilities of a company. For example, a major UK-based company whose balance sheet and accounts are reported in sterling may have the following asset and liability mix:

Assets		Liabilities	
Sterling	75%	Sterling	50%
US$	25%	US$	50%

12.5 If the US dollar appreciates in value relative to sterling, then the company's balance sheet must be affected detrimentally because the sterling equivalent of the US dollar-denominated liabilities will rise in absolute terms more than the sterling equivalent of the US dollar-denominated assets. The converse will apply if the US dollar depreciates against sterling, and in this situation there will be a translation gain.

12.6 These changes will show (be translated) in the balance sheet. Any net increase in assets will be balanced by an increase in the reported reserves and hence reported net worth of the business. Any net reduction in assets will be reflected in a reduced net worth.

12.7 Since lenders, creditors and shareholders study balance sheets and net worth when analysing the performance of a company, changes in net worth could affect attitudes and influence the ability of the company to raise money on favourable terms. In addition, translation losses or gains may influence shareholder attitudes in a takeover bid.

12.8 Sometimes a company can take a financing decision that results in the creation of both transaction and translation exposures. For instance, a company may have a sterling overdraft and decide to borrow US dollars, convert them to sterling and pay off the sterling borrowing. The rationale behind this action may well be that interest rates on US dollar borrowing are much lower than interest rates for sterling borrowing. Assuming the company does not have any income or assets denominated in US dollars, then it has incurred a translation exposure because of the US dollar liability, and a transaction exposure because of the need to provide US dollars to meet the interest payments on the US dollar loan. If the dollar appreciates in value after the loan has been made, the real cost of the interest payments will rise because more sterling will be required to obtain the dollars to cover the interest payments. Likewise, there will be a translation loss shown in the accounts because the sterling equivalent of the dollar loan will have increased.

Economic risk

12.9   Economic risk relates to the effects on the overall international competitiveness of a company resulting from exchange rate movements.

12.10   Companies need not be trading internationally to be affected by economic exposure. For example, suppose a British coal mine sells its coal only within the UK and only has one competitor, an Australian mine, for the sale of its coal in the UK. Any fall in the value of the Australian dollar against sterling will provide the Australian coal with a competitive advantage against British coal because the Australian coal will become cheaper in terms of sterling.

12.11   Exposure to economic risk is difficult to quantify and it is not reported in the published accounts of companies. Nevertheless, in the long run, failure to monitor and control economic exposure can result in a serious decline in international competitiveness.

Study Activities 14

1. Explain what is meant by the term 'transaction risk' in relation to exchange rate movements.   *(Paragraph 12.2)*

2. What is the importance of 'translation risk' to a company?   *(Paragraphs 12.4–12.8)*

3. Explain what is meant by the term 'economic risk' in relation to exchange rate movements.   *(Paragraphs 12.9–12.11)*

13   The hedging of foreign exchange-rate risk

Forward exchange contracts

13.1   A forward exchange contract is a contract between a customer and a bank whereby the parties agree a rate of exchange for the sale or purchase of a fixed amount of foreign currency at a fixed future date or between two set future dates. Banks are willing to enter into forward exchange contracts for most currencies for up to one year in advance of the agreed maturity date. For major currencies such as the yen, the US dollar or the Euro, banks may agree forward contracts for up to five-year periods. In effect, the forward contract fixes a rate of exchange today for a deal which it is agreed will take place at a set future date or within a set agreed period in the future.

13.2 It should be remembered that a forward exchange contract imposes an obligation on the customer to put into effect the transaction to which the contract relates. Hence, if the relevant foreign exchange rates have moved in favour of the customer at the time the contract matures, the customer must still deal with the bank at the agreed forward rate of exchange.

13.3 If the customer does not honour the obligation to deliver or take delivery of the foreign currency as specified in the forward contract, the bank will close out the contract. This involves the bank in honouring the customer's obligations by buying the currency at the spot rate and then selling back at the agreed forward rate if the contract was for the bank to sell currency. Alternatively, a closeout will involve the bank in selling the currency at the spot rate and then buying it back at the agreed forward rate if the forward contract was for the bank to buy. The resultant profit or loss on the closeout is then passed on to the customer.

13.4 Forward exchange contracts are appropriate when the customer is relatively certain of the amount and timing of future receipts or payments denominated in foreign currency, and when the customer expects exchange rates to move adversely. If there is a little uncertainty over the timing of the receipt or payment, then the customer could purchase an option forward contract. This gives the customer the choice of (say) a month in which to deliver the currency or sterling. If delivery is not made, then the contract is closed out. It should be noted that option forward contracts are expensive because of the additional risk taken on by the bank.

Currency options

13.5 A currency option operates in a similar manner to an interest-rate option (described in Unit 4). Thus, the holder has the right, but not the obligation, to buy or sell (depending on the type of option chosen) a set amount of foreign currency at a set future date or, if the option is an American option, at any time up to a set expiry date. The holder must pay a premium to acquire the option. This instrument should not be confused with an option forward contract.

13.6 Options are useful when the timing and amounts of payments or receipts denominated in foreign currency are uncertain, because the holder is under no obligation to complete the underlying foreign exchange transaction.

13.7 Options are also applicable when the holder expects the rate of exchange to move in its favour, but feels it necessary to protect against the possibility that rates move the other way. If the rate does move in favour of the holder it can abandon the option and deal at the spot rate. However, if rates move against the holder it can exercise the option and thus protect itself from these adverse foreign exchange movements.

13.8   Options are particularly applicable when a company makes a bid for a large contract with payment denominated in foreign currency. The company may wish to fix the sterling equivalent of the completion proceeds right from the start, but if a forward exchange contract is arranged there is a danger of a potential loss on a closeout if the contract is not subsequently awarded. However, if an option is used, there is no obligation on the holder to exercise it. Hence, if the contract is not awarded, the holder can abandon the option or, depending on which way rates of exchange have moved, the holder may be able to sell the option back to the bank for its intrinsic value.

Currency futures

13.9   Currency futures operate on exactly the same principles as interest rate futures. A company which has future monetary payments or receipts which are denominated in foreign currency may buy or sell a relevant futures contract at the outset, expecting that the resultant gain or loss on closing-out the futures contract may offset the loss or gain on settlement of the currency transaction. However, it should be noted that the standardised terms for futures contracts may mean that it is not possible to match the hedge required and the hedge available, thus giving rise to what is known as 'basis risk'.

Currency swaps

13.10   A currency swap arises when two parties agree to exchange equivalent borrowed sums of two different currencies, together with the associated interest commitments on those sums.

13.11   For example, let us suppose that a US company needs to borrow £10m to acquire a UK outlet, and a UK company needs to borrow $15m to take over a US business. Let us suppose that the current rate of exchange is $1.5 = £1. The US company could borrow $15m and the UK company could borrow £10m. The companies could then swap their respective borrowed principals and their respective servicing commitments. Thus, the UK company would acquire the necessary dollars whilst the US company would obtain the required sterling.

13.12   The effect of the swap is that each company has hedged its translation exposure by taking on liabilities in the currency in which the newly purchased assets are denominated. In addition, both companies will benefit so long as each is able to obtain better borrowing terms in their own domestic markets than they could in the overseas market. Hence the UK company has obtained a lower rates on dollar funds than it would have been able to obtain in its own market, whilst the US company obtains a lower rate on sterling funds than would otherwise be available.

13.13   In practice, the swap is usually arranged through an intermediary bank that guarantees the obligations of both parties. This is particularly important because each party is legally responsible for servicing its original borrowing and this commitment still remains even if the counter-party fails to honour its obligations under the swap.

Currency borrowing for exporters and currency deposits for importers

13.14 A UK company expecting to receive a foreign currency payment at a future date may borrow that amount of foreign currency immediately and convert it into sterling at the current spot rate, thus fixing the exchange rate on the transaction. When the foreign currency payment arrives it will be used to pay off the foreign currency loan. Some adjustment to the amount borrowed will be required in order to take account of the interest to be paid on the loan. Also, of course, the company takes the risk that the foreign currency payment will not materialise, and hence that it will be left holding a foreign currency debt requiring servicing.

13.15 Companies expecting to make foreign currency payments at a future date may use a similar device. In this case a UK company would purchase foreign currency at the current spot rate, and would then deposit the funds into an interest-bearing account in readiness to make the future foreign currency payment. The risk here is that the expected future transaction will not occur, and that the foreign currency funds will not be required, thus leaving the company holding foreign currency funds that have to be converted to sterling at the ruling spot rate.

Study Activities 15

1. What is a forward exchange contract? *(Paragraph 13.1)*

2. In what sense does a forward exchange contract impose an obligation on the parties to the contract? *(Paragraph 13.2)*

3. In what circumstances is the use of forward exchange contracts appropriate? *(Paragraph 13.4)*

4. What is a currency option? (Paragraph 13.5)

5. In what circumstances is the use of currency options appropriate? *(Paragraphs 13.6–13.8)*

6. What is a currency swap? *(Paragraphs 13.10 and 13.11)*

7. In what respect does a currency swap allow a company to manage its risks? *(Paragraphs 13.12 and 13.13)*

8. How might exporters use currency borrowing and importers currency deposits in order to manage risk? *(Paragraphs 13.14 and 13.15)*

Summary

Now that you have completed this unit you should be able to:

- define foreign exchange rates and cross rates;

- calculate a theoretical cross rate;

- describe the structure of the foreign exchange market;

- discuss the fundamental determinants of exchange rates;

- explain how a forward exchange rate is determined using the concept of covered interest parity;

- describe the structure of a country's balance of payments and its terms of trade;

- analyse how changes in the terms of trade affect a country's balance of trade and balance of payments;

- appreciate how changes in a country's balance of payments affect its currency's exchange rate;

- identify and understand the operation of the different types of exchange rate system;

- identify the types of foreign exchange risk, and the various financial derivatives which have been devised to manage such risk.

Self-assessment questions

Short-answer questions

1. As at 1998, where were the world's four major foreign exchange markets based?
2. What is the difference between a 'spot' currency transaction and a 'forward' currency transaction?
3. What is an option forward currency contract?
4. What is the purchasing power parity theory, and what is its relevance for the pattern of exchange rates?
5. What is likely to be the effect on a country's exchange rate if it experiences persistent and substantial balance of payments current account deficits?
6. What is the basic principle of a managed floating exchange rate regime?
7. What basic economic conditions are required for a fixed exchange rate regime to be successful in the longer term?
8. What economic conditions had to be met for the successful operation of the EMS?
9. Other things being equal, an increase in the UK interest rate on sterling funds is likely to cause the spot rate for sterling funds to rise relative to the US dollar, causing a premium to increase or discount to decrease, on forward sales of sterling for dollars. Why?
10. List the three types of exchange rate risk that might be faced by a company.

11. What is a forward exchange contract?
12. What is the difference between a European currency option and an American currency option?
13. Why do companies engage in currency swaps?

Multiple-choice questions

1. Foreign exchange markets

   (a) are located physically in all the Western world's major financial centres

   (b) exist through a sophisticated network of communications

   (c) engage in foreign currency denominated borrowing and lending activities

   (d) have not been subject to official intervention for many years in the UK

   (e) are regulated by the Bank for International Settlements.

2. Principals on the foreign exchange market make a profit by

   (a) buying and selling currencies for third parties

   (b) managing a bank's foreign exchange dealing room

   (c) administering the official government body responsible for dealing in foreign exchange

   (d) buying and selling currencies on their own account

   (e) using agents to act for them on foreign currency exchanges around the world.

3. The major long-term determinant of exchange rate movements is normally thought to be:

   (a) central bank intervention in the foreign exchange markets

   (b) political developments in major Western nations

   (c) industrial unrest in major Western nations

   (d) variations in the economic fundamentals

   (e) changes in the oil price.

4. For much of the period since the early 1970s, the exchange rate for sterling has been:

   (a) pegged to the US dollar

   (b) determined by agreement with other EU countries

   (c) determined within a clean floating exchange rate regime

   (d) determined within a managed floating exchange rate regime

   (e) aligned to the SDR.

5. In a clean floating exchange rate regime

    (a) a current account surplus must be balanced by a deficit on official financing

    (b) a balance of payments deficit must be balanced by a surplus on official financing

    (c) a current account surplus must be balanced by a deficit on the combined capital and financial account balance and balancing item

    (d) a current account surplus cannot occur

    (e) a country's net receipts from services should always balance a deficit on trade in goods.

6. The Exchange Rate Mechanism of the EMS involved

    (a) each member-country committing itself to keeping the value of its currency within a specified margin of an agreed amount of every other member currency

    (b) the fixing of exchange rates of all EU member states relative to each other

    (c) regular realignments of currency values in order to avoid the purchasing power parity theory taking effect

    (d) an agreement to introduce a single currency into the EU once the Single European Market was complete

    (e) members of the EMS depositing their reserve currencies with the ECB.

7. If a country raises its domestic rates of interest relative to those ruling in other major countries, the country's currency exchange rate will

    (a) probably depreciate

    (b) always appreciate, given time

    (c) probably appreciate, other things being equal

    (d) be largely unaffected in the short term

    (e) moved downwards and then upwards (the J-curve effect).

8. The medium-term objective of the EMS was to

    (a) bring about a single European currency

    (b) create a zone of monetary stability within the EU

    (c) cause EU interest rates to fall to the level of those experienced in Japan

    (d) bring about political union within the EU

    (e) bring new members into the EU.

9. If investors buy spot foreign currency to invest abroad at higher interest rates than those available in the domestic economy

(a) they will definitely make a profit as long as they arrange a forward contract to return the money to the domestic currency when the investment matures

(b) the higher overseas interest rates will always benefit them when they bring the money back home, even using spot rates

(c) they will make a loss on the deal even if they arrange a forward contract to repatriate the funds

(d) they will not gain by booking a forward exchange contract for repatriation of the funds on completion of the investment

(e) they need to sell the domestic currency forward to protect the investment abroad.

10. A UK-based company purchases all its raw material from within the UK and all its sales are within the UK. The competitors for the market of that company are a mixture of UK-based and overseas-based companies. The UK company is therefore exposed to

(a) transaction risk

(b) economic risk

(c) default risk

(d) translation risk

(e) default risk and translation risk.

11. A company has bid for a contract in an overseas country, and if the bid is successful a large payment, denominated in foreign currency, will be received. The company needs to protect the value of the potential foreign currency receipt in terms of home currency, but realises that if the contract is not awarded there will be no foreign currency. Which of the following would be the most appropriate hedging instrument?

(a) a forward exchange contract

(b) a currency future

(c) a currency option

(d) a currency swap

(e) a currency deposit.

12. Which of the following constitutes a right but not an obligation on the part of the holder?

(a) a forward exchange contract

(b) a forward rate agreement

(c) a currency option

(d) a financial futures contract

(e) a currency swap.

13. A currency swap arises when two parties

   (a) trade two different currencies with the same value

   (b) exchange equivalent borrowed sums of two different currencies, together with the associated interest commitments

   (c) exchange interest rate commitments on two separate borrowed sums

   (d) exchange currencies raised during trading operations in order to avoid domestic exchange controls

   (e) barter the currencies to avoid the foreign exchange

9
Portfolio Theory

Objectives

After studying this unit, you should be able to:

- understand the fundamental principles of portfolio theory;

- calculate the historic single-period investment return for a security or a portfolio of securities;

- calculate the expected return and the variability of expected return on a security or portfolio of securities;

- explain what is meant by the beta value of an equity share;

- appreciate the pricing of risk in equity and debt markets and the relevance of a share's beta value;

- assess the components of a portfolio's total risk: systematic risk and unsystematic risk;

- demonstrate how diversification of a portfolio of securities eliminates unsystematic risk;

- appreciate the nature of pricing efficiency and the implications for portfolio management;

- appreciate the nature of risk investors carry and the extent of the protection provided by portfolio diversification.

1   Introduction

1.1   In Unit 3 (Section 1) some basic concepts relating to efficient market theory were outlined. In particular, it was noted that the semi-strong version of the efficient market hypothesis argues that the price of securities reflects all publicly available information. Yet there is clear evidence that some securities do out-perform the market. Unfortunately for the investor, the view shared by most academics is that the only way persistently to beat the average return generated by the market is to assume more risk than the market average. Portfolio theory seeks to explain how the investor may reduce the risk that has to be assumed through portfolio diversification.

Return and risk

1.2   The return and risk characteristics associated with different types of securities vary tremendously. For example, the return on *National Savings* instruments is near certain. The Treasury guarantees the interest payments and they have fixed maturity values. The possibility of the government defaulting on its debt commitments is negligible. Therefore, in this sense, this type of asset is as near to being risk-free as might be achieved. By contrast, the return to be achieved on ordinary equity shares in an average company is far from certain. The dividend payments on the equity shares may prove to be higher or lower than expected when the investment was made, and the market price of the equities may not be stable. Overall, the investor faces the risk of making a loss on the investment. At the extreme, the company that issued the shares may get into difficulties and be liquidated – no dividend may be paid and the equity shares could prove to be worthless.

Calculating the historic single-period investment return

1.3   In order to measure the past performance of a security (or a portfolio of securities) it is necessary to calculate the actual return on the security (or the portfolio) taking into account:

●   Any change in the capital value of the security (or portfolio) during the relevant time period.

●   The dividend or interest payments received on the security or portfolio during the relevant time period.

The single period return may be calculated using the following formula:

$$R_l = \frac{P_1 - P_0 + D_1}{P_0}$$

where:

R_l = the return obtained by holding the security (portfolio) for the whole of period 1

P_0 = the market price of the security (portfolio) at the start of period 1

P_l = the market price of the security (portfolio) at the end of period 1

D_l = the dividend or interest income received on the security (portfolio) during period 1.

For example, if securities purchased at the start of 1999 for a price of £1,600 have a market value of £1,700 at the end of 1999, and if the interest and dividends received during 1999 amount to £120, the return on the investment is:

$$R_{1999} = \frac{1,700 - 1,600 + 120}{1,600} = \frac{220}{1,600} = 13.75\%$$

1.4   In relation to measuring the return on a portfolio of securities, care must be taken to ensure that the same assets are held throughout the whole of the relevant time period. Portfolios are often revised during an investment period, and hence it may be necessary to calculate the return on each security separately, with appropriate adjustment being made where they have not been held for the full investment period. However, the same (very simple) measurement principle still holds.

2   Measuring risk

2.1   The usual way to measure the risk associated with investment in a security is via calculation of the *probable variability of future returns*. In other words risk may be measured in terms of the *variance* (or *standard deviation*) of the expected return. The practical interpretation of this concept is explained in Section 3.2 below. For now it is sufficient to note that a security generating a stable return with little possibility of that return deviating from the expected level involves little risk and has a very small (or even zero) associated variance. This would apply, for example, to Treasury-guaranteed *National Savings* instruments. An investment in the equity shares of a high-risk company (that is, one operating in volatile market conditions) would involve the acceptance of possibly quite variable returns (and in some years losses). As the actual return might vary considerably from the expected return on a year-by-year basis, the associated variance of the return on the securities would tend to be high. *The higher the risk the higher the variance.*

Numerical examples

2.2   The easiest way to understand the concept of variance is through consideration of some simple numerical examples. *CASE 1*:

Outcome	Expected return	Probability of expected return occurring	Expected return weighted by probability
A	50%	0.1	5%
B	30%	0.2	6%
C	10%	0.4	4%
D	−10%	0.2	−2%
E	−30%	<u>0.1</u>	<u>−3%</u>
		1.0	10%

In Case 1, it is assumed that there are five possible outcomes, A to E. The probability of each outcome occurring is specified on the basis of past experience. For example, there is a 0.1 (i.e. 10%) probability that outcome A will occur. This outcome involves the occurrence of a 50% expected return on the security. If outcomes A to E cover all possible outcomes, then the combined probability must sum to 1.0 (i.e. 100%).

2.3   To calculate the overall expected return on the security, the expected return for each possible outcome is multiplied by the probability of that outcome occurring (to give the fourth column in the above table) and the weighted expected returns are summed. Therefore, it may be observed that whilst the security has possible expected returns ranging from 50% to –30%, the overall expected return is 10%.

2.4   To calculate the variance of the expected return on the security:

● Square the difference between the expected return for outcome A and the overall expected return and multiply the result by the probability that outcome A will occur.

● Repeat this step for each possible outcome.

● Sum the results generated for all possible outcomes.

Thus, for Case 1:

Variance =

$$0.1(0.5 - 0.1)^2 + 0.2(0.3 - 0.1)^2 + 0.4(0.1 - 0.1)^2 + 0.2(-0.1 - 0.1)^2 + 0.1(-0.3 - 0.1)^2$$

$$= 0.016 + 0.008 + 0 + 0.008 + 0.016$$

$$= 0.048.$$

2.5   The standard deviation is simply the square root of the variance. For Case 1:

Standard deviation = $\sqrt{0.048} = 0.2191$.

Standard deviation and variance are used interchangeably as measures of risk.

2.6   Case 2 has the same possible expected outcomes as Case 1, but the probability distribution is clearly different. There is a much greater chance of outcome C occurring, with the extreme outcomes being only half as likely.

2.7   The overall expected return on the security in Case 2 is again 10%. However, the smaller chance of the extreme outcomes occurring means that the variance and standard deviation are significantly smaller than for Case 1. In other words, the probability distribution of outcomes means that the security depicted in Case 2 is much less risky than the security depicted in Case 1.

CASE 2:

Outcome	Expected return	Probability of expected return occurring	Expected return weighted by probability
A	50%	0.05	2.5%
B	30%	0.10	3.0%
C	10%	0.70	7.0%
D	−10%	0.10	−1.0%
E	−30%	0.05	−1.5%
		1.00	10.0%

For Case 2:

Variance =

$$0.05(0.5 - 0.1)^2 + 0.1(0.3 - 0.1)^2 + 0.7(0.1 - 0.1)^2 + 0.1(-0.1 - 0.1)^2 + 0.05(-0.3 - 0.1)^2$$

$$= 0.008 + 0.004 + 0 + 0.004 + 0.008$$

$$= 0.024$$

Standard deviation $= \sqrt{0.024} = 0.15496$

2.8 So long as expected returns and probabilities of those returns can be specified for each possible outcome, the expected return and risk characteristics for a security may be specified concisely. Consequently, the selection of securities for investment purposes becomes more straightforward and scientific in its method.

2.9 It should, of course, be recognised that in practice the occurrence of unusually good returns on a security would not normally be regarded as a bad thing and hence would not be classified as risk in the normal run of events. However, so long as the possible outcomes are distributed fairly evenly around the expected return (i.e. the pattern of possible outcomes is symmetrical), the variance (standard deviation) measure does provide a reasonable indicator of risk.

Study Activities 1

1. According to accepted wisdom, what must an investor do in order to achieve average returns that are persistently above the average returns for the market as a whole?
(Paragraph 1.1)

2. In what sense are National Savings instruments as near to being risk-free as might be achieved?
(Paragraph 1.2)

3. What risk does the holder of equity shares issued by an average company face?
(Paragraph 1.2)

4. Specify the formula used for calculating the historic single-period investment return on a security or portfolio of securities. *(Paragraph 1.3)*

5. Explain in general terms how the risk associated with an investment in a security is normally measured. *(Paragraph 2.1)*

6. Explain how the expected return on a security is calculated.*(Paragraphs 2.2 and 2.3)*

7. Explain how the standard deviation of the return on a security is calculated. *(Paragraphs 2.4 and 2.5)*

8. Why is it important to have a symmetrical distribution of possible outcomes when measuring the risk associated with a security? *(Paragraph 2.9)*

3 The returns on a diversified portfolio of securities

3.1   The pattern of returns on an individual security may not be symmetrical, as was implied in the above illustrations (Cases 1 and 2). This is hardly surprising given the numerous factors affecting the performance of companies. However, the evidence would appear to suggest that the probability distribution of returns on a well-diversified portfolio of securities is often reasonably symmetrical.

3.2   If returns on a portfolio are distributed symmetrically, then an important approximation of the likelihood of particular outcomes may be used. That is:

● 68% of actual returns on the portfolio tend to fall within one standard deviation of the expected return.

● 95% of actual returns on the portfolio tend to fall within two standard deviations of the expected return.

Therefore, for example, if the expected return on a portfolio is 10% and its standard deviation is 0.035 (i.e. 3.5%), the investor can be reasonably confident that:

● returns will fall between 17% p.a. and 3% p.a. for 95% of the time; and

● returns will fall between 13.5% p.a. and 6.5% p.a. for 68% of the time.

In other words, concentrating on the downside risk, there is a 16% chance of return falling below 6.5%, but only a 2.5% chance of the return falling below 3% p.a.

3.3   It cannot be emphasised too strongly that in practice all portfolios of securities, irrespective of the diversity of their content, carry with them some risk. Selecting low-risk assets may reduce the variability of returns, but it does not eliminate the chance that in any given year losses will be made. Experience also shows that a portfolio of low-risk assets generally implies a portfolio of low-return assets. As stated above, a higher than average expected return can only be achieved persistently by the investor taking on a higher than average level of risk. This means that the investor must be willing to accept the possibility that losses may be made in a greater number of investment periods as the price of raising the average return earned on the portfolio.

4   Reducing risk within a portfolio

4.1   Whilst investors cannot escape from the inherent return-risk trade-off, they may nevertheless construct their portfolios in a manner that aims to minimise the risk assumed at any given desired rate of return. *Modern Portfolio Theory* seeks to explain this behaviour. The theory derives from the seminal work of Markowitz undertaken in the 1950s.

Modern portfolio theory

4.2   The central principle of modern portfolio theory is that it is possible to construct a portfolio of securities which has a return that is less risky than the return on any individual security contained therein. In order to do this it is necessary that the returns on the individual component securities should not be perfectly correlated. If the performance of securities is affected in an identical way by a particular event, then it is not possible to reduce the risk of being adversely affected by the event simply by holding a portfolio of those securities.

4.3   The relative variability of returns on two securities is known as their *covariance*.

- Where the returns on the two securities have a very close positive correlation (i.e. the returns move up and down together in response to particular events) the covariance of the returns on the securities is high and positive.

- Where the patterns of variability in returns have a fairly random relationship, the covariance of the two securities is small and may be positive or negative in sign.

- Where there is a near perfect negative relationship between the variability of the returns on the securities, the covariance is high and negative.

4.4   If the returns on two securities have a high negative covariance, it is possible to eliminate much of the risk faced in holding each individually by instead holding both securities in a portfolio. Consider the following example:

Security	X	Y
Returns in years with a good harvest	30%	–10%
Returns in years with a bad harvest	–10%	30%

Assuming that the harvest is either good or bad (and hence that all possible outcomes are covered):

- Investing in Security X produces a good return in years when the harvest is good, but generates a loss in the years when the harvest is bad. If an investor holds just Security X, then a series of bad harvests could be very damaging financially. A domestic agricultural company might have issued Security X.

- Investing in Security Y produces a good return in years when the harvest is bad, but a poor return when the harvest is good. A food import company might have issued Security Y.

- By dividing investment funds evenly between Securities X and Y, the investor will receive:

  - a return of 10% when the harvest is good – i.e. (0.5 x 30% return on Security X) + (0.5 x –10% return on Security Y); and

  - a return of 10% when the harvest is bad – i.e. (0.5 x –10% return on Security X) + (0.5 x 30% return on Security Y).

  Therefore, irrespective of the quality of harvest, the return is made constant from year-to-year by holding the two-security portfolio, as opposed to holding just one or other of the securities. In this purely theoretical case it would appear that the risk associated with the return on the two securities has been eliminated entirely.

4.5 In reality it is most unlikely that the returns on two securities would be so perfectly matched as to eliminate entirely the risk associated with their respective returns. However, the point is made that so long as the returns on the securities held within a portfolio do not respond in the same way to developments or economic events, the risk embodied in the portfolio is reduced through diversification.

4.6 It must be emphasised that holding just two different securities does not constitute a diversified portfolio. Twenty or more different securities is normally thought of as being the minimum number of securities required to achieve significant risk reduction.

4.7 The key to selecting a diversified portfolio is to be found in selecting securities that are influenced by different sets of economic and financial variables, or are affected differently by particular economic and financial variables. In practice, this means that risks can be reduced by selecting securities that emanate from different business sectors and from different countries, and by including securities issued by both the public sector and the private sector.

Study Activities 2

1. If returns on a portfolio are distributed symmetrically, what important approximations can be made in respect of the likelihood of particular outcomes?   *(Paragraph 3.2)*

2. What does the evidence suggest that an investor must do in order to achieve a persistently higher than average expected return on a portfolio of securities?

   (Paragraph 3.3)

3. What is the central principle of modern portfolio theory? *(Paragraph 4.2)*

4. What is a necessary condition for meeting the central principle of modern portfolio theory? *(Paragraph 4.2)*

5. What is the covariance of the returns on any two securities? *(Paragraph 4.3)*

6. What is the significance of having a high negative covariance in the returns on two securities? *(Paragraph 4.4)*

7. What is generally thought to be the minimum number of securities required in order to achieve a significant reduction in risk through diversification? *(Paragraph 4.6)*

8. What is the key characteristic of a portfolio selected so as to minimise associated risk? *(Paragraph 4.7)*

5 The pricing of risk

Systematic and unsystematic risk

5.1   The risk associated with the return on a security may be divided into two components:

- *Systematic risk* is the risk arising from the variability of security prices in general. The evidence shows that there is a tendency for prices of securities in general to move up and down with the market overall to some degree.

- *Unsystematic risk* is the risk arising from the specific factors that affect the return on a particular security. Specific factors might be, for example, the financial success of a company, the fruits of research and development activity, the discovery of a new oil field by an exploration company, a breakdown in labour relations, a health scare associated with particular types of foodstuffs, and so on.

5.2   *It is because of the existence of systematic risk that diversification does not normally eliminate all risk associated with the return on a portfolio*, irrespective of the number of different securities included. However, *diversification can reduce unsystematic risk*, on account of the uniqueness of its causes and effects in respect of the return on individual securities.

An equity share's beta (β) value

5.3   The extent to which the return on an individual equity share moves with the general trend of the average return on the market (i.e. its systematic risk component) is measured by its *beta value*. Some securities (and portfolios) tend to respond strongly to general movements in the market. The returns on other securities (and portfolios) tend to move less markedly, and may be relatively stable in the face of major market movements.

5.4 The mathematical derivation of beta values is complex. However, the interpretation of beta values is very straightforward. Quite simply, a market index (such as the FTSE 100) is given a beta value of 1. If an individual equity share has a beta value greater than 1, then the return on this share is prone to fluctuate more than the average return on the market index. For example, if the average return on the market index falls by 10%, the return on the share may fall by 15% – this would mean that the share had a beta value of 1.5. In contrast, if an equity share had a beta value of less than 1, then the return on this share is more stable than the average return on the market. For example, a beta value of 0.3 would imply that a 10% fall in the average return on the market index would be matched by a 3% fall in the return on the share. To summarise, for a given security:

- Beta = 1 means that it has the same risk characteristics as the market index. That is, the return on the share fluctuates *in proportion to* the returns on the market index.

- Beta > 1 means that its return fluctuates *proportionately more* than the returns on the market index. Hence, relative to the average of the market as a whole, it is a more risky security. Such securities are sometimes referred to as *aggressive investments*.

- Beta < 1 means that its return fluctuates *proportionately less* than the returns on the market index. Hence, relative to the average of the market as a whole, it is a less risky security. Such securities are sometimes referred to as *defensive investments*.

5.5 A perfectly diversified equities portfolio would effectively be an index portfolio and would have a beta value of 1. The systematic risk would remain and would be reflected in fluctuations in the average return on the market index. Experience has shown that this risk is significant as markets as a whole may rise and fall substantially over very short periods of time.

5.6 By selecting securities at random to include in a portfolio, the chances are that the average beta value for the securities will be around 1. The more of the randomly selected securities that are included, the more likely it is that the average beta value will be 1, but more importantly the more likely it is that average unsystematic risk will diminish. Research has shown that by the time that the portfolio contains in excess of 20 different (well-diversified) securities, with equal amounts invested in each, much of the unsystematic risk will have been eliminated.

5.7 If the securities selected for a portfolio are not chosen at random, but instead are selected according to their beta value, increasing diversification would still result in reduced unsystematic risk, but the beta value for the portfolio overall need not be 1. For example, if all the securities selected had a beta value of less than 1, then the portfolio overall would be a defensive portfolio, with returns tending to fluctuate proportionately less than the average returns of the market as a whole.

The capital asset pricing model

5.8 It is argued that rational risk-averse investors will:

● Require additional expected returns to compensate for taking on additional risk.

● Construct a diversified portfolio of securities.

Therefore, the return that investors require, and the return that the market is willing to pay, will be determined by that component of risk that cannot be eliminated by diversification; i.e. by systematic risk, which cannot be avoided. In other words, the capital asset pricing model suggests that:

● The *return required* on any given security (or portfolio of securities) will depend upon its *beta value*.

● The *total risk* associated with the return on any security is *irrelevant* to the determination of the required return; i.e. because it is relatively easy to eliminate unsystematic risk, investors will not receive any premium for that risk.

5.9 The operation of efficient markets in securities should ensure that diversified portfolios containing securities with the same average beta value should attract the same return, irrespective of the total risk associated with the individual securities. If this was not the case then investors holding diversified portfolios would seek to purchase the securities attracting the higher returns (presumably those with greater associated unsystematic risk) and sell securities earning the lower returns. This action would push up the price of the riskier securities and push down the price of the less risky securities. This adjustment would continue until the returns from securities with the same beta values were equalised.

Implications for portfolio selection

5.10 UK Treasury-guaranteed *National Savings* instruments are effectively risk-free investments. As their return does not alter with movements in the average return in the equities market the beta value of such securities is zero. The return on these instruments is likely to be relatively low and may be thought of as the risk-free rate of interest. The average return on a portfolio of equities with an average beta value of 1 (effectively the equity market index portfolio) is likely to be greater than the risk-free rate of interest *in the long run*. However, on a year-by-year basis there will be fluctuations in the returns on the equities portfolio. In some years, substantial losses may be made; in other years the returns may be positive, but below the risk-free rate of interest; in other years the returns will be substantially greater than the risk-free rate of interest.

5.11   By selecting securities so as to raise the average beta value of the portfolio held, the long-run average returns may be raised, but so too will the associated risk. Today, investors are assisted in this choice process by the provision of estimated beta values for securities by a number of commercial investment organisations.

5.12   The beta value is used rather than the variance or standard deviation of returns on securities for the asset selection process as it is assumed that rational investors will hold securities in diversified portfolios. The beta value measures the risk brought to the portfolio by a particular security and hence is the relevant variable for determining the required return on the portfolio.

Study Activities 3

1. Explain the difference between systematic risk and unsystematic risk as they relate to the return on a security.   (Paragraph 5.1)

2. Explain why portfolio diversification can only reduce the risk associated with the returns on a portfolio, but can never eliminate that risk.   (Paragraph 5.2)

3. What is a beta value?   (Paragraph 5.3)

4. What is the implication of an individual security having a beta value of 1?
                                                               (Paragraph 5.4)

5. What is the implication of an individual security having a beta value greater than 1?
                                                               (Paragraph 5.4)

6. What would be the average beta value of a perfectly diversified equities portfolio?
                                                               (Paragraph 5.5)

7. What is generally thought to be the minimum number of diversified securities required in a portfolio in order to eliminate much of the unsystematic risk?   (Paragraph 5.6)

8. Why might an investor deliberately select securities according to their beta value?
                                                               (Paragraph 5.7)

9. What does the capital asset pricing model say about the importance of total risk associated with the return on a security?   (Paragraph 5.8)

10. Why is an efficient securities market mechanism important to the operation of the capital asset pricing model?   (Paragraph 5.9)

11. What type of security is likely to generate a beta value of zero?   (Paragraph 5.10)

12. Why is the beta value (rather than standard deviation or variance) the relevant measure of risk when an investor is considering adding a security to a diversified portfolio?   (Paragraph 5.12)

Summary

Now that you have completed this unit, you should be able to:

- understand the fundamental principles of portfolio theory;

- calculate the historic single-period investment return for a security or a portfolio of securities;

- calculate the expected return and the variability of expected return on a security and on a portfolio of securities;

- explain what is meant by the beta value of an equity share;

- appreciate the pricing of risk in equity and debt markets and the relevance of a share's beta value;

- assess the components of a portfolio's total risk: systematic risk and unsystematic risk;

- demonstrate how diversification of a portfolio of securities eliminates unsystematic risk;

- appreciate the nature of pricing efficiency and the implications for portfolio management;

- appreciate the nature of risk investors carry and the extent of the protection provided by portfolio diversification.

Self-assessment questions

Short-answer questions

1. Explain briefly how the risk associated with a security may be measured.

2. What is the central principle of *Modern Portfolio Theory*?

3. Explain briefly the concept of covariance as it relates to the return on two securities.

4. In general terms, what is the key to selecting a portfolio of securities designed to minimise the investor's risk at any given level of desired returns?

5. What is the relevance of unsystematic risk to the selection of a security by an investor?

Multiple-choice questions

1. The variance of the returns on a security

   (a) is the difference between the highest and the lowest possible returns on the security

   (b) is the sum of the possible returns on a security weighted according to their probability of occurring

   (c) would be zero if there was absolute certainty as to the returns

(d) grows with the expected returns on the security

(e) is only relevant when the security is marketable.

2. For a particular security, experience has shown that there is a 0.5 probability that the return will be 20% and a 0.5 probability that the return will be 0%. Therefore

(a) there is no risk associated with the security as no losses will be made

(b) the expected return on the security is 20%

(c) the variance on the expected return on the security is 0.01

(d) the standard deviation on the expected return on the security is 0.01

(e) the variance on the expected return on the security is 20%.

3. A well-diversified portfolio of securities has an overall expected return of 8% p.a., with a standard deviation of 0.05. The investor can be reasonably confident that

(a) there is a 95% chance that the return will be 8% p.a.

(b) here is a 95% chance that the return will be between 3% p.a. and 13% p.a.

(c) the return will never fall below 0% p.a.

(d) the return will never rise above 13% p.a.

(e) there is an 84% chance that the return will be greater than 3% p.a.

4. In order to reduce the risk associated with a portfolio of securities through diversification, it is necessary to ensure that

(a) there is perfect positive correlation between the returns on the individual component securities

(b) there is a covariance greater than 1 between the returns on each pair of component securities

(c) the sum of the covariance on the returns generated by the component securities is zero

(d) at least some of the additional securities are risk-free gilt-edged securities

(e) the returns on the individual component securities are not perfectly correlated.

5. The return required by a rational investor on a diversified portfolio of securities

(a) depends upon the combined measures of systematic risk and unsystematic risk

(b) depends upon the systematic risk associated with the returns on the portfolio

(c) will be reduced to the extent that a greater proportion of the securities held have a low associated unsystematic risk

(d) becomes larger the longer is the investment horizon of the investor

(e) is unaffected by holdings of risk-free Treasury-backed securities.

6. The beta value of a security larger is

    (a) the greater is the unsystematic risk associated with that security

    (b) the less likely it is that a rational investor will wish to hold the security

    (c) the more attractive is the security to a risk-averse investor

    (d) the greater is the sensitivity of the return on the security to the general trend in the overall market return

    (e) the more suitable it becomes for holding in a defensive investment portfolio.

10
Corporate Sector Finance

Objectives

After studying this unit, you should be able to:

- discuss the broad trends in corporate sector financing in the UK and identify the various financing alternatives available to companies of different sizes;

- understand the role of equity, bank debt and non-bank debt in corporate sector balance sheets;

- appreciate the role of rating companies and the importance of credit ratings in the pricing of corporate sector debt;

- appreciate the impact of internal cash flow and the business environment on corporate requirements for external funds;

- understand the basic corporate financing role of various debt and equity instruments;

- describe the various mechanisms by which shorter-term (working capital) and longer-term (investment) requirements may be funded;

- appreciate the nature of business and financial risk faced by companies;

- understand the basic principles of interest rate and exchange rate risk management;

- describe the operation and qualities of basic corporate financial risk management instruments.

1   Background issues

1.1   One of the most important functions of the financial system is to meet the financing requirements of the corporate sector, i.e. all private sector companies that are not classified as banks or other financial institutions. Companies are major borrowers from the banking sector, as well as being important customers for other banking services. They are also the source of equity and debt securities, the issue and trading of which dominate capital market activities; and a significant proportion of the turnover of the money markets relates to short-term corporate financing. Therefore, the financing operations of the corporate sector have crucial implications for the prosperity and development of financial institutions and markets.

1.2 In recent years the overall financial position of the corporate sector has been rather variable. In aggregate, between 1988 and 1992, the corporate sector generated substantial financial deficits, with the peak value deficit being £18.7bn in 1990. This continual increase in net indebtedness over this period was in sharp contrast to the position between 1981 and 1987 when the sector was a substantial net provider of funds to other sectors of the economy. During 1993, the sector returned to an overall surplus and in 1994 this rose to £12.6bn, reflecting the recovery in economic conditions and the improved state of company finances. The sector returned once again to deficit in 1995, and following a short-lived improvement in 1996, the position deteriorated rapidly with the deficit standing at £26.9bn in 1998. This recent deterioration has been due more to an increase in capital expenditure and investment in securities (of both UK and overseas companies) than to changes in internal funds generation.

UK corporate sector aggregate balance sheet

Financial assets

1.3 These consist of:

- Notes and coin – a small fraction of the total, largely held by retail outlets for day-to-day transactions.

- Public sector debt instruments – secure, interest-bearing investments.

- Bank deposits – an important item, showing steady growth in recent years; the main liquid asset held.

- Building society deposits – much less important than bank deposits following a significant reduction in recent years, reflecting the conversion of many of the larger building societies to bank status.

- Claims on other businesses – these are the dominant items, and include trade credit outstanding, holdings of UK and overseas company securities, and direct and other investment overseas (which is the largest single item amongst the financial assets). It should be noted that the value of marketable securities depends upon market forces, and that movements in exchange rates may influence the sterling value of foreign currency denominated assets.

Financial liabilities

1.4 These consist of:

- Public sector lending – this largely relates to purchases of commercial bills by the Bank of England, the significance of which has declined markedly in recent years.

- Bank lending – a major item of corporate sector debt which grew steadily until 1990, contracted somewhat during the recession of the early 1990s, but which has grown again in recent years.

- Other financial institution lending – demonstrates a similar pattern to bank lending, but is of much less significance.

- Trade credit – an important element of debt which has grown steadily in recent years.

- Securities issues – by far the largest item, effectively representing the nominal value of equities and marketable debt issued by companies. New issues and redemption of securities influence the total value outstanding, and stock market conditions influence the attraction of this source of finance. Also, it must be emphasised that equities do not represent creditors' claims. Their inclusion under the liabilities heading is conventional within the official statistics.

- Overseas direct and portfolio investment – this has grown significantly in recent years, reflecting the relative attractions of investment in the UK.

1.5   In recent years, the UK corporate sector has had substantial net financial liabilities. However, the special position of equity claims on companies must be recognised, as must the fact that in a capitalist economic system individuals ultimately own a large proportion of all national wealth, either directly or indirectly (via claims on financial institutions). Also, the corporate sector holds substantial amounts of tangible assets, such as buildings, plant and equipment, stocks and work-in-progress. Over the longer term the net asset value of the corporate sector has tended to be positive.

UK corporate sector sources and uses of funds

1.6   Examination of a balance sheet shows the relative importance of various assets and liabilities held at a specific point in time. However, in order to understand how companies are financed and the uses to which they put their net inflows of funds, we must consider the sector's sources and uses of funds data.

Sources of funds

1.7   For any company, the sources of funds may be divided into internal and external sources.

- *Internal funds* basically relate to the net income generated by a company that has been retained rather than distributed to shareholders.

- *External funds* relate to borrowing from banks and other financial institutions, issuing of securities (both equity and debt), and flow of other investment funds.

1.8   The importance of internal funds grew significantly between 1989 and 1994, as the amount of funds raised externally fell markedly (with the exception of the 1993 flow, which staged a short-lived recovery). Since 1995 external funding has risen substantially, with bank funding showing a major turnaround to produce large net borrowing positions in 1995 through to 1998.

1.9   In each year between 1991 and 1994 there were unprecedented net repayments of bank loans by the sector, whilst fairly substantial share and other capital issues occurred. It was the reduction in bank borrowing during the early 1990s that bore the brunt of the corporate sector's financial adjustments during the recession of that period. This development was quite understandable in the light of the uncertain economic environment, and following the pressures placed upon banks themselves to take extra care to avoid unnecessary risk. The subsequent recovery in economic conditions and the more stable financial environment explain the more recent positive attitude to bank borrowing. However, since 1995, a much more important source of external funding has been capital market issues, with substantial ordinary share, debenture and preference share issues taking place against the background of a generally buoyant stock market. Interestingly, the largest single source of external funding in 1997 was overseas investment, despite the strength of sterling and the uncertainty surrounding the UK's commitment to a single European currency. Indeed, it should also be noted that overseas sources have for many years made important contributions to the external funds used by UK companies, via the purchase of securities, direct investment and overseas bank loans. It was only during the period 1991 to 1994, at a time when major overseas economies were themselves slipping into recession, that the inflows of direct investment funds from overseas diminished temporarily, and, to some extent, these were counter-balanced by higher inwards portfolio investment.

Uses of funds

1.10   Between 1989 and 1992 there was a substantial reduction in the total amount of funds used by UK companies. A major factor explaining this trend was the deteriorating state of business prospects. However, during this period and subsequently, the sector continued to build up its holdings of liquid assets, and especially its holdings of bank deposits. Attractive returns available on wholesale deposits, and the desire to provide for unforeseen contingencies were probably key factors underlying this trend. The major reductions in the use of funds were in respect of stock building, investment in UK companies' securities and investment overseas. Quite simply, the deteriorating state of the world economy in general, and the UK economy in particular, at the beginning of the 1990s, made investments in both UK and overseas companies rather unattractive and fairly risky.

1.11   Since 1993, the total amount of funds used by UK companies has risen substantially, reaching a record level of £171bn in 1998. Stock building was an important factor between 1993 and 1996, but the dominant items have been investment in UK companies' securities, which increased substantially, and gross domestic fixed capital formation (real capital investment), which reached £92bn in 1998. Also, the position in respect of investment overseas has strengthened substantially since 1993.

1.12   In recent years there have been some fundamental changes in the patterns of UK corporate sector finances. These changes have had important effects on the corporate financing facilities provided by both banks and other financial institutions. As the UK economy exhibits reasonably steady growth, the nature of competition between financial institutions for corporate business and the continuing evolution of the financial markets will be critical in determining the future patterns of corporate financing.

Types of external finance commonly used by companies

1.13   There are many different sources of external finance that may be used by companies. These may be categorised as follows:

Short-term debt finance

● Overdraft facilities

● Short-term LIBOR-linked loan facilities – committed and uncommitted

● Acceptance credits

● Commercial paper

Long-term debt finance

● Bank loans

● Sterling debentures

● Eurobonds

Equity finance

● Ordinary shares

● Preference shares

● Cumulative preference shares.

1.14   It should be recognised that there is some overlap between the debt categories, primarily because of questions on the appropriate definition of the short-term as opposed to the long-term. For example, it might be argued that medium-term notes, which are a particular variety of sterling commercial paper (with an initial maturity of between one and five years) should be identified separately either in a *medium-term debt* class of instruments or amongst the long-term debt instruments. Also, companies may rollover short-term debt to turn it into *de facto* medium-term or long-term debt, and, of course, long-term loans may be retired prematurely. However, far more important than the grouping of instruments is being aware of their individual characteristics and understanding how they may be used to meet corporate financing needs.

Study Activities 1

1. In general terms, why is the corporate sector of major importance to the operations of the financial system? *(Paragraph 1.1)*

2. What has been the overall financial position of the corporate sector in recent years? *(Paragraph 1.2)*

3. What are the most important groups of financial assets on the corporate sector's balance sheet? *(Paragraph 1.3)*

4. What is the importance of bank lending to the corporate sector, and in what way did its position change during the early 1990s? *(Paragraph 1.4)*

5. What are the most important groups of financial liabilities on the corporate sector's balance sheet? *(Paragraph 1.4)*

6. What does internal financing for companies mean? *(Paragraph 1.7)*

7. What is meant by external financing for a company? *(Paragraph 1.7)*

8. In what ways have the sources of funding used by UK companies altered since the late 1980s? *(Paragraphs 1.8 and 1.9)*

9. In what ways have the uses of funds for UK companies altered since the late 1980s? *(Paragraphs 1.10–1.12)*

10. List the main types of external finance that may be used by a company. *(Paragraph 1.13)*

2   Overdraft facilities

2.1   Overdraft facilities are provided by banks and allow corporate customers to overdraw their current accounts up to an agreed maximum amount. Interest is charged on the overdrawn balance at close of business each day. The facility usually lasts for one year, and then can be renewed by mutual agreement.

2.2   The *benefits* of the overdraft from the point of view of corporate borrowers are that:

- The facility is flexible and is ideal for financing day-to-day working capital needs.

- The facility is not tied to any specific transactions. In this respect, it is different from an acceptance credit.

- The documentation is simple and can be quickly arranged.

- Interest is charged on the daily debit balance and thus interest costs are minimised.

- If the facility is secured, a lower rate of interest may be available because of the lower risk for the lender.

- As an uncommitted facility, there is no non-utilisation fee, although there is normally an initial arrangement fee.

2.3 The *drawbacks* of overdraft facilities from the borrower's point of view are that:

- Overdraft facilities are, in theory, repayable on demand. However, it is unlikely that a bank would exercise this right unless the position of the borrower had deteriorated dramatically. Nevertheless, it should be remembered that in difficult times companies would be safer with committed facilities, such as loans, which cannot be called in unless there is a breach of one of the covenants in the loan agreement.

- Overdrafts are sometimes linked to base rate whereas other facilities for major corporate borrowers could be linked to LIBOR. Generally speaking, base rate will be higher than LIBOR.

- The borrower is exposed to interest rate fluctuations as interest rates are linked to base rate or LIBOR. However, base rate does not experience such volatile movements as other interest rate benchmarks, such as LIBOR.

2.4 There is also a drawback for lenders, when companies draw cheques for large amounts on their current accounts – whether in debit or credit – as this may cause substantial swings in the operational balances of the banks involved. The need to keep these balances at the target levels agreed with the Bank of England can cause extra work for the treasury dealers who manage the banks' liquid assets. Hence, the margin over LIBOR at which the overdraft is priced will be set so as to reflect this risk created for the bank. In addition, the margin is designed to make overdrafts unattractive as core borrowing facilities.

3 Short-term LIBOR-linked loan facilities

Committed LIBOR-linked loan facilities

3.1 These are known as committed facilities because a bank allows its customer to take out various LIBOR-linked loans of varying maturity (usually one to three months), subject to a maximum total amount outstanding at any one time. The minimum total facility is usually £250,000 and the minimum individual loan is usually £100,000. The maximum facility and individual loan size are fixed by negotiation between the bank and the customer.

3.2 The *benefits* of a LIBOR-linked loan facility for the corporate borrower are that:

- The documentation is standardised and simple.

- There are many banks which offer these facilities, hence the margins over LIBOR are kept relatively low because of competitive pressures amongst the providers of such finance.

- The facility is committed, hence the borrower knows that the funds will be available if needed (except in the comparatively rare case where the bank has insisted on a demand clause whereby the facility may be withdrawn without notice after a demand is made and not immediately met).

- As with overdrafts, there is no need for the loans to be tied to specific transactions.

3.3   The *drawbacks* from the corporate borrower's point of view are that:

- A non-utilisation fee is payable on unused facilities, thus making these loans more appropriate where the borrower has a fairly certain financing requirement. In addition, the bank may well charge a commitment fee for setting up the facility.

- The borrowing is linked to three-month sterling LIBOR which is more volatile than base rate. Hence, there is a greater interest-rate exposure than would apply with an overdraft linked to base rate.

Uncommitted LIBOR-linked loan facilities

3.4   Major companies with high credit ratings (and normally whose shares are included in the *FTSE-100* Index) can *enter the money market directly* for the purposes of raising immediate short-term funds. There are no commitment fees or non-utilisation fees to pay since the facility is uncommitted. The minimum amount via this direct borrowing facility is usually £1m. The margin over LIBOR is narrower than for the committed LIBOR-linked loans raised in the normal way, because the company deals directly with a bank which wishes to make a deposit for the period and amount which matches the borrower's requirements.

4   Acceptance credits

4.1   Companies may raise short-term finance via the drawing of *bills of exchange* as the *counterpart to commercial transactions*. Where goods are sold on credit, the vendor may draw a bill (which is effectively a claim on the purchaser of the goods). The bank *accepts* the bill of exchange in return for a fee. By accepting the bill, the bank is effectively *guaranteeing payment* to the holder at maturity. Once a bill has been accepted by a bank, the company should easily be able to find a third party who will discount the bill (that is, purchase the bill for an amount below its face value at maturity). The difference between the face value of the bill and the amount paid when it is discounted represents the effective rate of interest; the lower the difference (or discount), the lower the effective rate of interest.

4.2   When a bank has accepted a commercial bill, it becomes a *commercial bank bill* and if that bank is an eligible bank, then the bill becomes an *eligible bank bill*. (Eligible banks are banks that meet the minimum criteria of the Bank of England for the quality of their acceptance business, market standing and, for foreign banks, the treatment of UK banks in the relevant overseas market.) The finest rates of discount apply to eligible bills, because these bills may be discounted at the Bank of England.

4.3 The bill itself must be related to an *underlying trade transaction*, and there must be a brief mention of this transaction on the bill itself. The original term of the bill must not exceed 187 days and the bill must be payable in the UK.

4.4 Companies may arrange an *acceptance facility* with their bank, which will allow them to have bills accepted automatically up to a fixed limit. The minimum facility is usually around £500,000, and minimum denomination of bills is £50,000. A commitment fee has to be paid for this facility, in addition to the acceptance fee. However, as these payments are known in advance, and the discount is fixed at the time that the bill is sold, the total cost of funds will be known precisely.

4.5 The *benefits* of acceptance credit finance for companies are that:

- Depending upon the fees involved, bill finance may be cheaper than funds raised via short-term bank loans, with the discount rate on eligible bank bills often being below LIBOR.

- Discount (that is, the effective rate of interest) is fixed at the outset, hence the cost of borrowing is not affected by subsequent interest rate changes.

- The facility is flexible since bills can be drawn for varying amounts and at varying maturity up to 187 days.

- The facility is self-liquidating, provided the underlying trade transaction is completed and the debtor pays.

- There is no tie to the accepting bank and bills may be discounted with another organisation if that organisation offers a better discount rate.

4.6 The *drawbacks* to acceptance credit finance are that:

- The facility is only available if there is an underlying trade transaction.

- The discounted bill may subsequently be re-sold (rediscounted) to another party. Thus, the drawer's name and the underlying transaction (which must be specified on the bill) could become public knowledge, with obvious implications for the drawer's commercial position.

Study Activities 2

1. Describe the key characteristics of an overdraft facility.   *(Paragraph 2.1)*

2. List the benefits and drawbacks of an overdraft facility for a corporate borrower.
   (Paragraphs 2.2 and 2.3)

3. What is a short-term committed LIBOR-linked loan facility?   *(Paragraph 3.1)*

4. What are the benefits of a committed LIBOR-linked loan facility for a corporate borrower? *(Paragraph 3.2)*

5. List the drawbacks of a committed LIBOR-linked loan facility for a corporate borrower. *(Paragraph 3.3)*

6. What types of companies may raise funds directly from the money markets? *(Paragraph 3.4)*

7. What are the advantages of raising money directly from the money markets for a corporate borrower? *(Paragraph 3.4)*

8. What is an acceptance credit? *(Paragraphs 4.1–4.3)*

9. Describe a typical acceptance facility. *(Paragraph 4.4)*

10. What are the benefits of using acceptance credits for a corporate borrower? *(Paragraph 4.5)*

11. What are the drawbacks to acceptance credit finance for a corporate borrower? *(Paragraph 4.6)*

5   Commercial paper and medium-term notes

5.1   Commercial paper relates to marketable, unsecured promissory notes issued by companies and purchased directly by investors. The notes are issued at below their face value but are redeemed at par by the issuing company. The discount rate for sterling commercial paper is usually linked to the London Inter-bank Bid Rate (LIBID). This form of corporate borrowing bypasses the normal financial intermediary (since investor and borrower deal direct) and hence the process provides a good example of disintermediation.

5.2   The three main commercial paper markets are US dollar commercial paper (USCP), Euro-commercial paper (ECP) and Sterling Commercial Paper (SCP). If the paper is issued with an initial maturity of between one and five years, it is known as medium-term notes (MTNs).

5.3   Commercial paper is usually issued under a *programme* managed by a bank or syndicate of banks, while MTNs are often issued as part of a *Note Issuance Facility* arranged and managed by a syndicate of banks.

5.4   The *benefits* of commercial paper finance for companies wishing to raise finance are that:

- It does not have to be tied to an underlying trading transaction, thus giving greater flexibility.

- On account of the disintermediation process, whereby the traditional bank deposit/lending function is omitted, it is possible for borrowers to obtain funds at lower cost whilst investors receive higher rates of return.

- The facility is flexible, since commercial paper can be issued with original maturity of between seven days and five years.

5.5 The major *disadvantages* of commercial paper are that:

- The minimum denominations are relatively high (£100,000 for an individual note for SCP, as opposed to £50,000 for individual bills with acceptance credits).

- It is necessary to make fairly regular issues of commercial paper to establish a high market profile and to maintain investor interest.

- The documentation requirements may be demanding.

- There is a minimum net asset requirement (of £25m in the case of SCP) which precludes many companies from using this facility. Also for SCP the company's shares or those of its guarantor must be listed on the London Stock Exchange or on a comparable overseas stock exchange.

- For USCP and ECP, it is usually necessary for the borrower to obtain a r ating from one of the commercial rating organisations such as Moody's or Standard & Poor. These ratings are costly to obtain and so set an initial cost for entry into the market. However, if the rating is high enough the company may be able to issue commercial paper at relatively attractive discounts (i.e. at lower effective interest rates). In some instances, the guarantee of a first class bank may be an acceptable alternative to a commercial credit rating.

- There is no guarantee that investors will always take up any issue of commercial paper and thus it may be necessary to arrange stand-by funding, perhaps from a bank, in order to cover the risk of an issue being under subscribed. Naturally, the bank will charge a commitment fee for the stand-by facility.

5.6 In the UK, initially SCP could only be issued with a maturity of up to one year. Since the enactment of the Companies Act 1989, it has been possible for companies to issue SCP with an original maturity of up to five years. As mentioned above, issues with original maturity in excess of one year are normally referred to as medium-term notes. This market was given a further boost in January 1990 by the Bank of England's announcement that the range of short-term paper which could be issued without the need for a prospectus would be extended to cover issues with an original maturity of between one and five years.

6 Long-term bank loans

6.1 In today's competitive market, banks are willing to structure bank loans on a made-to-measure basis to meet the specific needs of corporate customers. Consequently, it is difficult to generalise on the nature of bank loans. However, it is possible to appreciate the vast range of lending packages available from banks by considering the main characteristics of a bank loan.

6.2   The *term to maturity* can be anything from one to 10 years, but it is not uncommon for loans to be made with repayments scheduled over 30 years.

6.3   *Repayment of capital* may be spread over the life of the loan or may be deferred for fixed periods. *Early repayment* of fixed term loans is possible but the bank may levy a cancellation fee.

6.4   *Interest can be fixed or variable.* Variable rates can be linked to LIBOR or to base rate. There can be an arrangement whereby fixed interest rates will only apply for part of the loan period and then rates will be subject to renegotiation for the remainder of the loan. There may also be options to switch at pre-determined points in time, and interest may sometimes be deferred at the start of the loan period.

6.5   The majority of long-term loans are *secured* against specific assets of the borrower, or alternatively there may be a floating charge covering all the assets. Failure to service the debt within the terms of the loan agreement may threaten the long-term survival of the company.

6.6   There will usually be covenants in the loan agreement by which the company agrees to *maintain minimum financial ratios* such as gearing (ratio of debt to equity).

6.7   The majority of banks charge *commitment fees* for arranging the facility and there may well be specific charges to cover the cost to the bank of tying up its capital in the loan.

6.8   Where the amount required by a single customer is too great for one single bank (because the bank does not wish to become too exposed to one borrower or to one market sector), *syndicated loans* may be offered. Here, one bank acts as lead bank and undertakes negotiations with the borrower on behalf of a syndicate of banks. Syndicated loans enable banks to obtain business that would not otherwise be available and to spread the risk among their number. They enable the borrower to obtain a loan with lower transaction costs than would have applied if the funds had been raised through a number of separate loans from different banks for smaller amounts.

6.9   At times when confidence in the economic system is high, syndicated loans are not as popular as other facilities such as commercial paper that involve disintermediation. However, when confidence ebbs, companies prefer the safety of a loan. This was illustrated by the surge of syndicated loans that occurred just after the October 1987 world stock market crash.

6.10   An important use of syndicated loans is in the financing of acquisitions. Stock Exchange rules require that quoted companies must have committed funds available to finance proposed acquisitions. Syndicated loans are an efficient and flexible way of providing this finance. Once the acquisition has received shareholder and regulatory approval, normally the company will then refinance the syndicated loan facility through the capital markets. In this case the syndicated loan is being used as bridge finance for the acquisition.

6.11   A variant of the normal form of bank loan is the use of leasing capital assets. Large companies often acquire the use of capital assets via *lease finance from a bank*. The bank acquires the capital assets, obtaining any associated tax allowances on the capital expenditure, and then gives the company use of the assets for an agreed period. The implications for the security of the bank's funds are fairly clear, as are the potential tax allowances, especially where the user of the assets is unable to take advantage directly of capital allowances.

Study Activities 3

1. What is commercial paper?   *(Paragraph 5.1)*

2. What are the three main commercial paper markets?   *(Paragraph 5.2)*

3. What are the benefits for a company of raising finance through an issue of commercial paper?   *(Paragraph 5.4)*

4. What are the main disadvantages for a company of raising finance through an issue of commercial paper?   *(Paragraph 5.5)*

5. List the key characteristics of long-term bank loans.   *(Paragraphs 6.2–6.7)*

6. What is a syndicated bank loan?   *(Paragraph 6.8)*

7. Under what conditions are syndicated loans likely to prove popular with corporate borrowers?   *(Paragraph 6.9)*

8. What role may be played by syndicated loans in corporate acquisitions?
                                                                     (Paragraph 6.10)

9. What are the advantages to banks and their customers of using lease finance for the purchase of capital assets?   *(Paragraph 6.11)*

7   Sterling debentures

7.1   Sterling debentures (sometimes called sterling bonds) are transferable registered secured loan stocks by which a company can raise funds. The stocks are issued by way of an offer for sale to the general public or by a private placing with the clients of a merchant bank or other major financial institution. The debentures of public listed companies are quoted on the London Stock Exchange.

7.2   The sterling debenture is only suitable for raising large amounts of funds, with a typical issue being in the range of £30–100m. The original maturity period must exceed five years. (The medium-term note market has superseded the sterling debenture market for issues of less than five years' original maturity.)

7.3 The launch of corporate bond PEPs provided a stimulus for managers of unit trusts and investment trusts to purchase more sterling debentures than has been their practice. However, such bonds carry an interest-rate risk and no possibility of substantial capital gain. If secured, their credit risk is less than that of equity shares.

7.4 The *benefits* of sterling debentures to the corporate borrower are that:

- the rate of interest is fixed for the period of the loan.

- the cost of servicing is fixed for the whole loan period.

- the company issuing the debentures may be able to repurchase them in the market, subject to certain legal formalities, and this will prove beneficial if interest rates in general have fallen and refinancing at lower cost is available.

7.5 An important determinant of the price of corporate bonds (effectively the return that must be offered for investors to take up an issue) is the *credit rating of the issuer*. Companies achieving the highest rating (AAA or Aaa) may raise funds at a very small margin above the comparable risk-free benchmark government security. The lower the credit rating, the higher the yield required by investors. High-yield bonds are often referred to as *junk bonds* on account of their perceived poor quality.

8 Eurobonds

8.1 Eurobonds are foreign-currency-denominated bearer securities that may be issued by way of an offer for sale to the general public or by a private placing with investors. Public issues are normally made through a syndicate of banks, which underwrites the bonds and distributes them to investors. Public issues are usually listed on one of the major stock exchanges whereas private placements are rarely announced publicly and are rarely listed on any stock exchange. Clearly, the private placements will tend to result in a narrow ownership with fewer opportunities for the holder to sell the bond prior to maturity.

8.2 Eurobonds are only suitable for raising large amounts of funds with a typical acceptable minimum issue being in the region of US$75m or its equivalent. Therefore, the market is only relevant to large companies. Companies that have a high credit rating, an international presence and a widely recognised name achieve the best rates on eurobonds, which provide a useful means of raising foreign currency funds without having to enter overseas financial markets.

8.3 Eurobonds are unsecured and this helps the issuer to maintain creditworthiness with other providers of finance, as it is unnecessary to commit assets as security for eurobonds. Such assets may therefore be used to support other types of financing.

8.4   The most popular type of eurobond is a fixed-rate bond with the whole of the principal debt repaid on maturity.

8.5   Eurobonds may be issued as *convertibles* or with *warrants* attached, which give the holder a right to purchase ordinary shares in the issuing company at a predetermined price.

8.6   Floating rate bonds are linked to LIBOR. As interest rates on eurobonds tend to reflect those ruling in the country from where the currency of denomination originates, it may be possible to raise funds more cheaply than in domestic markets. However, unless the borrower anticipates having incomes denominated in the same currency as the bonds, unexpected adverse exchange rate movements could make the real debt servicing costs much higher than the nominal rate payable on the bonds.

8.7   The role of the *credit rating agencies* is vital to the pricing of eurobonds. Even a modest downgrading of the credit rating may cause a significant increase in the yield required by investors on the bonds.

Study Activities 4

1. What are sterling debentures?   *(Paragraph 7.1)*

2. For what type of fund-raising are sterling debentures appropriate?   *(Paragraph 7.2)*

3. What are the benefits for a corporate borrower of using sterling debentures to raise funds?   *(Paragraph 7.4)*

4. What are junk bonds?   *(Paragraph 7.5)*

5. What is the importance of credit rating agencies in the pricing of corporate bonds?   *(Paragraph 7.5)*

6. What are eurobonds?   *(Paragraph 8.1)*

7. For what type of fund-raising are eurobonds appropriate? *(Paragraphs 8.2 and 8.3)*

8. Describe some of the different types of eurobonds.   *(Paragraphs 8.4 and 8.5)*

9. Why might it be cheaper for a borrower to raise funds via the issue of eurobonds than through comparable domestic markets?   *(Paragraph 8.6)*

10. What risk might a borrower face in raising funds through the issue of eurobonds rather within the comparable domestic market?   *(Paragraph 8.6)*

9   Equity finance

9.1   Equity finance is a method of raising long-term funds by issuing shares; the most common of which are *ordinary shares*. Ordinary shareholders are part owners of the company and their return comes by way of dividends and capital gains on the shares. Ordinary shareholders have a claim to the residual profits of the company after all other claims have been met; they have the right to vote at general meetings, and can vote to elect or dismiss the directors.

9.2   In the event of liquidation, the ordinary shareholders are entitled to participate in the surplus, if any, which is left after all outside creditors have been paid in full and after the claims of any prior equity holders, such as preference shareholders, have been met. Thus ordinary shares are the most risky investments in a company, but are potentially the most profitable.

9.3   The *benefits* of ordinary shares as a means of finance from the company's perspective are:

● Dividends can be paid only from available profits (from the current year or from profits retained from past years) and, even if profits are available, dividends need not be paid. The directors recommend the rate of dividend, subject to available profits, and whilst ordinary shareholders can vote to reduce the dividend, they cannot vote to increase it. By contrast interest due on a loan is a commercial debt and must be paid irrespective of profits.

● Equity capital is not generally redeemable, except with the consent of the courts or the shareholders, so long-term capital is committed to the company which does not have to be serviced if trading conditions are unfavourable.

9.4   The *disadvantages* of ordinary shares are:

● Dividends are not tax-deductible expenses, whereas interest *is* tax-deductible. This adds to the effective cost of equity finance relative to debt finance.

● If a new issue of ordinary shares is made, the decision-making power of the original shareholders can be diluted as the new shareholders become part-owners. However, new issues may be made by way of rights issues, which means that the original shareholders are given the opportunity to buy the shares on favourable terms. Nevertheless, it is almost inevitable that some of the new shares will subsequently find their way on to the open market.

9.5   Companies may also raise equity finance via the issue of *preference shares*. Normally these shares pay a fixed dividend and give prior claims over ordinary shareholders. Preference shareholders can only receive a dividend if there are available profits. However, their return is likely to be higher than on comparable debt instruments, as shares are more risky, with the possibility that dividends may be waived in poor trading conditions. In liquidation, preference shareholders rank behind all outside creditors although they rank before ordinary shareholders. In normal circumstances preference shareholders have no voting rights.

9.6   *Cumulative preference shares* provide the facility for dividends to be carried forward should the company feel unable to make dividend payments in any given year. As this reduces the holders' risk relative to that associated with the basic preference shares, the fixed return tends to be slightly lower.

The importance of capital structure

9.7   It is important that a company does not attempt to rely too heavily on short-term sources of funds, as this may create cash flow problems should the lenders decide not to rollover the debt. It may also distort the company's business strategy, as emphasis may be placed on short-term cash generation rather than long-term profits. However, in some instances, perhaps when interest rates are expected to fall and long-term floating rate funds are difficult to raise, a company may feel that it has little alternative but to cover its financing needs via short-term funds.

9.8   The company must also seek to obtain *a suitable balance between equity and debt* within its capital structure. This balance is often considered in terms of the *gearing ratio* of the company, which measures the proportion of interest-bearing debt to total funds within the capital structure. The greater the amount of interest-bearing debt taken on, the higher will be the gearing ratio, other things being equal. As there is a legal commitment to service debt as payments fall due, whilst dividends can be waived, it is argued that a higher gearing ratio implies a greater risk associated with the company's financial position. Nevertheless, a company may raise its gearing in order to take advantage of relatively cheap debt finance. The shareholders may be willing to agree to this move, in the belief that the funds will generate a return sufficiently greater than their servicing cost to justify the addition risk entailed.

9.9   At times of economic prosperity, companies with a high gearing ratio will benefit. The profits of such companies would be expected to rise, but the interest paid to debt holders will only increase if interest rates rise on floating rate debt. Thus, equity holders are likely to gain the bulk of the extra earnings. However, as companies become more highly geared they also become more risky. Consequently, their shareholders will suffer a disproportionate downturn in earnings at times of recession.

Study Activities 5

1. What are the rights of ordinary shareholders?   *(Paragraph 9.1)*

2. What is the position of ordinary shareholders if the company in which they hold shares goes into liquidation?   *(Paragraph 9.2)*

3. From the point of view of a company, what are the benefits of ordinary shares as a means of raising funds?   *(Paragraph 9.3)*

4. From the point of view of a company, what are the disadvantages of ordinary shares as a means of raising funds? *(Paragraph 9.4)*

5. What are preference shares? *(Paragraph 9.5)*

6. What are the relative merits and demerits of preference shares and ordinary shares from an investor's perspective? *(Paragraphs 9.1, 9.2 and 9.5)*

7. What are cumulative preference shares and in what way are they more attractive to an investor than ordinary preference shares? *(Paragraphs 9.5 and 9.6)*

8. What problems may be caused for a firm if it relies too heavily upon short-term sources of funds? *(Paragraph 9.7)*

9. Why is it important for a company to obtain the 'right' balance of debt and equity in relation to its capital structure? *(Paragraph 9.8)*

10. What are the implications for shareholders of their company having a high gearing ratio during periods of recession and boom? *(Paragraph 9.9)*

10 Corporate sector risk management

10.1 As financial transactions become ever more sophisticated, the associated risks for the participants in such transactions tend to grow. During periods of change in financial markets, when uncertainty in respect of interest rate movements tends to be high, the need increases for both borrowers and lenders to be able to manage their interest rate risk positions effectively. Similarly, the need for exchange rate risk management for traders and investors committed to making and receiving payments in foreign currency grows with uncertainty in respect of exchange rate movements. Consequently, in recent years there has been a significant growth in the provision of risk management facilities by financial institutions for their corporate customers. Indeed, many such institutions are active in the markets for risk management instruments as a means of dealing with the risks that they themselves find unavoidable in the modern financial environment.

Interest rate risk

10.2 As borrowers normally have to commit themselves to either a fixed or a floating (variable) rate of interest on borrowed funds for a given period of time, they must necessarily face risk in the uncertain financial environment.

- If the borrower decides to accept a fixed rate, the future cash flows associated with the debt servicing will be known in advance. However, if market rates of interest subsequently fall, the cost of the borrowed funds may become high relative to the cost incurred by other borrowers with floating rate debt. If the borrower's competitors have raised their funds via floating rate debt, the competitive position of the borrower is therefore undermined.

- If the borrower takes on floating rate debt, any downward movement in rates will be beneficial, but upward movements will mean increased debt-servicing charges. Hence, floating rate debt not only introduces uncertainty into the calculation of future servicing costs, it may also undermine competitiveness relative to other firms that have fixed rate debt in times of rising interest rates.

10.3   Lenders face opposite risks to those incurred by borrowers:

- When funds are lent at a market-related floating rate, the lender loses out if market rates of interest fall below the level that was initially expected.

- When fixed rate loans are made, there is no opportunity to earn higher interest rates even if market rates of interest rise.

10.4   The factors that influence the choice between fixed rate and floating rate borrowing/lending are:

- Expectations of future interest rate movements during the period of the loan.

- The current level of fixed interest rates which are on offer.

- The margin over LIBOR or base rate which is available.

- The risk associated with the company's activities as a whole. Companies that face high risks in their markets will generally prefer fixed rate debt. Indeed, credit rating agencies generally award higher ratings to companies with fixed rate debt as opposed to those with floating rate debt.

10.5   Financial intermediaries such as banks face the opposite risks to those of borrowers when they lend money. When funds are lent at floating rates the bank loses out if rates in general fall. When loans are made at fixed rates of interest the bank loses if rates in general rise. Clearly, such losses can be mitigated if the bank raises funds (that is, deposits) which match the lending in maturity and type of interest (fixed or floating).

10.6   For financial intermediaries obtaining a suitable balance between fixed and floating rates on both assets and liabilities is of crucial importance to profitability, as well as to the financial risk faced by the business.

Study Activities 6

1. What factors might explain the significant growth in the provision of risk management facilities to companies?   *(Paragraph 10.1)*

2. What risk does a borrower taking on floating rate debt face?   *(Paragraph 10.2)*

3. What risk does a borrower taking on fixed rate debt face?   *(Paragraph 10.2)*

4. In what sense do lenders face opposite risks to borrowers in respect of interest rate movements?   *(Paragraph 10.3)*

5. What factors influence the choice between fixed and floating rate borrowing?

(Paragraph 10.4)

6. Why is it important for banks to maintain a suitable balance between fixed and floating rate assets and liabilities? *(Paragraph 10.5)*

Management of interest rate risk

10.7   There are many different approaches to the management of interest rate risk. For example, companies may:

- Reduce exposure to interest-bearing debt by shifting the balance of financing towards equity capital.

- Use fixed rate debt so as to remove the cash flow risk, but the competitive threat remains if other companies have floating rate debt and interest rates fall.

- Reduce dependence on short-term bank loans by using factoring services (to turn outstanding debtors into cash) or by leasing capital equipment, rather than buying it outright.

- Adopt a 'portfolio approach', whereby targets are set for the mix of fixed rate and floating rate debt depending upon broad expectations of market conditions.

However, most attention tends to be focused upon the so-called *external approaches* to the hedging of interest rate risk.

10.8   The main external techniques for hedging interest rate risk are:

- Forward rate agreements;

- Interest rate options;

- Interest rate swaps; and

- Financial futures.

Detailed discussion of these derivative products is to be found in Unit 4. However, it is useful to summarise the key characteristics of these products from the perspective of a company wishing to hedge interest rate risk.

Forward rate agreements (FRAs)

10.9   FRAs are a technique that enables a company to fix an interest rate for a specific period of time in advance and independently of the principal sum borrowed. Thus, a borrower with a floating rate loan outstanding may wish to hedge against a possible increase in the market rate of interest beyond a certain level. If the market rate rises above this level, the bank entering into the FRA (which is not necessarily the bank from which the loan was obtained) will cover the excess interest payments. If the market rate falls below the agreed level, the borrower will pay the difference between the actual rate and the agreed rate to the bank. Naturally, the notional principal of the FRA will need to match the amount of the underlying borrowing.

10.10 *Major limitations* of FRAs are that they are normally only available when the principal sum on which they are based is £100,000 or more, and FRAs to cover borrowings in excess of a year are rarely available.

Interest rate options

10.11 An interest rate option endows a *right*, but not an obligation, to take up an FRA for a specified notional principal at a set rate of interest (the striking rate), for an agreed period of time which commences on a known future date. The company will pay a premium to the bank for this right.

10.12 In the case of an option to borrow, the borrower will decide on the expiry date of the option whether to exercise the right to take up the FRA at the striking rate. If interest rates in general are below the striking rate at the expiry of the option the borrower will allow the option to take up the FRA to lapse and will borrow at current market rates. If interest rates are above the striking rate the option will be exercised and the FRA will be taken up. The compensation payment under the FRA will offset the extra interest on the underlying borrowing.

10.13 Thus, for a premium, the company can fix the maximum borrowing costs of a known future commitment, but if interest rates subsequently fall, the company can abandon the option and can take advantage of the favourable interest rate movements.

10.14 One further benefit of the option is that if the borrowing is not in fact required, the option can be sold back to the writer if interest rates in general have risen at expiry date. Such an option is said to have an intrinsic value, since the right to take up an FRA at below current market rates must be worth something.

10.15 OTC interest rate options can be tailor-made by banks to meet the specific perceived borrowing (or depositing) requirements of a corporate customer.

Interest rate swaps

10.16 Interest rate swaps were first developed when two companies borrowed funds independently for the same principal sum and for the same borrowing period. However, one borrowed at a fixed rate and the other at a floating rate of interest, or one borrowed at a rate linked to LIBOR whilst the other borrowed at a rate linked to base rate. The two companies then swapped their associated debt servicing commitments. From the point of view of hedging interest rate risk, interest-rate swaps were and are useful for smaller companies that may not be able to borrow at fixed interest rates.

10.17   In practice, swaps are normally arranged through a bank or other specialist institution. The principles are similar to those associated with financial intermediation. The contractual obligations under the swap are between the bank or other specialist institution and the counter-parties. There is no contract or obligation between the counter-parties.

Financial futures

10.18   A financial future is an agreement to buy or sell a standard quantity of a specific financial instrument at a future date and at an agreed price. Other financial futures have their payoffs based on an index such as LIBOR or FTSE100. For futures contracts which hedge interest rates, if interest rates rise the prices of the relevant futures contracts fall.

10.19   If a company wants to hedge a perceived future borrowing requirement against a rise in interest rates it can sell futures contracts. If interest rates do rise by the time the underlying borrowing is taken up, the interest cost of that borrowing will be greater than would have been the case if the interest rate had been fixed at the same time as the futures contract was sold. However, the company can cancel out its obligations under the futures contract by buying back the same number of contracts at the lower price. Hence, the gain on the sale and subsequent repurchase of the futures contracts will offset the extra interest costs on the underlying borrowing.

10.20   If interest rates were to fall by the time the borrowing was due to be taken up the lower cost of borrowing would be offset by the loss on the futures contracts. The price of the futures contract would have risen by the time the company had to cancel its obligations by repurchasing futures contracts.

10.21   It is not always possible to buy a number of interest rate financial futures contracts to match exactly the potential extra interest rate costs if rates rise, because financial futures contracts are for standard amounts and periods. These standard periods on offer from the futures contracts may not exactly match the borrowing requirements of the company.

Interest rate caps, floors and collars

10.22   These are all types of interest rate options or combinations of interest rate options. As with all derivatives, the rights under caps, floors and collars are totally independent of the rights and obligations under any associated borrowing/lending. A *cap* may be purchased from a bank in order to protect the holder of an existing floating rate loan from the interest rate moving upward beyond the level specified by the cap contract. The borrower is still able to benefit if interest rates fall, but may claim any excess interest charge over the cap level from the seller of the cap. The cap works in the same way as the interest option described earlier.

10.23   A *floor* has the same characteristics as a cap, except that it protects an investor or depositor against a floating rate of interest falling below the specified floor level. The purchaser is still able to benefit from increases in interest rates, but is protected if the market rate falls.

10.24 A *collar* is effectively a combination of a cap and a floor. It may be purchased by a company wishing to protect itself against the interest rate on outstanding debt going beyond a capped level, but prepared to forgo the gain from the interest rate falling below a lower specified level in exchange for a lower premium on the cap.

Study Activities 7

1. In what ways might a company reduce its interest rate exposure without resorting to external approaches involving derivatives? *(Paragraph 10.7)*

2. What is a forward rate agreement? *(Paragraph 10.9)*

3. What are the major limitations of forward rate agreements? *(Paragraph 10.10)*

4. What is an interest rate option? *(Paragraph 10.11)*

5. Under what circumstances will the buyer of an interest rate option allow it to lapse? *(Paragraph 10.12)*

6. In what sense does an option have a market value? *(Paragraph 10.14)*

7. Give an example of the operation of an interest rate swap. *(Paragraph 10.16)*

8. What are the benefits in having interest rate swaps arranged via a bank? *(Paragraph 10.17)*

9. What is a financial future? *(Paragraph 10.18)*

10. Explain how a borrower may use financial futures. *(Paragraphs 10.19 and 10.20)*

11. Describe the use of caps, floors and collars. *(Paragraphs 10.22–10.24)*

Exchange rate risk

10.25 Any financial transaction denominated in a foreign currency necessarily involves risk in relation to unexpected exchange rate movements. For example, a UK-based borrower may raise a loan denominated in US dollars, in order to take advantage of a lower interest rate on dollar funds relative to sterling funds. However, unless the borrower is expecting future incomes denominated in dollars, the actual cost of the loan may prove to be much higher than was initially anticipated, if the value of the dollar should rise relative to sterling. In other words, a depreciating value for sterling means that larger amounts of sterling have to be given up in order to service the interest and repayments on the dollar loan. Of course, an appreciation in the value of sterling relative to the dollar has the opposite effect and the real cost of the loan falls.

10.26 A similar problem arises in respect of any payments or receipts due in foreign currencies. Exchange rate movements may alter the domestic currency value of the foreign currency funds significantly, and may turn an otherwise profitable project into one that generates a loss.

10.27   As was explained in Unit 8, exchange rate risk may take three different forms:

● *Transaction exposure* – This arises from normal international trading activities where the prices of exports or imports are fixed in foreign currency terms. Movements in exchange rates will alter the domestic currency value of transactions, and if these are unexpected they may have a serious impact on the profitability of the business.

● *Translation exposure* – This arises when a company has assets and liabilities which are not matched in terms of currency of denomination. Therefore, any movement in exchange rates will alter the net asset value of the company when the balance sheet is translated into a single currency.

● *Economic exposure* – This relates to the impact on the overall international competitiveness of a company resulting from exchange rate movements. For example, if sterling depreciates without any corresponding rise in domestic inflation, then the UK exporter acquires an improved competitive position, other things being equal.

Management of exchange rate risk

10.28   Avoidance of translation exposure requires the company to maintain a balance of assets and liabilities in terms of their currency of denomination.

10.29   Economic exposure requires careful management of the company's operations, in order to maintain the maximum level of efficiency and profitability. The diversification of sources of materials and markets for final output over a range of different countries is also likely to reduce this particular aspect of risk.

10.30   Companies may seek to reduce their transaction exposure by using *internal risk management devices*. These include:

● The use of *foreign currency bank accounts*, where there are receipts and payments in the same currency. This not only avoids the risk of exchange rate movements between the time that foreign currency is received and the time that it is spent, but also avoids the payment of commissions and fees that would be required if currencies were traded.

● *Multilateral netting* (where a group of companies effectively pools its foreign currency transactions, and then hedges the net exposure).

● In the longer term, a larger company selling output overseas may move some of its production facilities to its export markets, as a means of *aligning more closely foreign currency revenues and costs*.

- Companies may have *exchange rate protection clauses* written into contracts, although such actions may make it more difficult to win overseas orders.

10.31 The risks associated with individual foreign currency transactions may be managed via a range of external hedging instruments, which include:

- Forward exchange contracts.

- Currency swaps.

- Currency options.

- Currency futures.

- Currency borrowing for exporters and currency deposits for importers.

The broad characteristics of these instruments and their suitability in different circumstances were summarised in Unit 8.

Study Activities 8

1. Outline the circumstances within which a foreign currency loan would pose no greater risk to a borrower than a domestic currency loan.   *(Paragraph 10.25)*

2. Describe transaction, translation and economic exposure within the context of the exchange rate risk that may be faced by a company.   *(Paragraph 10.27)*

3. How might foreign currency translation exposure be avoided?   *(Paragraph 10.28)*

4. How might foreign currency economic exposure be managed?   *(Paragraph 10.29)*

5. What are the internal risk management devices for dealing with foreign currency transaction exposure?   *(Paragraph 10.30)*

6. List the external hedging instruments that may be used to manage foreign currency transaction exposure.   *(Paragraph 10.31)*

Summary

Now that you have completed this unit you should be able to:

- discuss the broad trends in corporate sector financing in the UK and identify the various financing alternatives available to companies of different sizes;

- understand the role of equity, bank debt and non-bank debt in corporate sector balance sheets;

- appreciate the role of rating companies and the importance of credit ratings in the pricing of corporate debt;

- appreciate the impact of internal cash flow and the business environment on corporate requirements for external funds;

- understand the basic corporate financing role of various debt and equity instruments;

- describe the various mechanisms by which shorter-term (working capital) and longer-term (investment) requirements may be funded;

- appreciate the nature of business and financial risk faced by companies;

- understand the basic principles of interest rate and exchange rate risk management;

- describe the operation and qualities of the basic corporate financial risk management instruments.

Self-assessment questions

Short-answer questions

1. A creditworthy company, the shares of which are listed on the London Stock Exchange, wishes to borrow for capital expenditure purposes. Why is an acceptance credit facility unlikely to be available for this purpose?

2. Why will a lender normally accept a lower rate of interest for secured as opposed to unsecured lending?

3. What are the benefits of overdraft facilities for corporate borrowers?

4. What are the possible disadvantages of sterling commercial paper from the point of view of corporate borrowers?

5. How do preference shares differ from ordinary shares?

6. Why is a highly-geared company considered to be more risky than a low-geared company, other things being equal?

Multiple-choice questions

1. Since the early 1990s, the UK corporate sector has

   (a) had holdings of notes and coin which have far outweighed deposits with banks and building societies

   (b) had holdings of sterling bank deposits which have declined steadily

   (c) experienced fluctuations between deficit and surplus in its overall financial position

   (d) remained in deficit in its overall financial position

   (e) maintained substantial net financial assets in its overall balance sheet.

2. Bank borrowing for the UK corporate sector

   (a) has never been a major source of funding

   (b) is the main internal source of funding

   (c) rose substantially during the early 1990s, due to the difficulties experienced in raising equity funds

(d) saw an unprecedented reduction during the early 1990s

(e) is now by far the largest financial liability in the overall balance sheet.

3. Which one of the following can be considered as a disadvantage of an overdraft facility as opposed to a loan, from the point of view of a corporate borrower; the overdraft is

(a) less flexible than a loan

(b) calculated on the closing debit balance each day

(c) repayable on demand

(d) only available for the borrowing of sums in excess of £1m

(e) not usually available in a foreign currency?

4. Which of the following borrowing facilities must be linked to an underlying trade transaction

(a) an overdraft

(b) a LIBOR-linked bank loan

(c) sterling commercial paper

(d) an acceptance credit

(e) a medium-term note?

5. What may be the original maturity of medium term notes

(a) 187 days

(b) 187 days to one year

(c) one to five years

(d) less than one year

(e) over five years?

6. In order to be eligible to issue sterling commercial paper, a company must

(a) have net assets of no more than £50m

(b) be included amongst the top 100 companies quoted on the London Stock Exchange

(c) have a credit rating from a major credit rating agency

(d) have net assets of at least £25m

(e) receive prior authorisation from the Bank of England.

7. An important motive for a company raising finance through an issue of ordinary shares, as opposed to through long-term debt instruments, is that

10

(a) this reduces the gearing ratio and hence improves the financial stability of the company

(b) equity finance is much cheaper than debt finance

(c) this protects the existing owners' control of the business

(d) the dividends which are paid on equity shares are tax-deductible for the company, whilst interest payments on debt are not

(e) ordinary shares are far more flexible with regard to covering short-term finance for working capital requirements.

8. A corporate borrower raising long-term funds through a floating interest rate bank loan

(a) is continually at risk from translation exposure

(b) could reduce its capital gearing by reducing its equity capital base

(c) may hedge the associated interest rate cash flow risk by taking out an equal size fixed interest-rate loan

(d) will find itself with a competitive advantage if market rates of interest subsequently rise

(e) could hedge its associated cash flow risk via the use of a forward rate agreement.

9. A major disadvantage of using an interest rate option to hedge interest rate risk is that

(a) there is a cost to the buyer of the option if it proves not to be required

(b) the buyer is unable to benefit if market rates move in his or her favour

(c) options are only available for fixed amounts for fixed periods via an options exchange

(d) the buyer must offer security against the value of the option

(e) the buyer is exposed to unlimited risk if the underlying transaction fails to materialise.

10. The management of foreign currency transaction exposure

(a) requires the matching of assets with liabilities according to their currency of denomination

(b) may only be undertaken through the use of internal risk management devices such as multilateral netting and invoicing of overseas customers in the domestic currency

(c) focuses upon the improvement of the international competitiveness of the company

(d) is best undertaken through a process of diversification of sources of materials and markets for final outputs over a range of different countries

(e) may involve the use of external hedging instruments such as forward exchange contracts, currency options and currency futures.

11
Personal Sector Finances and the Housing Market

Objectives

After studying this unit, you should be able to:

- analyse the structure of the personal sector balance sheet;

- name the sources and uses of funds for the personal sector;

- appreciate the economic and financial risks faced by the personal sector;

- appreciate the broad nature of the financial risks inherent in various saving and borrowing products;

- describe the ways in which members of the personal sector may seek to manage financial risk;

- understand the 'life-cycle' approach to borrowing and investment decisions faced by the personal sector;

- appreciate the importance of home ownership, income uncertainty and pension provision for personal sector financial decision-making;

- appreciate the general nature of borrowing and investment vehicles available to individuals;

- understand the broad nature of the UK housing market, housing finance and how house prices are determined;

- identify the main types of mortgage loan and the associated types of interest payments and repayments of principal.

1   The structure of personal sector finances

The personal sector within the UK economy

1.1   The UK personal sector is defined as comprising all individuals resident in the UK, as well as unincorporated businesses (such as sole traders and partnerships), and non-profit-making institutions (such as registered charities and trade unions).

1.2   With the exception of a short period at the end of the 1980s, the personal sector has been a major net provider of funds to the other sectors of the economy in recent years. In 1988, in the 'mortgage' boom, a record financial deficit was generated by the personal sector with the amount spent on consumption and investment in real capital assets exceeding personal disposable income by £13bn. A large part of this net borrowing (which financed the extra spending on house purchase) was from building societies and retail banks, in the form of mortgage loans. By 1990, the sector had returned to an overall financial surplus, which grew rapidly to reach a record £32.5bn in 1995. The impact of the recession on consumer confidence, and the downturn in the housing market were crucial factors underlying this return to a surplus. Since 1995, the personal sector financial surplus has fallen and in 1998 it stood at £17.6bn. This pattern reflects the steady recovery in the economy, the gradual strengthening of the housing market and the return of consumer confidence.

1.3   Personal sector financial requirements are of crucial importance to the operation of the UK financial system. A large proportion of the activities of the retail banks, and almost all of the activities of the building societies, are directed towards satisfying the demands of personal sector customers, who also dominate the work of pension funds and many insurance companies, unit trusts and investment trust companies.

UK personal sector aggregate balance sheet

1.4   Care must be taken in respect of the interpretation of the data on personal sector finances, as most of the information available has to be collected indirectly, from financial institutions, and some figures quoted are estimates or residuals. Nevertheless, the broad patterns of personal sector financing are clear, and the key aspects of the balance sheets are summarised below.

Financial assets

1.5   These consist of:

- *Notes and coin* – total holdings have grown steadily, but their relative importance has diminished, as would be expected given the evolution of payments methods and increased financial sophistication.

- *UK government securities and National Savings* – holdings reflect the demands of UK public sector finances and grew steadily during the first half of the 1990s, but have fallen somewhat in recent years. They have remained modest relative to total financial assets held.

- *Bank and building society deposits* – these are extremely important for the personal sector, accounting for 17% of total financial assets at the beginning of 1999.

- *Trade credit* – relates to credit granted by unincorporated businesses and has been relatively stable in amount in recent years.

- *Company securities* – direct holdings are significant (around 17% of total financial assets at the beginning of 1999), but of much greater importance are indirect holdings via investments in life assurance, pension funds and unit trusts.

- *Life assurance and pension funds* – now comprising over half of the personal sector's financial assets. As we have seen, these financial intermediaries invest in gilt-edged securities and property as well as in equities, but around a half of all personal sector financial assets are in the form of company securities, both directly and indirectly.

Financial liabilities

1.6   These consist of:

- *Bank lending* – for purposes other than the purchase of residential property, bank lending accounts for around 15% of the sector's total outstanding financial liabilities. However, the rate of new bank lending fell markedly during the early 1990s. Total outstanding debt actually fell during 1992 and 1993, as a result of the writing-off of bad debts and an apparently widespread desire within the personal sector to rein in financial commitments. Since 1997 total outstanding non-mortgage debt to banks has grown steadily.

- *Loans for the purchase of residential property* – by far the largest category of debt (around 70% of the total), continued to grow throughout the recession of the early 1990s, although at a much reduced rate. The dominant providers of these funds have been the building societies, with banks making a significant contribution and gradually increasing their share.

- *Trade credit and credit extended by retailers* – have maintained their importance in recent years, although overall growth has been relatively slow.

1.7   Total personal sector financial liabilities and financial assets have both grown steadily in recent years, although a healthy balance of net financial assets has been maintained. The personal sector also holds substantial amounts of tangible assets, the most important element of which is residential property. The importance of financial institutions for personal sector finances is without question. Banks and building societies have a crucial role on *both* sides of the balance sheet, although non-bank financial intermediaries dominate the assets side, with life assurance companies, pension funds and unit trusts being especially important. Banks and building societies dominate the liability side of the balance sheet.

UK personal sector sources and uses of funds

1.8   The personal sector balance sheet shows the relative importance of various assets and liabilities held at a specific point in time. However, in order to understand the nature of personal sector financing, in terms of the generation and disposition of its funds, we must consider the sector's sources and uses of funds data.

Sources of funds

1.9   These may be divided into saving and borrowing. The ratio of saving to personal disposable income has risen substantially since the mortgage boom of the late 1980s. The ratio stood at the historically low level of 3.9% in 1988; by 1992 it had reached a recent peak of 11.5%. In 1988, 25% of the sector's sources of funds came from saving; in 1992 the corresponding figure was about 73%, although since that time the relative importance of saving has fallen somewhat.

1.10   During the early 1990s there was a massive reduction in the flows of borrowed funds, with bank lending for purposes other than the purchase of residential property largely collapsing. Indeed, in 1993 the personal sector made a net repayment of debt to banks of £1bn. The weak state of the UK economy, lack of consumer confidence, high unemployment and the debt overhang from the 1980s are thought to be the main factors underlying this trend. The more recent economic recovery and apparent gradual return of consumer confidence probably underpinned the significant increase in bank borrowing between 1993 and 1998.

Uses of funds

1.11   Total amounts of funds utilised by the personal sector remained relatively stable during the early 1990s, but have increased substantially since 1993. Also, there have been some important shifts in the pattern of uses of funds. In particular, the amount of funds withdrawn from holdings of company securities was relatively high between 1995 and 1998, following more moderate withdrawals during the early years of the 1990s. Also, 1995 to 1998 saw a massive increase in the additions made to deposits with banks and building societies, following a fairly steep downward trend in such deposits between 1989 and 1994. The basic economic factors, and especially the trends in unemployment, are likely to have affected the pattern of deposits with banks and building societies. In addition, stock market performance and the possibility of building society members earning bonus payments in the event of their societies converting to plc status, almost certainly have also influenced personal sector financial decisions.

1.12   The two main uses of personal sector funds have continued to be investments in life assurance policies and pension funds and the purchase of fixed assets and stocks (the most important element of which has been purchases of residential property). The weakness of the economy, and especially fears of unemployment, and bad publicity in respect of certain insurance and pension products were major factors holding back the growth of the flow of funds into these longer-term assets during the early to mid-1990s. Purchases of public sector debt have largely reflected the public sector's borrowing requirement, and both were substantial during the first half of the 1990s. Since 1996, a significant amount of funds has flowed out of holdings of UK government securities.

1.13 Holdings of liquid assets have continued to rise, with a substantial increase in the rate of growth being observed between 1995 and 1997. During the early years of the 1990s, financial pressures on members of the personal sector and falling returns on liquid assets were probably responsible for a much-reduced rate of growth in liquid asset holdings. One outcome of this occurrence was an intensification of competition between financial institutions, involving fixed interest rate offers and a broadening of services made available as a means of attracting customers. Banks and building societies have also taken increased interest in the provision of longer-term investments such as pension schemes and insurance products.

Study Activities 1

1. What has been the overall financial position of the personal sector in recent years?
   (Paragraph 1.2)

2. What major economic factors are reflected in the pattern of personal sector financing observed in recent years?
   (Paragraph 1.2)

3. What types of financial institutions are heavily dependent upon the financial needs of the personal sector?
   (Paragraph 1.3)

4. List the main groups of financial assets held by the personal sector in order of their importance in the sector's balance sheet.
   (Paragraph 1.5)

5. List the main groups of financial liabilities held by the personal sector?
   (Paragraph 1.6)

6. To what extent are banks important to the personal sector's balance sheet?
   (Paragraphs 1.5 and 1.6)

7. In broad terms, how have the sources of funds for the personal sector altered in recent years?
   (Paragraphs 1.9 and 1.10)

8. In what ways have the uses of personal sector funds altered in recent years?
   (Paragraphs 1.11–1.13)

2   Financial risks faced by the personal sector

2.1 Members of the personal sector face a number of financial risks that may cause them serious financial problems and threaten their economic welfare. The existence of these risks helps to explain why individuals tend to hold a diverse range of financial and other assets, and why specific types of liabilities are incurred, and why both asset and liability portfolios tend to be altered in structure over time. The main risks relevant to the personal sector may be categorised as relating to:

- Default
- Inflation
- Changes in financial requirements
- Interest rate movements
- Changes in government policy.

Default

2.2   The most obvious default risk for the personal sector relates to the granting of trade credit by unincorporated businesses to buyers of their products. Quite simply, debtors may be unwilling or unable to discharge their debt, and creditors may then be forced to write off the debt or perhaps initiate expensive legal action. This type of risk is potentially very damaging, especially in areas of business where the granting of substantial amounts of trade credit is regarded as part of the normal terms of trade. The only protection is for creditors to screen carefully the creditworthiness of potential debtors before credit is granted. Also, traders may consider withdrawing credit facilities altogether, and offering discounts for cash in order to maintain the level of business.

2.3   The bulk of personal sector financial asset holdings represent claims on financial institutions. An institution may fail, due to inept management or fraud, and depositors/investors may lose all of their deposits/investments. However, in the UK this occurrence is rare due to the existence of officially sponsored depositor/investor protection schemes, as outlined in earlier units. The liquidation value of failed institutions is also available to compensate depositors/investors, such as those who had substantial deposits in BCCI.

2.4   Direct ownership of company securities is inherently risky, especially when they relate to smaller, unlisted companies. It is rare for long-established, well-managed 'blue chip' companies to go into liquidation. The more likely occurrence is that such companies may experience gradual erosion of their trading performances, which will be reflected in their share values. Investors are wise to hold diversified portfolios of securities and to seek professional advice.

2.5   Government securities issued by major Western countries are effectively free of default risk, but if investments in such securities have to be realised before their maturity dates capital losses may still be incurred (if interest rates in general have risen since the securities were purchased). In practice, the only truly capital safe investments are *National Savings* instruments. These may be liquidated for their full nominal values on demand or after a short period of notice; but even here the investor might have to forgo the higher returns on the instruments that would have been available had they been held until their natural maturity date. Also, *National Savings* instruments are only available in limited quantities for individual investors.

Inflation

2.6   The main problem is in predicting the future rate of inflation. If the actual rate of inflation turns out to be significantly different from the rate expected, either the borrower or the lender will experience unanticipated gains or losses. Unexpectedly high inflation will effectively transfer wealth to the borrower holding a fixed-interest debt. Linking interest payments to market rates of interest or to a suitable price index may help to alleviate this problem, although uncertainty in relation to actual cash payments is then introduced into the transaction.

2.7   Purchasing company equity shares or residential property may serve as a hedge against inflation, but experience has shown that this may only be true in the longer term. Short-term price fluctuations may make such investments particularly risky.

2.8   Personal sector financial behaviour may be affected in a general sense because inflation may alter the balance between saving and consumption. Whilst some people may seek to spend their funds before their value is eroded by inflation, the evidence suggests that the opposite reaction occurs. The uncertainty created by inflation causes saving to rise to protect financial security, and to try to preserve the real value of wealth holdings.

Changes in financial requirements

2.9   Unanticipated change in personal circumstances may cause serious problems for both borrowers and lenders. For example, someone with a large mortgage loan may be unable to cope with the servicing commitments if income is reduced due to illness, loss of employment, the break-up of a relationship, and so on. Sensible financial planning is always important – if possible there should be flexibility to adjust commitments in response to changes in circumstances, without fundamentally disrupting living standards. Various forms of insurance may be taken out in respect of some eventualities, but these always entail cost and so may not be taken up. In any event full insurance cover may not be available in respect of some risks, or may only be available at prohibitive cost. In practice, it is probably impossible to protect fully against the effects of unanticipated changes in financial circumstances. The minimisation of the associated risks can only occur against the background of prudent financial decision-making that avoids all unnecessary financial commitments, and leaves flexibility to alter asset portfolio composition as events unfold.

2.10   For a lender, the choice is often between relatively low-risk liquid assets, which pay only modest returns, or higher return, illiquid risky assets. Once a portfolio has been selected, unanticipated changes in circumstances may result in the forced sale of securities, with associated risk of capital loss, or the premature withdrawal of deposits, which may incur interest penalties. Indeed, where access to funds is either not possible or would involve excessive costs, the investor may be in the invidious position of having to borrow funds at rates of interest higher than the returns being earned on the investments held. This possibility provides a good reason for investors to hold diversified portfolios of assets, as far as their personal circumstances will allow. However, for many individuals the freedom of choice of portfolio is limited by their pension and life assurance needs and their outstanding debt commitments.

Interest rate movements

2.11   The interest rate risks faced by members of the personal sector are basically the same as those faced by companies (see Unit 10). Thus, variable rates of interest lead to uncertainty in respect of future cash flows, whilst fixed rates mean that benefits of favourable interest rate movements may be forgone. The market value of fixed interest securities is also likely to be affected by movements in market rates of interest, and the market value of company shares may alter depending upon the perceived impact of interest rates on company profitability and cash flows.

2.12   Other than not holding interest-bearing claims and not borrowing funds, there is little that members of the personal sector can do to avoid interest rate risk entirely. The holding of diversified portfolios of assets helps to spread risk and borrowers should ensure that they are able to cope with the cash flow implications if interest rates were to rise to the maximum level which appears realistically possible.

Government economic policy changes

2.13   Sudden changes in government economic policies may have adverse effects on personal sector finances. Monetary policy, affecting interest rates, inflation, bankruptcies and unemployment, will impact as implied above. Constraints on money supply growth may limit the ability of financial institutions to lend. The policy overall is likely to influence the broad economic environment, and affect consumer confidence and attitudes to investment and borrowing.

2.14   Fiscal policy changes may lead to alterations in the tax regime in respect of interest earnings, or payments, or capital gains. The balance of portfolios may need to be altered if the tax privileges granted to pension schemes, *PEPs/ISAs* and *National Savings* were to be changed or removed. The public sector's expenditure plans and overall budgetary position will not only influence broad economic developments but will also affect the availability of and returns on public sector debt instruments. Business and consumer confidence is also likely to be affected if excessively large public sector borrowing is forecast.

2.15   Changes in almost any aspect of economic policy may have potentially serious effects on personal sector finances. Both direct and indirect impacts on decision-making should be recognised. Unfortunately, there is little that can be done to protect against the impact of government policy changes, other than to maintain some diversity in asset holdings and to behave prudently in respect of the assumption of financial commitments.

Study Activities 2

1. Outline the types of default risk faced by members of the personal sector.
   (Paragraphs 2.2-2.4)

2. What actions might members of the personal sector take in order to reduce the default risk that they face?   *(Paragraphs 2.2–2.5)*

3. Why is the occurrence of inflation a problem for someone lending money?
   (Paragraph 2.6)

4. How might the balance between saving and consumption in the personal sector be affected by the occurrence of inflation?   *(Paragraph 2.8)*

5. Give some examples of the problems that might be caused for both borrowers and lenders as a result of changes in their personal circumstances.
   (Paragraphs 2.9 and 2.10)

6. In what ways might both borrowers and lenders be adversely affected by interest rate movements?   *(Paragraph 2.11)*

7. How might individual borrowers and lenders attempt to limit the adverse impact of movements in interest rates?   *(Paragraph 2.12)*

8. In what general ways might changes in government monetary policy adversely affect personal sector finances?   *(Paragraph 2.13)*

9. In what general ways might changes in government fiscal policy influence personal sector financial decisions?   *(Paragraph 2.14)*

10. What actions might individuals take to protect against the adverse impact of changes in government economic policies?   *(Paragraph 2.15)*

3   Life-cycle investment and borrowing decisions

Investment decisions

3.1   The basic factors influencing an individual's asset portfolio selection are often listed as being:

● The trade-off between return and risk associated with each asset.

- The reduction in risk that comes from being able to hold investments for a longer period.

- The benefit to be obtained from regular saving/investment across all stages of the financial market cycle.

- The individual's capacity to assume risk.

- The individual's attitude toward risk.

3.2   The historical data are quite clear. As a rule, *it is only possible to increase the return on an investment portfolio by taking on greater risk.* This risk is manifest in the volatility of returns on the portfolio, which may, at the extreme, include the total loss of an asset. It cannot be emphasised too strongly that the return/risk trade-off relates to a well-diversified portfolio of assets.

3.3   *The length of the period over which an asset may be held* makes the stage in the individual investor's life cycle at which an investment takes place a critical variable in the investment decision. Take, for example, the case of government bonds. The regular coupon payments and the maturity value are as near to being guaranteed as it is possible to achieve. If a bond with a twenty-year maturity is purchased, then the holder has near certainty in respect of the return to be earned so long as the bond is held for the full twenty-year period. However, if the funds are required after, say, five years, the return is much less certain. If market rates of interest have risen substantially since the bond was purchased, the market value after five years might be much less than the purchase price. In relation to equity investments the position is more complex, but the same principle still holds and the evidence is quite clear. That is, so long as a diversified portfolio of equities is held, the return in any single year is uncertain, but the return over the longer term tends to be much better than could be earned from investment in other financial assets (e.g. bonds, bank deposits and so on). As the longer term could be ten, twenty or more years, the implications for portfolio selection are that, other things being equal, the longer is the investment horizon the less risky it is to increase the proportion of the portfolio invested in equities.

3.4   By purchasing bonds and equities at regular intervals of time (perhaps monthly or quarterly) it is possible to take advantage of a concept often referred to as *'pound-cost averaging'*. Quite simply, this means that the investor is able to ensure that the whole of his/her portfolio is not purchased at a time when equity and bond prices are artificially inflated. Conversely, at least some equities and bonds are likely to be purchased when prices are unusually low. The only practical problem to be aware of in this regard relates to the transaction costs of purchasing small amounts of equities and bonds at regular intervals. Transaction costs per pound invested are usually much lower for large investments.

3.5   As suggested above, *an individual's investment decisions will reflect his/her age.* In general, the closer that an individual moves toward retirement, the less able he/she becomes to rely upon earned income to compensate for losses on investments. In other words, other things being equal, it is likely that as people approach retirement they will become less willing to assume financial risk. This does not, of course, mean that individuals of different ages will be unwilling to purchase the same types of assets.

3.6   It may be the case that *different individuals have different attitudes to risk*. Some people are psychologically more prone to taking risk than others. Also, the mix of assets within each individual's portfolio may be different. For example, the purchase of a high risk and potentially high yield asset for £1,000, to be added to a portfolio that contains solely gilt-edged securities and bank deposits with a nominal value of £100,000, may be quite compatible with the investment strategy for someone nearing retirement. The same purchase may be equally compatible with the investment strategy of a young person in a high-income occupation and holding a portfolio consisting exclusively of equally high-risk assets with a current market value of £50,000.

Borrowing decisions

3.7   The life cycle concept is *equally relevant to the acquisition (and ultimate discharge) of financial liabilities*. During the early years of adult life many people take out loans to finance education, the purchase of consumer durable items and, most importantly, to purchase residential property. Some commentators have argued that borrowing funds through the use of credit cards has become too easy. There are many sad cases of people being overwhelmed by debt, and being unable to make the interest payments, let alone repay the debt. However, in order to obtain credit, especially the substantial amounts required to finance the purchase of cars and residential property, it is usually necessary for potential borrowers to establish their creditworthiness. Their ability to service any loans extended is crucial, and the security that they are able to offer (as a means of reducing the risk faced by the lender) may determine whether or not a loan is to be made.

3.8   From the viewpoint of the lender, *the age and personal circumstances of the prospective borrower are crucial*. Thus, a reasonably young person, holding a secure well-paid job and having a clean credit record may be able to raise substantial sums of money to finance the purchase a wide variety of goods and services. An older person who is already heavily indebted, and especially if close to retirement age, will normally find it difficult to raise additional loans, at least, that is, on attractive terms and probably not without the provision of security.

3.9   In respect of mortgage loans, the lender holds a claim on the mortgaged property as security for the loan. However, given the costs associated with arranging a loan and taking the mortgage as security, let alone taking possession of a property should the borrower default, the lender always seeks to establish the ability of a prospective borrower to service the loan. Again, the age and other personal circumstances of the prospective borrower are crucial in determining whether or not a loan is made, and in determining the terms upon which it is made, including its term to maturity. The more creditworthy is the prospective borrower and the better quality is the security, the greater is likely to be the proportion of the value of the property that the lender is willing to finance.

Life-cycle profile

3.10 Considering the pattern of a typical individual's life-time earned (as opposed to investment) income and his/her ability to save and finance major expenditures during the early years of working life, it is possible to build up a life-cycle profile of net financial wealth for an individual:

- It is reasonable to suggest that during the early years of working life a typical individual will take on substantial debt, in order to finance education, the purchase of consumer durable items and, in particular, residential property. Unless the individual has inherited substantial wealth (or been unusually fortunate with investments or lottery tickets) he/she is likely to have financial assets outweighed by financial liabilities. The ability to service a net debt position is vital.

- During the middle years of life (say middle/late thirties through to early fifties), so long as earned income continues to flow and ideally to rise, debt will gradually be paid off and saving/investment (especially into pension plans) will rise. At some point during this middle period, financial assets are likely to overtake financial liabilities in value. By the end of this period, the mortgage loan may have been repaid, and the value of pension plans and investments may give a healthy net financial asset value.

- The later earning years, through to retirement, are normally a period of consolidation of financial wealth involving the accumulation of investments and pension rights, with earned income comfortably exceeding expenditure commitments.

- The final stage of the life cycle is the retirement period, where the individual largely depends upon the income generated by investments and pension plans to cover expenditures. Net financial assets may be run down during this period, with the pension earnings being guaranteed by a pension fund or through an insurance company annuity.

Study Activities 3

1. Why is it important to think in terms of a diversified portfolio of assets when considering the balance of return and risk on an investment?   *(Paragraph 3.2)*

2. Why is the investment horizon critical to the investment decision of an individual?
          (Paragraph 3.3)

3. Explain why there are circumstances within which even a gilt-edged security might be a risky investment for an individual. *(Paragraph 3.3)*

4. What does 'pound-cost averaging' mean? *(Paragraph 3.4)*

5. What practical problem might limit the gains to be generated by using the 'pound-cost averaging' concept? *(Paragraph 3.4)*

6. Why is it reasonable to believe that as people approach retirement they will become less willing to assume financial risk, other things being equal? *(Paragraph 3.5)*

7. Why might it not be irrational for two individuals to purchase similar investments despite the fact that one is nearing retirement and the other is relatively young and holds a well-paid secure job? *(Paragraphs 3.5 and 3.6)*

8. Explain why the life-cycle concept is just as relevant to the acquisition of financial liabilities as it is to the acquisition of financial assets. *(Paragraphs 3.7 and 3.8)*

9. In what ways do the personal circumstances of prospective borrowers affect their ability to obtain mortgage loans on the terms and conditions that they would desire? *(Paragraph 3.9)*

10. Map out a possible life-cycle profile for the net financial wealth of a typical person. *(Paragraph 3.10)*

4 The UK housing market and house prices

4.1 For many people, the ownership of residential property is their single most important investment, and the purchase of such property is probably the largest single expenditure that most people will ever make in their personal capacity. However, as most people entering the housing market for the first time or trading up to more expensive property need to borrow funds for this purpose, the provision of housing finance is an extremely important aspect of personal sector finances.

4.2 To obtain a clear understanding of the nature of UK housing finance, the structure of the UK housing market and the broad factors affecting the determination of house prices must be understood. (Note that in the following sections, the terms 'residential property' and 'houses' are used interchangeably, although the former is the more accurate description.)

UK housing market

4.3 As is shown in Table 11.1, owner-occupation dominates housing tenures in the UK. Currently, around two-thirds of all housing tenures in the UK are in owner-occupation. This is one of the highest proportions amongst Western nations, and its popularity has grown steadily this century.

4.4 A large proportion of purchases of residential property is financed, at least in part, by mortgage loans. In other words, houses are bought and sold, rather than inherited; the average length of a mortgage is around 9 to 10 years. For the UK personal sector in aggregate, such loans dominate total financial liabilities. In 1980, mortgage loans accounted for 57% of financial liabilities; by 1999 this proportion was near to 71%.

The housing market and the economy

4.5　The nature of the UK housing market and its associated financing has important implications for the implementation of government economic policy and the Bank of England's monetary policy and the operation of the economy. Changes in interest rates may have significant effects on the spending power of people with outstanding variable-rate mortgage loans. As such people often have high propensities to consume, the impact on the economy as a whole may be substantial. Also, changes in the real value of residential property may affect personal sector expenditure decisions. When the real value is rising, owners may feel better off and hence may spend a higher proportion of their disposable income, thus underpinning economic growth and supporting business confidence. This, in turn, may encourage people to enter the housing market for the first time or to trade up to more expensive property, which may push up house prices further. A virtuous cycle may be created. This pattern occurred in the UK in the late 1980s, fed by the competition between mortgage lenders. Unfortunately, if underlying economic conditions alter, the accumulated mortgage debt may cause serious problems.

Table 11.1 UK housing tenure, 1985 to 1996 (end-year figures)

Year	Owner-occupied		Public sector rented *		Private sector rented		Housing association rented		Total dwellings
	m	%	m	%	m	%	m	%	m
1985	13.5	60.5	6.0	26.8	2.3	10.2	0.6	2.5	22.4
1986	13.9	61.5	5.9	26.1	1.3	9.8	0.6	2.5	22.6
1987	14.3	62.6	5.8	25.3	2.2	9.5	0.6	2.6	22.8
1988	14.8	64.0	5.6	24.2	2.2	9.1	0.6	2.7	23.1
1989	15.2	65.2	5.4	23.0	2.1	9.0	0.7	2.8	23.3
1990	15.5	65.8	5.2	22.1	2.1	9.1	0.7	3.0	23.5
1991	15.6	65.9	5.1	21.4	2.1	9.4	0.7	3.1	23.7
1992	15.8	66.1	5.0	20.8	2.2	9.6	0.8	3.4	23.9
1993	16.0	66.4	4.9	20.3	2.3	9.6	0.9	3.7	24.1
1994	16.2	66.6	4.8	19.7	2.3	9.6	1.0	4.0	24.2
1995	16.3	66.8	4.7	19.2	2.4	9.7	1.0	4.3	24.4
1996	16.5	67.0	4.6	18.8	2.4	9.7	1.1	4.5	24.6

* From local authorities or new town corporations.

Source: Housing and Construction Statistics, Department of the Environment, Table 2.23

The determination of house prices

4.6 House prices are determined in the free market by the forces of supply and demand. The key characteristics of the housing market, which must be borne in mind, are:

- Residential property is extremely durable;

- The vast majority of the population is housed at any point in time;

- The total stock of houses can only be increased at a very slow rate;

- The bulk of house purchases/sales relate to second-hand houses;

- First-time buyers have considerable discretion over the timing of entry into the market.

4.7 The net supply of houses for sale on the market is the sum of:

- New houses made available;

- Houses vacated as a result of the owner's death, emigration or move to rented accommodation;

- Houses transferred from rental status, but not involving sitting tenants.

4.8 The net supply is reduced to the extent that properties are demolished for slum clearance or redevelopment purposes. Houses placed on the market by owner-occupiers wishing to move have no net effect on supply, as they create an equal demand (albeit possibly for a different type of property).

4.9 The net supply is likely to be influenced by the general state of the economy, and expected trends in earnings, unemployment, inflation and interest rates. This is especially so in respect of the activities of property developers. When economic conditions are good, more houses are likely to come on to the market. The only qualification relates to people with financial difficulties who may have to withdraw from owner-occupation as economic conditions deteriorate.

4.10 The sources of net demand for houses are potential first-time buyers and separated partners. This demand is influenced by the general economic conditions as noted above and in the longer-term by demographic factors and social conventions. The availability of alternative types of tenure is also important.

4.11 The interaction of supply and demand determines prices, but demand is able to adjust much more quickly than supply. Therefore, if economic conditions are favourable, expectations in respect of employment and earnings are good, and interest rates are felt to be relatively low, at least in the short term the boost to demand is likely to place upwards pressure on prices. The speed of adjustment of supply will determine the extent and persistence of the price rise. Ultimately, the impact on building costs and land prices, and expectations of property developers will be the key factors. Supply may never catch up with demand, and prices may continue to drift upwards until there is a change in conditions sufficient to reduce the level of demand. In this case, excess supply may arise in the market. As property developers do not wish to hold stocks of vacant houses, and as some owner occupiers feel obliged to sell their houses due to pressing financial problems, there may well be downward pressure on house prices.

UK house prices

4.12   Trends in UK house prices in recent years are easy to explain. During the late 1980s the UK economy was growing steadily, unemployment was falling, income taxes had been reduced, and there was a high level of competition between mortgage lenders. Thus, despite relatively high rates of interest, house prices were pushed up significantly. The word 'gazumping' was coined, describing instances where sellers broke their undertakings to sell when another buyer offered a higher price. The apparent investment values of houses merely reinforced demand.

4.13   At the beginning of the 1990s, consumer confidence was dented by rising unemployment, and interest rates remained high. The boom of the late 1980s had left many people with unmanageable debts and the levels of arrears on mortgage loans and repossessions began to rise. The actions of lenders in selling repossessed properties cheaply in order to recover funds and cut their losses just made matters worse. The housing market stagnated, undermining confidence still further, and unprecedented reductions in housing prices (in nominal terms) became widespread.

4.14   The appearance of negative equity – where the value of a property falls below the outstanding associated mortgage debt – for some borrowers also made matters worse. Thus, if the property is sold, the owner must raise additional funds to discharge the debt. Technically, mortgage lenders find themselves with unintended unsecured loans. The risks involved for borrowers and lenders are fairly obvious, and the negative equity overhang was one of the factors that held back recovery in the housing market during the mid-1990s. Uncertainty on economic conditions was the other major factor. It is believed that the extent of negative equity in the UK peaked in 1993. The more recent improvement in the housing market and the continuing repayment of mortgage loans has had a significant impact on the number of households affected by negative equity.

Study Activities 4

1. What proportion of housing tenures are accounted for by owner-occupation?
                                                                        (Paragraph 4.3)

2. What is the importance of mortgage loans amongst personal sector financial liabilities?
                                                                        (Paragraph 4.4)

3. In general terms, how might changes in the state of the housing market affect economic activity?
                                                                        (Paragraph 4.5)

4. List the key characteristics of the housing market. *(Paragraph 4.6)*

5. What factors determine the net supply of houses for sale on the market?
(Paragraphs 4.7–4.9)

6. What are likely to be the most important factors determining the level of house prices?
(Paragraphs 4.7-4.11)

7. Describe and explain the recent trends in the UK house prices.
(Paragraphs 4.12–4.14)

5 Types of mortgage loans

5.1 All types of mortgage loans commit the borrower to make regular payments to the lender, usually for a period of 20–25 years:

Annuity (repayment) mortgage

5.2 This involves the repayment of the loan plus interest by equal instalments (assuming that the mortgage interest rate does not alter) over the life of the loan. During the early years of the loan, a large proportion of each instalment is consumed by the interest element, and only a small amount of the principal is repaid.

Endowment mortgage

5.3 This links the loan to an endowment assurance plan. The borrower pays only interest to the lender during the term of the loan, but at the same time pays a regular premium to an insurance company. The proceeds from the matured policy should be sufficient to pay off the loan and leave a residual sum for the borrower. This was the dominant form of mortgage loan between the mid-1980s and the mid-1990s. Whilst these loans are attractive when the stock market performs well and house prices rise steadily, the repayment arrangements are relatively inflexible. There has also been criticism of lenders being too eager to push this type of loan in order to earn the substantial commissions generated on the sale of the endowment policies.

5.4 Endowment mortgages are of three types, distinguished by differences in the endowment policy that repays the mortgage. The borrower pays interest on the whole mortgage loan for the whole period, unlike a repayment mortgage, where the debt reduces over the whole period, with the final year's payments comprising almost wholly repayments of principal.

With profits endowment policy

5.5 Each year, the value of the policy rises in line with reversionary bonuses that are added to the capital sum assured and never deducted. In addition, at the end of the term of the policy, a variable bonus (the terminal bonus) is also added. In recent years the reversionary bonuses have fallen and insurance companies have had to announce cuts in their reversionary bonuses for forthcoming years. The result has been that in some cases the proceeds of endowment policies may not be sufficient to repay mortgage loans as intended, especially if their initial term was around 12 or 15 years rather than the traditional 25 years. Accordingly, some borrowers faced with a possible financing gap are being advised to take out savings plans. The 'up-front' charges of an extra life policy would probably make it an unattractive way of topping up the repayment, as would the fact that the borrowers would face higher premiums because they are older than when they initially took out the mortgage loan.

Unit-linked policy

5.6   This type of policy has neither reversionary bonus nor a terminal bonus attached, but its value fluctuates in much the same way as the price of a unit trust fluctuates.

Low-cost endowment mortgage

5.7   Here, the life cover provided by the policy is below the value of the debt, with the difference being covered by a mortgage protection policy (a sort of extended term life policy). The advantage for the borrowers is that they do not have to pay such large premiums but, of course, they cannot take all the profits when the policy matures. Instead, most of the profits go to repay the loan, and what remains (if anything) is paid to the borrower.

Pension mortgage

5.8   This involves the borrower paying only interest to the lender during the term of the loan, whilst contributing to a pension scheme. On retirement part of the lump-sum pension payment is used to discharge the loan. The borrower gains from the tax relief on the pension contributions. For legal reasons they are more risky than endowment mortgages for lenders.

Interest-only mortgage

5.9   This involves a commitment only to pay interest for the term of the loan. The borrower must make separate arrangements for the ultimate repayment of the debt; e.g. a savings plan may be set up. Until ISAs replaced them, the use of PEPs had become increasingly popular in this context.

6   Types of interest payments

6.1   In the UK the vast majority of mortgage loans are associated with variable rates of interest, although some lenders are willing to fix rates for a period of, say, 2 or 3 years, and a very few have recently fixed rates for the whole term of some loans. The advantages and disadvantages of fixed and variable rates for the borrower are the same as those for any type of loan, and are in terms of cash flow certainty and possible opportunities forgone when market rates of interest alter. For the lender, an important advantage of variable rates is that short-term funds may be raised to finance long-term mortgage loans without exposure to risk from short-term rates rising. Short-term funds are normally cheaper than long-term funds, and hence the borrower is also likely to benefit.

6.2   Variable rate loans may dampen the impact of monetary policy (working through movements in interests) on the housing market and house prices. Potential borrowers will tend to view extreme levels of interest rates as being only temporary aberrations from normal levels, and will expect their interest commitments to adjust appropriately in the future. However, memories of repossessions, negative equity, falling house prices and two base-rate rises announced on 'Black Wednesday' will be slow to fade.

6.3   It should be noted that there is now a close link between changes in the base rate and the variable mortgage rate. A number of mortgage lenders now offer a base rate tracker mortgage loan, which has proved to be popular with borrowers. One reason for this popularity is probably concern that at low interest rates some mortgage lenders may be reluctant to pass on further reductions in interest rates on account of the impact on savings rates or their interest rate spread.

Study Activities 5

1. List and describe the operation of the main types of mortgage loan.
    (Paragraphs 5.1–5.9)

2. What is the dominant form of interest arrangement associated with mortgage loans in the UK?
    (Paragraph 6.1)

3. What are the advantages and disadvantages of fixed and variable rate mortgage loans for borrowers?
    (Paragraph 6.1)

4. What are the advantages and disadvantages of fixed and variable rate mortgage loans for lenders?
    (Paragraph 6.1)

5. In what way might variable rate mortgage loans interfere with the implementation of monetary policy?
    (Paragraph 6.2)

6. What factor might explain the popularity of base rate tracker mortgage loans?
    (Paragraph 6.3)

7   Structure of UK housing finance

7.1   As Table 11.2 shows, the dominant providers of housing finance in the UK are the *retail banks*. At January 1999 they accounted for 70% of the UK housing finance market (with *building societies* accounting for just 23%). This dominance is a very recent phenomenon, and has resulted from the conversion of a number of major building societies to bank (plc) status. At June 1996 the building societies accounted for 57% of the UK housing finance market. At the beginning of the 1980s the building societies were even more important in the market (accounting for 80% of the total), and the second largest provider of housing finance was then the public sector. The retail banks were only minor players in the market at that time; however they rapidly grew in importance in the market following deregulation of the financial sector. In 1992 the banks provided about 36% of all new mortgage loans. By 1988, before the conversion of Abbey National Building Society to bank status, the banks' share of outstanding loans had reached 20%. By June 1996 the banks' share was 36%.

Table 11.2 Providers of housing finance in the UK, £bn outstanding, 1985 to 1998 (end-year figures)

Year	Building societies	Banks	Insurance companies and pension funds	Public sector	Other financial institutions	Total
1985	97.2	21.1	2.7	5.4	1.0	127.4
1986	116.6	25.9	3.2	5.0	3.5	154.2
1987	131.6	35.9	4.0	4.6	7.5	183.6
1988	155.3	45.3	4.5	4.4	14.2	223.7
1989	152.3	79.2	4.5	4.3	17.4	257.9
1990	176.7	85.7	3.2	3.9	24.0	293.4
1991	197.6	90.4	2.9	3.0	26.2	319.7
1992	209.9	96.4	2.8	2.5	25.1	336.8
1993	217.7	108.5	2.1	2.2	22.7	253.2
1994	231.2	115.9	2.3	1.9	25.4	376.7
1995	223.2	139.9	1.8	1.8	23.5	390.2
1996	224.4	158.2	1.7	1.6	23.4	409.3
1997	97.6	305.7	1.7	0.6	25.1	430.7
1998	107.4	320.6	1.8	0.4	27.4	457.6

Source: Financial Statistics, Central Statistical Office, Table 3.2C

7.2   *Specialist mortgage lenders* funded entirely from wholesale sources first appeared in the market in the mid-1980s. By 1990 they accounted for around 10% of new advances, although they were badly affected by the downturn in the housing market, and have reduced their exposure to the market. Some building societies, seeking to expand in a depressed market, bought the 'mortgage books' of some of these lenders, who then withdrew from providing mortgages. At January 1999 their share of outstanding mortgage loans was 6%.

7.3   In line with government policy, the *public sector* has largely withdrawn from the mortgage loan market. *Insurance companies and pension funds* in aggregate are also relatively minor players, having reduced their exposure to the market somewhat since the late 1980s. However, it is interesting to note that more recently the growth of bancassurance has brought with it aggressive competition in the mortgage market from some insurance companies (for example, Standard Life).

8   Competition in the UK housing finance market

8.1   Since the beginning of the 1980s, there has been a significant increase in the level of competition in the market for housing finance in the UK. Major factors influencing this trend were the:

● Removal of unofficial barriers to competition, such as the abandonment in 1983 of the interest-rate fixing cartel by the building societies;

● Easing of monetary controls on retail banks;

● Enactment of the Building Societies Act 1986, allowing building societies to engage in a wider range of financial activities;

● Advances in technology; and

● Increased financial sophistication within the personal sector.

8.2   The main outcomes of increased competition have been:

● The end to mortgage queues, which were common before 1980, when building society head offices gave monthly mortgage allocations to their branches;

● Interest rates now reach market clearing levels (in 1990 they reached a new peak);

● Some upwards pressure on both mortgage interest rates and retail deposit rates initially due to excess demand for mortgage loans;

● Pressure for mortgage lenders to improve their efficiency and reduce their costs;

● Increasing innovation and product differentiation;

● Some backwards integration by mortgage lenders attempting to improve access to potential customers (for example, via the purchase of estate agency chains); and

● Increased marketing and advertising.

8.3   Competition for market share was probably also responsible for an increasing proportion of the purchase price of property being covered by mortgage loans, and loans growing relative to borrowers' earnings. Together with squeezed profit margins, these developments increased the risk associated with mortgage lending in the late 1980s. The outcome was clear to see during the early 1990s, with record levels of mortgage arrears and repossessions. The subsequent weakness of the market curtailed the excesses of free market competition, although the more recent aggressive competition from new entrants into the mortgage market has been putting pressure on retail banks to reduce their interest spread on mortgage business.

9 Over-funding of the housing market

9.1 This is sometimes referred to as *equity withdrawal*, and relates to leakage of funds from the housing market. There is controversy associated with this occurrence as mortgage loans, which have had a privileged tax position, have been used for purposes other than the purchase or improvement of residential property. Effectively, the consumer credit market has been distorted, as a state subsidy has been inadvertently paid on one type of interest charges but not on others.

9.2 Leakage may occur when borrowed funds are used:

- to purchase a house owned by someone who has died – the beneficiaries of the estate may spend the proceeds as they wish, but the borrower, in this case, has genuinely used the funds for a house purchase;

- by an existing owner-occupier moving house, but where not all of the net proceeds from the sale of the initial property are reinvested in the newly-acquired property;

- for purposes other than the purchase or improvement of residential property, but where residential property is used as security (often as a second mortgage) – this is a genuine withdrawal of equity.

9.3 The planned abolition of tax relief on mortgage interest payments (in April 2000) will finally remove this distortion to the consumer credit market. The problem had, in fact, been diminishing throughout the 1990s, as the level of tax relief was progressively reduced and as positive equity diminished (and in some cases became negative equity) in a stagnant housing market. Nevertheless the importance of residential property as security for loans in general should not be ignored. A first or second legal charge on the property will generally enable the owner to obtain more favourable terms on borrowing than would be possible with various types of unsecured personal lending.

Study Activities 6

1. Describe the pattern of the provision of housing finance in the UK during the early 1990s. *(Table 11.2)*

2. In what ways has the pattern of housing finance provision altered since the early 1980s? *(Paragraphs 7.1 and 7.2)*

3. Where do the specialist mortgage lenders raise their funds for lending?

   (Paragraph 7.2)

4. What factors might explain the increased level of competition occurring in the market for housing finance since the beginning of the 1980s? *(Paragraph 8.1)*

5. In what way has the increased competition in the housing finance market altered the characteristics of that market? *(Paragraph 8.2)*

6. What factors contributed to the increased risk associated with mortgage lending in the late 1980s? *(Paragraph 8.3)*

7. What is meant by equity withdrawal from the housing market? *(Paragraph 9.1)*

8. Why did equity withdrawal become less of a problem in the late 1990s?

   (Paragraph 9.3)

Summary

Now that you have completed this unit you should be able to:

- analyse the structure of the personal sector balance sheet;

- name the sources and uses of funds for the personal sector;

- appreciate the economic and financial risks faced by the personal sector;

- appreciate the broad nature of the financial risks inherent in various saving and borrowing products;

- describe the ways in which members of the personal sector may seek to manage financial risk;

- understand the 'life-cycle' approach to borrowing and investment decisions faced by the personal sector;

- appreciate the importance of home ownership, income uncertainty and pension provision for personal sector financial decision-making;

- appreciate the general nature of borrowing and investment vehicles available to individuals;

- understand the broad nature of the UK housing market, housing finance and how house prices are determined;

- identify the main types of mortgage loan and the associated types of interest payments and repayments of principal.

Self-assessment questions

Short-answer questions

1. What is the importance of company securities to personal sector financial asset holdings?

2. Which groups of financial institutions dominate the assets side of the personal sector balance sheet?

3. List the main types of financial risk which members of the personal sector face.

4. What are the basic principles that are often regarded as influencing financial asset portfolio selection?

5. Explain the concept of 'pound-cost averaging'.

6. What are the component parts of the net supply of houses for sale on the market?

7. What have been the main factors influencing the trend towards increased competition in the market for housing finance since the beginning of the 1980s?

Multiple-choice questions

1. Between 1988 and 1995 the UK personal sector:

   (a) moved from a position of record financial deficit to one of record financial surplus

   (b) persistently generated financial deficits

   (c) persistently generated financial surpluses

   (d) moved from a position of small financial deficit to one of record financial deficit

   (e) moved from a position of small financial surplus to one of record financial surplus.

2. Loans to the personal sector for the purchase of residential property:

   (a) are of minor significance to the activities of the retail banks

   (b) account for around 80% of all personal sector financial assets

   (c) are by far the largest category of debt on the personal sector's balance sheet

   (d) increased dramatically during the early 1990s

   (e) account for around 30% of all personal sector financial liabilities.

3. In relation to the UK housing market:

   (a) renting property from the public sector has largely disappeared due to the government's policy on home ownership

   (b) almost one half of all tenures are in the form of owner-occupation

   (c) the recession of the early 1990s led to a substantial reduction in the level of home ownership

(d) the most significant change since 1988 has been a substantial rise in privately rented housing

(e) there is one of the highest ratios of owner-occupation in the Western world.

4. Annuity mortgage loans:

(a) involve proportionately larger amounts of the principal sum borrowed being repaid as the debt approaches maturity

(b) have been criticised on the grounds that they involve the payment of large commissions to lenders on the sale of the associated endowment (insurance) policy

(c) involve only the commitment to pay interest for the term of the loan

(d) were the dominant form of housing finance in the UK between the mid-1980s sand the mid-1990s

(e) assist elderly people to eke out their savings.

5. In respect of the provision of housing finance in the UK:

(a) building societies dominated the provision of housing finance until 1998

(b) insurance companies and pension funds withdrew completely from the market during the 1980s

(c) specialist mortgage lenders (using wholesale funding sources) grew far more rapidly than any other group of providers of finance during the second half of the 1980s, but have since diminished somewhat in importance

(d) the building societies accounted for less than a half of outstanding mortgage debt during the early 1990s

(e) housing associations are the fastest growing source of housing finance.

6. A major outcome of the increase in competition in the housing finance market since the early 1980s has been:

(a) a reduced need for lenders to differentiate their mortgage products

(b) the elimination of mortgage queues

(c) interest rates for borrowers being lower than they otherwise would have been

(d) interest rates paid by mortgage lenders for their funds being lower than they otherwise would have been

(e) the entry of foreign banks into the mortgage market.

12

Examination Questions

Suggested answers to the following questions are set out in Appendix 2.

1. (a) What attributes must an asset possess in order to be considered liquid? [5]

   (b) To what extent do the following assets possess the attributes referred to in (a) necessary for them to be considered liquid?

   (i) Treasury bills;

   (ii) gilt-edged stock;

   (iii) bank notes;

   (iv) building society term shares;

   (v) certificates of deposit issued by a commercial bank;

   (vi) sterling commercial paper. [10]

   (c) Classify the assets set out in (b) according to whether they are included in the measures of money stock in the UK. [5]

2. (a) Explain the basic role of financial intermediaries. [10]

   (b) Classify the main types of financial intermediary in the UK according to whether their liabilities are included in official measures of the money supply. [10]

3. (a) What are the basic benefits arising from financial intermediation? [10]

   (b) What do you understand by the term 'disintermediation'? [4]

   (c) Outline the clearing banks' response to challenges from the building societies in the area of financial intermediation. [6]

4. Discuss the effects of each of the following on a clearing bank's balance sheet and interest rates:

   (a) regulations concerning capital adequacy; [6]

   (b) the need for liquidity; [8]

   (c) an increased demand for advances. [6]

5. Why and how does a bank raise funds in the following markets?

    (a) the retail market; [5]

    (b) the wholesale market; [7]

    (c) the capital market. [8]

6. (a) Explain why 'liquidity' and 'capital' are important to commercial banks. [8]

    (b) Outline the basic principles underlying the current prudential controls relating to banks' liquidity and capital adequacy. [12]

7. (a) Discuss the role of the parallel sterling money markets in London. [14]

    (b) Is it still valid to distinguish the parallel markets from the discount market? [6]

8. Discuss the significance of the following in the UK financial system:

    (a) the inter-bank market; [7]

    (b) commercial (eligible) bank bills; [5]

    (c) the London Stock Exchange, including reference to the changes introduced by 'Big Bang'. [8]

9. (a) What is meant by bank lending in 'eurocurrencies'? [6]

    (b) Consider the impact of the following on the eurocurrency bank lending market:

    (i) securitisation;

    (ii) liberalisation in the domestic markets. [14]

10. (a) Discuss the factors which determine the level of eurocurrency interest rates. [10]

    (b) Why are changes in euro-dollar rates of importance to the foreign exchange market? [10]

11. (a) Define an interest rate swap and outline its main features. [8]

    (b) A UK bank has made a fixed-rate mortgage loan for a 5-year period at 8%. It is funding this loan with 3-month maturity deposits paying interest at 3-month LIBOR that is currently at 5.6%. A swap dealer currently quotes the following swap rates against 3-month LIBOR: 7.5% – 7.6%. Explain how the UK bank could use the swap to fix its interest rate margin between the loan and the 3-month deposits, and outline the benefits and drawbacks for the bank. [12]

12. (a) Discuss the factors which affect the level and pattern of money market interest rates in the UK. [10]

    (b) To what extent do changes in money market rates lead to changes in commercial banks' base rates? [10]

13. (a) What is meant by the term 'yield curve'? [5]

(b) Examine:

(i) the factors which, in normal conditions, produce higher rates for long-term than for short-term maturities;

(ii) the relationship between short-term inter-bank rates and commercial bank lending rates. [15]

14. In seeking to achieve the ultimate objectives of monetary policy, the authorities can set intermediate targets.

(a) Discuss the intermediate targets that might be selected. [14]

(b) List the techniques that could be used to achieve these targets. [6]

15. (a) A country is experiencing a rate of inflation approaching 10% p.a.. Examine the likely effects on:

(i) the functions of money; [10]

(ii) interest rates. [5]

(b) If a country's inflation rate is higher than that of its major trading partners, what will be the likely consequences for the exchange rate? [5]

16. (a) Outline the different techniques available to monetary authorities for controlling the money supply. [12]

(b) Discuss the techniques for controlling the money supply which have been used in the UK since the early 1980s. [8]

17. (a) How can a government rectify:

(i) a deficit on the current account of the balance of payments? [10]

(ii) a deficit on the capital and financial account of the balance of payments? [6]

(b) What is the purpose of a country's foreign exchange reserves? [4]

18. In the absence of official intervention in the foreign exchange market, what factors are likely to influence changes in a country's exchange rate? [20]

19. (a) Distinguish between a country's 'balance of trade' and its 'terms of trade'. [10]

(b) To what extent can a government influence its balance of trade and its terms of trade? [10]

20. (a) Within the context of corporate finance, what is meant by the terms 'internal funding' and 'external funding'? [6]

(b) Outline the main types of external funding available to a large company. [14]

21. (a) Outline the broad types of exposure to foreign currency exchange rate risk which a company may face. [8]

(b) Summarise the benefits and drawbacks of forward exchange contracts as hedging techniques. [6]

(c) A UK company tenders for major capital goods projects in the USA against several other major competitors. What particular difficulties arise in the management of this particular exposure? [6]

22. (a) What risks are faced by a company which borrows substantial amounts of long-term funds:

(i) at a market-related rate of interest;

(ii) at a fixed rate of interest? [10]

(b) Explain how a company may use interest rate swaps as a means of managing interest rate risk. [10]

23. (a) In relation to the housing market, what do you understand by the term 'negative equity'? [4]

(b) What problems might the existence of negative equity entail for:

(i) an owner-occupier;

(ii) a provider of housing finance? [8]

(c) Discuss the main factors likely to influence the average price of new houses. [8]

24. Discuss the significance of the following for the UK personal sector's finances:

(a) building societies; [7]

(b) life assurance companies and pension funds; [7]

(c) company securities. [6]

25. (a) What are the main types of financial risks faced by a personal sector investor? [10]

(b) Describe the actions that might be taken by a personal sector investor in order to minimise the risks identified in (a). [10]l

Appendix 1
Answers to Self-Assessment Questions

Unit 1

Short-answer questions

1. The desirable features of money are portability, divisibility, durability, homogeneity, recognisability and stability of purchasing power.

2. The essential function of money is to act as a medium of exchange. Other functions that money can perform are store of value, unit of account and standard of deferred payment.

3. It is normally the case that assets having a high degree of liquidity are financial assets paying only relatively low rates of interest. Therefore, in times of inflation the return on a liquid asset may be insufficient to cover the erosion of purchasing power embodied in the asset, thus making it a relatively poor store of value. By contrast, an illiquid asset, such as real estate, may prove to be a good store of value in times of inflation.

4. The true or correct value of a financial asset is calculated by summing the expected future cash flows associated with the asset discounted at an appropriate rate.

5. Risks associated with financial assets may be divided into systematic risks and unsystematic risks. Systematic risks derive from general market conditions that affect all issuers of securities. These risks cannot be avoided by portfolio diversification and hence the market will compensate investors for assuming these risks. Unsystematic risks derive from factors specific to individual issuers of securities. Holding a diversified portfolio of financial assets may reduce these risks. In an efficient market, compensation will not be paid to investors for this type of risk.

Multiple-choice questions

1. (b)
2. (b)
3. (c)
4. (e)
5. (d)

Unit 2

Short-answer questions

1. Expected return, risk, liquidity and transaction costs.

2. A higher rate of interest may persuade a potential lender to lend more funds for a longer period at a greater risk than would otherwise have been the case. Conversely, the potential borrower may be willing to reduce the amount of funds required and accept a shorter duration of loan.

3. This phenomenon is known as maturity transformation of funds, and it is possible due to the law of large numbers. This allows an intermediary to hold a relatively small proportion of its assets in liquid form to cover withdrawals of funds. Experience of day-to-day flows of funds and business judgement determines the maximum proportion of funds that it is advisable to lend long term.

4. Loans will generally be available for a longer period of time, in larger amounts, attracting a lower rate of interest and involving lower transaction costs than would be the case with direct borrowing.

5. Insurance companies, pension funds, unit trusts and investment trusts.

6. It may seek to increase its interest-rate margin, reduce its operating costs and reduce losses due to defaults.

7. A branch network, but this is increasingly being superseded by more telephone banking, PC banking and the use of Internet sites.

8. The fixed costs of the banks are much lower – both total fixed costs and average fixed costs.

9. Cash, cheques, bank giro credits, standing orders, direct debits, debit cards, CHAPS.

10. No. Almost all offer some wholesale facilities.

11. They comprise about 70% of total assets and liabilities.

12. Opening their branches for longer each day, introducing more ATMs and telephone banking facilities, paying interest on current accounts, introducing more savings accounts and interest rate tiers.

13. Bidding for term deposits and making term loans, often involving foreign currency funds.

14. Balancing the maturity, currency and type of interest rate (fixed or floating) of specific assets with comparable liabilities. For example, perfect matching would mean that if two-year loans in currency Z at fixed interest rates form 4% of total assets, then 4% of total liabilities will be two-year loans in currency Z at fixed interest rates.

Multiple-choice questions

1. (c)

2. (a)

3. (c)

4. (c)

5. (a)

6. (c)

7. (d)

8. (c)

9. (b)

10. (a)

Unit 3

Short-answer questions

1. Borrowing and lending of short-term wholesale funds.

2. Discount market and open gilt repo market, together with the following parallel markets: sterling inter-bank, sterling certificates of deposit, sterling commercial paper, inter-company, finance house and local authority.

3. Bank of England, the major clearing banks and the British merchant banks.

4. To keep short-term interest rates stable and at a level consistent with the its monetary policy objectives.

5. By keeping the market short of liquidity and then relieving the shortage at a repo rate of its choosing.

6. All transactions are unsecured and also because the Bank of England does not supply day-to-day liquidity to the parallel money markets.

7. The banks receive funds that are not repayable until the CDs mature; yet the purchasers of the CDs can obtain cash immediately by selling in the secondary market.

8. Primary markets raise new money. Secondary markets enable owners of financial assets to sell them – they are markets in existing securities.

9. Gilt-edged securities issued by the Treasury, bonds issued by companies and public-sector bodies, and shares issued by companies.

10. Undergo stringent vetting of its recent trading record and accounts by the exchange authorities.

11. An offer for sale involves inviting members of the public to buy the new shares. A placing is where a merchant bank or stockbroker buys all the shares for sale to its clients. Members of the public have to buy in the secondary market, using a stockbroker.

12. It gave the institutions much lower dealing costs, especially in connection with overseas securities that are also traded on overseas stock exchanges.

13. Eurocurrency bank deposits are wholesale deposits denominated in a foreign currency, e.g. US dollars deposited in a bank in Zurich.

14. Narrow interest-rate margins have attracted more depositors and borrowers to the eurocurrency markets.

15. Eurocurrency bank deposits are attractive to international companies because the interest rates are favourable and the companies are able to avoid exchange-rate risk and currency-switching commissions.

16. Eurocurrency transactions are normally very large and hence there are substantial economies of scale available for market participants.

Multiple-choice questions

1. (c)
2. (a)
3. (c)
4. (b)
5. (c)
6. (b)
7. (d)
8. (a)
9. (a)
10. (c)
11. (c)
12. (a)
13. (b)
14. (d)
15. (b)

Unit 4

Short-answer questions

1. Derivative markets give investors a choice of location within which they can change their portfolios. They also act as 'price discovery' markets that clarify the opinions of investors as to the future course of prices. They need not attract speculators but, if they do, then the presence of speculators will increase the liquidity of the markets.

2. Derivative markets are exchange-based or OTC markets. Derivative transactions on exchanges are strictly controlled by the exchanges themselves, whereas OTC markets rely on self-regulation by the ISDA and prudential regulation of their members by the relevant authorities in the countries concerned.

3. (a) The borrower can seek a fixed-rate mortgage from a lender who has purchased caps and collars so as to offer stable interest rates for some years ahead.

   (b) This is also called a 'money purchase' pension and its final value depends totally on the performance of the fund managers, who need to hedge the value of the assets in the pension fund. Index options could be used to achieve this.

   (c) The fund manager, to hedge the value of the assets in the life fund, could use derivatives.

   (d) Unfortunately, unless the remittances are very large, the person in the UK is unlikely to be able to purchase the currency forward or buy a currency option on Canadian dollars. If the remittances were very large, the forward purchase of currency and the use of currency options would allow certainty in transfers to be purchased.

4. The primary market in gilt-edged securities comprises investing intermediaries whereas that in interest-rate swaps is likely to involve corporate borrowers and deposit-taking financial intermediaries (such as banks and building societies). The gilt-edged securities market is exchange-based, whereas the interest-rate swap market is an OTC market.

5. Forward rate agreements are effectively forward contracts in interest rates. Forward rate agreements relate to the fixing of an interest rate for a specific period of time in advance and independently of the principal sum borrowed. Interest rate swaps are agreements between two parties to exchange cash flows on a notional borrowed principal for some future period according to a prearranged formula. With an interest-rate swap there is a constant flow of cash between the parties.

Multiple-choice questions

1. (a)

2. (b)

3. (a)

4. (e)

5. (e)

6. (b)

Unit 5

Short-answer questions

1. Under the Banking Act 1987 a bank must satisfy certain minimum criteria before it can receive authorisation. These criteria require that:

   (a) The bank's directors, controllers and managers are 'fit and proper' persons to hold such positions;

   (b) The bank is effectively directed by at least two individuals;

   (c) For banks incorporated in the UK, there must be as many non-executive directors as the Financial Services Authority considers being appropriate;

   (d) The business is conducted prudently, with regard to liquidity, capital adequacy, foreign currency exposure, provisions for bad and doubtful debts, accounting and other records and internal management controls;

   (e) The institution has net assets of not less than ECU (now Euro) 5m when authorisation is granted.

2. There are basically three ways in which a bank may ensure that it has sufficient liquidity to meet its obligations when they fall due:

   (a) Cash and other liquid assets may be held.

   (b) Assets may be matched with liabilities in respect of their maturity, so as to ensure an appropriate cash flow from maturing assets.

   (c) The bank may seek to maintain a diversified deposit base and an appropriately high standing in the markets, so that it is able to attract deposits without undue cost, as and when required.

3. The BIS proposals specify risk weightings for assets held by banks, as well as the items that may be included in core capital and supplementary capital. It is required that all banks involved in international business must hold capital equal to at least 8% of their risk-weighted assets; and of this capital, at least one-half must be in the form of core capital. These proposals led to a tightening-up of the Bank of England's approach to capital-adequacy supervision, in the sense that formerly it declined to specify minimum standards that would be applied to all banks. Instead, the Bank had taken each bank on its own merits, and set trigger and target capital ratios on a case-by-case basis. The Bank continued to apply these ratios where they were greater than the minimum BIS

requirement. The Financial Services Authority has carried forward the Bank of England's approach to the regulation of capital adequacy.

4. The closure of BCCI was followed by serious criticism of the role of banking regulators. It was argued that the standards of banking supervision in a number of countries, including the UK, had proven to be inadequate, and that as a consequence a large number of depositors had suffered needlessly. Therefore, in response to this criticism a number of enquiries were set up, including one in the UK which led to the Bingham Report. Whilst this Report was not unduly critical of the Bank of England or of the basic system of banking supervision in the UK, it did make a range of recommendations for strengthening the supervisory framework and for enhancing the rigour with which regulatory requirements should be implemented. All the recommendations were accepted by the UK authorities, and most were acted upon quickly. Bodies such as the EU Commission and the BIS also recommended a similar tightening of supervision.

5. The SIB (the Securities and Investment Board) was at the heart of the regulatory mechanism for UK investment businesses, as established by the Financial Services Act 1986. The SIB had delegated powers from the Treasury in respect of the regulation and supervision of investment businesses, and itself delegated operational responsibility for day-to-day supervision to self-regulatory organisations each responsible for a particular sector of the investment industry. The SIB was absorbed into the new Financial Services Authority that is now the regulatory body responsible for the bulk of financial services and banking activities in the UK.

6. No. Whilst the bulk of investment business activities were taken within the SIB structure, certain activities remained the responsibility of other regulatory bodies. For example, the Bank of England was responsible for the regulation of the gilt-edged securities market, and the Department of Trade and Industry and subsequently the Treasury had important powers in respect of the operations of insurance companies and unit trusts.

7. The Building Societies Commission has had considerable powers in respect of the activities of building societies. In the first instance, societies have had to meet the Commission's criteria for prudent management if they were to obtain and then maintain authorisation. In addition, the Commission has been able to issue directions to societies on financial restructuring if specified financing and lending ratios were violated. It could also issue prohibition orders forbidding the provision of particular services by individual societies; and it could direct that advertising be amended or withdrawn if it considered it to be misleading.

8. The Treasury operated under the requirements of the Insurance Companies Act 1982 and had overall responsibility for the authorisation and supervision of insurance companies operating in the UK. The Treasury had the power to grant or revoke authorisation for all types of insurance business; to stipulate solvency margins; to monitor the activities of insurance companies; and to intervene in their operation if necessary. The Financial Services Authority has now assumed these powers.

Multiple-choice questions

1. (d)

2. (b)

3. (c)

4. (a)

5. (d)

6. (e)

Unit 6

Short-answer questions

1. This is because in order to calculate a real rate of interest from a fixed nominal rate it is necessary to deduct the concurrent rate of inflation. Even for a past time-period, inflation is measured using price indices that relate to particular samples of goods and services, and hence only provide an approximation of the rate of inflation for any individual. Therefore, it is only possible to obtain an approximate measure of the real rate of interest. For future real rates of interest the situation is even more problematic as it is only possible to work in terms of expectations, which means that there is additional uncertainty introduced into the calculation.

2. Money is irrelevant to the Classical theory, in the sense that it is held to determine only the absolute level of prices and does not affect the amounts of real saving or real investment (that is, the amounts of loanable funds supplied and demanded). An increase in the money supply will merely raise the nominal amounts of saving and investment by the same proportion.

3. A term structure of interest rates shows the spread of interest rates that are paid on the same type of assets with different terms to maturity.

4. There are so many different rates of interest because there are so many different types of borrowing and lending transaction. Each transaction comprises a set of characteristics, such as the risk attached, term to maturity, tax implications, size of loan/deposit and so on. It is these characteristics which will determine the supply of and demand for the type of transaction and hence its price (that is, the rate of interest charged). Different sets of characteristics may lead to different prices for different transactions.

5. Risk;

    Term to maturity;

    Expectations of changes in interest rates;

    Size of loan/deposit;

    Interest rates elsewhere;

Expectations of inflation;

Tax considerations;

Marketability of the asset (where securities are involved);

Business strategy of financial intermediary;

Extent to which the rate of interest is fixed;

Type of loan/deposit;

Government intervention;

Market imperfections.

6. A retail bank's lending rates will respond more quickly the narrower the bank's initial profit margin, the greater the increase in money market rates, the greater the expectation that the higher money market rates are to persist, and the greater the proportion of funds raised from the money markets.

7. The economic environment in the countries concerned;

An expectation of movements in exchange rates;

Actual and expected rates of inflation in the countries concerned.

Multiple-choice questions

1. (b)

2. (d)

3. (a)

4. (b)

5. (c)

6. (d)

Unit 7

Short-answer questions

1. It is generally agreed that all of the world's governments would like to attain the following objectives, a:

    (a) High and stable level of employment;

    (b) Low and stable rate of inflation;

    (c) High rate of economic growth;

    (d) Satisfactory balance of payments position.

    Individual governments may seek to achieve additional objectives depending upon their political stance – for example, in respect of income and wealth distribution.

2. A major problem in implementing economic policy is that the objectives may often conflict. Thus, for example, a policy designed to reduce unemployment by way of raising domestic demand may also cause the balance of payments to deteriorate (by sucking in imports) and may push up inflation (if bottlenecks occur in domestic production). Consequently, the authorities are likely to require a set of policies aimed at achieving a set of policy objectives. It is most unlikely that just one policy (say, of raising demand or reducing monetary growth) will cause all policy objectives to be achieved, especially in the shorter term. Different policies may, therefore, be aimed at achieving different specific objectives.

3. The importance attached to monetary policy within the government's policy package will depend upon the views it holds as to how the economy operates (and hence, as to the impact of interest rates and the money supply on economic activity). It will also be influenced by the priorities that the government has in respect of its policy objectives. For example, a high priority for the defeat of inflation from a government committed to monetarist principles will cause monetary policy to be applied to the single most important element of the policy package.

4. If the authorities attempt to control the supply of money, the free market demand will determine the price (the rate of interest). Conversely, an attempt to peg interest rates must mean that private-sector demand for money is accommodated, irrespective of its level. If the authorities attempt to control both the money supply and interest rates, this can only be done by overriding the free market mechanism; for example, by dictating to banks how much they may lend and at what rates. However, because individual potential borrowers are frustrated by these controls they are likely to seek out funds from channels not involving the controlled institutions. If the latter are restricted in their lending, they have only limited requirements for funds, and hence the rates they are willing to pay for deposits are likely to be less than potential lenders would hope for. Thus, the circumstances exist for disintermediation to occur. Borrowers and lenders may come together directly and funds may be exchanged at rates different from those ruling in the controlled sector. This also raises questions about the extent to which the authorities are actually controlling a meaningful money supply variable.

5. The rates of growth of the money supply.

    The level and/or structure of interest rates.

    Expected rates of inflation.

    Exchange rates.

    Credit creation by banks and building societies.

    Nominal domestic expenditure (or nominal national income).

6. Whilst cash is only a relatively small part of the money supply, it is a vital element of the reserve base for credit creation. Hence, if the authorities are able to limit the growth of the cash base they may be able to exert pressure on the growth of the money supply overall.

7. The major policy objective specified by the government has been the control of inflation. The results of policy in this respect have been somewhat mixed. Certainly the rate of inflation fell to relatively low levels during the middle years of the 1980s, but by 1990 the rate had crept back up towards the level which the government inherited in 1979. However, more recently the rate of inflation has been held at a relatively low level. Furthermore, in general, the UK's rate of inflation has tended to remain above that experienced by the majority of its major trading partners.

Multiple-choice questions

1. (c)
2. (a)
3. (c)
4. (c)
5. (b)
6. (b)

Unit 8

Short-answer questions

1. UK

   USA

   Japan

   Singapore.

2. A spot currency transaction takes place at the current quoted market exchange rate, and settlement must take place within two business days of the transaction. By contrast, a forward transaction relates to an agreement to exchange currencies beyond two working days after the deal and before a future date (or between set future dates) at a premium or discount to the spot exchange rate.

3. An option forward contract gives the purchaser the option over when to deliver the currency (which is the subject of the contract) between the two set future dates. The option does not relate to whether the currency is delivered. The currency must be delivered at some point between the set dates at the agreed premium or discount to the spot rate.

4. The purchasing power parity theory states that the equilibrium exchange rate between any pair of currencies will only be achieved when the domestic purchasing power of each currency is equal. Where this is not the case, it will be worthwhile for traders to import goods and services from the country with the relatively cheap products into the country with relatively expensive products. The deterioration in the latter country's balance of payments is likely to push the exchange rate downwards; whilst the other

country will experience an appreciating exchange rate. This adjustment will continue until purchasing powers are brought into line and adjustments in trade flows cease. The main relevance of the purchasing power parity theory is that it explains why countries with inflation rates persistently greater than their major trading partners' tend to experience steadily depreciating exchange rates. As the purchasing power of a given amount of domestic currency diminishes more quickly than in other countries, the exchange rate will tend to adjust under pressure from balance of payments flows.

5. The exchange rate of the country's currency is likely to drift downward over time relative to the currencies of countries experiencing balance of payments surpluses. Not only must a current deficit be financed period by period, with the obvious demands for foreign currencies from domestic residents, but also overseas suppliers of funds will begin to question the country's ability to service its debt, which is likely to grow (as reserves are finite). However, it should be recognised that, at least in the shorter term, capital inflows for investment purposes may be able to swamp the effect of the current deficit, and the exchange rate may be supported at its existing level or even pushed upwards.

6. A managed floating exchange rate regime attempts to combine the gradual adjustments in exchange rates which may occur in a clean floating system with the stability of rates which may be achieved when the authorities are committed to intervene in the foreign exchange markets to limit undesired fluctuations in rates. In the long term it is expected that market forces will determine the broad trend of exchange rates; however, the authorities are willing to intervene on a day-to-day basis to iron out short-term fluctuations which may undermine international business confidence.

7. As fixed exchange rates are held within their set margins by official intervention in the foreign exchange markets, the fixed rate system can only operate successfully if the required intervention is kept within manageable limits. This will only occur when the economic performances of the countries concerned converge over time. An especially important factor is the relative rate of inflation. If the countries concerned have markedly different rates of inflation, their relative international competitiveness will alter (with fixed exchange rates), balance of payments problems will probably arise and pressure will build up on the structure of exchange rates. As there are limits to any country's reserves and international borrowing power, it is likely that sooner or later the countries with growing balance of payments deficits will be forced to devalue their currencies, thus violating the spirit of stability embedded in a fixed rate system.

8. The successful operation of the EMS implied that members' exchange rates would be stabilised and realignments of parity values would be avoided. In order to bring this about, member states' economic performances had to be broadly similar, and to this end there had to be general agreement on economic policy objectives and the means of achieving these objectives. In particular, policies would have to be aimed at bringing EMS members' inflation rates broadly into line at a relatively low level. In addi-

tion, interest rate differentials would have to be narrowed in order to avoid excessive international short-term capital movements, and balance of payments imbalances would have to be kept to a minimum.

9. An increase in interest rates on sterling funds, other things being equal, is likely to increase the demand for sterling from investors wishing to take advantage of the more attractive returns. This will have the immediate effect of pushing up the spot rate for sterling on the exchange market against other major currencies, including the US dollar. In respect of rates for forward transactions, the premium or discount relative to the spot rate will depend upon the differential between interest rates on comparable funds denominated in the two currencies concerned. Thus, for a future sale of sterling for US dollars, any premium required (because interest rates on dollar funds are lower than those paid on sterling) will be raised, as the forgone interest earnings of the bank willing to sell the dollars will be increased. Alternatively, if dollar interest rates are above comparable sterling interest rates, the increase in the latter will make the discount available fall (as the interest benefit to the bank selling the dollars at the future date will be reduced).

10. Transaction risk.

    Translation risk.

    Economic risk.

11. A forward exchange contract is a contract between a bank and one of its customers, whereby the parties agree a rate of exchange for the sale or purchase of a fixed amount of foreign currency at a fixed future date or between two set future dates.

12. A European option relates to a right to buy or sell a set amount of foreign currency at a set future date. An American option may be exercised at any time up to a set expiry date.

13. Companies may engage in currency swaps to exploit imperfection in markets, whereby each can borrow in particular markets at different rates to those at which the other can borrow. Thus, a UK firm may wish to borrow Euro but may be charged a higher rate of interest than a French company wishing to borrow Euro. Similarly, a French company may require sterling funds but may be charged more than a UK company for such funds. It may, therefore, make sense for the UK company to raise sterling funds and the French company to raise Euro, and for the two companies to swap the funds and the associated servicing commitments. Companies are also able to manipulate the balance of their assets and liabilities in terms of their currencies of denomination by using swaps, thus hedging translation exposure.

Multiple-choice questions

1. (b)

2. (d)

3. (d)

4. (d)

5. (c)

6. (a)

7. (c)

8. (b)

9. (d)

10. (b)

11. (c)

12. (c)

13. (b)

Unit 9

Short-answer questions

1. Risk is normally measured in terms of the variance or standard deviation of the expected return on the security. Drawing upon past experience, a probability distribution of future returns is drawn up from which the variance or standard deviation is calculated. The broader is the range of possible outcomes, the more uncertain is the return on the security, and this will be reflected in a higher variance or standard deviation.

2. The central principal of modern portfolio theory is that it is possible to construct a portfolio of securities the return on which is less risky than the return on any one of the individual securities contained therein. Whilst it is not possible for an investor to escape the return-risk trade-off associated with the holding of securities, it is possible for the investor to minimise the risk assumed at any given desired rate of return through careful portfolio selection. The key to this selection is to ensure that the returns on the individual component securities are not perfectly correlated.

3. The concept of covariance as applied to the returns on two securities relates to the relative variability of the returns. For example, if the returns on two securities have a very close positive correlation, then the covariance of the returns is high and positive. By contrast, where there is a fairly random relative variability, the covariance is small in value and may be either positive or negative in sign. The importance of the concept of covariance is to be found in the construction of portfolios designed to minimise the risk assumed by the investor at any level of desired return.

4. The key to selecting a diversified portfolio relates to the factors influencing the returns on the component securities. Specifically, it is necessary to choose securities the returns on which are influenced by different sets of economic and financial

variables, or that are affected in different ways by particular economic and financial variables.

5. Unsystematic risk arises from the specific factors that affect the performance of a particular security. For example, the quality of the issuing company's senior management team, the discovery of a potentially lucrative production process, a health scare relating to particular products, and so on. If the investor is considering holding just a single security, the associated unsystematic risk is crucial to the selection. In this case the investor would be taking a very significant risk with the purchase of any individual security, other than one backed by the Government. However, if the investor holds a well-diversified portfolio, the unsystematic risk associated with a security considered for addition to the portfolio is irrelevant. Increasing diversification progressively removes the effect of unsystematic risk from the portfolio. The return that the investor seeks, and the only return that the market is willing to pay, will then relate to the degree of systematic risk embodied in the portfolio. Systematic risk cannot be removed by diversification, and is measured by the average beta value of the portfolio.

Multiple-choice questions

1. (c)
2. (c)
3. (e)
4. (e)
5. (b)
6. (d)

Unit 10

Short-answer questions

1. Quite simply, acceptance credit facilities are available only if there is an underlying trade transaction to which the associated bills of exchange may be attached. Thus, raising money for general capital expenditure is not possible by this means. In addition, capital expenditure implies a long-term commitment of funds that should ideally be financed by long-term sources of funds. Acceptance credits are short-term financing instruments.

2. With secured lending the lender obtains a legal claim to realisable assets owned by the borrower. In the event of the borrower being unable or unwilling to service the debt, the lender may activate the security and force the borrower to meet his/her commitments by realising the assets in question. Where lending is unsecured, the lender has to depend upon the good name of the borrower and, in the event of default on the debt, cannot fall back upon a legal claim to property owned by the borrower. Therefore,

secured loans normally attract a lower rate of interest than unsecured loans as the lender is less exposed to the risk of losses on the transaction.

3. Overdraft facilities are easy to arrange with simple documentation. Interest is charged on a daily basis on the closing debit balance. The funds are not tied to specific transactions, and hence overdrafts provide a useful source of working capital. There is no non-utilisation fee, as there is with committed facilities.

4. The main disadvantages of sterling commercial paper are the relatively high minimum denominations (£100,000), the associated documentation requirements and the requirement in respect of minimum net assets (£25m), which may exclude many companies from the market. In addition, it is necessary to make fairly regular issues of commercial paper in order to establish a high market profile and maintain investor interest.

5. Preference shares give their owners preferential treatment over ordinary shareholders in their company's dividend payments and in the case of the liquidation of the company. Thus, in any given year, if dividends are to be paid preferential shareholders will be paid before any distributions are made to ordinary shareholders. However, the dividends on preference shares tend to be a fixed amount (when paid), whereas dividends on ordinary shares tend to vary with the company's profitability. If the company goes into liquidation, the proceeds from the sale of its assets are used, firstly, to meet the claims of creditors and only then to make payments to shareholders. Before ordinary shareholders can receive any payment the preferential shareholders must have been paid their due amount. Finally, whilst ordinary shareholders have voting rights at general meetings of the company, it is only in extreme circumstances (such as when liquidation is proposed) that such rights are extended to preferential shareholders.

6. Gearing measures the ratio of long-term loan capital to equity capital held by a company: the higher the gearing ratio the greater the amount of interest-bearing debt of a company relative to its share capital. Thus, the greater the gearing ratio, the greater the commitment for the company to make regular interest payments. Consequently, the stability of the company depends upon its being able to generate sufficient profits (before interest and tax) to meet these interest payments. Hence the company is in a more risky situation than if it had depended more heavily on equity finance (where dividends can be waived in times of low profitability).

Multiple-choice questions

1. (c)

2. (d)

3. (c)

4. (d)

5. (c)

6. (d)

7. (a)

8. (e)

9. (a)

10. (e)

Unit 11

Short-answer questions

1. Company securities are of great importance in the personal sector balance sheet. Around a half of all the personal sector's financial assets are in the form of company securities, although their value may fluctuate according to market forces. Direct holdings of company securities are significant, but of much greater importance are indirect holdings via investments in life assurance, pension funds and unit trusts.

2. Non-bank financial intermediaries dominate the assets side of the personal sector balance sheet. Life assurance companies, pension funds and unit trusts are especially important.

3. The main types of financial risk faced by the personal sector relate to:

   ● Default

   ● Inflation

   ● Changes in personal financial circumstances

   ● Interest rate movements

   ● Changes in government economic policy.

4. The basic principles influencing portfolio selection are often listed as being:

   ● The trade-off between risk and return.

   ● The reduction in risk that comes from being able to hold investments for a longer period.

   ● The benefits to be obtained from regular saving/investment – pound-cost averaging.

   ● The individual's capacity to assume risk.

   ● The individual's attitude toward risk.

5. Pound-cost averaging relates to the benefits to be gained by an investor making regular investment in equities and/or bonds. By doing this, irrespective of the general condition of the markets, the investor is able to ensure that the whole of his/her portfolio is not purchased at a time when equity and bond prices are artificially inflated.

Conversely, at least some equities and bonds are likely to be purchased when prices are unusually low.

6. The net supply of houses for sale on the market is the sum of:

- New houses made available;

- Houses vacated as a result of the owner's death, emigration or move to rented accommodation;

- Houses transferred from rental status, but not involving sitting tenants.

The net supply is reduced to the extent that properties are demolished for slum clearance or redevelopment purposes. Houses placed on the market by owner-occupiers wishing to move have no net effect on supply, as they create an equal demand (albeit possibly for a different type of property).

7. The main factors influencing the trend towards increased competition in the housing finance market have included:

- the removal of unofficial barriers to competition (such as the abandonment of the interest-rate fixing cartel operated by the building societies);

- the easing of monetary controls on retail banks; the Building Societies Act 1986 (allowing building societies to engage in a wider range of financial activities);

- technological advances;

- increased financial sophistication within the personal sector.

Multiple-choice questions

1. (a)
2. (c)
3. (e)
4. (a)
5. (c)
6. (b)

Appendix 2
Answers to Examination Questions

Question 1

(a) An asset is said to be liquid if it can be realised quickly and cheaply and without capital loss or interest loss. The liquidity of an asset is a matter of degree, depending on how well it fulfils the criteria set out above. Cash is, by definition, the most liquid of assets and it acts as a benchmark against which other assets are judged.

Assets that are easily saleable may not necessarily be liquid. For instance, stocks and shares in major companies quoted on the London Stock Exchange are easily saleable, but their price fluctuates in accordance with market conditions.

Assets which are close to maturity and which have a guaranteed price are liquid. For example, a gilt-edged security that is one week away from maturity may be regarded as a liquid asset. The original time between first issue and maturity date is irrelevant in this context. The key factor is how long there is between the present time and the maturity date.

(b) (i) Treasury bills – Treasury bills are government guaranteed and have been issued with 31, 63, 91 or 182 day maturity and are redeemed at par on maturity. Being negotiable, bills can be sold at any time at a price determined by market conditions. Clearly the price cannot be too far below face value because of the imminent redemption date. The bills are generally regarded as being fairly liquid assets.

(ii) *Gilt-edged stock* – Gilt-edged securities are government guaranteed with an original maturity of five years or more. Some gilt-edged securities are undated. There is an active secondary market in these securities and they may be sold quickly for cash, although there is always the risk of capital loss. Clearly, gilt-edged securities with longer terms to maturity and undated gilt-edged securities are not liquid assets. Whilst gilt-edged securities become more and more liquid as redemption approaches, in general, they are not regarded as liquid assets.

(iii) *Banknotes* – By definition, banknotes are the most liquid of assets since they represent immediate purchasing power. The attractiveness of their liquidity is undermined by the fact that notes do not pay interest. Therefore, there is no protection against the detrimental effect of inflation on their store of value function.

(iv) *Building society term shares* – These are deposits with building societies that are committed for a fixed term. The deposits cannot be withdrawn on demand and there is no secondary market. These assets cannot be considered liquid on basic criteria, but as maturity approaches the shares become increasingly liquid. Although some societies allow premature withdrawals against an interest penalty, such shares could not be considered as liquid.

(v) Certificates of deposit issued by commercial banks – These instruments are normally issued with an original maturity of between three months and five years. The certificates are negotiable and can be easily sold on the secondary market for the current market price. Certificates can be denominated in sterling or foreign currency. The liquidity of certificates of deposit can be considered to be similar to that of short-dated gilt-edged securities (see above). The closer a certificate of deposit moves to its maturity date, the more liquid it becomes.

(vi) Sterling commercial paper – These assets should be secure, being issued by quoted companies with minimum net assets of £25m. Thus the considerations are similar to those for Treasury bills, with liquidity increasing as maturity approaches. However, market prices on the secondary market could be affected by credit considerations at times of stock market uncertainty. This factor would not apply to Treasury bills. Hence, a Treasury bill with the same residual maturity would always be more liquid than sterling commercial paper.

(c) (i) Banknotes: these are included in all monetary measures, including M0.

(ii) Gilt-edged securities, Treasury bills and sterling commercial paper: these are not included in any of the measures of the money supply.

(iii) Building society term shares: included in M2, M4 and M3H.

(iv) Sterling certificates of deposit are included in M4 and M3H; foreign currency certificates of deposit are included in M3H.

Question 2

(a) The most fundamental role of financial intermediaries is to channel funds between those who wish to lend (those with budget surpluses) and those who wish to borrow (those with budget deficits). It is important to appreciate, though, that financial intermediaries do *not* just act as 'agents' or 'middlemen', and that they are responsible for *transforming* the funds that pass through their hands, creating new financial assets in the process. An individual might, for example, deposit funds with a building society on the basis of seven days' notice of withdrawal; this deposit is an asset of the depositor but a liability of the building society. All or part of those funds may be lent to an ultimate borrower; in the case of a building society it might be for a period of 25 years. That loan is an asset of the building society but a liability of the borrower. Thus, the process of financial intermediation has led to a *maturity transformation of funds*. The ultimate lender holds a claim on the financial intermediary that is more liquid than the claim that the financial intermediary holds on the ultimate borrower; that is, the financial intermediary's liabilities are more liquid than its assets.

The ability of the financial intermediary to undertake the maturity transformation of funds is dependent upon the 'law of large numbers'. The financial intermediary uses its experience to show that on any one day the net withdrawal of funds will only amount to a relatively small proportion of total deposits. As a consequence, so long as adequate liquid reserves are maintained, the financial intermediary will be able to remain solvent whilst utilising a large proportion of its funds to purchase fairly illiquid assets. In addition, the law of large numbers allows the financial intermediary to spread the risk of lending between a large number of ultimate lenders. Defaults on interest payments and repayments of principal by ultimate borrowers are not attributable to any individual lender.

A financial intermediary also acts to aggregate the small savings of individuals into sums that are large enough to be of use to ultimate borrowers. On the borrowing side of a financial intermediary's business there are economies of scale in the collection and the interpretation of financial information in relation to investment opportunities. The ultimate lender effectively obtains a stake in a diversified portfolio managed by professionals. The borrower also gains through the easier access to funds, probably at a lower rate of interest than would otherwise be the case.

(b) *Banking institutions'* liabilities are included in all currently used measures of the money supply, although for M0 only Bank of England Banking Department liabilities are relevant. Also, in respect of M2, it is only those deposits that constitute retail transactions balances that are included. Both sight and time sterling deposits are relevant for M2, M3H and M4. Bank sterling certificates of deposit are included only in the broad measures M3H and M4, whilst foreign currency deposits and certificates of deposit appear only in the M3H measure.

Building society sterling retail deposits and shares are included in M2. All forms of building society sterling deposits and shares and sterling certificates of deposit are included in M3H and M4, whilst foreign currency deposits and certificates of deposit appear only in the M3H measure.

The liabilities of *other non-bank financial intermediaries* (the most important of which are the long-term investment institutions; i.e. the insurance companies, pension funds, unit trusts, and investment trust companies) are not included in any of the currently used measures of the money supply. The deposits of finance houses and credit unions also do not feature in the money supply data.

Question 3

(a) The term *financial intermediation* refers to the activity of channelling funds between those who wish to lend (those people and institutions with budget surpluses) and those who wish to borrow (those with budget deficits). Most people think of financial intermediaries as including banks, building societies and the like, but it is important to understand that whenever an individual or institution undertakes, as a business venture, the channelling of funds between borrowers and lenders, then the process of financial intermediation takes place. This process forms an extremely important aspect of the modern financial system, and hence it may be concluded that it generates significant benefits for all parties involved and for society as a whole.

The major benefits generated by the financial intermediation process may be thought of within the context of its *key characteristics*:

(i) *Maturity transformation of funds* – It is often the case that the assets of a financial intermediary are less liquid than its liabilities. For example, the average maturity of deposits with a bank may be seven days, whilst the average maturity of its loans and investments may be one year. The bank is able to perform this maturity transformation by utilising the 'law of large numbers'. That is, because it has a large number of depositors it is able to estimate fairly accurately the maximum likely net withdrawal of funds on any given day, and hence it needs to cover only a small percentage of its total deposits with immediately liquid assets. Consequently, a large proportion of its funds may be used for long-term lending. The ultimate borrower benefits from access to funds that are likely to be available for longer than would have been the case had they been obtained directly from the ultimate lenders. The latter benefit from holding claims against the financial intermediary which are likely to be more liquid than had the funds been lent directly to an ultimate borrower.

(ii) *Risk spreading* – As the financial intermediary normally lends to a large number of individuals and/or institutions, any defaults on debt may be regarded as losses from the intermediary's overall portfolio of assets. The losses are not attributable to any individual ultimate lender, but are shared between all lenders supplying funds to the financial intermediary. However, such losses are normally absorbed within the operating margin of the intermediary, and so are rarely recognised by the ultimate lenders. Thus, there is a reduced risk for the ultimate lender, whilst the ultimate borrower will probably be able to raise funds at a lower cost than would have been the case had direct borrowing been necessary (with the consequently higher risk for the lender).

(iii) *Reduction of transaction costs and aggregation of savings* – Financial intermediaries are often able to take advantage of economies of scale. This is in respect of the accumulation and interpretation of financial information, to spread the fixed overheads often associated with financial transactions, and to employ specialist personnel capable of assessing the creditworthiness of potential borrowers and the earnings potential of available investments. Also, they are able to advertise their presence and so reduce search costs for both prospective borrowers and lenders. Indeed, as many lenders often have only relatively small amounts of funds available, financial intermediaries are able to bundle small deposits into amounts sufficient to meet the needs of ultimate borrowers.

The existence of financial intermediaries is also likely to generate *benefits for society as a whole*, through encouraging the lending of funds for innovative but risky projects which might otherwise not be able to elicit the necessary financial support. Thus, the economic growth of the nation may be enhanced.

(b) *Disintermediation* refers to the situation where ultimate lenders and ultimate borrowers come together directly, and thus bypass the established channels of financial intermediation. There are two major sets of circumstances that cause disintermediation activity to occur:

(i) Where artificial *restrictions* are placed upon the free market mechanism (such as the application of monetary controls on bank lending), it is quite possible that prospective borrowers will be unable to raise the funds they require from financial intermediaries. These borrowers may be willing to pay higher rates of interest than are currently being charged by the intermediaries, and it might be possible for an ultimate lender to earn a higher rate by lending funds directly rather than by lending through a financial intermediary. This rate of interest must, of course, be sufficient to persuade the lender to forgo the benefits normally offered by the deposit of funds with a financial intermediary. The sterling inter-company money market was formed on this basis in 1969.

(ii) Where the ultimate borrower possesses a very *high credit rating*, it may simply be cheaper for that borrower to raise funds directly from ultimate lenders, perhaps via the issue of marketable securities. The evolution of the sterling commercial paper market provides a good example of this form of disintermediation.

(c) The traditional role of building societies is the provision of long-term loans for the purchase of residential and other real property. A relatively small proportion of their assets has been held in the form of government and local authority securities, and hence they have also acted as financial intermediaries in this context. However, since the major provisions of the Building Societies Act 1986 came into force at the beginning of 1987, the building societies have had available the powers to extend significantly their financial intermediation activities, as well as the range of other financial services which they may offer. Of particular relevance is the ability of societies to make unsecured loans to customers, although initially the amount that could be lent to an individual customer was limited to £5,000 (this has since been raised to £10,000). In addition, the societies may now also establish and manage pension schemes, and through subsidiaries of associated companies establish and manage PEPs and unit trusts and engage in life and general insurance business. They may also offer investment services (agency brokerage, portfolio management and the provision of investment advice), trustees and executor services, land services (including estate agency and property development) and general banking services. When taken with their existing range of savings and current account facilities, it is clear that the building societies are now capable of providing a high level of competition to the banks over a broad front of activities, and especially in the personal savings and loans markets.

The banks' response to these developments has taken several forms and understandably has focused upon the maintenance of the personal customer base. In particular, the banks have broadened the range of savings facilities available and have improved the flexibility of access to funds, whilst offering more competitive interest rates. Interest-bearing current accounts are becoming increasingly common and various automatic overdraft facilities and free banking services have been introduced. Banks have also attempted to attack the building societies in their own traditional area of mortgage lending. Not only have they allocated large amounts of funds to this purpose, but they have also introduced various innovations, including fixed-rate mortgage loans for fixed periods. In addition, the banks have become somewhat more aggressive in their marketing and advertising strategies, trying to acquire a more up-to-date and accessible image. There is now much more explicit recognition of customer needs, through longer opening hours and the provision of ATMs. Indeed, the banks have once again been seen to take the initiative in the implementation of computer technology. It is also interesting to note that a number of building societies have been taken over by banks as a means of gaining rapid expansion in the personal savings and mortgage loan markets. Also, the situation has been made more complex by the conversion of several leading building societies to plc (bank) status, sharpening further the competitive pressures within the banking sector.

Question 4

(a) The capital of a bank is basically the difference between the value of its assets and the value of its liabilities. The capital base effectively comprises the bank's paid-up share capital and accumulated capital reserves, together with certain special forms of loan stock. Capital is vital for the protection of a bank's depositors from losses on assets (i.e. defaults on loans and capital losses on investments), and hence for the maintenance of confidence in the bank. The adequacy of a given capital base will depend upon the quality of assets held by the bank. The more risky are the assets held, the less adequate a given amount of capital will be in respect of protecting depositors. Conversely, the more risky are assets, the greater will be the amount of capital required in order to maintain a given level of protection.

The regulations as currently applied flow from internationally-agreed principles put forward by the Committee on Banking Regulations and Supervisory Practices of the Bank for International Settlements (BIS) in July 1988. These specify risk weightings for assets, ranging from a zero weight for cash through to a 100% weight for commercial loans, and define the balance sheet items which are acceptable as capital. The regulations require that all banks that undertake international activities must hold capital with a value *at least* equal to 8% of risk-weighted assets. Of this capital requirement, at least a half must be in the form of Tier 1 (or core) capital, which comprises shareholders' equity and disclosed reserves; the remaining capital is known as Tier 2 (or supplementary) capital, and includes revaluation reserves, general provisions, hidden reserves and subordinated debt. In the UK, these minimum requirements are applied to all banks, and the Financial Services Authority has reserved the right to apply higher ratios to individual banks, depending upon the quality of their management and the nature of their operations.

Clearly, the above-specified capital adequacy requirements have important implications for the structure and growth of banks' balance sheets. The total of risk-weighted assets can only grow so long as there is sufficient capital to allow this to occur, although the book value of assets may be raised by switching to lower-risk assets, hence reducing the risk weighting per unit of assets. If the bank does not wish to restructure its assets portfolio, and is already operating on the minimum capital ratio allowed, it can only expand its assets base by raising additional capital. Raising more share or loan capital in the market or by ploughing back profits and thus increasing capital reserves may do this.

The raising of capital funds involves a commitment to pay dividends or interest, and hence the bank's costs will be raised, thus putting pressure on profit margins. Indeed, if the bank decided instead to reduce the risk associated with the assets held, this would probably have a similar effect, as less risky assets also tend to be those which are less profitable. Therefore, in order to raise the level of capital adequacy, or to maintain the level in the face of balance sheet growth, it is probable that a bank will be forced to widen its interest-rate margin if it is to maintain its profitability.

In order to generate extra profits, interest rates charged to borrowers are likely to be higher, and rates paid to depositors are likely to be lower than they would have been had the bank not been obliged to adhere rigidly to the capital adequacy requirements. The bank is also likely to take special care when considering making marginal loans to all but the most creditworthy of borrowers, as expected profitability will be vital for the internal generation of capital funds.

(b) All banks need liquidity, in order to be able to meet demands from depositors for withdrawals of funds, inter-institution indebtedness, unforeseen borrowing requests from customers, and so on. In the UK the Financial Services Authority requires that banks should manage prudently their liquidity positions, and the broad objective of current regulations is that banks should be able to meet their obligations when they fall due. Other than requiring large retail banks to adhere to minimum standards in respect of the holding of a stock of liquid assets, the Financial Services Authority does not specify formal liquid assets ratios. Rather it lists the major types of obligations that banks must take into account (including sight deposits, time deposits, commitments to lend at a specific date, and unutilised overdraft facilities, where the timing of commitments is uncertain), and then specifies the various means by which these obligations may be covered. An important aspect of this liquidity cover is the holding of cash and other liquid assets, which has obvious implications for a bank's balance sheet structure. The types of liquid assets that are held, in addition to cash, include operational balances with the Bank of England, Treasury Bills, eligible bank bills, inter-bank deposits and certificates of deposit. In addition, careful management of asset portfolios, such that asset maturity is matched, at least to some extent, with that of liabilities, is important to the maintenance of a satisfactory liquidity position. Finally, by maintaining a diversified deposit base and a good reputation within the financial markets, a bank will be able to raise additional funds relatively easily without undue cost, and hence will be able to supplement its liquidity if required. The Financial Services Authority takes each bank on its own merits, and has to be satisfied that its total liquidity cover is adequate in the light of its particular operations and the management expertise which it has available. However, within this constraint, each bank is left to determine its own combination of approaches to liquidity management.

In relation to the effect on banks' interest rates, it must be remembered that liquid assets tend to pay lower returns than many other forms of assets. Hence the need for liquidity is likely to cause interest rates charged on loans to be somewhat higher than they would be in the absence of liquid asset holdings. Also, by limiting the extent of mismatch between the maturity of assets and liabilities, a bank is likely to forgo some of the benefits of maturity transformation of funds (i.e. borrowing short-term at relatively low rates of interest, and lending long-term, at relatively high rates). Therefore, the bank may widen its interest-rate margins so as to make good some of this loss. Indeed, in simply maintaining the quality of operations, and hence a good market standing, costs are likely to be incurred which will be reflected in the interest rates charged on loans and paid on deposits.

(c) If a bank wishes to meet an increased demand for advances it may do this by running down holdings of other assets. Thus, it may have excess liquid reserves that may be turned into loans, although this may involve the need to sell short-term instruments with the associated risk of capital loss if funds are required immediately. Alternatively credit creation may take place on the basis of existing reserve assets. This will inflate both sides of the balance sheet (a deposit will be created on the liabilities side to match the loan created on the assets side), at least until funds are withdrawn or transferred to other financial institutions.

In many cases, an increase in the demand for advances will necessitate the raising of additional funds by a bank. In the short term, these are likely to come from money market sources, and especially via inter-bank deposits and issues of certificates of deposit. Clearly, this form of adjustment would cause both sides of the bank's balance sheet to grow. However, it must be emphasised that balance sheet growth would only be feasible if the bank held sufficient capital to support its larger portfolio of risk-weighted assets. Also, liquidity constraints would have to be borne in mind, and it might be necessary for the bank to hold some of its additional funds in liquid asset form. An increased demand for advances persisting into the longer term is likely to cause the bank to consider its strategy in the market for retail funds, and it may make positive efforts to increase inflows of funds from this source.

If the increased demand for advances was sufficiently large, it is probable that the consequently higher demand for funds from banks would push upwards wholesale money market rates (and perhaps retail deposit rates in the slightly longer term). In turn, this higher cost of funds will put pressure on banks to raise their on-lending rates to borrowers. Thus, the overall effect is likely to be a general upward movement in interest rates.

Question 5

(a) Retail banks raise funds in the *retail market* in order to finance their lending activities. As these funds are normally raised from a large number of personal and small business customers, the banks are also likely to attempt to develop the business relationships formed as a basis for marketing other banking products and services. The opportunity to cross-sell insurance and investment products, plastic card-based credit and payments services, financial advice, and so on, is seen as being of great importance to the prosperity of retail banks in the increasingly competitive business environment.

In order to attract retail funds, the banks offer a range of current and savings accounts for customers. Current accounts are characterised by their associated money transmission services, with the traditional chequebook, direct debit and standing order facilities increasingly being supplemented by various forms of plastic card-based electronic payments mechanisms. Many current accounts now also pay interest on credit balances, which provides a further attraction for depositors. Indeed, in recent years, the distinction between current and savings accounts has become increasingly blurred. At the same time, the variety of terms, conditions and interest returns on savings accounts has been extended significantly in an attempt to meet the needs of the widest possible range of retail savers.

The retail banks have been helped in their task of raising retail funds by being able to utilise their extensive branch networks. The convenient location of branches in major centres of population and business activity and their increasingly extended opening hours have been an important competitive factor in being able to tap the retail market. The spread of ATMs, and the introduction of telephone banking facilities, is of increasing importance.

(b) Banks may use the *wholesale market* to raise funds for lending. For retail banks, such funding may be seen as supplementing their retail market sources; for wholesale banks undertaking no retail operations, the wholesale market is their sole source of funding for lending. The nature of wholesale funds means that they are used extensively by all types of banks in respect of liquidity management operations. Wholesale term deposits, ranging in maturity from overnight upwards, may be raised quickly at competitive market rates, thus allowing banks to maintain a prudent balance of maturity within their assets and liabilities portfolios. The raising of foreign currency denominated funds on the eurocurrency markets also allows banks to manage their foreign currency exposure, and hence minimise the risk which might otherwise arise from unexpected movements in currency exchange rates.

A major source of wholesale funds is the parallel sterling money markets. In particular, fixed-term borrowing on the inter-bank market and the issue of sterling certificates of deposit (£CDs) on the primary CD market are of great significance to UK banks. Inter-bank borrowing may also take place on the eurocurrency markets where foreign currency funds are required, and various forms of foreign-currency denominated marketable instruments may be issued on the relevant eurocurrency market.

Banks may also raise funds by selling part of their holdings of marketable securities. For example, holdings of £CDs, issued by other financial institutions, may be sold on the secondary CDs markets, or eurocurrency instruments may be sold on the relevant secondary eurocurrency market. Alternatively, holdings of commercial or Treasury bills may be sold on the discount market.

(c) The capital of a bank may be defined as the value of its net assets (i.e. total assets less total liabilities). The capital base effectively comprises the bank's paid-up share capital, its accumulated capital reserves, and, under certain circumstances, issues of hybrid debt/equity instruments such as subordinated loan stock. A bank may raise funds in the *capital market* as a means of contributing to its capital base, which is vital for the protection of its depositors, and hence for the maintenance of general confidence in its operations, and for the underpinning of its long-term stability and growth. If the bank suffers from defaults on advances or incurs losses on investments, these will reduce the value of net operating profits. However, large provisions for bad debt may be greater than the concurrent gross operating profits of the bank, and hence the excess loss will have to be absorbed by the bank's capital base. In other words it is the bank's shareholders that incur the loss (through reduced capital reserves, as well as lower dividends), rather than the bank's depositors.

The adequacy of any given capital base depends not only upon the absolute volume of assets to be covered, but also is affected by the quality of the bank's assets. Thus, the more risky are the assets, the greater must be the cushion of capital funds, other things being equal, in order to maintain a given level of capital adequacy. It should be recognised that the Financial Services Authority, in compliance with the Basle Agreement on capital standards and relevant EU Directives, lays down official requirements in respect of capital adequacy. Basically, in order to maintain authorisation to operate in the UK, a bank must hold capital equal in value to at least 8% of its risk-weighted assets (with the weights attaching to each category of assets being specified by the authorities). At least a half of this minimum capital requirement must be in the form of Tier 1 (core) capital, which comprises ordinary paid-up share capital plus disclosed reserves. The remaining capital, termed Tier 2 (supplementary) capital, may comprise undisclosed reserves, asset revaluation reserves, general provisions and hybrid debt/equity instruments (including subordinated loan stock).

A bank may add to its capital base, and hence, other things being equal, raise its capital adequacy, by issuing equity shares on the capital market. If the bank is making a public issue of shares for the first time in the UK it may float the shares on the London Stock Exchange. Alternatively, a rights issue of shares may be made to existing shareholders. In addition to ordinary shares, a bank may issue other types of equity, such as preference shares or convertible preference shares, but for official regulatory purposes the precise nature of the equity will be of importance. As stated above, only ordinary paid-up share capital is included in Tier 1; preference share capital is included in Tier 2. The capital market may also be used for the issue of hybrid debt/equity instruments including loan stock, which will bolster Tier 2 capital so long as it meets the specified official requirements.

Question 6

(a) The liquidity of a commercial bank relates to its ability to meet its obligations as they fall due. An important factor in this respect is the broad structure of its assets portfolio, although the liquidity position of the bank involves its general ability to raise new funds and its expected future cash flows from maturing assets.

Banks require adequate liquidity, relative to their commitments, in order to maintain the confidence of their customers (particularly their depositors) and their shareholders. The specific reasons for banks requiring liquidity include the need to:

- be able to cover withdrawals of funds by customers;

- meet inter-bank indebtedness, which may arise on a day-to-day basis following the payments clearing process;

- be able to meet any unforeseen borrowing requests from customers;

- be able to cope with interruptions to their normal cash inflows.

- meet official requirements laid down by the Financial Services Authority in respect of banks' liquidity positions.

The capital of a commercial bank may be defined as the value of its net assets (that is, total assets less total liabilities). The capital base normally comprises the bank's share capital, various forms of accumulated capital reserves and certain types of subordinated loan stock.

The capital base of a bank is vital for the protection of its creditors (its depositors) and hence for the maintenance of general confidence in its operations and the underpinning of its long-term stability and growth. If the bank suffers from defaults on advances or incurs losses on investments these will reduce the value of operating profits. However, large provisions for bad debts may be greater than the concurrent operating profits of the bank, and so these excess losses will have to be absorbed by the bank's capital base. In other words, it is the bank's shareholders that incur the loss (through reduced capital reserves, as well as through lower dividends) rather than the bank's depositors.

The adequacy of any given capital base depends not only upon the absolute volume of assets to be covered, but is also affected by the quality of those assets. Thus, the more risky the assets, the greater must be the cushion of capital funds, other things being equal, to maintain a given level of capital adequacy. It should also be recognised that the Financial Services Authority lays down official requirements for capital adequacy, and so capital adequacy is necessary for a bank to obtain and keep its authorisation to operate.

(b) The current prudential controls on banks' liquidity have the broad objective that institutions should be able to meet their obligations when they fall due. In this context, banks' major obligations are their sight deposits, time deposits, commitments to lend at a specific date, and unutilised overdraft facilities. Institutions are expected to be able to cover demands for funds made in respect of these obligations by one or more of three means:

- by holding cash or other liquid assets;

- by careful asset-management designed to provide an appropriate cash flow from maturing assets;

- by the maintenance of a diversified deposit base which allows funds to be raised quickly and without undue cost.

The basic principle of liquidity controls is one of *self-regulation* by institutions. That is, within the official guidelines an individual institution is able to select the combination of assets and liabilities that it believes to be optimal, given its own commercial objectives. In order to ensure adequate liquidity, the management of an institution may choose any combination of the above-mentioned approaches. However, as all banks are required to make regular accounting returns to the Financial Services Authority, close monitoring of banks' liquidity positions takes place.

An important qualification to the general rule relates to the position of large UK retail banks, which are expected to adhere to a common minimum standard in respect of sterling liquidity. The standard is designed to ensure that at all times each bank maintains a stock of high quality liquidity that can be mobilised quickly and discreetly to replace funding that has been withdrawn because of a perceived problem in the bank. The types of liquid assets that are acceptable for meeting the minimum requirement include cash, operational balances at the Bank of England, UK Treasury bills and gilt-edged securities, UK eligible bank and local authority bills and secured overnight and callable deposits with Stock Exchange money brokers and gilt-edged market makers.

If it is felt that an institution is not pursuing appropriately prudent liquidity management policies it will undoubtedly be warned by the Financial Services Authority.

Failure to act on such a warning risks the suspension of its authorisation, and hence its ability to continue in business.

The official approach to measuring capital adequacy is to evaluate the various risks attached to a bank's assets portfolio, and then to weight the portfolio according to its associated risk. The more risky the assets held, the greater the risk weighting given to the assets, and hence the larger the amount of capital required in order to maintain a given degree of capital adequacy. The Financial Services Authority also provides a clear definition of the items that may be included within the capital base for regulatory purposes.

Since the implementation of the Basle Accord, the UK authorities have applied a common minimum capital-adequacy standard to all UK banks, specified in terms of a ratio (8%) of capital to risk-weighted assets. However, it must be emphasised that the Financial Services Authority is able to set higher capital adequacy ratios for individual banks if it is believed that their activities warrant such action. In practice, the required minimum ratios set by the Authority reflect its assessment of each bank's ability to manage its risk position, the profitability of the business and its general prospects.

A recent innovation in the prudential control of capital adequacy relates to the implementation of a revised EU Capital Adequacy Directive (1998), which is compatible with the amended Basle Accord. This sets minimum capital requirements for market risks in trading books of banks and investment firms. An interesting aspect of this development is that the authorities have agreed, subject to certain conditions being met, to allow banks to use their own in-house value-at-risk models as the determinant of supervisory capital requirements for market risks. This recognises the increasing complexity of the assessment and management of risk, and also emphasises the willingness of the authorities to work with commercial organisations to produce prudential requirements that are not damaging to business interests.

Question 7

(a) The parallel sterling money markets are one component of the London money markets. All money-market activity relates to short-term, wholesale borrowing and lending transactions. In sterling markets, the minimum transaction is normally in the region of £50,000 to £100,000, with the term to maturity of loans or debt instruments rarely being in excess of one year, and often being for periods of three months or less. Transactions in the parallel markets are unsecured, and consequently the lender has to depend upon the good name of the borrower. As a result, there tends to be a somewhat greater risk attached to lending in the parallel markets than in the (secured) discount market.

The *inter-bank market* is probably the most important of the parallel sterling money markets, due to its large size and its position within the financial system. This market serves to smooth the fluctuations in banks' cash flows, providing banks with a convenient means of adjusting their day-to-day liquidity positions. Thus, banks with surplus short-term funds are often willing to lend them to other banking institutions through the inter-bank market. Interest rates tend to be marginally greater than those earned on funds placed on the discount market, in recognition of the additional risks involved. The market also acts as an indicator of general trends in interest rates, in particular through the three-month London Inter-Bank Offered Rate (LIBOR). This rate is used as a measure of the cost of marginal funds to an individual bank, and hence changes in its value have important implications for the setting of rates on bank lending. LIBOR has a strong influence on movements in bank base rates, and so ultimately on the trend in mortgage and other longer-term rates.

The major role of the *sterling certificates of deposit market* is to provide the banking sector with an important alternative source of wholesale funds. Sterling CDs are negotiable bearer securities issued by banks in amounts ranging from £50,000 up to £1m, and are normally for terms ranging from twenty-eight days to five years. Sterling CDs provide a useful way for the issuing bank to raise large sums of money for fixed periods at fixed rates of interest, thus reducing risk in portfolio management operations. Margins are very competitive and flows of funds tend to be sensitive to small changes in interest rates paid. Technically, the banks issuing the sterling CDs form the primary market in these instruments, whilst institutions which deal in issues, irrespective of whether or not they are the issuing banks, form the secondary market. The efficient operation of this secondary market is vital to the maintenance of the sterling CDs' liquidity, and hence their attractiveness to borrowers.

The *finance house market* relates to the raising of wholesale funds by UK finance houses. This market has become progressively less important since a number of the larger finance houses gained full bank status in the late 1970s and began to raise funds on the inter-bank market as a consequence. Nevertheless, the market is still very active, with regular issues of commercial bills by the finance houses. The non-bank finance houses also raise wholesale funds directly from banking institutions, as well as from insurance companies, pension funds, non-financial companies and individuals.

The *local authority market* relates to the raising of funds by local authorities in the bill market and the bond market and through wholesale bank loans. The attractiveness of the instruments issued by local authorities has been significantly enhanced by their implicit support from the Treasury. In more recent years the market has diminished in importance as a result of the government's attempts to hold back local authority expenditure and as it has sought to exert a greater direct influence over their borrowing activities.

The *sterling commercial paper (SCP) market* is the newest of the parallel sterling markets. SCP relates to short-term, marketable, unsecured promissory notes with a fixed maturity, typically between seven days and three months, that are issued in bearer form at a discount to their maturity value. SCP may be issued by companies (including banks) in the UK which have a net asset value of £25m or more, and where either they or their guarantors have a listing on the Stock Exchange. The major role fulfilled by the SCP market is that of allowing companies to raise short-term funds through the issue of marketable instruments that are *not* the counterpart to specific commercial transactions; unlike commercial bills, they may be issued for general business financing purposes. Some companies, owing to their financial standing, are able to borrow more cheaply through the issue of SCP than by taking out bank loans, and yet the purchasers of the paper may obtain higher returns than they would through making bank deposits. The development of the SCP market represents a further form of disintermediation and is becoming increasingly popular with larger companies in the UK, with a corresponding growth in the size of the market.

The *inter-company market* is the smallest of the parallel markets. This market allows lending by companies with surpluses directly to other companies who wish to borrow, making use of the agency of a broker. The market originated in 1969 in response to the difficulties faced by fundamentally creditworthy companies in raising finance through normal banking channels. With the relaxation of bank lending restrictions, the relative attractiveness of this disintermediation activity has diminished somewhat, and consequently the market now only operates on a modest scale.

(b) It is widely agreed that it *is* still valid to distinguish between the parallel sterling money markets and the discount market, despite the fact that there are similarities between the two types of market.

A major reason for distinguishing between them is that the discount market still plays an important role in official money-market intervention operations. On a day-to-day basis the Bank of England seeks to smooth flows of funds between private sector and government accounts held at the Bank, and may also harness these cash flows as a means of influencing short-term interest rates. The Bank does this by either purchasing (or selling) bills outright from (to) the markets, or engaging in repo transactions including some relating to bills.

It is also valid to distinguish between the two types of market because the transactions within the discount market are *secured* while those within the parallel markets are *unsecured*. Also, the main participants in the discount market are the major clearing banks, certain merchant banks and the Bank of England's Banking Department. Therefore, it is to be expected that the rates at which funds are borrowed and lent in this market are the finest available and are often significantly less than those rates generated by comparable transactions within the parallel markets.

While recognising the important sources of difference between the two types of market, the similarities also need to be recognised. In particular, the banks which have access to the discount market will consider competing opportunities for the adjustment of their liquidity positions. These banks will look for the best deal for depositing surplus funds on either the discount market or the inter-bank market, and the purchase of sterling CDs provides a further use for such short-term funds. Similarly, to cover short-term deficiencies in liquidity, the discount market, the inter-bank market and the issue of sterling CDs provide alternative sources of funding.

Question 8

(a) *The inter-bank market*

The activities of the sterling inter-bank market involve the borrowing and lending of short-term wholesale funds between banks, often via the agency of a broker. It is the largest of the parallel sterling money markets. The funds are borrowed and lent on an unsecured basis, and hence transactions in this market are slightly more risky than those which take place with the discount market where the transactions are both secured and have the lender-of-last-resort facility of the Bank of England available for support.

The importance of the inter-bank market has progressively increased since the mid-1970s, primarily because it provides the banks with a means of adjusting their liquidity positions relatively quickly and efficiently. On a day-to-day basis, banks are able to place surplus funds on the inter-bank market and thus earn a reasonably good return whilst maintaining some degree of liquidity for those funds. Conversely, banks experiencing pressure on their liquidity or seeing immediate on-lending opportunities may raise substantial amounts of funds within the market at competitive rates. The use of the market has tended to develop alongside the trend towards liability management whereby, rather than adjusting their assets to accommodate their liabilities, banks seek to adjust their liability position to reflect their assets.

The inter-bank market is also responsible for establishing the inter-bank rates that determine the marginal cost of funds to the commercial banks. Movements in inter-bank rates are therefore carefully monitored by the banking community, with the key rate in this respect being the three-month London Inter-Bank Offered Rate (LIBOR) which is taken as a crucial indicator of market trends. Substantial amounts of commercial bank lending, especially to the corporate sector, are now charged at a percentage over LIBOR, and hence changes in this rate have an immediate impact on the financing position of borrowers with such loans outstanding. In addition, changes in inter-bank rates will also have implications for the setting of bank base rates.

(b) *Commercial (eligible) bank bills*

A commercial bill is a bill of exchange that is issued as the counterpart to a commercial transaction. It is upon acceptance by a bank that the commercial bill becomes a *commercial bank bill*. If the bank accepting the bill happens to be classified by the Bank of England as an eligible bank, the bill then becomes an *eligible bank bill*. Eligibility status is awarded to banks meeting certain minimum criteria laid down by the Bank of England, which ensures that they command very fine rates of discount. This is in turn enhanced by the fact that eligible bills may be rediscounted at the Bank of England.

The origin of eligible bank bills is plainly in the short-term financing of trade and commerce. These self-liquidating instruments are attractive to issuers as they allow short-term funds to be raised at rates that may be below LIBOR. For investors, the instruments provide relatively secure and liquid assets generating a market level of return. However, it may be argued that their greatest importance relates to the operation of official monetary controls. In particular, prior to the recent changes in the emphasis of market intervention it was primarily through dealing in such bills that the Bank of England smoothed cash flows between the government sector and the private sector of the economy, and through which it sought to influence short-term interest rates. Whilst outright purchases and sales of eligible bills still form an important aspect of official market intervention, repo transactions, especially in gilt-edged securities, now provide the dominant form of intervention, although some repo activity does focus upon eligible bank bills.

(c) *The Stock Exchange*

The London Stock Exchange is the major constituent of the UK capital market. Activities within the London Stock Exchange relate to the issue of long-term securities (primary market activity) for both private sector companies and public sector organisations, and to the trading of existing securities (secondary market activity).

The primary market is of obvious importance for raising funds to support capital investment in industry and commerce. Funds may be raised through the issue of various forms of equity shares that constitute claims upon the profits of the companies issuing them. Companies may also raise capital funds through the issue of interest-bearing debt instruments such as debentures. Purchasers of these instruments normally have a claim to regular interest payments and are creditors of the issuing company. This mechanism for raising funds provides an important alternative to taking out bank loans. In the government sector, the issue of gilt-edged securities has traditionally been an extremely important aspect of budget deficit financing. The ability to issue large quantities of such debt to the non-bank, non-building society private sector is of great importance for monetary control purposes.

The secondary market is also of crucial importance, as it provides holders of both equities and interest-bearing securities with the opportunity to liquidate their investments at very short notice. Indeed, whilst a large proportion of the interest-bearing debt is dated, and hence would mature automatically at some point, some debt instruments, such as consolidated loan stock, have no fixed maturity date, and the bulk of equities are irredeemable (unless the issuing company deems otherwise). Thus, without the facilities offered by the London Stock Exchange, it would be considerably more difficult for private companies and the public sector to raise long-term funds, as borrowers would be required to take on highly illiquid assets together with the associated risks.

It should also be recognised that the London Stock Exchange is not only of importance for financing domestic businesses and the UK government sector. It also provides an active market for trading securities issued by foreign companies and overseas governments and official institutions. In addition, the London Stock Exchange has become increasingly involved with trade in eurobonds.

During the mid-1980s there was significant deregulation of London Stock Exchange activities. Since March 1986 it has been possible for non-members of the London Stock Exchange to purchase a 100% stake in London Stock Exchange member firms. This has resulted in a large proportion of former brokers and jobbing firms either being taken over by, or going into partnership with, other financial institutions, including many major banking organisations. This take-over and merger activity has also led to a significant increase in the capital backing for London Stock Exchange firms, which was thought to be vital if such firms were to become serious contenders in the securities business on an international level. In October 1986 further substantial changes in activities occurred within the framework of what became known as 'Big Bang'. These changes included the abolition of fixed minimum commissions on London Stock Exchange transactions, thus introducing a competitive pricing basis for trading in the secondary market. The distinction between brokers (who acted as agents for non-London Stock Exchange members, and who were not allowed to act as principals by holding securities on their own account) and jobbers (who acted as market-makers and were only allowed to deal with other London Stock Exchange members) was also abolished. There is now a single category of member, namely the broker/dealer, who may act as both a broker and a market maker. In other words, if London Stock Exchange members so wish, they may take on dual capacity dealing. In addition, the gilt-edged securities market was opened up to a larger number of primary dealers.

A significantly freer competitive environment within the primary and secondary markets was the major intention of these developments, with the London Stock Exchange offering an improved service to both investors and those wishing to raise finance. As things have turned out, there has been a great deal of restructuring within the capital market, and commissions paid by the larger institutional investors would appear to have been reduced significantly. The same cannot be said for small investors, the services for whom were formerly subsidised by the fixed-commissions framework. There is now also a greater choice of instruments available through a wider variety of institutions for those organisations wishing to raise funds and for those investors seeking longer-term investment opportunities.

Question 9

(a) Bank lending in eurocurrencies refers to wholesale bank lending that is denominated in foreign currencies. Thus, for example, a bank located in Sydney that makes a wholesale loan denominated in yen would be making a euro-yen loan; a bank located in Paris that makes a wholesale loan denominated in sterling would be making a euro-sterling loan, and so on. The term 'wholesale' in this context relates to transactions that normally involve the equivalent of at least US$1m. The 'euro' prefix is given purely because the eurocurrency markets originated in Europe; it should be appreciated that eurocurrency loans can be made by banks located in any country (provided that the local banking regulations permit) and may be made in any (convertible) currency.

(b) (i) Securitisation refers to the process whereby borrowers issue marketable securities as an alternative to raising funds by means of bank loans. The popularity of this method of borrowing by the corporate sector has increased recently, with the result that the growth of bank lending has tended to fall, including the growth in the eurocurrency markets. An important factor stimulating the growth of this activity has been the deregulation of financial markets, since this has allowed companies greater freedom to issue securities, but the major driving force behind the trend towards securitisation has been the cost of borrowing for those companies with high credit ratings. Many large companies are now able to borrow *more cheaply* by issuing securities directly to the ultimate lenders than by borrowing from banks. The reason for the lower cost associated with issuing securities is that companies frequently have credit ratings equal to those of commercial banks, itself partly a consequence of the downgrading of many banks as a result of their earlier sovereign and corporate debt problems. Although there are administrative costs associated with issuing securities, these may be lower than the charges (excluding interest) that are effectively levied on loans by banks. The result is that the corporate borrower may be able to raise funds at a lower total cost than if the funds had been raised through bank loans. At the same time the ultimate lender may be able to earn a higher return on funds than would be available through making deposits with banks.

Whilst securitisation has undermined the growth of eurocurrency bank lending, it should be emphasised that it has not necessarily harmed the eurocurrency markets in general. The reason for this is that many companies (and indeed official institutions) raise long-term funds through the issue of eurobonds, while euro-notes and euro-commercial paper issues meet shorter-term requirements. However, even here the banks do not lose out entirely, since they often provide underwriting facilities for euro-notes issues and act as agents for euro-commercial paper issues.

(ii) A reduction in the rate of growth of eurocurrency bank lending has also come about as a consequence of the removal of official restrictions and the easing of regulatory requirements for activities in *domestic* financial markets. An initial stimulus to the growth of the euro-markets was the freedom that they offered relative to the comparable domestic markets. The need to comply with fewer regulatory requirements than in domestic markets allowed participants in the euro-markets to operate on very fine margins. This meant that they were able to pay higher rates to suppliers of funds than could be obtained in domestic markets, whilst often charging borrowers lower rates than available for domestic funds. Therefore, as domestic financial markets have been liberalised, the relative cost advantages of the euro-markets have diminished, thus tending to reduce their popularity. This trend has been supported by the wider array of business financing opportunities now available within domestic markets for both banks and their corporate customers. Many new forms of financial instruments and modes of operation have been introduced in recent years, within the evolving regulatory framework. It is now possible for a high proportion of the constantly changing corporate financing needs to be met without difficulty by the domestic markets. Since the late 1970s important aspects of the liberalisation of the domestic markets have included:

- the removal or reduction of foreign currency exchange controls (particularly on capital account items);

- the removal of direct monetary controls which tended to constrain banks' purely domestic operations (as in the UK before 1981);

- the easing of banking regulations on the allowable scope of domestic activities (for example, the removal of certain restrictions on interstate banking in the USA);

- the removal of restrictions on the issue of certain forms of securities by domestic companies (for example, the issue of sterling commercial paper by UK companies);

- the general deregulation of domestic capital markets, allowing many banks to become much more directly involved with activities in areas of the financial markets that were previously prohibited to them.

Question 10

(a) The level of interest rates paid on eurocurrency deposits and charged on eurocurrency loans is broadly determined by the forces of supply and demand for eurocurrency funds. However, given the special nature of the eurocurrency markets it is possible to identify a number of specific key factors which affect the level of interest rates in these markets:

(i) The rate of interest paid on a eurocurrency deposit or charged on a eurocurrency loan will reflect the level of *interest rates ruling in the country from which the relevant currency originates* (rather than the rates ruling in the country where the eurocurrency market is based). The reason for this is that, for activities to take place, banking institutions must obtain foreign currency funds and these will only be forthcoming if the rates of interest offered on deposits are at least as good as those available in the country where the currency originates. Therefore, the factors that affect the level of interest rates within any particular domestic market will also influence the level of rates to be found in the corresponding overseas eurocurrency market. Thus important factors include:

- the current and expected rates of domestic *inflation*;

- the official *monetary policy* position of the domestic authorities;

- the general *economic environment* including the international payments position and prospects for future economic growth;

- the *confidence* of investors in future economic and financial prospects;

- the *risk premium* required by investors in the light of the inherent political and economic stability of the country.

(ii) Until fairly recently, eurocurrency market activity was largely *unregulated*. Intermediaries were not required to hold low-yield liquid assets or to maintain specific capital backing relative to their risk-weighted assets, and hence they were able to operate on very *fine margins*. The large scale of transactions has also tended to hold down unit administration costs. Thus, for any given maturity of funds, the rates paid on eurocurrency deposits have tended to be somewhat *higher* than those rates paid on comparable domestic deposits; whilst the rates charged to borrowers have often been *lower* than rates charged for comparable domestic loans. However, since the mid-1980s the comparative advantage of the eurocurrency markets has been eroded by the movement towards the *harmonisation of regulation* within international banking markets. This has come about both through the strengthening of domestic supervisory requirements and through the pressures exerted by the Basle Committee agreement that required all banks to achieve minimum capital-adequacy standards. In consequence, the differentials between eurocurrency and comparable domestic interest rates have tended to narrow somewhat in recent years.

(iii) Notwithstanding the moves outlined above, which have tended to reduce the risk faced by providers of funds to the eurocurrency markets, the nature of activities in the markets generally involves *higher levels of risk* than those experienced in comparable domestic markets. Thus, the higher rates paid on deposits may be largely justified in terms of the risk premium required by depositors.

(iv) A very small number of Western countries still maintain some form of *exchange controls* on movements of capital funds. Where this occurs, the differential between interest rates in eurocurrency markets and the rates in comparable domestic markets may be greater than can be explained purely on the basis of economic factors.

(b) As the level of euro-dollar rates shows the nominal return which may be earned on dollar deposits held with banks outside the USA, it would seem reasonable to suggest that, other things being equal, an increase in such rates will tend to raise the volume of euro-dollar deposits. However, in order to make dollar deposits, investors must obtain the necessary dollars. Consequently, and irrespective of the precise portfolio adjustments undertaken, a *higher* level of *euro-dollar interest rates* is likely to lead to an *increase* in the *US dollar spot exchange rate* as investors raise their demand for dollars. A lower level of euro-dollar interest rates is likely to have the opposite effect, as investors liquidate their euro-dollar deposits and switch to investments denominated in currencies which now offer relatively more attractive returns.

Changes in euro-dollar rates, other things being equal, will also have implications for forward transactions on the foreign-currency exchange markets. This is because the *premiums and discounts on forward exchange rates* reflect the *differences between interest rates* on assets denominated in the currencies involved. The relationship can best be explained by a simple example. A UK-based bank may agree to sell dollars to a customer in three months' time. The bank will immediately purchase an appropriate amount of dollars on the spot market and will then use these dollars to make a euro-dollar deposit with a three months' maturity. Thus, the bank effectively converts a quantity of funds that would otherwise have been held as interest-bearing *sterling* assets into an equal value of interest-bearing *dollar* assets. If the *rate of interest* that can be earned on the *euro-dollars* is *less* than that which can be earned on *comparable sterling assets* on the domestic market, the bank will charge a *premium* on the forward trans-action. This is in order to cover the interest-rate differential, which amounts to a cost imposed on the bank. (This premium is in addition to charges that the bank will make for the various administrative expenses incurred.) Consequently, the higher the rate of interest that the bank is able to earn on the euro-dollar deposit, the smaller the premium that it will charge the customer. The existence of competitive financial markets will ensure that the premium is reduced and that benefits from the higher euro-dollar rate are passed on to the customer. Alternatively, if the *rate of interest* paid on the *eurodollar* deposit is initially *higher* than that which could be earned on domestic *sterling deposits*, the bank will offer a *discount* on the forward sale of dollars for sterling relative to the ruling spot rate. In this case, an increase in the euro-dollar rate will cause the discount to be raised, as the bank benefits from the increased interest-rate differential in favour of euro-dollars. A fall in the euro-dollar rate would lead to a reduction in the discount or an increase in the premium on forward dollar sales to the bank's customer, depending upon the magnitude of the reduction of the euro-dollar rate and the value of the initial interest-rate differential.

Question 11

(a) An interest rate swap occurs when two borrowers raise funds independently and then exchange the associated streams of interest payments. For example, one party may borrow at a fixed rate and the other at a floating rate of interest. The two parties then swap their debt servicing commitments.

The main features of interest rate swaps are:

- Only the interest payments are swapped; there is no exchange of principal.

- The interest rates and terms for swaps are agreed at the outset on the basis of an agreed notional principal.

- Transactions are usually governed by a standardised swap contract, although the amount and terms are not standardised.

- The rights and obligations under the swap are entirely separate from the rights or obligations associated with any underlying borrowing.

- Initial periods normally cover anything from 1 year to 10 years or more.

(b) The swap transaction is best explained through the use of a simple diagram:

Quite simply, the bank earns a fixed 8% from the borrower, but pays the LIBOR for deposits. The bank agrees the swap giving a LIBOR inflow in exchange for a fixed payment of 7.6%

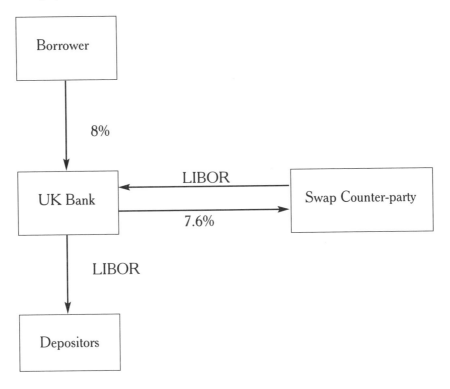

The outcome is that the UK bank's margin on the intermediation transaction is fixed at 0.4% for the full five-year period. A major benefit to the bank is that it will be unaffected by changes in LIBOR during that period.

The underlying loan and deposits are not disturbed by the swap agreement.

Ideally, the notional principal on the swap agreement should match the mortgage loan made by the bank, in both amount and maturity, but in practice such precision may be difficult to achieve.

In addition, the UK bank will incur costs and fees payable to the other bank managing the swap transaction, reflecting the settlement and counter-party risk. There is also the problem that if the borrower wishes to repay the mortgage loan early, the UK bank will still have to pay the fixed 7.6% on the swap transaction in exchange for a LIBOR inflow. If LIBOR then falls, the exposure is clear. It is for this reason that the UK bank may insist on a penalty clause in the mortgage loan contract, so that it will receive compensation if early repayment is made.

Question 12

(a) Money market activity involves the borrowing and lending of wholesale funds for relatively short periods of time (usually for less than one year and often for periods ranging from overnight up to three months). The short-term nature of the market implies that the supply of and the demand for liquidity influence the overall level of interest rates, although there are many important considerations underlying this relationship. A particularly important factor relates to the position of the Bank of England, which, for many years, has been closely involved with the operations of the primary (discount) money market, and is now a key participant in the gilt repo market. These are important channels for monetary controls and the adjustment of liquidity within the financial system. Furthermore, as all the London money markets (including the parallel sterling markets and the eurocurrency markets) are to some extent interconnected, the Bank's influence may percolate quickly throughout the whole market system.

On a day-by-day basis the Bank of England attempts to maintain stability within the money markets, through appropriate intervention actions to deal with any forecast cash imbalances. However, for monetary policy reasons the Bank may wish to alter short-term interest rates, and hence influence interest rates throughout the economy. On such occasions it will alter appropriately its official repo rate (which equals the discount rate that it applies to purchases of bills), and so affect the cost of liquidity to the market. The Bank concentrates its market intervention on instruments with a maturity of 14 days or less.

Looking towards longer-term rates within the money markets, the standard term-structure analysis applies. Consequently, when there are no general expectations of interest rate movements, the longer the term to maturity the higher the rate will be. This reflects the liquidity preference of lenders and the increased risks over time, so that the yield curve slopes upward. However, once expectations of future changes in rates are recognised the situation is not so simple. An expected rise in rates will tend to increase the demand for long-term fixed-rate funds but will reduce the supply, which tends to make the yield curve steeper. Expected falls in rates will increase supply relative to demand for longer maturity funds and may even lead to a negatively sloped yield curve. Government policies, exchange rate movements, general economic/inflation conditions and so on, will frame the expectations.

Interest-rate differentials between different money market instruments (for example, Treasury bills, local authority deposits, sterling CDs) with the same maturity will be influenced by the set of characteristics which each instrument embodies. Factors such as inherent risks, specific demand and supply conditions, ease of marketability, liquidity and so on will be important.

(b) The importance of money markets for commercial banks' liquidity positions cannot be overemphasised, for it must be remembered that it is virtually impossible for a bank to adjust its short-term liquidity position through its retail funds flows. Thus, for all practical purposes, the marginal cost of funds for commercial banks is broadly reflected by money market rates, and in particular by the three-month sterling LIBOR. Therefore, bank base rates will tend to be strongly influenced by money market rates over time, but they only follow the broad trends, not the temporary fluctuations.

The setting of banks' base rates will be affected by longer-term considerations, including expectations of future movements in money market rates, and hence the factors listed above. The critical factor is, of course, the Bank of England's official repo rate, which measures the marginal cost of liquidity to the money markets. A change in this rate will almost inevitably lead to a widespread corresponding change in bank base rates as money market rates move into line.

Retail banks must consider customer loyalty, as ordinary retail customers may be inconvenienced by continually changing interest rates, and indeed their finances may not be able to cope with such changes. In addition, the number of retail customers is now so large that the mechanics of altering retail deposit and base rates involve substantial costs for banks, despite the advances of computer technology. Consequently, their interest rates tend to be 'sticky' relative to the more volatile money market rates.

Clearly, as all interest rates are inter-linked, changes in money market rates will always have some influence on bank interest rates in the broadest sense, and consideration by banks of their longer-term profitability in respect of the raising and on-lending of funds will affect the nature of that influence. The decision as to whether or not to alter interest rates following a change in market rates will be influenced by the proportion of total funds raised at market rates, the proportion of funds on-lent at market-related rates, and the size of the initial overall interest rate margin.

Question 13

(a) A yield curve shows the relationship between yields on a particular type of asset with different terms to maturity. Yield curves can only exist for instruments which carry fixed interest rates and have fixed maturity dates: for example, gilt-edged securities, certificates of deposit and eurobonds.

A 'normal' yield curve shows that the longer the term to maturity of the asset, the greater the yield generated. The curve tends to level off as maturity becomes longer, since beyond a certain time into the future it becomes almost impossible to differentiate between different degrees of risk and liquidity preference, which are the basic factors responsible for the upward slope.

If there are general expectations that interest rates are going to rise in the future, this will tend to make the yield curve steeper as investors hold back on longer-term commitments to lend until rates have risen. Conversely, expectations of future reductions in interest rates will tend to cause the yield curve to become flatter as lenders increase long-term lending as a means of taking advantage of currently high rates of interest, whilst borrowers hold back their requirements in readiness for future lower rates of interest.

(b) (i) *The two basic factors which cause yield curves to slope upward from left to right are risk and liquidity preference.*

The longer the term to maturity of an asset, the greater the risk which must be accepted by the holder of the asset. For example, whilst a borrower might appear to be highly creditworthy at the time a loan is made, the longer the period for which the funds are to be lent the greater the risk that conditions may alter, and hence the greater the risk of default. Therefore, the lender will seek a higher return in order to compensate for this higher risk. Similarly, the further one looks into the future, the harder it becomes to predict accurately the rate of *inflation*, and hence the degree of erosion of real capital value which might be expected in a nominal amount of funds lent or invested. Again, the lender will seek a higher return to cover this greater risk of *capital loss*. Indeed, concern over the risk of capital loss may be extended to the possibility of adverse movements in interest rates making the premature sale of marketable instruments unattractive, and hence perhaps causing difficulties if the lender's personal situation necessitates a reappraisal of his/her financial portfolio.

Lenders usually require compensation for the loss of access to *immediate purchasing power* which is entailed when funds are used to make fixed-term loans. The longer the term to maturity, the greater the amount of compensation that will be required by the lender. The liquidity issue is still relevant even when marketable debt is purchased, as the risk of capital loss from premature sale of the debt means that liquidity is lost in the strict sense.

The existence of risk and liquidity preference explains why longer-term rates of interest are higher than shorter-term rates, when there are no specific expectations of interest movements; that is, in what are sometimes referred to as 'normal' circumstances. However, when expectations of interest rate movements do exist, additional forces are exerted on the shape of the yield curve. Specifically, if there are general expectations of an increase, this will tend to push up long-term rates relative to short-term rates. This occurs because lenders, wishing to avoid being locked into relatively low-yield assets, will increasingly prefer to lend short-term hoping that when the loans mature they will be able to reinvest the funds at the expected higher rate. Thus, there is an increase in the supply of short-term funds and a corresponding reduction in the supply of long-term funds. Conversely, borrowers will wish to borrow long-term today at the currently relatively low rate of interest. They would be foolish to borrow short-term only to have to borrow the funds again at higher rates of interest at some time in the future. Thus, there will tend to be an increase in the demand for long-term funds and a reduction in the demand for short-term funds. Considering the behaviour of both lenders and borrowers, the effect of an expected increase in interest rates is to create an excess demand for long-term funds and an excess supply of short-term funds at the initial term structure of interest rates. This will tend to result in market forces pushing down short-term rates and pushing up long-term rates, which makes the yield curve steeper.

(b) (ii) Short-term inter-bank interest rates provide a good measure of the *marginal cost of funds* to individual banks attempting to adjust their liquidity positions. The importance of the inter-bank market cannot be overemphasised, for it must be remembered that it is virtually impossible for a bank to adjust its short-term liquidity position through its retail funds flow. By contrast, the inter-bank market is sensitive to relatively small changes in rates, terms for individual transactions are negotiated separately, and the sophisticated communications networks ensure that financing needs can be met quickly and efficiently.

The effect of changes in short-term inter-bank interest rates on commercial bank lending rates depends very much upon the *types of lending activity* involved and upon the *nature of the changes* in inter-bank rates. In relation to lending at a *fixed margin above inter-bank rate*, the relationship is direct. For example, a wholesale loan may be made to a corporate customer at a fixed percentage over the three-month LIBOR, and consequently an increase in inter-bank rates will cause an immediate increase in the rate charged to the corporate customer.

Where lending rates are *linked to base rates* the relationship is somewhat more complex. The Bank of England's official repo rate largely determines decisions on base rates. Consequently, lending rates tend to follow the general trend in short-term inter-bank rates, but are not adjusted to reflect every short-term fluctuation in such rates. The reason for this is that the cost of inter-bank funds is only one factor in the determination of lending rates. The direct effect on a bank's operating margin of having to pay a higher rate for inter-bank funds would have to be weighed against the cost of adjusting lending rates, both in terms of the administration expenses and the effect on customer loyalty. Banks will be more willing to raise lending rates:

- the greater the increase in inter-bank rates;

- the more permanent the increase in inter-bank rates is expected to be;

- the larger the proportion of total funds that the bank raises at inter-bank rates;

- the finer the bank's pre-existing operating margin;

- the greater the response from competing financial intermediaries.

Finally, it should be recognised that some lending by commercial banks takes place at *fixed rates*. However, changes in inter-bank rates are still likely to influence the average of such rates, as term loans mature and are renegotiated and as new loans are made at rates reflecting the new (and future expected) cost of funds to the bank.

Question 14

(a) Intermediate targets are those variables through which the authorities intend to achieve their economic policy objectives. In turn, the intermediate targets are themselves influenced by the authorities' policy instruments (that is, those policy variables over which they have reasonably close control). In addition, some intermediate targets may be manipulated to affect other target variables, which will then, it is hoped, influence the ultimate policy objectives.

The intermediate targets of monetary policy include the following:

(i) *The level and/or structure of interest rates* – The fundamental idea is that by altering interest rates the authorities may be able to influence interest-sensitive expenditure relating to both business investment and consumer spending. Changes in interest rates may also have implications for international currency flows, and hence for the balance of payments. In addition, it is important to recognise that changes in interest rates may be used as a means of influencing other intermediate target variables, and hence may be part of a chain of intermediate targets. For example, an increase in the level of interest rates may be effected by the authorities in the hope of damping down the demand for bank and building society credit, and thereby reducing the rate of growth of the money supply and hence aggregate demand within the economy.

(ii) *The rates of money supply growth* – This became a more important intermediate target of monetary policy, during the 1980s in particular, as a consequence of the increased popularity of monetarism. Monetarists would argue that the rate of growth of the money supply must be controlled if the price level is to be stabilised. Unfortunately, a major problem in utilising this target variable is in determining which measure of the money supply to use. This caused particular difficulties in the UK in the 1980s.

(iii) *Bank and building society credit creation* – It is sometimes argued that members of the non-bank, non-building society private sector obtain credit primarily to finance expenditure on goods, services and real assets. Hence, there is likely to be a predictable relationship between the extension of bank and building society credit and the total level of private sector expenditures.

(iv) *Projected rate of inflation* – When the actual rate of inflation is the policy objective, it may be appropriate to use some measure of projected inflation rates in future periods as the intermediate target. Market expectations are likely to provide a reasonable indication of inflationary pressures, and hence give direction to the adjustment of policy.

(v) *Exchange rates* – The exchange rate of a country's currency may be a target variable, to affect the relative prices of exports and imports, and hence influence the current account of the balance of payments, domestic output and employment and the rate of inflation.

(vi) *Nominal domestic expenditure (national income)* – It is quite acceptable to consider the level of domestic expenditure as a target for policy, as ultimately the manipulation of this variable may be expected to have an influence upon the rate of inflation and/or the levels of output and employment.

(b) The *techniques* that may be used by the authorities in order to achieve their monetary policy targets include the following:

(i) *The central bank's repo or discount rate* may be changed, as a means of affecting the marginal cost of funds for the financial system, and hence interest rates in general.

(ii) *Open market operations* may be undertaken in either the discount market or the gilt repo market, with the intention of affecting the structure of financial assets held by the private sector and/or the level and structure of interest rates. The authorities may engage in repo transactions (involving both gilt-edged securities and bills in the UK) or in outright purchases/sales of bills and other debt instruments.

(iii) *The authorities may intervene in the foreign exchange market* by purchasing and selling currencies in order to influence the domestic currency's exchange rate, and possibly international currency flows.

(iv) *Direct controls* may be imposed on lending by financial institutions. These could be in the form of lending ceilings or qualitative guidelines.

(v) *Special deposits*, or the imposition of *restrictive reserve requirements* by the authorities, may influence the reserve bases of financial institutions.

(vi) *Moral suasion* may be applied to financial institutions in an attempt to persuade them to restrain their lending activities.

(vii) The authorities may set *maximum target growth rates for interest-bearing deposits* with financial institutions, as a means of limiting their willingness to bid for funds for lending. Penalties may be enforced against institutions violating the target rates. *Interest rate ceilings* may be imposed with a similar aim in mind.

Question 15

(a) (i) *Medium of exchange* – With annual inflation at around 10% there is *unlikely to be any significant effect* on the use of money as a medium of exchange. Experience has shown that inflation rates have to rise considerably above this value before people stop using money in the transaction process. The convenience of money is so great and the loss in purchasing power so small that reverting to the use of commodity monies or barter is out of the question.

Store of value – The impact of inflation on the store-of-value function of money depends very much upon the particular definition of money being considered. Thus, where money bears *no interest* (as in the case of cash and ordinary current account deposits) any amount of inflation erodes its *real purchasing power*, and hence it is likely that people will switch to holdings of other assets as *hedges against inflation*. However, a large proportion of the money stock as defined by the broader measures of money does pay interest, and this offers at least some *compensation* for the effects of inflation. If the real rate of interest on money is positive (which implies a nominal rate greater than 10% within the context of the question), then it is unlikely that people will move into non-money assets to any great extent (given the convenience factor associated with holding wealth in money form). Expectations of persistent inflation at even higher rates may cause a somewhat more substantial shift to other types of assets with better inflation-hedging qualities.

Unit of account – The performance of money as a measure of value would be increasingly *undermined* the longer inflation persisted. Comparisons of money values over time would become increasingly difficult. With inflation at 10% the interpretation of company accounts could be distorted, especially if costs and revenues were compared at different points in time. To assess the true financial performance of a company it might be necessary to use inflation-adjusted accounting methods.

Standard for deferred payment – The existence of inflation will undoubtedly undermine the *credit function* of money. Unless funds are lent on an index-linked basis, both lender and borrower will face *uncertainty* as to the real rate of interest to be received or paid. If funds are lent at a fixed rate of interest and inflation turns out to be higher than expected, the borrower will gain at the expense of the lender. Quite simply, the real value of the amount owed will diminish over time. Unless real interest rates are positive, the lender will not even receive sufficient compensation to make good the loss in purchasing power of the funds lent, let alone a return for the risk and loss of liquidity incurred.

(a) (ii) If the rate of inflation rises towards 10%, it is likely that *nominal rates of interest* will also *increase*. There are basically two reasons for this: firstly, the lender will seek to *protect the purchasing power* of his outstanding loans and hence will push for higher nominal rates of interest. If he has in mind a desired real rate of interest, then nominal rates will have to be held above the concurrent rate of inflation. Indeed, financial institutions may feel obliged to raise the rates offered on savings deposits to dissuade savers from shifting their funds into other forms of assets that offer hedges against inflation.

Secondly, a rising rate of inflation will probably cause the authorities to tighten their *monetary policy* and so engineer an increase in nominal interest rates. Higher rates of interest are seen as a means of damping down the demand for credit and therefore money supply growth; and higher borrowing costs associated with outstanding debt will reduce the ability of borrowers to purchase goods and services, thus helping to reduce *inflationary pressures*. In addition, higher rates of interest will tend to support the *exchange value* of the domestic currency (by providing compensation to overseas investors for the effects of domestic inflation), and so help to hold down import prices whilst putting pressure on domestic producers to contain their costs.

(b) If a country's inflation rate is higher than the rates experienced by its major trading partners then, other things being equal, its exports will become *increasingly less competitive* in overseas markets, whilst *imports* become *increasingly attractive* in the domestic market. Assuming that the *price elasticity of demand* for traded goods and services is sufficiently high, then the country will find its current account deteriorating. In the short term, it may be able to draw upon its accumulated currency and gold reserves to cover any deficit or it may borrow from overseas, possibly pushing up interest rates in the process. However, as both reserves and international borrowing power are limited for any particular country, it is likely that in the longer term international *confidence* in the country's ability to pay its way will be undermined, and the domestic currency's *exchange rate* will begin to *depreciate*. The exchange rate movement may be seen as a necessary adjustment for the effects of above-average inflation on the country's international competitiveness. This natural adjustment mechanism is explained by the *purchasing power parity theory*, which states that, in the long run, movements in exchange rates are determined by the inflation differential between the relevant countries. Equilibrium exchange rates will only be achieved when the domestic purchasing powers of equivalent amounts of the relevant currencies are equal. However, in the short run capital flows may counteract the effects of inflation differentials on exchange rates.

Question 16

(a) The instruments of monetary control may be divided into three broad groups:

  (i) instruments of market intervention;

  (ii) instruments of portfolio constraint;

  (iii) longer-term control mechanisms.

  The instruments of market intervention comprise the Bank of England's *open-market operations* and the setting of its *repo (discount) rate*. This latter rate is effectively the price charged by the Bank for funds supplied to the markets in the event of a general shortage of liquidity. In recent years it has normally represented the rate that the Bank has applied to its repo transactions relating to gilt-edged securities, eligible bills (Treasury bills, eligible local authority bills and eligible bank bills) and Bank of England Euro bills. This is the same rate as the discount rate applied to the Bank's outright purchases of bills, which supplement the repo transactions. The influence of the repo rate on the financial system is pervasive, as it measures the marginal cost of funds to the system as a whole. Changes in the repo rate give important signals in respect of the likely future trend of interest rates in general, but especially the trend in short-term rates.

  Open-market operations occur when the Bank intervenes in the markets for securities, either buying or selling or using repo agreements, depending upon its objectives in relation to the level and structure of interest rates and/or the volume of liquidity in the financial system. The Bank trades extensively in the discount market and open gilt repo market and its greatest influence is exerted upon short-term interest rates, concentrating on instruments with a maturity of 14 days or less.

The instruments of market intervention are likely to have a fairly generalised effect on financial conditions. Thus, if interest rates are pushed upward, this may dampen the demand for mortgage loans from building societies and hire purchase credit from finance houses as well as the demand for bank loans.

Although the instruments of portfolio constraint could be applied broadly, in practice they have been normally applied to specific groups of financial institutions, and hence they tend to operate in a discriminatory manner. This is clearly inequitable, and the controls may generate conditions that undermine their own effectiveness in the longer term. In other words, disintermediation may occur as non-controlled institutions attempt to take up any business driven away from the controlled parts of the financial system. The major portfolio constraints are reserve requirements, special deposits and supplementary special deposits, moral suasion and direct controls. Currently, they are in abeyance.

In order to create deposits, banks and building societies must hold a *reserve asset base*, usually in the form of cash or other liquid assets. When the institution reaches its desired minimum reserve ratio, assuming that there are unsatisfied demands for loans, it either has to turn away potential borrowers or it has to attract more deposits and/or purchase reserve assets. In either event, it is likely that interest rates will be pushed upward, which will restrain the demand for loans. Thus, if the authorities are able to influence the total supply/price of reserve assets or the required reserve ratio, they should be able to exert pressure on the level of deposit creation and hence the rate of growth of the money supply.

Special deposits are funds that must be deposited by (banking) institutions with the Bank of England. The Bank has the right to call for special deposits in amounts related to individual institutions' eligible liabilities. These special deposits do not count as part of institutions' reserve bases, and hence calls have an immediate effect on their ability to create credit. Special deposits have a similar ultimate effect to open-market operations, although they tend to act quicker and are useful for mopping up excess reserves within the banking system without having an undue destabilising effect. After a call has been made, banks are able to adjust their reserve positions steadily over time. *Supplementary special deposits* referred to the 'penalty' which had to be paid by institutions in violation of a fixed maximum target growth rate for a certain category of their deposit liabilities. When this system operated in the UK it was referred to as the 'corset' mechanism and focused attention directly upon a major element of the money supply. Special deposits were paid on a scale related to the degree of target overshoot and banks could not use them as part of the reserve base. Also, they attracted no interest payment from the Bank of England (unlike ordinary special deposits).

Moral suasion occurs when the Bank applies informal pressures on financial institutions to act in a manner which is conducive 'to the national interest', although this might not be in the best commercial interest of the institutions. The Bank may make suggestions about lending priorities and may ask institutions to limit the amount of credit granted to certain categories of customers.

Direct controls limit the freedom of financial institutions to pursue their commercial objectives. The Bank of England might, for example, issue directives limiting the volume of credit creation for some or all borrowers; it may specify qualitative lending guidelines; or it may set ceilings on interest rates (thus limiting the ability of institutions to bid for new deposits).

Finally, there are a number of policies that may be applied with a view to influencing the rate of growth of the money supply in the *longer term*. In particular, the authorities may seek to reduce the level of *public sector borrowing* or increase the size of *public sector debt repayment*. If public sector borrowing is to be reduced this not only has a direct effect on the demand for borrowed funds within the economy but also the supply of potential bank reserve assets is limited. In addition, for any given size of public sector borrowing requirement, the greater the proportion which is covered by the issue of gilt-edged securities and National Savings instruments to the non-bank, non-building society private sector, the smaller the monetary implications of the deficit financing. Indeed, as existing debt matures, the authorities may pursue a *funding policy* that is aimed at reducing the stock of liquid assets in the economy suitable for reserve asset purposes. In the case of a debt repayment, funds are withdrawn from the private sector and the money supply will be reduced, unless the authorities use these funds to retire debt held by the non-bank, non-building society private sector. Clearly, the greater the debt repayment the greater the opportunity for reducing money supply growth.

(b) Since the authorities introduced the new monetary control provisions in August 1981 the emphasis has been placed upon the use of market intervention and the implementation of policies directed towards the longer-term control of the money supply. Portfolio constraints have been largely abandoned. Since spring of 1997 the Bank of England has used announcements of changes in its repo rate as a means of influencing interest rates in general.

The emphasis of monetary controls since the early 1980s has been focused upon the manipulation of *short-term interest rates*. The Bank has achieved this through the use of open-market operations, changes in the Bank's repo (discount) rate and, on occasions, somewhat more direct pressures. In addition, the government pursued a policy of holding down public sector borrowing, initially within its Medium Term Financial Strategy framework. Clearly, such policies have important implications for taxation and public expenditure decisions. It is hoped that reduced public-sector dependence on bank finance will take the pressure off interest rates at all levels and will encourage corporate borrowers to raise funds in the capital markets rather than through bank loans.

Finally, the authorities have also attempted to facilitate their monetary objectives through the careful implementation of *funding policy*. In fact, during part of the 1980s extensive *over-funding* of the PSBR took place, which means that sales of gilt-edged securities and National Savings instruments to the non-bank, non-building society private sector often exceeded the concurrent PSBR, thus having a negative impact on the growth of M4.

Question 17

(a) (i) *The following measures could be implemented with the objective of reducing a current account deficit:*

(i) The authorities could seek to *reduce the exchange rate for the domestic currency.* This action would be aimed at reducing the foreign currency price of domestic exports, whilst raising the domestic currency price of foreign imports, other things being equal. Whilst it is probable that the domestic demand for imported goods and services would be depressed, total expenditure on imports would only fall if the *price elasticity of demand* for these imports was greater than one. That is, the proportionate reduction in the quantity demanded must be greater than the proportionate increase in the domestic currency price of the goods and services. Similarly, whilst the volume of exports would probably increase, overseas earnings would only rise if the price elasticity of demand for exports was greater than one. Clearly, for there to be an overall improvement in the balance of traded goods and services, it is not necessary that both these elasticity conditions should be met. Strictly, if the sum of the two elasticities is greater than one, the balance of trade will improve (this is known as the Marshall-Lerner condition).

The required adjustment in exchange rates may be brought about by the authorities allowing market pressure to depress the value of the domestic currency (which would probably occur at some point due to the existence of a current account deficit). Alternatively, the downwards pressure could be intensified by official exchange market intervention involving sales of the domestic currency, or by a loosening of monetary controls with the aim of pushing interest rates downwards and hence undermining the attractiveness of domestic deposits for foreign investors. However, a possible side effect of this type of policy action is that domestic money supply growth may be stimulated, and hence the level of demand within the economy may be raised, thus counteracting at least some of the effect of the policy on the level of imports. In addition, it should also be noted that irrespective of the means by which the exchange value of the domestic currency is reduced, there may be a J-curve effect to contend with. That is, as it takes time for trading patterns to adjust, in the short-term it is likely that the deficit will be made worse. It is only as the demand for the now cheaper export goods and services begins to rise that export earnings will recover; and it is only as the demand for the now more expensive imports falls that total expenditure on such items will fall back. The final outcome will depend upon the relevant price elasticity of demand, as mentioned above.

(ii) *Demand management policies* may be directed towards reducing the volume of imports. Specifically, the authorities could tighten monetary policy (although higher interest rates could place upward pressure on the domestic currency's exchange rate, through the attraction of foreign currency funds), reduce the level of government spending or raise taxes. The ensuing reduction in aggregate demand would not only depress the demand for imports, but also would possibly lead to the creation of spare capacity in the domestic economy, thus providing industry with the ability (and the motivation) to service export markets more effectively.

(iii) *Direct controls* could be introduced as a means of making imports less attractive to domestic consumers, or simply limiting the volume of such imports. For example, the authorities might apply tariffs to specific imports in order to raise their price within the domestic market, and hence improve the relative competitiveness of domestically pro-duced goods. So long as the price elasticity of demand for the imports is greater than zero, demand would fall, and, other things being equal, total payments made to foreign exporters would be reduced. The problem with this measure is that it may lead to retal-iation by overseas countries, which may adversely affect domestic exports. So too may the application of quotas (physical limits) on imports. Any subsequent price increases for the imports would offset the benefit for the current account payment flows.

(iv) The authorities could introduce *exchange controls* so as to restrict foreign curren-cy usage by domestic residents. This measure would effectively require the authorities to give their explicit permission before domestic residents could spend foreign curren-cy, and hence their ability to purchase goods and services from overseas would be severely restricted.

It should be recognised that both exchange controls and direct controls would raise serious issues for many industrialised countries, in respect of their international com-mitments to support free trade and capital movements.

(v) *Overseas investment by domestic residents might be encouraged* as a means of improving the net inflow of interest, profits and dividends in the longer term. However, the feasibility of this policy, in the face of current account deficits, would depend upon the availability of foreign currency reserves, and a willingness to see those reserves run down.

(vi) Any policy designed to *improve the quality* of domestically-produced goods and services and their associated *marketing* on an international level, would help to improve the current account position, although probably only in the longer term.

(vii) The government might seek to *reduce its net payments* to official institutions and organisations overseas, and its expenditure on military and diplomatic commitments overseas. However, the feasibility of such actions is likely to be severely restricted by political factors.

(a) (ii) The following measures could be implemented with the objective of reducing a capital and financial account deficit:

(i) The authorities may use monetary policy as a means of *raising domestic interest rates*, and hence making domestic interest-bearing assets more attractive to international investors. This policy may also help to depress inflationary pressures, and hence give increased confidence to investors in respect of the holding of assets denominated in the domestic currency.

(ii) An official commitment to the maintenance of a *stable currency exchange rate* will reduce the perceived risk of losses, in international purchasing power terms, from the holding of assets denominated in the domestic currency.

(iii) The broad stance of the *government's economic policy* will be important to foreigners' expectations of the possible future development of the domestic economy. Policies may be used to promote stable economic growth, and hence to raise the rate of return on direct investment. They may also be formulated in a manner designed to generate confidence in international financial markets.

(iv) *Direct controls* may be introduced in the form of limits on the amounts of foreign currency that may be withdrawn from the country for overseas capital investment purposes. Alternatively, direct limits may be imposed on the amounts of overseas investment that may be undertaken by domestic residents. Unfortunately, such policies may lead to retaliation by other countries, which may see a direct threat to their own capital account position.

(v) The government may offer *incentives for investment* in the form of grants, subsidies or tax-free allowances, which may be directed either towards the potential foreign investor in the domestic economy, or towards the domestic investor on the brink of investing abroad. Indeed, the authorities may use the threat of taxation as a weapon to dissuade domestic residents from investing abroad.

(vi) The government may *reduce its own capital expenditure overseas*, perhaps by drawing back from political and military commitments. It may also encourage foreign governments to undertake capital expenditure within the domestic economy. However, the nature of such expenditure could generate serious political problems.

(vii) In relation to the *official financing* elements of the capital account, the authorities might seek to lengthen the repayment period on any outstanding official overseas debt. They may also negotiate with international monetary authorities and overseas central banks to raise official overseas borrowing, and may borrow from private capital markets via bond issues.

(b) The possession of official foreign currency reserves allows the authorities to support the exchange value of the domestic currency. If a country operates a managed floating exchange-rate regime, official reserves may be used to purchase the domestic currency as a means of preventing an undesired depreciation in its value. Where the authorities are committed to pegging the value of the domestic currency to some other currency or group of currencies, the possession of official reserves is vital for day-to-day foreign exchange market intervention. The reserves are used to iron out fluctuations in the balance of supplies of and demands for currencies which might threaten the stability of the domestic currency's value.

For countries with weak current account positions, and especially for developing countries with poor credit ratings, holdings of foreign exchange reserves provide overseas companies with confidence that they will be paid for imports into such countries. An adequate level of reserves, measured in terms of the cover they provide for imports, is therefore likely to enhance the prospects of international trade taking place.

Question 18

The exchange rate of a currency is its *price* relative to other currencies, with the exchange rate for any particular currency being dependent upon the supplies of and the demands for that currency on the foreign exchange markets.

The following factors have important effects on international trade and capital flows, and hence are likely to influence exchange rates:

(a) *Relative inflation rates* – A country with relatively high inflation will tend to lose competitiveness against its trading partners. Assuming that the price elasticity of demand for traded goods is sufficiently high then, other things being equal, the value of exports/imports will fall/rise, and downward pressure will be put on the exchange rate. The purchasing power parity theory may be relevant here.

(b) *Relative interest rates* – Changes in interest rate differentials between nations may cause a reallocation in international investment portfolios. However, raw nominal interest rates have to be taken with the expected inflation rates and exchange rate changes to form a meaningful calculation of relative real yields. In addition, transaction costs and official impediments to flows may limit such influences.

(c) *Expectations of economic condition* – Foreign exchange markets may anticipate the likely effects on the balance of payments position of actual or expected events, and hence currencies may strengthen or weaken before the events have noticeable effects on the balance of payments. For example, expected changes in oil prices have implications for the future trading position of oil exporters; or expected interest rate or productivity changes may imply future capital movements.

(d) *Non-economic factors* – Actual or expected changes in the political/social environment may have implications for a country's future trading/economic position, and hence foreign currency flows. Political unrest can badly undermine confidence.

(e) *Government economic policies* – Even without direct intervention on the foreign exchange market, a government can have a significant influence on the exchange rate. This may arise not only through the general stance of its monetary and fiscal policies (affecting business confidence, and so on), but also through the specific effects of the policies on the demand for imports, supply of export goods, general inflation rate, and so on. Import controls, investment incentives and government expenditure overseas might also be included, as might policies to improve the quality and marketing of exported products.

Question 19

(a) The *balance of visible trade* measures the difference between the value of visible exports and the value of visible imports. Visible imports and exports involve trade in:

(i) food, beverages and tobacco;

(ii) basic raw materials;

(iii) fuel;

(iv) manufactured goods.

The *terms of trade* can be defined as:

$$\frac{\text{Index of export prices}}{\text{Index of import prices}} \times 100$$

At a particular base-date, both indices are given a value of 100, and so the starting point of the terms of trade is also 100. If there is a subsequent rise in the average price of imports with the average price of exports remaining constant, the terms of trade will fall below 100; conventionally this is described as a 'deterioration' in the terms of trade. A fall in the index of export prices relative to import prices would have the same effect. If the opposite adjustments occur, there is said to be an 'improvement' in the terms of trade. Therefore, in effect, movements in the terms of trade show changes in the real purchasing power (in terms of imports) of a given quantity of exports. If the terms of trade improve, for every unit of goods exported the country will obtain a larger quantity of imports; the converse is true for deterioration in the terms of trade.

(b) The government is able to influence the *balance of trade* to the extent that it is able to affect overseas trade flows. The major approaches that may be taken include the following;

(i) *Alteration of currency exchange rates* – For example, by reducing the exchange value of the domestic currency, other things being equal, the overseas price of exports will be reduced whilst the domestic price of imports will rise. As long as the price elasticity of demand for exports is greater than one, the additional demand for exports will be sufficiently great to cause the value of exports to rise. Similarly, as long as the price elasticity of demand for imports is greater than one, the reduction in the demand for imports will be large enough to cause the value of imports to fall. Clearly, as long as the elasticity of demand for traded goods taken in aggregate is high enough, the balance of trade will move in favour of the country reducing the value of its currency. In addition, there should be sufficient spare capacity in the economy to enable the output to export markets to be increased. An increase in the value of the currency will have the opposite effect on the balance of trade.

(ii) *Domestic demand management* – If the authorities are able to depress domestic demand, the flow of imports is likely to be reduced and spare capacity created within the domestic economy for the production of additional goods for export. This may be brought about through an increase in taxation, government spending cuts or a tightening of monetary policy, Indeed, depressed home markets are likely to act as a stimulus to domestic businesses to seek out overseas markets for their products. In addition, reduced demand within the domestic economy is likely to ease inflationary pressures and so help domestic producers to maintain their competitive position in overseas markets. Expansionary economic policies would have the opposite effect on the economy and hence on the balance of trade.

(iii) *Direct controls* – Notwithstanding international free-trade agreements, the authorities may introduce import controls, export incentives or exchange controls. To the extent that imports are held back or exports are raised, the balance of trade may be improved. However, it is important to recognise that such direct controls may simply lead to retaliation by overseas governments and so domestic exports may also be adversely affected, making the overall effect questionable.

Clearly, the authorities have a wide range of means through which they may seek to influence the balance of trade, and potentially the effects may be great.

The government's influence over the *terms of trade* is likely to be much more limited than its influence over the balance of trade. The reason for this is that in order to affect the terms of trade the authorities must alter the relative prices of export and import goods, and these are very much at the mercy of *world market prices*. Thus, whilst the government may be able to alter the terms of trade by an adjustment in the domestic currency's exchange rate, a subsequent change in market conditions which alters the prices of traded goods may wipe out the effect on the terms of trade. Nevertheless, by implementing policies which affect the level of domestic prices relative to prices overseas, the government will have some influence on the terms of trade.

As we mentioned above, alterations in the *domestic currency's exchange rate* will affect the terms of trade, for given sets of domestic prices. Alternatively, the authorities may introduce policies to hold down the rate of *domestic price inflation*. The objective here is to keep price rises below those experienced by overseas countries. This approach, which might involve a tightening of monetary or fiscal policies, would tend to cause the terms of trade to deteriorate. It seems unlikely that a government would attempt to cause domestic inflation as a means of improving the terms of trade. A far more sensible approach would be to encourage domestic industries to produce high-quality output and undertake aggressive marketing in overseas markets. Thus, if overseas demand for domestic exports can be stimulated, the prices of these goods may be pushed upwards (and hence the terms of trade improved) as a by-product of a favourable shift in trading patterns.

Question 20

(a) Internal funding occurs when a company raises funds from internal sources such as from the sale of assets or from the retention of profits. If a company can reduce its dividends or boost profits then it will be raising funds internally.

Such funds do not have to be repaid or serviced in any way. However, internally generated funds can involve a cost, in that reduced dividends may result in shareholder dissatisfaction and a reduction in assets may result in reduced productive capacity.

Externally raised funds are funds raised by borrowing or by the issue of new shares for cash. Borrowings have to be serviced to meet both interest obligations and agreed capital repayments. New shares do not involve any servicing costs but the holders of the shares will expect to receive dividends. If new shares come into the hands of new shareholders, as opposed to being taken up by the existing shareholders as in a rights issue, then there will be some dilution of control in the company.

(b) The main means by which companies can raise external finance are as follows:

(i) *Overdraft facilities* – There is a maximum borrowing limit marked on the current account, and the balance can fluctuate at will up to the maximum permitted overdraft limit. Overdrafts are repayable on demand. Interest is usually at floating rates and is charged on the closing daily debit balance.

(ii) *LIBOR-linked loans* – Within an agreed total limit the company may withdraw blocks of funds of maturity normally of between one and three months. The minimum facility is usually £250,000 and the minimum individual loan is usually £100,000. The bank usually commits the total facility, since the bank guarantees to keep the total facility available for a certain minimum period. A commitment fee is payable if the facility is committed, and banks usually charge a non-utilisation fee on any part of the facility which is not drawn.

LIBOR is usually more volatile than base rate, so interest costs are likely to be less predictable than for a base-rate-linked facility such as an overdraft.

(iii) *Acceptance credits* – A company draws a bill of exchange which is accepted by a bank. If the bill fulfils the following criteria, it becomes an eligible bill that can be discounted at the Bank of England:

(1) the bank must be deemed 'eligible' according to the Bank of England criteria;

(2) the bill must have a maximum original term of 187 days;

(3) the bill must be issued in connection with some underlying trade transaction, brief details of which must be noted on the bill itself.

Because eligible bills can be rediscounted at the Bank of England, the holder can discount the bill at a fine rate that can be below LIBOR.

The minimum total facility is usually £500,000 and the minimum amount for an individual bill is usually £50,000.

(iv) *Commercial paper* – This consists of unsecured promissory notes issued by companies to investors at a discount to face value. The minimum amount is very large (for example, £100,000 for a single promissory note with sterling commercial paper, as opposed to the £50,000 minimum for a single bill under an acceptance credit).

Sterling commercial paper is more flexible than acceptance credits because there is no need to link the issue to an underlying trade transaction. However, SCP requires a higher effective rate of interest than does an acceptance credit because of the lower security of SCP.

Sterling commercial paper has an original maturity of between seven days and five years, but the one to five year maturity issues are called Medium Term Notes.

Other commercial paper markets are the US commercial paper market and the euro-commercial paper market.

(v) *Bank loans.* Given the competition between banks, there is a tremendous variety of loans available to suit the needs of company borrowers. Terms to maturity can be from one to ten years, but in suitable cases 30-year maturity can be arranged. Interest can be fixed or floating, and floating rates can be LIBOR-linked or linked to base rate.

Security will normally be required for longer-term loans and there may be covenants in the loan documentation, which bind the company to maintaining certain minimum financial ratios.

(vi) *Sterling debentures* – These are registered transferable loan stocks that usually pay a fixed rate of interest and are redeemable at par on the set maturity date. The stocks are listed on the London Stock Exchange. The minimum original maturity period is now five years, since stocks with an original maturity of fewer than five years must now be issued as Medium Term Notes on the sterling commercial paper market.

Large amounts of funds can be raised, with the typical range being £30–100m.

(vii) *Eurobonds* – Eurobonds are foreign currency denominated bearer securities that may be issued by way of an offer for sale to the general public or via a private placing with investors. A syndicate of banks that underwrite the bonds and place them with investors normally makes public issues. Such bonds are normally listed on one or more of the main stock exchanges. Private placements are rarely listed on a stock exchange.

Eurobonds are only applicable where large amounts of funds are required, with a typical issue being in excess of US$75m or its equivalent. Issuers must be major corporate bodies with an international reputation and a first-class credit rating. Companies which have issued a Eurobond find that this gives them added credibility with other providers of finance, thus ensuring that if additional funds are ever required, they can be raised at the finest rates.

(viii) *Leasing* – Assets such as aircraft, ships and machinery may be obtained with the aid of lease finance from a bank or group of banks. Even the largest companies occasionally use this source of external finance, whereas the factoring of book debts tends to be used primarily by smaller companies.

(ix) *Equity shares* – New issues of equity capital provide long-term funds without the need to service the repayment of capital or to make interest payments. There are two main classes of equity capital: ordinary shares and preference shares.

Ordinary shareholders are legally the owners of the company, with the power to appoint directors by a majority vote at meetings. Dividends can only be paid from available profits and within that constraint the directors recommend the rate of dividend. In the event of liquidation ordinary shareholders rank last, but they are entitled to the whole of the surplus, if any, remaining after the claims of all creditors and prior ranking preferential shareholders have been met.

Preferential shareholders rank behind all outside creditors in the event of liquidation and are entitled (usually) to repayment at par if there is a sufficient surplus. The dividend on preference shares is fixed and it ranks before the ordinary shareholders' dividend. Preference dividends can be paid only from available profits, and indeed there is no compulsion on the directors to recommend payment of the preferential dividend. However, ordinary shareholders cannot receive any dividend if the preference dividend for the year has not been met.

The higher is the ratio of equity capital to loan capital the lower is the gearing ratio. Other things being equal, low-geared companies are less risky than high-geared ones. However, debt finance is usually cheaper than equity because interest is tax deductible whereas dividends are not.

It is a matter of great concern that a company employs the optimal mix of debt and equity finance. If there is too little debt the cost of capital is too high; whereas if there is too much debt, the high gearing ratio causes providers of capital to demand higher returns to compensate for the greater perceived risk.

Question 21

(a) The three broad types of exposure to exchange rate risk are normally classified as:

(i) transaction risk;

(ii) translation risk;

(iii) economic risk.

Transaction risk arises from normal trading activities when foreign currencies are used in settlement. Exporters invoicing in foreign currency will lose if the foreign currency has depreciated against the home currency between invoice date and settlement date. The converse applies to an importer who will gain if the foreign currency depreciates against the home currency between invoice date and settlement date.

Translation risk applies whenever there is a mismatch between the mix of currencies in which the assets are denominated and the mix of currencies in which the liabilities are denominated. For balance sheet reporting purposes, the value of the foreign-currency-denominated assets and liabilities must be changed (translated) into home currency. Thus, if foreign-currency-denominated assets exceed foreign currency denominated liabilities, and if the foreign currency has appreciated against the home currency between the previous balance sheet date and the current balance sheet date, there will be a reported translation gain. If foreign-currency-denominated assets exceed foreign-currency-denominated liabilities and if the foreign currency has depreciated during this period, the new balance sheet will show a translation loss.

Any translation gain will be matched by an increase in reported net worth, whereas any translation loss will be matched by a reduction in net worth. Changes in net worth affect the reported gearing ratios and thus can affect the attitudes of shareholders, creditors and bankers.

Economic risk is difficult to quantify and cannot be reported in the published accounts. It reflects the extent to which a company can suffer a competitive disadvantage because of adverse movements in exchange rates. For example, a UK company with all its operations and sales within the UK could be at a competitive disadvantage if the currency of the country of a competitor were to depreciate against sterling.

(b) The main benefits of forward exchange contracts are that they are:

- Easy to arrange and understand.

- Relatively low cost, involving only a bid/offer spread.

- Useful for smaller businesses which need to hedge all their exposure.

- Over-the-counter instruments that can be tailor-made to meet the user's requirements.

The main drawbacks of forward exchange contracts are that they are:

- Inflexible, with no opportunity to exploit potentially advantageous movements in the exchange rate.

- Not suitable for hedging uncertain cash flows. If the underlying deal is not completed, the forward contract creates an exposure due to the potential loss or gain at close out.

- Treated as a credit facility by banks, and hence reduce the availability of borrowing facilities for the user.

(c) There is a pre-transaction exposure arising from the submission of a tender for a capital project. By the time that the contract is awarded, the spot rate may have changed significantly, so that the expected profitability of the project may be altered. Unfortunately, it is inappropriate to cover this type of exposure by using forward contracts. If the tender were not accepted, a forward contract would have to be closed out, which could result in either a gain or loss. A more suitable hedging devise for the company would be the use of options. Failure in the tender would then mean that the maximum cost to the company is the premium paid on the option. If the option is not required it can either be allowed to lapse or exercised if it has an intrinsic value.

Question 22

(a) When a company borrows a substantial amount of long-term funds it is taking on a major commitment to service the debt, which will have important implications for its financial position, irrespective of the form of interest rate payable or the currency of denomination of the debt. In particular, if the borrowing is large relative to the scale of the company's operations, the impact on the company of unexpected movements in interest rates or exchange rates may be serious.

(i) If the company borrows at a market-related rate of interest, the main risk that it faces is that of market rates proving to be much higher than expected. The borrower is normally required to service the debt regularly, and hence higher rates of interest mean higher cash outlays. This does not only mean that the company faces possible pressure on its cash-flow position, but also it may find itself at a competitive disadvantage if competing companies have raised their borrowed funds at fixed rates or if they have little outstanding debt.

(ii) If the company borrows at a fixed rate it is able to avoid the cash-flow risk which arises from unexpected increases in market rates of interest. However, there is still the risk that competing companies might have borrowed funds at market-related rates, and then those rates fall, thus leaving the company with fixed-rate debt having to carry relatively expensive debt servicing costs.

The above discussion assumes that the company is committed for a long period to one particular type of interest payment. In reality, it is often possible for borrowers to elect to switch between fixed and floating rates at predetermined times during the loan period. Nevertheless, some commitment has to be made for a certain minimum length of time, and it is likely that the lender, to reflect the changing conditions in the financial environment, will adjust levels of fixed rates and margins required over floating rates. Consequently, it is most probable that some element of risk will also be present even where switching between commitments is possible. Furthermore, the matter of foreign currency borrowing has been ignored in the above discussion. If the company does in fact raise funds denominated in foreign currencies, it may add to the risks which it faces, unless sufficient of its expected revenues are also denominated in the same foreign currencies. Where expected revenues and interest commitments are denominated in different currencies, any movements in the exchange rates between those currencies may place unforeseen burdens on the borrower (or may lead to unexpected gains), when all flows are converted to a common currency. This exchange-rate risk merely compounds the underlying interest-rate risk problem, and again may generate implications for the borrower's competitiveness.

(b) An interest rate swap occurs when borrowers raise funds independently and then swap the associated debt servicing commitments on equal sums. Borrowers may engage in swap transactions merely because their expectations differ as to future interest rate movements. For example, a borrower with outstanding floating rate debt may believe that interest rates are set to rise substantially, and hence may seek a counter-party with fixed rate debt outstanding who is willing to swap commitments. Clearly, for a swap to be agreed, the counter-party must regard the floating rate commitment as being more attractive than the fixed rate. This may mean that the counter-parties have different expectations of interest rate movements. Alternatively, it may be that the interest payment pattern associated with the floating-rate debt is thought to be more attractive, than that on the fixed-rate debt, by the borrower willing to give up the commitment to the latter. Irrespective of the ultimate reason for the counter-parties' agreement to swap, the transaction allows the initial holder of the floating-rate debt to obtain certainty in respect of the future cash flows required for interest payments, and hence this particular element of risk is avoided. However, the risk is accepted that competing companies with floating-rate debt will subsequently be placed at a competitive advantage if market interest rates fall, thus reducing their debt servicing costs. In a similar way, companies may manage their interest-rate risk position by swapping different forms of floating-rate debt.

It is important to appreciate that the counter-parties to a swap transaction maintain their original responsibilities to the lenders of the funds. Therefore, whilst the counter-parties may have hedged certain interest-rate risks, they must be willing to accept counter-party risk, in the sense that if a counter-party defaults on a commitment to make interest payments, the original borrower is still liable for the debt servicing. Consequently, complex legal problems may arise in respect of swap transactions, which may deter borrowers from becoming involved.

Finally, it should be noted that in practice a bank would normally be responsible for arranging a swap transaction. The intermediary bank will act as principal rather than an agent, and will guarantee the obligations of the counter-parties. Standard bank documentation can be used to simplify and clarify the legal position. Normally the bank makes its return on this activity through the bid/offer spread.

Question 23

(a) Within the context of the housing market, negative equity arises where the market value of residential property falls below the outstanding associated mortgage debt. For example, an owner-occupier may have an outstanding mortgage debt of £60,000 relating to a property the market value of which has fallen to £55,000. In this case the negative equity amounts to £5,000. This means that if the owner-occupier wished to sell the property, the proceeds would be insufficient to discharge the debt.

(i) Assuming that a mortgage lender would not normally lend in excess of 100% of the market value of a mortgaged property, the existence of negative equity implies that the owner-occupier has incurred a capital loss, and this may affect the owner-occupier's spending patterns adversely. The reduction in the value of personal wealth may encourage the owner-occupier to raise his/her saving ratio as a means of rebuilding the amount of wealth held.

The main problem for an owner-occupier, arising from negative equity, occurs if there is a desire to sell the property and move elsewhere. By definition, the funds realised from the property sale will be insufficient to discharge the outstanding mortgage loan. This means that the owner-occupier must raise an unsecured loan or run down savings in order to meet the legal commitment of the mortgage loan. If the owner-occupier is unable to call upon savings, the raising of an unsecured loan in such circumstances may be difficult (especially if economic conditions in general are unfavourable, which they are likely to be if the housing market is stagnant). Furthermore, the need for an unsecured loan implies that the owner-occupier will have little, if any, funds to contribute towards the purchase of another property, thus creating substantial difficulties in raising a new mortgage loan. In this case there may be little alternative but to move into rented accommodation.

(b) (ii) An important problem for a mortgage lender, where negative equity arises, is that, by default, it finds itself with a loan outstanding which is partly unsecured. This is particularly awkward for building societies that, in normal circumstances, are limited in the extent to which they are able to make unsecured loans. However, until the borrower wishes to move from the property, the negative equity is not realised, although this does not diminish the risk associated with the mortgage loan for the lender. As indicated above, a borrower may be able to discharge the whole of a mortgage loan upon moving house by using savings. Also, where the borrower is fundamentally creditworthy with a stable income, the risks in making an unsecured loan to cover the negative equity are relatively small. The main difficulty is likely to arise if a borrower with negative equity becomes unemployed or otherwise unable to service the mortgage loan. When this happens there is the serious risk that the borrower will literally walk away from the debt (and the negative equity). The lender then has the expensive task of obtaining possession of the property and attempting to realise as much of its value as possible.

(c) Basically, the price of new houses is determined by the interaction of the supply of and the demand for new houses. However, as existing houses are close substitutes for new houses, supply and demand conditions relating to second-hand houses must be taken into account when considering the determination of the price of new houses. The greater is the supply of new houses coming on to the market, other things being equal, the lower is likely to be the price of new houses. The supply of new houses depends upon the rate of completions by builders, the stock of previously unsold new houses being offered for sale, and the ability of builders to agree sales before houses have been completed. This supply in total is likely to be influenced by factors such as the general state of the economy, and expected trends in unemployment, earnings, inflation and interest rates. Property developers are more likely to invest in construction of residential property if they are optimistic about being able to sell it. Hence supply is likely to rise if real earnings are growing and employment prospects appear good; by contrast, rising unemployment and high interest rates are likely to lead to a reduction in supply.

The total supply of houses on the market will be higher than the number of new houses being made available. This is on account of houses being transferred from rental status (where transfers do not involve sitting tenants) and houses being vacated as a result of the owner's death, emigration or move to rented accommodation. The rate of transfer from rental status is likely to increase during periods of buoyancy in the housing market, which in turn will be encouraged by favourable economic conditions. The factors causing the supply of houses on the market to rise for other reasons are unlikely to be linked to shorter-term economic developments, except where houses are vacated due to mortgage loan-servicing problems, which is more likely when the economy is depressed and the housing market stagnant. Overall, to the extent that the supply of second-hand houses rises, other things being equal, the price of all houses (including new ones) is likely to be depressed. It is important to note that houses placed on the market by owner-occupiers wishing to move into other owner-occupied houses have no net effect on the supply of houses available, although there may be some impact on the supply of and demand for different types of houses.

As far as a potential purchaser of a house is concerned, new houses and second-hand houses may be very close substitutes. Individual preferences, relative prices and locations of houses will influence the extent of the substitutability. However, as far as the determination of the price of new houses is concerned, the crucial factor is the net demand for houses overall, and this depends upon potential purchasers entering the market for the first time. Existing owner-occupiers moving between houses have no impact on net demand. The factors that affect the demand from first-time buyers at any point in time are those that have been listed above as factors affecting supply. In the longer term, demographic trends (particularly changes in population and age profiles) and social conventions (including the occurrence of single-person households and single-parent families) affect the number of first-time buyers. The availability of alternative forms of suitable accommodation is also of importance, and hence government policies in respect of local authority house building, rent levels and private sector rented property developments are of relevance. These longer-term factors are also likely to influence the expectations of future trends in demand held by property developers, and hence will probably affect the supply side of the market. It should also be recognised that changes in government economic policies, in so far as they affect the broad development of the economy and especially the factors listed above as being relevant for the supply of and the demand for houses, are likely to influence the price of new houses. Interest rates affect both the cost of financing the purchase of houses, i.e. the demand,

and the costs of building new houses and of 'bridging' the ownership of two houses, i.e. the supply of houses.

As stated above, it is the interaction of the supply of and the demand for new houses that determines their price. Thus, for example, if economic conditions improve, and favourable trends are expected in personal sector earnings and job prospects, it is likely that both demand and supply will be stimulated. But as demand is able to adjust much more quickly than supply, there is likely to be upwards pressure placed on house prices, at least in the short term. The extent of any increase in house prices will depend upon the speed of adjustment of net supply and ultimately the impact on building costs and land prices. It is possible that the pressure of demand will push up the price of building land, with only a marginal impact on the total supply made available. Consequently, supply may never catch up with demand, and prices of new houses may continue to drift upwards until the trend in demand itself alters. If demand was to fall, perhaps due to the economy moving into a period of recession, the above situation could be reversed with the given supply on the market becoming excessive relative to demand. As property developers do not wish to hold stocks of vacant houses, and as some owner-occupiers with pressing financial problems feel that they have no option but to sell their properties, the pressure on house prices will be downwards. The market price of new houses may then only stabilise once the level of net demand stabilises and the net supply on the market falls to a comparable level.

Question 24

(a) *Building Societies*

For many years building societies dominated the provision of mortgage loans, which comprise around 70% of all personal sector financial liabilities, and deposits (mainly shares) with building societies formed the largest single element of the sector's liquid asset holdings. Despite the recession in the UK during the early 1990s, and in particular the downturn in the housing market, the amount of building society mortgage debt outstanding and the total value of shares and deposits held with building societies continued to grow. However, this was at a slower rate than that experienced during the boom years of the late 1980s. Since the mid-1990s, the situation has changed fundamentally as many of the largest building societies have converted to retail bank status. Whilst maintaining an importance to personal sector financial arrangements, by 1999 building societies had become minority providers of mortgage loans (accounting for only about one quarter of outstanding mortgage loan debt) and of savings facilities.

The increased competition in the personal savings and loans markets, unleashed by the financial deregulation which took place during the 1980s, had tended to erode the building societies' pre-eminence in respect of their specialist financial intermediation roles. The retail banks have shown themselves to be particularly aggressive competitors in certain areas of business. However, it must be recognised that deregulation has opened up new opportunities for building societies to service a wider range of personal sector financial requirements. The major development in this respect was the enactment of the Building Societies Act 1986 (and subsequent amendments), which allowed the building societies for the first time to make unsecured loans and to provide a range of payments and other banking services, including some relating to international transactions.

In addition, many building societies are now active in the provision of facilities designed to meet the longer-term investment needs of the personal sector. For example, it may be possible for individuals to invest in unit trusts, insurance-based products and personal pension plans through their building societies. The total holdings of these types of investment by the personal sector are huge, although such investments purchased through building societies are still relatively modest. Some building societies also offer share-dealing facilities for customers with direct holdings of company shares.

Finally, it should be recognised that as building societies become increasingly like retail banks in the provision of personal sector financial services, their staff is becoming better equipped to offer advice to customers on the management of their finances.

(b) *Life assurance companies and pension funds*

Claims on life assurance companies and pension funds are the largest single item amongst the personal sector's financial assets, accounting for around a half of the total of such assets. In recent years the flows of funds into life assurance companies and pension funds have been one of the two main uses of personal sector funds. They have been of similar magnitude to the amounts of funds spent on the purchase of residential property and other fixed assets by the sector. It is through life assurance companies and pension funds that the personal sector holds the bulk of its claims on the corporate sector; direct shareholdings are relatively small in comparison. Ultimately, the value of company securities depends upon market forces, and hence a boom on the stock market may raise the relative importance of claims on life assurance companies and pension funds without there being corresponding inflows of new funds. By the same token, the importance of such claims may diminish if stock market conditions stagnate.

Investments with life assurance companies and pension funds are long-term in nature. Indeed, the contractual arrangements associated with most of these investments are such that it is not possible for the investor to receive a return until a particular event has occurred. In the case of a pension fund, the retirement of the contributor activates the fund's commitment to pay a pension for the remainder of the contributor's life, and often beyond in respect of dependent relatives. In respect of life assurance, there may be some access to accumulated funds before the maturity of a policy or the death of the person whose life is insured, but the terms are often such that the surrender value represents a poor return on the funds invested. However, a small market in second-hand endowment policies has begun recently. Consequently, whilst investments with life assurance companies and pension funds are of vital importance to the long-term security of members of the personal sector, they cannot be viewed in the same way as deposits with banks and building societies. The latter are generally liquid assets held to meet shorter-term financing requirements and to cover unforeseen demands for funds without excessive transaction costs being incurred.

(c) *Company Securities*

Direct holdings of company securities form an important element of the personal sector's total financial assets (around 17% of the total in recent years), with the bulk of these holdings relating to UK companies. However, of much greater importance for the personal sector are the indirect holdings of company securities represented by investments in life assurance companies, pension funds and unit trusts. Claims on these financial intermediaries amount to over a half of personal sector financial assets, and company securities comprise around 70% of the assets held by these intermediaries. Therefore, in total, around a half of the personal sector's financial asset holdings ultimately relate to company securities, although about three-quarters of these are effectively locked away in life assurance policies and pension funds, and hence cannot be realised at will (as explained in part (b) above). As the value of company securities is at the mercy of market forces, changes in stock market conditions can have a substantial impact on the value of personal sector wealth. Also, whilst the overall return on investments in company securities is often greater than that on deposits with banks and building societies, significant risks are associated with the holding of company securities, as was demonstrated by the stock market collapse of October 1987.

In recent years, flows of personal sector funds into company securities via investments in life assurance companies and pension funds have remained at very high levels, despite the depressed economic conditions at the beginning of the 1990s. However, the personal sector has withdrawn substantial amounts of funds from direct holdings of securities.

Question 25

(a) The most extreme form of risk faced by any investor is that of default on interest payments or repayment of debt. The most obvious default risk run by the personal sector relates to the granting of trade credit by unincorporated businesses (which are included in the personal sector). Quite simply, debtors may be unable or unwilling to discharge their debt, and hence creditors may be forced to write-off the debt or perhaps initiate expensive legal action. However, the bulk of personal sector financial assets are in the form of claims on financial institutions. There is always some risk that an individual institution will fail, due to inept management or fraud, and hence that depositors/investors will lose the entire value of their deposits/investments. The latter occurrence is rare in the UK, as there are often officially sponsored depositor/investor protection schemes, which provide at least a limited safety net. There is also the liquidation value of a failed institution, which may allow for some repayment of creditors.

Direct ownership of company securities is inherently risky, although it is rare for well-managed blue-chip companies to go into liquidation. The more likely occurrence is that the trading performance of a company will be eroded, and consequently the level of returns on, and the capital value of, its securities will fall. Government securities, issued by major Western nations, are effectively free of default risk but, if such instruments are to be realised before their maturity dates, investors may incur capital losses if the general level of interest rates has risen since the time that the instruments were purchased.

When an investor purchases a fixed-term asset paying a fixed rate of interest, there is the risk that the rate of inflation may prove to be higher than was expected at the time that the purchase was made, and hence that the real return will be unexpectedly low. Indeed, if the rate of inflation rises above the nominal rate of interest earned, the real return on the investment is negative, as the interest earnings are insufficient even to cover the erosion of the purchasing power of the principal sum lent. In addition, to the extent that inflation generates uncertainty in financial markets, it may undermine business activities, especially at an international level, and this may increase the risk associated with investments in companies susceptible to such effects.

Against a background of economic uncertainty, it is difficult for members of the personal sector to predict with any accuracy their future financial needs, particularly several years in advance. Consequently, decisions on the deployment of financial asset holdings may entail significant risk arising from unanticipated changes in financial or personal circumstances. Investors tend to be faced with a choice between holding relatively low-yield liquid assets or holding higher-yield illiquid assets that are more risky. Once a portfolio has been selected, an unanticipated change in financial circumstances may necessitate the forced sale of securities, with the associated risk of capital losses, or the premature withdrawal of deposits from financial institutions, which may incur interest penalties.

As mentioned above, investors holding fixed-term assets that pay fixed rates of interest are at risk from unexpectedly high rates of inflation. They also forgo the opportunity for earning higher returns if market rates of interest should rise. Unfortunately, variable interest rates on assets are equally risky, as the cash earnings on such investments depend upon movements in market rates of interest, and if these rates were to fall, the investor would have been better placed holding fixed-rate assets. Also, interest rate movements are likely to affect the capital value of fixed-interest marketable securities, thus generating a further source of risk for the investor.

Finally, it should be noted that possible changes in government economic policy provide yet another source of risk for the investor. For example, changes in the stance of monetary policy are likely to lead to alterations in the level of interest rates, with the types of effect mentioned above. Again, changes in fiscal policy may affect the tax regimes relating to investments in pension funds, National Savings instruments and ISAs, as well as investment earnings in general. Thus the relative benefits attached to particular portfolios of assets may be altered. In fact, the government's economic policy as a whole is likely to be a crucial determinant of the broader economic and financial environment, and hence returns on all forms of investments are potentially vulnerable in one way or another.

(b) Personal sector investors may take a number of actions in order to minimise the financial risks identified in part (a), although it must be recognised at the outset that the sophisticated hedging instruments available to corporate financial managers are largely inappropriate in this context. Rather, prudent management of finances and the application of common sense in financial decision-making are at the root of limiting exposure to risk.

In respect of risk of default, unincorporated businesses should undertake careful screening of the creditworthiness of potential debtors before credit is granted. In fact, there may be a case for curtailing the provision of credit, and instead offering discounts for cash payment as a means of retaining customers.

Investors in financial intermediaries would be well advised to ensure that they only place funds with institutions which have a good reputation and which are part of a sector covered by an investor/depositor protection scheme. Also as most such schemes are designed to protect smaller investors, and hence have strict limits on the cover offered, it may also be advisable for investors to distribute their funds between a number of institutions, so as to spread risk and to maximise the effective insurance coverage. A disadvantage of holding relatively small amounts of funds with a range of institutions is that higher returns might have to be forgone where tiered interest rates are offered.

For investors in marketable securities, the holding of a diversified portfolio of instruments is perhaps the best way of spreading the unsystematic risk, particularly for company equities where performances may vary markedly. Professional advice should also be sought before funds are committed to such uses. The holding of government securities removes the risk of default, but premature realisation may lead to capital losses. Therefore, consideration may be given to the purchase of National Savings instruments, which are the only truly capital-safe instruments. These may be liquidated for their full nominal values either on demand or after a short period of notice, although higher returns might have to be forgone as the price for early redemption. Also National Savings instruments are only available in limited quantities for individual investors.

In order to avoid unexpected transfers of wealth between lender and borrower when inflation rates prove to be higher than expected lenders may seek to have their interest earnings linked to market rates of interest or to a suitable price index. The latter approach removes the risk in respect of real returns on loans, but the lender must be willing to accept the uncertainty created in respect of cash receipts. Alternatively, interest-bearing debt may be avoided altogether, and instead funds used to purchase company equity shares, the capital value of which and the income from which tend to rise with inflation, although holdings of such instruments open up other forms of risk for the investor. In a similar way, residential property, land or other real assets may be purchased as a hedge against inflation. However, whilst such assets often prove to be good investments in the longer term, there are often prolonged periods over which their prices fall, and at any time individual purchases may lead to substantial losses.

It is impossible for personal sector investors to hold interest-bearing debt and yet avoid risk. Fixed-rate instruments secure cash returns, but these may prove to be relatively poor returns if market rates of interest rise, or if inflation is higher than anticipated. Variable-rate debt leads to uncertainty in respect of cash earnings. Movements of funds into other forms of investment bring their own particular risks. Therefore, the investor would be wise to hold a diversified portfolio of instruments, perhaps containing a range of different types of interest-bearing assets, company equities and real property. Within a portfolio it will probably be necessary to forgo some higher-return assets in order to maintain a sufficient degree of liquidity. This will give the flexibility of finances to meet unanticipated changes in financial circumstances, and also to respond appropriately to changes in government policy, which may impinge upon the relative returns on financial assets.

Index